Lecture Notes in Computer Science 4373

Commenced Publication in 1973
Founding and Former Series Editors:
Gerhard Goos, Juris Hartmanis, and Jan van Leeuwen

Koen Langendoen   Thiemo Voigt (Eds.)

Wireless Sensor Networks

4th European Conference, EWSN 2007
Delft, The Netherlands, January 29-31, 2007
Proceedings

 Springer

Volume Editors

Koen Langendoen
Delft University of Technology
2628 CD Delft, The Netherlands
E-mail: K.G.Langendoen@tudelft.nl

Thiemo Voigt
Swedish Institute of Computer Science
Box 1263, SE-164 29 Kista, Sweden
E-mail: thiemo@sics.se

Library of Congress Control Number: 2006939921

CR Subject Classification (1998): C.2.4, C.2, F.2, D.1.3, D.2, E.1, H.4, C.3

LNCS Sublibrary: SL 5 – Computer Communication Networks and
Telecommunications

ISSN   0302-9743
ISBN-10   3-540-69829-9 Springer Berlin Heidelberg New York
ISBN-13   978-3-540-69829-6 Springer Berlin Heidelberg New York

Springer is a part of Springer Science+Business Media

springer.com

© Springer-Verlag Berlin Heidelberg 2007
Printed in Germany

Typesetting: Camera-ready by author, data conversion by Scientific Publishing Services, Chennai, India
Printed on acid-free paper   SPIN: 11976370   06/3142   5 4 3 2 1 0

Preface

This volume contains the proceedings of EWSN 2007, the fourth European conference on Wireless Sensor Networks. The conference took place at TU Delft, January 29–31, 2007. Its objective was to provide a forum where researchers with different experience and background, from hardware to applications, would present and discuss the latest developments in the exciting field of wireless sensor networks.

Since the interest in sensor networks has been rapidly expanding, it was no surprise that EWSN received a record number of 164 submissions, of which 22 papers were selected for the final conference. It was a pleasure to observe that, although based in Europe, the conference serves as a truly international forum with submissions originating from all five continents: 35% from Europe, 35% from Asia, 26% from America, 3% from Australia, and 1% from Africa. The selection process involved more than 500 reviews with most papers being evaluated by at least three reviewers. The final program covered a wide range of topics, grouped into seven sessions: networking, tracking, algorithms, applications and support, medium access control, OS and tools, and localization.

In addition to the papers published in these proceedings, the conference also included a poster and demonstration session, of which separate proceedings are available. Tutorials and keynotes complemented the program, together making for a truly interesting conference.

In closing, we would like to express our sincere gratitude to everyone who contributed to EWSN 2007. In particular, the members of the Program Committee and external reviewers responsible for the strong technical program, the local TU Delft people for streamlining the conference logistics, and Springer for their excellent cooperation in putting these proceedings together.

January 2007   Koen Langendoen and Thiemo Voigt
                                                            Program Chairs

Organization

EWSN 2007, the fourth European conference on Wireless Sensor Networks, took place in Delft, The Netherlands, January 29–31, 2007. It was organized by the department of Electrical Engineering, Mathematics and Computer Science, Delft University of Technology, The Netherlands.

Executive Committee

General Chair: Koen Langendoen (TU Delft, The Netherlands)
Program Co-chairs: Koen Langendoen (TU Delft, The Netherlands) and Thiemo Voigt (SICS, Sweden)
Publicity Co-chairs: Pedro Marrón (University of Stuttgart, Germany) and Andreas Savvides (Yale, USA)

Local Arrangements

Muneeb Ali (Delft University of Technology, The Netherlands)
Laura Zondervan (Delft University of Technology, The Netherlands)

Program Committee

Tarek Abdelzaher (University of Illinois at Urbana Champaign)
Michael Beigl (TU Braunschweig)
Jan Beutel (ETH Zurich)
Athanassios Boulis (National ICT Australia)
Torsten Braun (University of Bern)
Rebecca Braynard (Duke University)
Nirupama Bulusu (Portland State University)
Srdjan Capkun (ETH Zurich)
Mun Choon Chan (National University of Singapore)
Maarten Ditzel (TNO)
Jean-Pierre Ebert (IHP microelectronics)
Carlo Fischione (KTH Stockholm)
Vipin Gopal (United Technologies Research Center)
Takahiro Hara (Osaka University)
Paul Havinga (University of Twente)
Mike Hazas (Lancaster University)
Wendi Heinzelman (University of Rochester)
Holger Karl (University of Paderborn)
Bhaskar Krishnamachari (University of Southern California)
Koen Langendoen (Delft University of Technology)

Chenyang Lu (Washington University in St. Louis)
Pedro J. Marrón (University of Stuttgart)
Amy L. Murphy (University of Lugano)
Chiara Petrioli (University "La Sapienza" Rome)
Marcelo Pias (University of Cambridge)
Hartmut Ritter (FU Berlin)
Utz Roedig (University College Cork)
Christian Rohner (Uppsala University)
Kay Römer (ETH Zurich)
Andreas Savvides (Yale)
Thiemo Voigt (SICS)
Klaus Wehrle (RWTH Aachen)
Dirk Westhoff (NEC)
Andreas Willig (TU Berlin)
Adam Wolisz (TU Berlin)
Wei Ye (USC/ISI)

Additional Reviewers

Henoc Agbota
Roberto Alesii
Muneeb Ali
Markus Anwander
Frederik Armknecht
Aline Baggio
Zinaida Benenson
Jonathan Benson
Thomas Bernoulli
Sangeeta Bhattacharya
Urs Bischoff
Eric-Oliver Blass
Alvise Bonivento
Marcin Brzozowski
Ricardo Chaves
Yu Chen
Octav Chipara
Karthik Dantu
Roberto Di Pietro
Daniel Dietterle
Fred Dijkstra
Cormac Duffy
Stefan Dulman
Anna Egorova-Förster
Leon Evers
Laura Feeney

Chien-Liang Fok
Matthias Gauger
Amitabha Ghosh
Joao Girao
Stefan Goetz
Ben Green
Yong Guan
Yukang Guo
Gertjan Halkes
Ahmed Helmy
Alban Hessler
Hans-Joachim Hof
Pai-Han Huang
Er Inn Inn
Johan Janssen
Sverker Janson
Akimitsu Kanzaki
Shyam Kapadia
Kevin Klues
Albert Krohn
Andreas Lachenmann
Caspar Lageweg
Olaf Landsiedel
Lars-Åke Larzon
Yee Wei Law
Jae-Joon Lee

Maria Lijding
Hua Liu
Dimitrios Lymberopoulos
Sanjay Madria
Mihai Marin-Perianu
Raluca Marin-Perianu
Marinus Maris
Gaia Maselli
Rene Mayrhofer
Alessandro Mei
Andreas Meier
Dragan Milic
Daniel Minder
Sridhar NagarajaRao
Tony O'Donovan
Tom Parker
Sundeep Pattem
Kaustubh Phanse
Krzysztof Piotrowski
Maxim Piz
Axel Poschmann
Olga Saukh

Robert Sauter
Zach Shelby
Adam Silberstein
Alberto Speranzon
Cormac Sreenan
Avinash Sridharan
Thomas Staub
Affan Syed
Hwee-Xian Tan
Shao Tao
Thiago Teixeira
Stefano Tennina
Daniela Tulone
Markus Waelchli
Gerald Wagenknecht
Zhiguo Wan
Xiuchao Wu
Guoliang Xing
Kiran Yedavalli
SunHee Yoon
Mingze Zhang
Benigno Zurita Ares

Supporting Institutions

Delft University of Technology, The Netherlands

Table of Contents

Versatile Support for Efficient Neighborhood Data Sharing

Andreas Lachenmann, Pedro José Marrón, Daniel Minder, Olga Saukh,
Matthias Gauger, and Kurt Rothermel

Universität Stuttgart, IPVS, Universitätsstr. 38, 70569 Stuttgart, Germany
{lachenmann, marron, minder, saukh, gauger,
rothermel}@ipvs.uni-stuttgart.de

Abstract. Many applications in wireless sensor networks rely on data from neighboring nodes. However, the effort for developing efficient solutions for sharing data in the neighborhood is often substantial. Therefore, we present a general-purpose algorithm for this task that makes use of the broadcast nature of radio transmission to reduce the number of packets. We have integrated this algorithm into *TinyXXL*, a programming language extension for data exchange. This combined system offers seamless support both for data exchange among the components of a single node and for efficient neighborhood data sharing. We show that compared to existing solutions, such as Hood, our approach further reduces the work of the application developer and provides greater efficiency.

1 Introduction

As sensor networks gain momentum and applications are increasingly developed by experts in the application domain rather than experts in sensor networks, there is a growing need to simplify standard tasks while achieving the efficiency of optimized applications. To address this issue both programming abstractions and efficient general-purpose algorithms have to be considered.

In sensor network applications one such standard task is data sharing among neighboring nodes. For example, the location of neighboring nodes [1,2] or information about their current role [3] are used by several algorithms and applications. Typically, developers create application-specific protocols for this task. This approach tends to incur significant development overhead and, for example, with a tight development budget, might often lead to inefficient solutions. Therefore, a general-purpose algorithm would not only reduce the development effort but also make neighborhood data sharing more efficient. In this paper we describe such an algorithm for neighborhood data sharing that strives to minimize the number of bytes transmitted. In addition, we use this algorithm as the basis of programming abstractions to facilitate the development of efficient applications that use data from neighboring nodes.

Although neighborhood data sharing only involves communication in a limited part of the sensor network and the size of such data is often small, the data of all nodes throughout the network adds up to considerable amounts.

K. Langendoen and T. Voigt (Eds.): EWSN 2007, LNCS 4373, pp. 1–16, 2007.

Therefore, optimizing such transmissions locally on each node can result in significant improvements regarding the number of messages sent and enhance the energy efficiency of the whole network. So far, however, most work has focused on disseminating data to all nodes in the network (e.g., [4,5,6]) or on data-centric algorithms that transmit data to a sink node (e.g., [7]). In contrast, sharing data efficiently within the neighborhood has not been studied in sufficient detail yet. Even work dealing with programming abstractions for data sharing left the actual data transmission algorithm to be created by the application developer [8], or only provided simple ones [9].

There are two classes of data sharing algorithms: push-based and pull-based approaches [10]. With push-based approaches a node providing data sends it without having received an explicit request for it. Obviously, such approaches can lead to inefficiencies when the node's neighbors do not need this data. Especially in heterogeneous networks a node cannot necessarily infer what data its neighbors need because they may execute different code. Thus nodes might transmit unnecessary data or omit data that is actually required.

The second class of data sharing algorithms is composed of pull-based approaches. Here nodes only send data when they have received a request for it. This approach is better suited for heterogeneous networks, since each node may request the data it actually needs. The only shared assumptions are that neighbors can provide the requested data and use the same naming scheme. However, a pull-based approach can incur significant overhead for sending requests.

Therefore, we have developed *Neidas* ("**NEI**ghborhood **DA**ta **S**haring algorithm"), an efficient pull-based algorithm for neighborhood data sharing. Similar to network-wide dissemination approaches, our algorithm makes use of overhearing requests and data from neighboring nodes. It leverages the advantages of both pull-based and push-based strategies: The algorithm works well with heterogeneous networks and reduces the overhead for requests.

Typically, data is not just shared among neighboring nodes but also between the software components of a single node. We address this problem with *TinyXXL* [11], an extension to the nesC programming language [12]. *TinyXXL* simplifies cross-layer data sharing and decouples the components accessing data. Its runtime component, the *TinyStateRepository*, provides efficient access to such data. We have integrated *Neidas* into *TinyXXL* to create a comprehensive approach for data sharing among components on a single node and on neighboring nodes, which reduces the effort for the developer.

The rest of this paper is organized as follows. Section 2 describes related work. In Section 3 we present our data sharing algorithm and in Section 4 its integration into *TinyXXL*. Section 5 evaluates our approach. Finally, Section 6 gives an outlook on future work and concludes this paper.

2   Related Work

Publish/subscribe systems have been used in different domains to make data available. In sensor networks several algorithms following a publish/subscribe-like paradigm have already been proposed. Perhaps the best-known example is SPIN [4], which uses such an approach to disseminate data in the network. However, these approaches typically require explicit interaction between every two nodes publishing and subscribing to data, which is not needed by our algorithm.

Gossiping algorithms are flooding-like approaches where nodes randomly forward data packets that they have received. Trickle [5] uses a gossiping variant to efficiently distribute information about code images in the whole network. It has been integrated into Deluge [6], a code distribution algorithm, and adapted for the Drip protocol [13] to transmit queries to all nodes in the network. *Neidas* is inspired by the concepts of Trickle but deals with multiple nodes requesting potentially different data. Trickle, in contrast, can assume a single or few data sources and just one kind of data. In addition, with *Neidas* changes of data are kept local whereas Trickle disseminates them through the network.

Hood [8] is a programming abstraction that tries to ease neighborhood data exchange in sensor networks. However, it leaves important parts to be added by the application developer, e.g., data transmission policies that are responsible for sending data and requests. This allows for more flexibility than our system but increases the development effort. In addition, Hood does not strive to provide a comprehensive system for both intra-node and neighborhood data exchange.

Likewise, abstract regions [9] provide programming primitives for local communication. An abstract region is defined using radio connectivity or the location of nodes, for example. Extending the neighborhood beyond immediate neighbors within radio range is something not considered by our approach yet. Like Hood, abstract regions only include a very basic data transmission algorithm. Similarly, logical neighborhoods [14] can be used for communication within a set of nodes that are not necessarily just the nodes in radio range. However, with this system a data sharing mechanism would still have to be implemented by the application developer based on other primitives.

There are numerous algorithms and applications that make use of data obtained from their neighbors. Most of them include custom solutions for neighborhood data sharing. Prominent examples are algorithms for self-organization [3], routing [1], and medium access control [15]. By factoring out the transmission of data using *TinyXXL*, developers could focus more closely on the actual purposes of their algorithms and applications.

3   Neighborhood Data Sharing Algorithm

Neidas is a data sharing algorithm that retrieves data from all neighboring nodes in radio range and continuously transmits updates when this data changes. It is based on the observation that – even in heterogeneous networks – there are typically several nodes within radio range that are interested in the same data. Therefore, our algorithm can take advantage of polite gossiping, which was first introduced in the Trickle algorithm [5]. With this approach nodes wait a random time before sending data or a request for data from neighboring nodes. If during this time k_r neighbors send the same request, polite gossiping suppresses

(1) In each request round:
    Wait for the listen-only period and random interval
    For each data item needed from neighbors:
        If less than k_r identical requests have been received:
            Send request
(2) In each data send round:
    For each data item requested by other nodes:
        If data item not requested in last data send rounds:
            Remove request
    Wait for listen-only period and random interval
    For each data item requested by other nodes:
        For local data and data received from neighbors:
            If less than k_d copies of data with same version
            number have been received from this node:
                Send data including version number
    Double duration of data send round
(3) If new neighbors arrive:
    Reset duration of data send round to one request round
(4) Request received:
    Mark data as requested
    Increment counter for request
(5) Data received:
    If data requested and data is from node in neighborhood:
        If version number > stored version number
            Store data, source node, and version number
        Else if version number == stored version number
            Increment counter for this data

Fig. 1. Overview of the *Neidas* algorithm

the transmission of redundant messages. Therefore, this algorithm leverages the broadcast nature of radio transmission: If several nodes have the same request, making each node send it would be unnecessary. Similarly, *Neidas* uses the same mechanism to locally forward the data provided by neighbors.

To deal with transmission failures and dynamic topologies *Neidas* periodically resends requests and data in so-called request and data send rounds. Fig. 1 gives an overview of the basic operation of the algorithm. Our algorithm is executed: periodically in each request round (1) and data send round (2), when new nodes arrive in the neighborhood (3), and when requests (4) or data packets (5) are received. The following subsections describe the *Neidas* algorithm in more detail.

3.1   Neighborhood Management

Since *Neidas* retrieves and stores data from neighboring nodes, it needs to know which nodes are in the neighborhood. Our current implementation includes an algorithm that intercepts all *Neidas* packets to build this neighborhood table. This algorithm does not incur any message overhead because it does not send

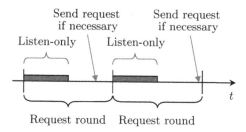

Fig. 2. Actions within request rounds

any packets itself. If it has not received any packets within a predefined interval, it removes this particular node from the table.

If there is already an algorithm available that provides the required interfaces, it can be used instead to avoid duplicate data in memory. For instance, neighborhood information can be retrieved from the *TinyStateRepository* (our cross-layer data repository [11]), SP's neighbor table [16], or accessed directly from the algorithm providing the data. To demonstrate this flexibility we implemented several such algorithms.

3.2 Sending Requests

Neidas is a pull-based algorithm, i.e., nodes send requests for data that they need. It takes advantage of overhearing messages by suppressing requests if other nodes have already sent the same one. The algorithm periodically resends requests to deal with dynamic neighborhoods and transmission failures. Therefore, it divides time into fixed-length request rounds, which are shown in Fig. 2.

Starts of rounds do not have to be synchronized on neighboring nodes. This can lead to an increased number of messages if nodes send their requests early at the beginning of a round. To avoid this problem, each round starts with a listen-only period [5] in which a node just listens for messages from its neighbors (see Fig. 2). In the rest of the round each node randomly selects a point of time at which it will send its request if by then it has not overheard at least k_r identical ones. Otherwise, it suppresses its own request in the current round.

Since neighborhoods may overlap, not necessarily all the neighbors of a node receive a request when the node overhears one. Therefore, a node might suppress its own transmission although not all of its neighbors have received the same request. This is especially a problem because there might be no other node in the neighborhood requesting that data item. Trickle can easily deal with this issue since all nodes transmit the same kind of information and because version numbers ensure that the most recent information is always sent. *Neidas*, in contrast, addresses this problem in the following way. First, the threshold k_r is set to a slightly greater value. We obtained good results with $k_r = 3$. Secondly, the random delay before sending a request ensures that not always the same nodes with the same set of neighbors send a request. Finally, following a soft-state approach with timeouts longer than a single round, nodes do not have to receive a request in every round. As shown in our simulations, in static topologies all nodes within radio range receive a request after some rounds.

If communication links are asymmetrical, i.e., node A hears node B, but B cannot receive messages from A, *Neidas* remains functional, since it does not necessarily require direct interaction between nodes to request and transmit data – given that there are other nodes with the same request. Thus *Neidas* fully makes use of the broadcast nature of radio transmission with its polite gossiping scheme.

3.3   Sending Data

Besides sending requests, *Neidas* takes care of sending the requested data itself. Nodes transmit this data in two cases. First, they send all their matching data periodically – including data received from neighboring nodes. This helps to make sure that after some retransmissions all neighbors have received it. Second, when the local data is modified, nodes send additional updates to their neighbors. This way the neighbors receive the most current data even before the next regular retransmission.

For sending data *Neidas* also takes advantage of polite gossiping: Nodes that have received data from one of their neighbors transmit it in addition to their local values. Since data is associated with a single node, only exactly the same data from the same node can suppress a transmission. In order to ensure that just the most current data is resent, the data includes a version number which is incremented whenever the data changes. To deal with version number overflows, receivers only accept data if this number is within a given range.

Since data is only relevant for the immediate neighbors and since only data originating from the same node can suppress its transmission, the polite gossiping threshold k_d for data can be smaller than k_r for requests. In addition, the version numbers define a prioritization where more recent data will not be silenced by older versions.

Nodes only accept data originating from one of the neighbors in radio range. This makes sure that data received via a third node is not disseminated throughout the network but kept within the neighborhood. Although *Neidas* currently only uses the radio range to define the neighborhood, with polite gossiping it would be easy to transmit data to differently defined groups of neighbors such as those proposed by abstract regions [9].

Data is not sent in every round in which it has been requested. The reason for this is that *Neidas* tries to reduce the number of packets. Since the data itself is often somewhat larger than a request message, it is important to minimize the number of data transmissions. Therefore, we have introduced data send rounds. All data requested in the last and current data send round is sent if k_d neighboring nodes have not already transmitted the same data. As Fig. 3 shows, a data send round is composed of one or more request rounds. The length of the data send round is doubled after each round (up to a predefined maximum

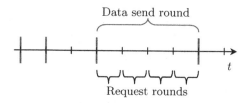

Fig. 3. Relation between request rounds and data send rounds

duration), in the figure from the length of one request round to four of them. It is reset to the length of a single request round when new nodes arrive in the neighborhood. This way these nodes receive prompt replies to their requests while greatly reducing the number of messages in static topologies. Note that changes to the length of the data send round are local to each node; they do not require any coordination among nodes. The length value reflects each node's estimate how often resends are necessary to make sure that all neighboring nodes receive a data item while keeping the rate of messages low.

We use a soft-state approach to remove requests after some time. Requested data, however, is not removed as long as the node stays within the neighborhood and there is enough memory available. So even after long data send rounds or several failed data transmissions, a node using *Neidas* still can access a previously received version of its neighbors' data from the local cache.

3.4   Further Optimizations

It is well known that radio communication consumes large amounts of energy [17]. In addition, there is also a significant MAC layer overhead associated with every packet. Therefore, reducing the number of messages is even more important than simply reducing the amount of data to be transmitted. In TinyOS and its standard MAC layer protocol [18], for instance, the MAC layer preamble, the header and the checksum included in all packets add between 17 (full duty cycle of receivers) and 2,663 bytes (low power listening with 1% duty cycle). Thus with a default data payload size of 29 bytes the overhead of sending a packet is between 58% and more than 9,000%.

Requests for neighborhood data and the data itself are expected to be comparatively small. Therefore, as an optimization *Neidas* accumulates several requests or data transmissions into a single packet. This is easily possible since *Neidas* uses small integer IDs instead of long names to identify the data and its type.

Sometimes even further optimizations are possible. Many applications and algorithms periodically send messages that do not fill the complete payload. Therefore, *Neidas* can take advantage of this free space by piggybacking its requests and data onto these messages. If the radio is operated in promiscuous mode, it does not even matter whether or not the packet is addressed to the same node as the piggybacked data, which – in our implementation – is always broadcast to all nodes in radio range. However, piggybacking is not feasible in all cases. For example, it is possible that the application does not send any data itself or that there are not enough free bytes available in the messages. Therefore, if after a time interval specified by *Neidas* the data has not been piggybacked, the piggybacking component sends a separate packet for this data.

This approach may incur some additional delays. During this time neighboring nodes might already have transmitted the same request, so that using polite gossiping it no longer has to be sent. Therefore, *Neidas* checks before actually sending the request if it is still necessary; otherwise, it cancels it.

Our implementation works with all packets sent by any TinyOS-based applications and protocols because it replaces the TinyOS components which provide the so-called active message interface immediately above the MAC layer. For both the higher-level and the MAC layer component itself piggybacking is completely transparent.

4   Programming and Runtime Support

4.1   Cross-Layer Data Exchange with *TinyXXL*

TinyXXL [11] is an extension of the nesC programming language [12] that decouples software components to ease cross-layer data exchange. With *TinyXXL* data shared among components is declared in a similar way to interfaces. Components using this data then can define dependencies without explicitly specifying the component providing it.

With automatic optimizations performed by the *TinyXXL* compiler, it is possible to develop applications that make use of cross-layer data from reusable components. For example, the compiler ensures that a single kind of data is stored only once in limited RAM and that no energy-intensive data gathering is performed redundantly. In addition, with its "virtual data items" *TinyXXL* allows the developer to create conversions and arbitrary database-like operators such as "count" and "average" to access data. This way not just the raw internal data of a component can be used by other ones but also derived data.

A pre-compiler translates *TinyXXL* source code into pure nesC code. It creates the components of the *TinyStateRepository* that stores the data at runtime. The *TinyStateRepository* offers a publish/subscribe interface with – for efficiency reasons – static subscriptions at compile-time.

4.2   Integration of Neighborhood Data Sharing

Previous versions of *TinyXXL* only allowed for data exchange among the components of a single node. To create a comprehensive system both for this kind of intra-node data exchange and for neighborhood data sharing we slightly modified *TinyXXL* to support accessing the data of neighbors and use *Neidas* in the *TinyStateRepository*. This combined system is called *TinyXXL/N*.

If a component wants to access data of its neighbors, it has to declare this property as a dependency. Then it may use the neighbors' data similar to an array

```
1  module DataAccessM {
2    uses interface Timer;
3    uses xldata RoleData as RoleDataLocal;
4    uses xldata RoleData as RoleDataN [];
5    ...
6    event result_t Timer.fired() {
7      uint8_t i;
8      for (i=0; i<Neighbors.count; i++) {
9        if (RoleDataLocal.role
10          == RoleDataN [Neighbors.nodes[i]].role) {
11    ...
```

Fig. 4. Accessing neighborhood data with *TinyXXL/N*

with the neighbors' node IDs. For instance, the code snippets in Fig. 4 show in
line 4 how a dependency for role information [3] of neighboring nodes is declared.
The brackets at the end of the line, which are not given for the dependency on the
corresponding local values (line 3), denote that data is requested from neighbors
and then accessed in an array-like fashion. With these declarations both local
role information and that of neighboring nodes can be accessed (see lines 9 and
10 in the figure). If the data of a node is accessed which has not been received
yet, a default value specified with the declaration of the data is returned (e.g.,
a reserved value indicating the absence of data). Since RAM is very limited on
sensor nodes, *Neidas* does not store separately which nodes have already sent
their data.

If data from neighboring nodes is declared to be accessed by at least one
component, the *TinyXXL* compiler reserves some memory for caching this data
locally. In addition, it adds calls to the *Neidas* algorithm to retrieve and continuously update the data. The compiler ensures that for each data item – even
if it is requested by several components – there is only one such request sent
and that the same data from a single node is stored only once in RAM. This
way applications can benefit from the advantages of *Neidas* without adding the
burden of implementing data exchange on the application developer. In fact, it
is possible to retrieve some arbitrary data from the *TinyStateRepository*. The
developer of the code running on the neighboring nodes does not have to be
aware of the fact that an already existing piece of data might be needed by
another node. This is an important advantage of our approach that facilitates
independent development of software in heterogeneous sensor networks as well
as reusability and exchangeability of components, whose data is automatically
shared with neighboring nodes when necessary.

One inherent assumption of this solution is that on neighboring nodes the
data is provided by a component and stored in the *TinyStateRepository*. Because of optimizations performed by the *TinyXXL* compiler, data is only gathered on a node if there is a component that needs to access it locally. Otherwise,
it removes the data gathering code to reduce runtime overhead. In this case

these nodes cannot answer requests for such neighborhood data. Therefore, like with manually implemented data sharing, the developer has to ensure that data needed from neighboring nodes is available.

If a node just accesses its local values and not those of its neighbors, there is almost no overhead associated with the integration of *Neidas*. In this case *Neidas* does not transmit any request messages. In addition, its RAM consumption is almost negligible: There is no need to reserve memory for local copies of neighborhood data, if the node does not use it. However, *Neidas* has to reserve two single bits for each kind of data in order to check if it has been requested by neighboring nodes within the most recent data send rounds.

Our solution offers the benefits of *TinyXXL* also for neighborhood data sharing. For example, it decouples components providing and accessing data: The component providing a piece of data that is needed by another node can be different from the one requesting data. In fact, in heterogeneous networks the component providing this data does not have to be part of the application requesting it. In addition, just like with local data it is possible to use virtual data items to transform data or perform some computations on it. Thus a neighboring node does not have to store a piece of data in order to provide it, as long as it can be converted to the target format. Furthermore, by taking advantage of the *TinyStateRepository*'s publish/subscribe mechanism the system can transmit updated data to its neighbors if it has been modified.

5   Evaluation

5.1   Experimental Setup

We have simulated *Neidas* and *TinyXXL/N* using Avrora [19], which accurately emulates the behavior of Mica2 nodes. Unless otherwise noted, each simulation scenario contains 50 nodes which are randomly placed in a 60 m × 60 m rectangular area. Since communication is only local to the neighborhood, we expect that the results are also valid for larger-size networks.

The nodes' radio model is set to a lossy model, which is based on empirical data and has a transmission range of about 15 m. The TinyOS MAC layer takes care of multiple accesses to the radio channel. The measurements shown are the average of 10 runs of 600 simulated seconds each. We have set *Neidas*'s polite gossiping thresholds k_r to 3 and k_d to 1. As described above, experiments have shown that good results can be obtained with these values. The duration of a request round has been set to 10 s for all algorithms but in long-running experiments this value can be neglected – as long as all algorithms use the same duration. Nodes are turned on randomly in the first 10 s and are not switched off before the end of the simulation. Unless otherwise noted, we have not made use of piggybacking optimizations.

5.2   Efficiency of *Neidas*

We have created straight-forward implementations of standard pull-based and push-based algorithms, which are likely to be integrated in similar form in real

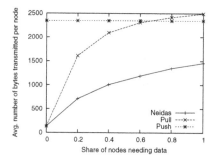

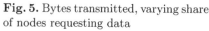

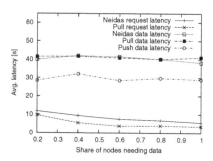

Fig. 5. Bytes transmitted, varying share of nodes requesting data

Fig. 6. Latency until requests and data have been received

applications. For a meaningful comparison, all of them use the same underlying data format and marshaling components as *Neidas*.

The pull-based algorithm periodically requests the data of neighboring nodes but does not suppress requests already heard. Similar to *Neidas* it does not service a request immediately but waits until the next round. However, it does not distinguish between request and data send rounds. The push-based algorithm periodically broadcasts its data without the need for requests. Neither of these algorithms resends data from neighboring nodes.

In our simulations all nodes provide a single data item of 10 bytes. We have varied the ratio of (randomly selected) nodes that needed this data. The only messages sent are those to request and transmit data.

Fig. 5 shows the total number of bytes transmitted by each node on average – including the packet header, preamble, etc. Since there are no big differences in the processing overhead of the three algorithms, overall energy consumption is dominated by the radio. Therefore, the energy consumed by the algorithms can be inferred from the number of bytes transmitted.

The push-based algorithm always transmits the same number of bytes because it does not distinguish between nodes that need data and those that do not. In contrast, for the pull-based algorithm the number of bytes transmitted grows with the percentage of nodes requesting data. If this percentage is greater than about 70%, the pull-based algorithm is less efficient than the push-based one because of the additional overhead for request messages. Even when all nodes request data, the overhead for these requests is relatively small. The reason for this is that the pull-based algorithm uses the efficient underlying techniques from *Neidas* to build packets. Therefore, requests are usually sent together with the data as a single message, and there is no overhead for the packet header, preamble, etc. Otherwise, the numbers of the pull-based algorithm would be up to 500% greater (not shown in the figure), because the payload is very small and thus the overhead of sending extra packets has even greater effects.

Neidas transmits much fewer bytes than these two algorithms. Depending on the number of nodes requesting data, it only sends between 30% and 62% of the

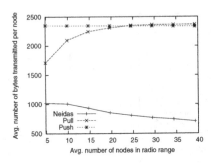

Fig. 7. Bytes transmitted varying the node density

number of bytes of the push-based algorithm and between 44% and 58% of the pull-based algorithm. Up to 20% of the savings compared to the corresponding pull-based approach are due to polite gossiping of requests. This percentage increases with higher node densities. Enlarging the length of data send rounds is responsible for the rest of the savings.

Fig. 6 compares the average latency until a node entering the neighborhood receives requests and data. The request latency of *Neidas* is up to 4 s greater than that of the pull-based algorithm because of suppressed request messages in overlapping neighborhoods. However, when comparing the latency of the data itself, the values for both algorithms are almost identical because with *Neidas* nodes are able to provide also data requested from their neighbors. The data latency of the push-based algorithm, of course, is even shorter, since with this algorithm nodes do not wait for requests before they send their data. The values for the data latency may seem comparatively high given the duration of the request rounds of 10 s. However, these numbers are average values until the data from *all* neighboring nodes has been received. Due to lossy links and collisions, some nodes have to send their data several times.

Fig. 7 shows the average number of bytes transmitted for different node densities. To get these values we have varied the total number of nodes from 25 to 200. The size of the area is kept constant and always 40% of the nodes request data from their neighbors. The figure shows that the values for the pull-based algorithm increase by about 38% with higher densities until all nodes are in the neighborhood of at least one node requesting data. For the push-based algorithm the number of bytes is constant, since each node sends its data independent of other ones. With *Neidas*, the number of bytes transmitted by each node even decreases by about 30% with higher densities although in these cases more nodes have to send their data. This is because more nodes overhear packets from their neighbors which avoids sending the same request several times.

As the results show, *Neidas* is suitable for both heterogeneous and homogeneous networks. Considering the benefits such as the small number of transmitted bytes shown in Fig. 5 and its ability to profit from high node densities (Fig. 7), for many applications *Neidas* offers a good compromise between efficiency and timely delivery of data.

5.3   Comparison with Hood

We have implemented a simple algorithm that builds a tree to route data to a sink node with both Hood and *TinyXXL/N*. In this example all nodes request their neighbors' depth in the routing tree. They then select the neighbor with the smallest depth as their parent and adjust their own depth value. Using Hood we have implemented two versions: The first one minimizes the number of messages by solely relying on Hood's auto-push policy that only broadcasts updates when the data changes. The second one is able to deal better with new nodes and transmission failures of lossy links by periodically requesting the neighbors' values in addition to the automatic updates. This version resembles more closely the properties of *Neidas* but with its forwarding of neighbor data *Neidas* is able to provide even better reliability. Depending on the properties required by the application, the solution actually implemented by the developer will probably lie somewhere within the boundaries defined by the two Hood versions. The *TinyXXL/N* implementation, however, automatically integrates *Neidas* so that the application developer does not have to deal with these low-level details.

Both the Hood versions and the *TinyXXL/N* version of the code use equivalent neighborhood management algorithms. These algorithms do not send any information themselves but use the node IDs transmitted with each request and data packet. It is an integral part of Hood's concepts that the neighborhood management algorithm has to be written by the application developer whereas in the *TinyXXL/N* version *Neidas*'s default neighborhood management algorithm is used.

Fig. 8 visualizes the total number of bytes sent by the Hood versions and the *TinyXXL/N* version for different node densities. Since the standard push-only version of Hood sends data just when it is modified, this algorithm transmits the smallest number of bytes. However, it is not able to deal with transmission failures and newly deployed nodes as it sends data only once. These two properties are fulfilled by the other two versions of the application. Therefore, these implementations offer different functionality and can hardly be compared. Thus we limit the following discussion to the *TinyXXL/N* variant and the Hood version including data pulls.

As expected, the number of bytes sent by *TinyXXL/N* decreases with high densities since it is based on *Neidas*. In contrast, the Hood version does not make use of overhearing messages and, therefore, has to transmit significantly more data if the number of nodes in radio range increases. For the highest node density the *TinyXXL/N* version sends only 24% of the number of bytes transmitted by Hood.

When compiled for Mica2 nodes, our sample application including the operating system components reserves 810 bytes of RAM in the Hood versions and just 608 bytes in the *TinyXXL/N* version (25% less). Most of *TinyXXL/N*'s savings are due to fewer variables used in the marshaling components as well as in the components storing data. With RAM sizes of just a few kilobytes such optimizations are crucial in order to be able to create complex applications.

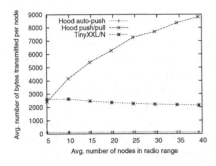
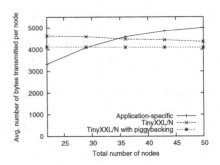

Fig. 8. Bytes transmitted compared with Hood

Fig. 9. Bytes transmitted for the Sense-R-Us application

From a developer's point of view creating the application with *TinyXXL/N* incurs significantly less overhead. The routing tree algorithm described above was implemented in 176 lines of code with Hood (for the version including data pulls) vs. 88 lines of code with *TinyXXL/N*. This means that the *TinyXXL/N* implementation needs 50% fewer lines of code than the Hood implementation. Most of these savings, however, are due to the fact that Hood requires the developer to implement a separate neighborhood management algorithm, which is already present in the *TinyXXL/N* solution. Although such numbers do not necessarily allow to draw conclusions about the complexity of the code, they can give a rough estimate about the effort needed by the application developer. Considering that Hood already reduces complexity compared to manual implementations [8], the overhead reductions of *TinyXXL/N* are even more significant.

5.4   Integration in Sense-R-Us

Sense-R-Us [2] is an application that uses a sensor network to provide the functionality of a smart environment where the current location of researchers in our department can be queried. In addition, Sense-R-Us is able to detect meetings using both sensory inputs and information about neighboring nodes. In this application there are stationary nodes placed in rooms and mobile ones that are carried by persons. The mobile nodes use neighborhood data from the stationary ones to localize themselves by requesting information about the location of neighboring nodes. A mobile node's location is set to the value of a neighboring node, which has been selected using the received signal strength.

We compare an implementation of Sense-R-Us that has been built using *TinyXXL/N* with the original one for which neighborhood data sharing has been implemented manually. This version uses Sense-R-Us's custom querying protocol, which tries to reduce the number of messages by intelligently selecting the nodes to be queried. However, it does not leverage broadcast communication and comes at the expense of significant development overhead.

In our experiments we simulated up to 50 nodes of which 22 ones are stationary. The remaining nodes are mobile and move using a random walk model.

Fig. 9 shows the number of bytes transmitted by the application-specific implementation of Sense-R-Us, a version using *TinyXXL/N*, and another *TinyXXL/N* version that takes advantage of the piggybacking optimization described in Section 3.4. These numbers also include packets transmitted by other components, e.g., to discover neighboring nodes. As the figure shows, for low densities with no or only few mobile nodes the performance of the *TinyXXL/N* versions is worse compared to the optimized application-specific solution. If, however, the node density is increased, the *TinyXXL/N* version can take advantage of overhearing messages and the number of bytes sent by each node decreases. For the application-specific implementation, in contrast, the number of bytes sent increases by almost 50% when adding more mobile nodes. The reason for this is that this implementation relies solely on point-to-point communication. Therefore, separate messages might have to be sent even if other nodes have similar requests. If *TinyXXL/N*'s piggybacking optimization is used, the number of bytes transmitted is reduced by between 8% and 13% compared to the other *TinyXXL/N* implementation. These savings are due to the reduced number of packets sent by this variant. Although piggybacking could also be incorporated in an application-specific solution, using *TinyXXL/N* has the advantage that it comes "for free" without requiring the developer to manually implement it.

6   Conclusions and Future Work

In this paper we have presented *Neidas*, a pull-based algorithm for neighborhood data sharing. Compared to other approaches it provides better efficiency by suppressing duplicate requests in the neighborhood. If the node density is high, the average number of bytes transmitted by each node decreases. We have integrated this algorithm with *TinyXXL*, an extension of the nesC programming language for cross-layer data sharing. The combined system, *TinyXXL/N*, is a comprehensive system for both data exchange among components and neighborhood data sharing. Using *Neidas* as its basis *TinyXXL/N* offers efficient data sharing at largely reduced development costs. For example, in heterogeneous networks the developer of a node providing data does not even have to be aware that this data might be required by another one. We are convinced that this combined system will lead to efficient applications which are developed with reduced effort.

Regarding future work we plan on making *Neidas* adaptable to the density of nodes requesting data by dynamically adjusting the threshold k_r. This will further reduce the number of requests in dense networks while increasing the share of nodes in the neighborhood that receive a request.

References

1. Karp, B., Kung, H.T.: GPSR: Greedy perimeter stateless routing for wireless networks. In: Proc. of the Conf. on Mobile Comp. and Netw. (2000) 243–254
2. Minder, D., Marrón, P.J., Lachenmann, A., Rothermel, K.: Experimental construction of a meeting model for smart office environments. In: Proc. of the Workshop on Real-World Wireless Sensor Networks, SICS Technical Report T2005:09. (2005)

3. Frank, C., Römer, K.: Algorithms for generic role assignment in wireless sensor networks. In: Proc. of the Int'l Conf. on Embedded Netw. Sensor Systems. (2005)
4. Heinzelman, W.R., Kulik, J., Balakrishnan, H.: Adaptive protocols for information dissemination in wireless sensor networks. In: Proc. of the Int'l Conf. on Mobile Computing and Networking. (1999) 174–185
5. Levis, P., Patel, N., Culler, D., Shenker, S.: Trickle: A self-regulating algorithm for code propagation and maintenance in wireless sensor networks. In: Proc. of the 1st Symp. on Networked Systems Design and Implementation. (2004) 15–28
6. Hui, J.W., Culler, D.: The dynamic behavior of a data dissemination protocol for network programming at scale. In: Proc. of the 2nd Int'l Conf. on Embedded Networked Sensor Systems. (2004) 81–94
7. Intanagonwiwat, C., Govindan, R., Estrin, D.: Directed diffusion: a scalable and robust communication paradigm for sensor networks. In: Proc. of the Int'l Conf. on Mobile Computing and Networking. (2000) 56–67
8. Whitehouse, K., Sharp, C., Brewer, E., Culler, D.: Hood: a neighborhood abstraction for sensor networks. In: Proc. of the 2nd International Conference on Mobile Systems, Applications, and Services. (2004) 99–110
9. Welsh, M., Mainland, G.: Programming sensor networks using abstract regions. In: Proc. of the Symp. on Network Systems Design and Impl. (2004) 29–42
10. Franklin, M., Zdonik, S.: A framework for scalable dissemination-based systems. In: Proc. of the 12th Conf. on Object-Oriented Programming, Systems, Languages, and Applications. (1997) 94–105
11. Lachenmann, A., Marrón, P.J., Minder, D., Gauger, M., Saukh, O., Rothermel, K.: TinyXXL: Language and runtime support for cross-layer interactions. In: Proc. of the Conf. on Sensor, Mesh and Ad Hoc Comm. and Networks. (2006) 178–187
12. Gay, D., Levis, P., von Behren, R., Welsh, M., Brewer, E., Culler, D.: The nesC language: A holistic approach to networked embedded systems. In: Proc. of the Conf. on Programming Language Design and Implementation. (2003) 1–11
13. Tolle, G., Culler, D.: Design of an application-cooperative management system for wireless sensor networks. In: Proc. of the Second European Workshop on Wireless Sensor Networks. (2005) 121–132
14. Mottola, L., Picco, G.P.: Logical neighborhoods: A programming abstraction for wireless sensor networks. In: Proc. of the Int'l Conf. on Distributed Computing in Sensor Systems. (2006) 150–168
15. Ye, W., Heidemann, J., Estrin, D.: An energy-efficient MAC protocol for wireless sensor networks. In: Proc. of IEEE INFOCOM 2002. (2002) 1567–1576
16. Polastre, J., Hui, J., Levis, P., Yhao, J., Culler, D., Shenker, S., Stoica, I.: A unifying link abstraction for wireless sensor networks. In: Proc. of the 3rd Int'l Conf. on Embedded Networked Sensor Systems. (2005)
17. Shnayder, V., Hempstead, M., Chen, B.r., Allen, G.W., Welsh, M.: Simulating the power consumption of large-scale sensor network applications. In: Proc. of the 2nd Int'l Conf. on Embedded Networked Sensor Systems. (2004) 188–200
18. Polastre, J., Hill, J., Culler, D.: Versatile low power media access for wireless sensor networks. In: Proc. of the 2nd Int'l Conf. on Embedded Networked Sensor Systems. (2004) 95–107
19. Titzer, B., Lee, D., Palsberg, J.: Avrora: Scalable sensor network simulation with precise timing. In: Proc. of the Conf. on Information Proc. in Sensor Netw. (2005)

An Energy-Efficient K-Hop Clustering Framework for Wireless Sensor Networks

Quanbin Chen, Jian Ma, Yanmin Zhu, Dian Zhang, and Lionel M. Ni

Department of Computer Science and Engineering,
The Hong Kong University of Science and Technology
{chenqb, majian, zhuym, zhangd, ni}@cse.ust.hk

Abstract. Many applications in wireless sensor networks (WSNs) benefit significantly from organizing nodes into groups, called clusters, because data aggregation and data filtering applied in each cluster can greatly help to reduce traffic. The size of a cluster is measured by the hop distance from the farthest node to the cluster head. Rather than 1-hop clustering, K-hop clustering is preferred by many energy-constrained applications. However, existing solutions fail to distribute clusters evenly across the sensing field, which may lead to unbalanced energy consumption and network inefficiency. Moreover, they incur high communication overhead. We propose an Evenly Distributed Clustering (EDC) algorithm. Constrained by the maximum cluster size K, EDC distributes clusters uniformly, and minimizes the number of clusters. By introducing a relative synchronization technique, EDC converges fast with low communication overhead. It also helps to improve the successful transmission rate from nodes to their cluster heads. The simulation results indicate that EDC outperforms other existing algorithms.

1 Introduction

Many applications for wireless sensor networks (WSNs), such as habitat monitoring [1], require each sensor node to sample the environment periodically and report the sensed data back to the base station. It is noticed that spatial locality exists prevalently among sensed data in these applications. Traffic can be reduced by data aggregation and data filtering techniques. Therefore, sensor networks can benefit significantly from organizing nodes into groups, called *clusters*. In each cluster, there is usually one responsible node, called *cluster head*. Other nodes in the group will send data to the cluster head, instead of reporting directly to the base station.

The clustering problem has been studied in the literature of WSNs. Most of the algorithms adopt heuristic approaches [12] [17], in which each sensor node exchanges information with its neighbors. 1-hop clusters can be formed based on 1-hop information. Similarly, by collecting information from all the nodes within 2 hops, 2-hop clusters can be made. However, 1-hop or even 2-hop clustering generates too many clusters, which may lead to energy inefficiency.

We define K-hop clustering, in which each node is either a cluster head or at most K hops away from a cluster head. K is decided according to the requirements of

K. Langendoen and T. Voigt (Eds.): EWSN 2007, LNCS 4373, pp. 17–33, 2007.

different applications. For example, when monitoring the temperature in a weather study application, the system requires only one reading from each sensing region, say 3000m², in a sampling cycle, because the temperature in a region varies slightly. Thus, if each sensor node has a communication range roughly between 10 meters to 15 meters, 3-hop clusters can approximate these equal-sized sensing regions and one temperature report from each cluster head is sufficient. However, optimizing the number of K-hop clusters, with a given K, is a well-known NP-complete problem [3].

Some algorithms, like MaxMin [3], attempt to address the K-hop clustering problem in the context of wireless ad hoc networks. However, the communication overhead in MaxMin is quite high, and the distribution of the clusters highly depends on the node ID distribution. The first K-hop clustering algorithm in wireless sensor networks [6] adopts a stochastic approach, which has very low traffic overload. Unfortunately, the distribution of clusters is rather poor. In wireless sensor networks, a good clustering should distribute clusters evenly across the sensing field, minimize the number of clusters in order to achieve energy efficiency, and maximize the successful transmission rate from the member nodes to their corresponding cluster heads. The extremely challenging issue lying in the clustering problem of wireless sensor networks is how to achieve good cluster distribution with small communication overhead.

In this paper, we propose an algorithm, namely Evenly Distributed Clustering algorithm (EDC), to establish a K-hop clustering network framework. It combines the positive features of traditional heuristic approaches and stochastic approaches, which can generate good cluster distribution and introduce small communication overhead, respectively. Furthermore, EDC can minimize the number of clusters and evenly distribute clusters across the sensing field. One of our main contributions is to reduce communication overhead significantly by introducing a relative synchronization technique. In addition, EDC helps to improve the successful transmission rate from nodes to their cluster heads. It can be employed independently of network topology, network scale, and node density. To the best of our knowledge, this is the first work to evenly distribute clusters across the sensing field, to minimize the number of K-hop clusters, and to concern the successful transmission rate between member nodes and cluster heads in order to achieve an energy-efficient network framework in wireless sensor networks.

The rest of the paper is organized as follows. Section 2 highlights the related work. We discuss the design principles and introduce basic assumptions in Section 3. Section 4 describes the Evenly Distributed Clustering algorithm (EDC) in detail. The simulation results and evaluations are illustrated in Section 5. Section 6 concludes the paper and lists some future work.

2 Related Work

Many efforts have been devoted to network clustering of ad hoc networks. From the perspective of algorithm approaches, there are three categories. In the first category, all the nodes have a global knowledge of the network. Decisions are made independently by each node [4] [5]. This approach is definitely not suitable for wireless sensor networks. In the second category, every node only has the knowledge

Fig. 1. Unevenly distributed cluster heads generated by the MaxMin algorithm. (K=3).

Fig. 2. Evenly distributed cluster heads in the ideal case. (K=3).

about its neighbors, or 2-hop neighbors. Cluster heads will be elected according to this local information [7] [8] [9]. This approach is adopted by many 1-hop clustering heuristics as it can achieve good network clustering with low overhead. Third, nodes do not need to exchange information with neighbors when self-electing cluster heads. Stochastic decisions are made independently upon some pre-determined parameters [6] [10]. This scheme introduces low communication overhead but produces poor distribution of the clusters.

From the perspective of parameters used in cluster head selection, early work usually employs node ID [3] [8] [9]. Node degree [11] is introduced in order to minimize the number of clusters; mobile status is taken into account in the context of mobile ad hoc networks aimed to maintain stable cluster organization; remaining energy [10] is considered to prolong the network lifetime. In some algorithms, all the above factors are integrated such that they are adaptive to different contexts [7].

Topology control [12] [13] [14], including the dominating set problem [15] [16] [17], is similar to clustering. It tries to select some nodes to form the network backbone. Other nodes are guaranteed to reach the backbone nodes within one hop.

However, most work mentioned above can only construct 1-hop clusters. In contrast, MaxMin [3] generates K-hop clusters. Every node elects the one with the largest ID in its K hops as a cluster head, and then associates to the head with the smallest ID, in order to balance the cluster size. However, communication overhead is relatively high, particularly when K is large. In addition, the clusters are not evenly distributed. It fails in some pathological cases, as shown in Fig. 1, in which node ID are assigned orderly according to the topology.

LEACH [10] is the first clustering solution specific in the context of wireless sensor networks. The algorithm does not require any communication overhead in electing cluster heads. Instead, each sensor node declares itself as a head with some probability. However, it is not guaranteed that every node is within K hops of a cluster head, and cluster heads cannot be evenly distributed by the probabilistic method. Moreover, the implementation of LEACH is constrained by two assumptions. First, the network size and the number of clusters are known in advance on each node. Second, all the nodes are well synchronized such that cluster heads can be re-elected periodically to balance energy consumption. A similar design is adopted in [6]. Each sensor node announces itself as a cluster head with a probability q. After the self-announcement process, the nodes lying farther than K hops away from any existing cluster heads will become cluster heads. Based on a mathematical model, the best q and K are calculated to minimize energy consumption in the many-to-one communication pattern. This algorithm, however, fails to provide even distribution of cluster heads, and may elect a large number of cluster heads.

3 Preliminaries

The first characteristic of a good K-hop clustering we discussed is to evenly distribute cluster heads across the sensing field. Evenly distributed clusters can balance energy consumption and achieve fair data fidelity, but few existing solutions focus on the even distribution of cluster heads. For example, in Fig. 1, all the nodes except the left three are elected as cluster heads if the MaxMin algorithm is applied. Indeed, only two cluster heads are sufficient in the ideal case, as Fig. 2 depicts. To formalize the even distribution feature, we introduce some restrictions as follows.

Condition 1: Every node is either a cluster head, or within K hops from one cluster head.

Condition 2: Every two cluster heads must be at least K+1 hops away from each other.

Condition 1 is the basic requirement of K-hop clustering. Condition 2 restricts that the distance between any two cluster heads is not shorter than K+1. These two conditions implicitly help to achieve an even distribution of cluster heads, while to minimize the number of cluster heads.

The second characteristic of a good K-hop clustering is to minimize communication overhead when forming clusters. When each node holds the information of all its K-hop neighbors, it might not be difficult for each node to determine whether to be a head or a member node. However, huge communication overhead occurs in this case. To select K-hop cluster heads based on 1-hop neighbors' information is the key issue we will solve in the EDC algorithm.

The third characteristic is to improve the successful transmission rate from the nodes to their corresponding cluster heads. Intuitively, a node that is located at the center of a cluster, and has good link quality to its neighbors should be an ideal head. Thus, a clustering parameter should be well designed to describe the suitability of a node as a potential head.

Before describing the EDC algorithm, we make several assumptions on wireless sensor networks as follows:

· Each node is stationary.
· The neighborhood of each node is fixed.
· Each node has a unique ID.
· Each link is symmetric.
· Messages broadcast by a node can be received correctly by all its neighbors.
· No location information is available on each node.
· No synchronization service is required.
· Neither routing nor multi-hop broadcast service is required.

The first three assumptions guarantee that we have a network topology which can be depicted by a graph. We mainly use a graph (it is not necessary to be a planar graph.) to help us analyze the algorithm. Stationary deployment of nodes is reasonable in wireless sensor networks, and asymmetric links can be filtered by some techniques in the MAC or the routing layer [2]. However, the fixed neighborhood can hardly be maintained in wireless sensor networks as the links are highly dynamic. Moreover, reliable broadcast is impractical in real environments. We claim that we make these assumptions in order to simplify the analysis of the algorithm. We will relax some of them to investigate the performance in simulation.

4 EDC Algorithm

In this section, we first present the basic idea of EDC, and introduce the data structures that each node maintains. Second, the key part of EDC, the head selection criteria is detailed. Third, we discuss some parameters defined in the EDC algorithm. At last, we prove the correctness of the algorithm.

4.1 Basic Idea

EDC is a heuristic approach, in which each node only exchanges its head selection with its neighbors. Based on neighbors' selection results, each node chooses the nearest head as its cluster head, satisfying Condition 1 and Condition 2. Selection will be updated once a node hears its neighbors' new selections. Finally, the algorithm finishes when there is no more update in the network, and every node is either a cluster head or a member node.

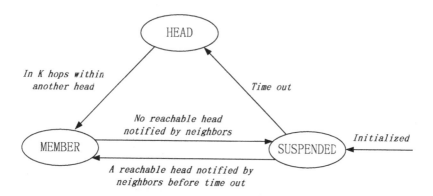

Fig. 3. Three states of a node in EDC

There are three states for nodes in EDC shown in Fig. 3, which are HEAD, MEMBER, and SUSPENDED. A node has declared itself to be a cluster head in the HEAD state, or has joined a cluster as a member node in the MEMBER state. A node in the SUSPENDED state is neither a cluster head nor a member node. Nodes may shift among the three states during the algorithm execution. When the algorithm terminates, each node is either in HEAD or in MEMBER.

For each node, the state is initialized as SUSPENDED, and an initialization timer t_{init} is triggered. When the timer expires, the node will change from SUSPENDED to

HEAD, and broadcast a notification to declare itself to be a cluster head. If a suspended node receives neighbors' notifications and joins a cluster before timeout, it will shift to MEMBER, and also broadcast a notification of its selection. A head node may change to a member node when it finds out that there is another head existing within K hops. If a member node originally joining a cluster cannot find any available head on its neighbors' new selections, it will be suspended and a timer t_{wait} is set.

When a node receives a notification from its neighbor, it reselects the cluster head, sets the state, and broadcasts a notification if there is any update.

4.2 Data Structures

The data structures of each node comprise of a number of locally estimated parameters, as well as the selection results of the node's 1-hop neighbors.

Clustering Parameter p. It estimates the suitability of a node as a potential head. Generally, the larger the p is, the more likely the node will become a cluster head. Clustering parameter is ready on commencement. We will discuss its selection later.

Initialization Timer t_{init}. It is set on each node when the algorithm is initialized. We try to fine-tune it for fast convergence.

Suspending Timer t_{wait}. When a node changes from MEMBER to SUSPENDED, a suspending timer is set.

Cluster Head Info. This is the information about the cluster head that a node chooses to associate to. It includes the head ID (h_id), the head's clustering parameter (h_p), the hop count (h_c), and the parent ID (p_id).

Neighbor Table. If a node has m 1-hop neighbors, its neighbor table has m entries. Each entry includes a neighbor ID (n_id), and the neighbor's cluster head info.

Notification. It is the message broadcast by nodes, which is supposed to be received by 1-hop neighbors only. Notification contains the node's cluster head info.

4.3 Head Selection Criteria

The most critical part of the EDC algorithm is to select the cluster head upon 1-hop neighbors' selection results in order to form K-hop clusters, and restrict every two cluster heads at least K+1 hops away with low communication overhead. To clearly illustrate the EDC design, it is necessary to introduce the following definitions.

Definition 1: A node's *reachable heads* are the heads chosen by its neighbors. Meanwhile, the following two conditions must be satisfied: 1) the head is reachable within K hops; 2) if a neighbor chooses the node as the parent, the neighbor's head selection should be ignored. The first constraint guarantees to generate K-hop clusters, and the second constraint is to avoid the slow convergence problem.

Definition 2: Head A is *stronger (weaker)* than head B, if the clustering parameter of A is larger (smaller) than that of B. If the clustering parameters of A and B are equal, the node ID will be used to break the tie.

Definition 3: Reachable heads of a node can be divided into two groups, *survivable heads* and *dying heads*. Dying heads are the heads which should change back to MEMBER from the node's point of view, and other heads are survivable heads. Every pair of its survivable heads is at least K+1 hops away from each other.

Sorting Head Candidates
1.   *Sorted Candidate Head List (CHL) = NULL*
2.   **for** *each neighbor*
3.   **if** (*p_id != node ID && h_c < K*)
4.   *CHL.InsertSort (h_p, h_id, h_c)* *

Filtering Dying Heads
1.   *num = length of CHL*
2.   *new flags[num], set 1 to each item*
3.   **for** *i = num*-1 : 0
4.   **if** (*flags[i] == 0*) *continue*
5.   **for** *j = 0 : i − 1*
6.   **if** (*CHL[i].h_c + CHL[j].h_c + 2 <= K*)
7.   *flags[j] = 0*

Getting Survivable Heads
1.   **for** *i = 1:num*
2.   **if** (*flags[i] == 1*)
3.   *Add CHL[i] to survivable heads set*

---

* CHL is sorted in the ascending order of clustering parameter and node ID. The item being inserted with a head ID which has already existed in CHL will be ignored, but the hop count will be updated to the smaller one.

Fig. 4. Pseudo-code to get survivable heads set

Suppose that some nodes have declared to be cluster heads, and every other node chooses the nearest reachable head as its cluster head. If there exist two heads within K hops, the conflict can be detected by some nodes between these two heads. The stronger one becomes a survivable head according to the definition, while the weaker one becomes a dying head. We show how to filter dying heads locally as depicted in Fig. 4. Each node sorts its reachable heads in the sorted candidate head list (CHL) according to clustering parameter. Node ID is used to break the tie. The "strongest" head is chosen from CHL to delete the heads which are lying within K hops from it. After filtering, the "strongest" head will be deleted from CHL, and put into the survivable heads set. Then, the remaining "strongest" head in the CHL is chosen to eliminate the dying heads again, after which it is deleted from CHL and added to the survivable heads set. The process will continue until the CHL has no head left.

The straightforward way to notify dying heads is to generate multi-hop messages destined to those dying heads. It, however, incurs traffic overhead, and it requires one-to-one routing service which is usually unavailable. Instead of doing this, the node in EDC just broadcasts its selection result to the 1-hop neighbors. The selection result reflects the conflicts and forces the neighbor nodes which have chosen the dying heads as the cluster heads to reselect. Finally, dying heads will detect the conflict by themselves, and then change to member nodes.

The selection criteria for each node are listed as follows. If the survivable heads set is not null, the nearest head in the survivable heads set will be chosen as the candidate. Node ID will be applied to break the tie.

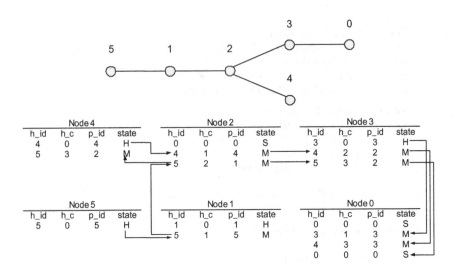

Fig. 5. An example of the head selection process of EDC when K=3. Arrows represent the notifications, which trigger updates.

Rule 1: (For member nodes) set the candidate as the cluster head; broadcast a notification if the head selection is updated.

Rule 2: (For suspended nodes) change to a member node after choosing the candidate as the cluster head; broadcast a notification; stop the timer t_{init} or t_{wait}.

Rule 3: (For head nodes) if the node is weaker than the candidate, it will change to a member node and broadcast a notification. Otherwise, no change is needed.

If the survivable candidate heads set is null, there's no available candidate.

Rule 4: (For suspended and head nodes) no change.

Rule 5: (For member nodes) change to SUSPENDED; broadcast a notification; set a timer t_{wait}.

An illustrative example is shown in Fig. 5. At a snapshot, node 0 and node 2 are still in the initialized SUSPENDED state, while the timers t_{init} of node 1, 3, 4, and 5 have just expired. We assume the clustering parameters to satisfy $p_5 > p_4 > p_3 > p_2 > p_1 > p_0$. For node 2, it first selects node 4 as its cluster head, and broadcasts a notification. When node 3 receives this notification, it is aware that a stronger head 4 exists and then changes back to a member node. Later, node 2 updates its selection to head 5 and broadcasts a notification again. After that, node 4 changes to a member node, and node 3 updates its selection to head 5. Then, node 1, 2, 3, 4 are member nodes which all choose node 5 as their cluster heads. Node 0 cannot find any available head from its neighbor node 3, and consequently it is suspended with a random timer t_{wait} being set. After this timer expires later, node 0 will declare itself to be a head, and finally node 3 will choose node 0 as its cluster head, while others remain unchanged.

4.4 Parameter Selection

4.4.1 Clustering Parameter

Clustering parameter p is defined to estimate the suitability of each node as a potential head. In EDC, we use it to determine which heads should be survivable when there are conflicts. Note that the selection of the clustering parameter will not affect the correctness of EDC, because node ID is the second parameter to break the tie.

In a cluster of sensor nodes, we mainly concern that member nodes can reach the cluster head through the routes with good path quality. In other words, the successful transmission rate from member nodes to the cluster head can be maximized. Therefore, it is appropriate to select the node with the best average path quality to all its K-hop neighbors as the cluster head. However, it is costly to obtain the path quality from a node to each of its K-hop neighbors. We use the following definition instead.

Definition 4: 1-*hop connectivity* of a node refers to the sum of link quality estimated to each of its 1-hop neighbors.

$$p^i_{1-connectivity} = \sum_{j \in \{id \,:\, i's\ neighbor\}} q_{j,i}$$

where $q_{j,i}$ represents the link quality from node j to node i.

Definition 5: *K-hop connectivity* of a node refers to the weighted sum of 1-hop connectivity of all the nodes within its K-1 hops (including the node itself).

$$p^i_{K-connectivity} = \sum_{j \in \{id \,:\, i's\ (K-1)-hop\ neighbor\}} \frac{p^j_{1-connectivity}}{d_{i,j} + 1}$$

where $d_{i,j}$ is the hop distance between node i and node j.

We choose K-hop connectivity as the clustering parameter p in EDC, as it can reflect the connectivity inside the node's K-hop neighborhood. With $d_{i,j}$, the nodes with many 1-hop neighbors are preferred. It does make sense from the aspect of higher successful transmission rate from nodes to head, and load balance among nodes. However, communication overhead is incurred to get the K-hop connectivity parameter, when K is larger than one. Particularly when K is large, the overhead cannot be ignored. In order to reduce traffic, we may adopt 1-hop connectivity, or fixed small hop connectivity instead. We will discuss them in simulation.

We do not aim to solve the optimization problem in the clustering, and instead we propose a simple yet effective way to estimate the suitability of each potential head. We argue that link quality is almost a free resource which can be usually attained from routing service, such as in TinyOS [2]. Asymmetric links also can be filtered in it. Connectivity-like parameter may cause some clusters having too many member nodes, which is not expected in wireless ad hoc networks. Fortunately, this is significantly alleviated in sensor networks, because topology control services can adjust the nodes to maintain proper density. In addition, our goal is to evenly distribute cluster heads across the sensing field, instead of balancing the number of nodes among clusters.

4.4.2 Initialization Timer

If there is no initialization timer, all the nodes declare themselves to be cluster heads at the same time. In this case, EDC can still generate a good clustering result which is guaranteed by the head selection criteria. However, we introduce the initialization timer in order to reduce most of the communication overhead.

Suppose all the nodes are suspended. The strongest node in the network declares itself to be a cluster head, forcing all the nodes in its K-hop neighborhood to associate to it. Then, the remaining strongest node which is still suspended, declares itself to be another head, and its K-hop neighbors may choose it as their head. Generally speaking, if the suspended nodes change to HEAD sequentially with a sufficient time interval, communication overhead is minimized. There are no conflicted heads which may lead to state fluctuation on nodes.

However, it is quite difficult to sort nodes globally, and synchronize them in the network. To solve the problem, we introduce a sink-initiated relative synchronization technique. It starts with the sink broadcasting a synchronization packet, containing an assigned initialization timer T^0_{init} and a clustering parameter p^0. On receiving the synchronization packet at the first time, each node will set its t_{init} according to the two parameters, and broadcast a synchronization packet embedded with its own t_{init} and clustering parameter p. The t_{init} is calculated by the following formula:

$$t^i{}_{init} = t^j{}_{init} + \left(p^j - p^i\right) \times T_c - T_{unit} + t_r$$

where $t^j{}_{init}$ and p^j are the parameters contained in the synchronization packet sent by one of its neighbors, T_{unit} is a constant referring to 1-hop transmission time of the packet, T_c is another constant which is set to be KT_{unit} (it implies that if node A is much stronger than any of its K-hop neighbors, node A will push them to associate to node A before their initialization timers expire.), and t_r is a random number smaller than T_{unit}. For the sink, p^0 is an estimated average value of nodes' clustering parameters, and $T^0{}_{init}$ is:

$$T^0{}_{init} = \left(p_{estimated-max} - p^0\right) \times T_c$$

where $p_{estimated-max}$ is the estimated maximum cluster parameter, such that all the calculated $t^j{}_{init}$ are positive values.

EDC is initialized with the sink-initiated relative synchronization process. Every node enters into SUSPENDED. Nodes with large cluster parameters set small timers, which tend to make themselves to be cluster heads. On the contrary, nodes with small parameters need to stay for a long time in SUSPENDED, waiting to join in clusters.

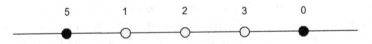

5   1   2   3   0

Fig. 6. Part of the network during EDC execution ($K=3, p_5 > p_0$)

4.4.3 Suspending Timer

In EDC, t_{wait} is set when a member node finds out that no reachable heads are available from its neighbors' selections. Even in this case, there may be a cluster head within the node's K hops. As shown in Fig. 6, node 5 and node 0 are in HEAD, while node 1 and node 2 choose node 5 as the cluster head, and node 3 chooses node 0. Assume that node 5 has detected a stronger head existing in exactly K hops away. Hence, it changes back to MEMBER. After that, node 1 cannot find any reachable head. Node 1 enters SUSPENDED with a timer t_{wait}. Node 2 then switches to adopt node 0 as its cluster head. If t_{wait} of node 1 expires before node 2's new notification, it will cause useless communication overhead. In this situation, if we set t_{wait} to be larger than two times T_{unit}, state fluctuation can be avoided on node 1.

We set t_{wait} according to the following formula, and we will show the reason why we choose it in the correctness part.

$$t_{wait} = KT_{unit} + t_r$$

4.5 Correctness

EDC does not terminate in fixed rounds, so the convergence of it should be proved first. Then, we show Condition 1 and Condition 2 proposed in Section 3 both can be satisfied by EDC.

Definition 6: A node in *stable state* means it will not change its state. A head in a stable state is called a *stable head*.

Lemma 1: There must appear at least one stable head during EDC execution.

Proof. Assume the sensor network has n sensor nodes, where $p_n > ... > p_2 > p_1$. If node n is a head or will become a head in a snapshot during the algorithm execution, it must be a stable head because it cannot change back to MEMBER or SUSPENDED following Rule 3 and Rule 4. If node n will not be a head, node $n-1$ must be a stable head once it changes to HEAD. If node n and node $n-1$ will not become heads, we consider node $n-2$ then. By induction, if nodes n, $n-1$ … and 2 will not become heads, node 1 must be a stable head when it enters the HEAD state. Therefore, there must appear at least one stable head during EDC execution.   □

Lemma 2: Nodes within K hops of a stable head cannot stay in or change to the HEAD state, when $t_{wait} > KT_{unit}$.

Proof. Assume node A is a stable head. Thus, there is no K-hop neighbor in HEAD which has a larger clustering parameter than node A has.

Assume node B is a node within K/2 hops of node A. Case 1: if node B is in HEAD or SUSPENDED, it will change to MEMBER on receiving neighbors' notifications; Case 2: if node B is a member node, it will choose node A as the cluster head only. That is because, even if node B notices some reachable heads nearer than node A, these heads must be dying heads, which are filtered by node B. Therefore, a stable head will keep its K/2-hop neighbors selecting itself as the clustering head.

Assume node C is a node within K hops of node A, but more than K/2 hops away. Case 1: if node C is in HEAD, it will change to a member node on receiving neighbors' notifications; Case 2: if node C changes from MEMBER to SUSPENDED, it means that the head that node C chose last time has become MEMBER, and all node C's neighbors cannot provide any reachable head, shown in the example of Fig. 6. Notifications claiming the lack of head selection will be propagated in a hop-by-hop way for at most K/2 hops until reaching a node which holds the head information of node A (all the nodes in K/2 hops of node A choose A as the cluster head.). Then, the head information of node A will be included in notifications and propagated back to node C in at most K/2 hops. The suspended node C obtains its new cluster head information within K-hop transmission time (KT_{unit}), before t_{wait} expires. Therefore, nodes within K hops of a stable head, but more than K/2 hops away, may change their states between MEMBER and SUSPENDED, but without entering HEAD.   □

Theorem 1: The EDC algorithm converges.

Proof. Assume there are n nodes in the network, denoted by set N. According to Lemma 1, there must appear a stable head during EDC's execution, and all the nodes within K hops of it cannot declare themselves to be heads by Lemma 2. Delete these nodes and the stable head from set N. Applying Lemma 1 again on set N, there must appear a stable head. Similarly, its K-hop neighbors cannot become heads. Delete them from set N. After several rounds, set N becomes null, and all the nodes are either stable heads, or cannot become heads any more.

Each non-head node chooses the nearest stable head as its cluster head. The selection is determined since the set of stable heads is fixed. Therefore, no update happens on nodes at this time. Thus, EDC converges.   □

Corollary 1: Each node is either a cluster head or within K hops from at least a cluster head.

Proof. Assume that the algorithm has already finished, and node A is not a cluster head, while there is no cluster head within its K hops. From the definitions of states in EDC, node A must stay in SUSPENDED, and its timer is still running. Therefore, it will declare itself as a cluster head when the timer expires. That's a contradiction.   □

Corollary 2: Every two cluster heads are at least K+1 hops away.

Proof. Assume that the algorithm has already finished, and nodes A and B are two cluster heads ($p_A > p_B$), which are in K hops from each other. There must be at least a boundary node for each cluster. Assume that the boundary node C belongs to cluster B. Node C must hold both the head information of A and B, as its neighbor from cluster A should have notified it. Therefore, node C should have detected the conflict, which would have forced it to join cluster A. That's a contradiction.   □

5 Performance Evaluation

In our simulation, we first build up a simulator according to the ideal network model we proposed in Section 3. The link layer adopts CSMA used in TinyOS of Mica2 nodes [18]. It takes 25ms (T_{unit}) to transmit a notification, similar to Mica2 nodes. The communication range of each sensor node is set to be exactly 15 meters, and traffic collision and hidden terminal effect are ignored such that each broadcast packet can be received correctly by neighbors. We set T_c to KT_{unit}, and adopt node degree as the clustering parameter. EDC is compared with three other algorithms: MaxMin [3], Degree, and Random. Degree is an algorithm using MaxMin heuristic while utilizing

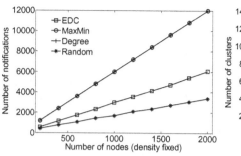

Fig. 7. Impact of network size on communication overhead

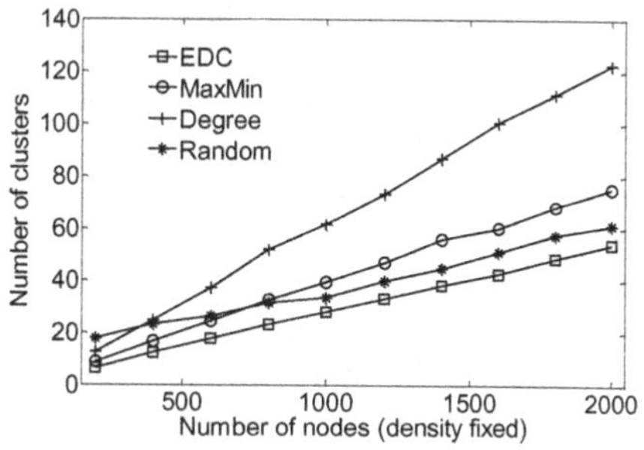

Fig. 8. Impact of network size on cluster number

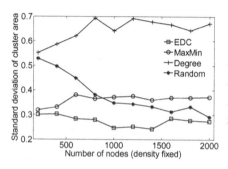

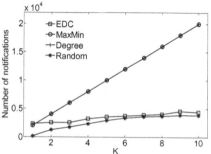

Fig. 9. Impact of network size on cluster distribution

Fig. 10. Impact of K on communication overhead

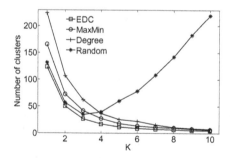

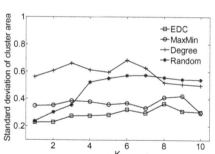

Fig. 11. Impact of K on cluster number

Fig. 12. Impact of K on cluster distribution

node degree as the clustering parameter instead of node ID. Random is based on [6], where q is calculated upon fixed K by a simple disk model. For example, if a node can cover 10 area units in K hops, a sensing field with 100 units should be covered by 10 clusters. Thus, q is 10% in this situation. Three metrics are adopted to evaluate these algorithms: 1) communication overhead measured by the number of notifications generated in the network; 2) number of clusters; 3) cluster distribution denoted by the standard deviation of cluster areas (cluster areas are calculated through voronoi diagrams.). We simulate and evaluate EDC in different scenarios. For each scenario, we randomly generate 10 connected sensor node topologies, and run four algorithms. The average values will be depicted in the figures.

Scalability of EDC is investigated first. In this scenario, K is set to 3, and the density of sensor nodes is fixed as 200 sensor nodes in 100m×100m. From Fig. 7, the communication overhead of EDC is much smaller than that of MaxMin and Degree, but larger than Random. EDC minimizes the cluster number, as it well controls every two cluster heads to be at least K+1 hops away, shown in Fig. 8. It is interesting that Degree adopts the same heuristic as used in MaxMin only with a different clustering parameter, but the performance of Degree from the perspective of cluster number is much worse than that of MaxMin. It is because the pathological case caused by node ID distribution, which is said to be rare in a random deployed sensor network, appears frequently when we change the clustering parameter from node ID to node degree. It is highly possible, that node degrees of sensor nodes decrease monotonously from dense area to sparse area. EDC also achieves the most even distribution of cluster heads among the four algorithms, shown in Fig. 9.

We also measure the performance according to different K, when there are 1000 nodes in a 224m×224m sensor field. The density is kept the same. As we expect, the value of K does not impact the communication overhead significantly in EDC and Random, while communication overhead rises linearly in MaxMin and Degree as shown in Fig. 10. EDC minimizes the cluster number for any K as depicted in Fig. 11. Surprisingly, the cluster number generated by Random increases dramatically after K=3. This is caused by the inherited drawbacks in probabilistic methods. When K increases, the estimated number of heads becomes smaller. Hence, it is more difficult to distribute heads evenly in the sensing field via a stochastic method. In this situation, the uncovered nodes all try to declare themselves to be the forced heads [6]. That's why the number of heads generated in Random increases with K. As Fig. 12 shows, EDC still outperforms others in terms of evenly distributed clusters.

Density is another important factor which may affect the performance of the clustering algorithms. We fix the sensor field to 100m×100m and increase the number of deployed sensor nodes from 100 to 500. As shown in Fig. 13 and Fig. 14, communication overhead per node decreases as density increases in EDC and Random, and the number of clusters almost stays the same in EDC when density changes. The reason why density has a strong impact on the number of clusters in Random can still be explained by the inherited drawbacks in probabilistic methods.

The relative synchronization technique we introduced tries to reduce communication overhead by avoiding state fluctuation on sensor nodes. Intuitively, as long as T_c is sufficiently large, there will not be any state fluctuation. Hence, communication overhead is minimized. As Fig. 15 shows, if all the nodes declare to be heads almost simultaneously (x=0), communication overhead is considerably high, particularly when K is large. We prefer to choose $T_c = KT_{unit}$ rather than $T_c = 10KT_{unit}$, because it can reduce overhead dramatically, while not much delay will be introduced. However, EDC with large T_c does not perform the best all the time. When K is equal to one, EDC with x=0 outperforms others. This is because if every node exchanges its information (declaring to be a head) with neighbors at the same time, EDC terminates immediately with only one selection update on each node. If nodes

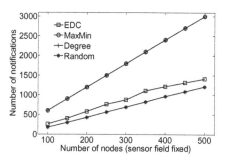

Fig. 13. Impact of density on communication overhead

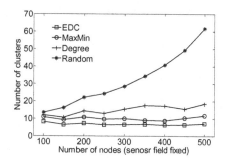

Fig. 14. Impact of density on cluster number

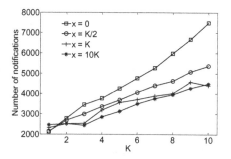

Fig. 15. Impact of the selection of T_{init} on communication overload ($T_c = xT_{unit}$)

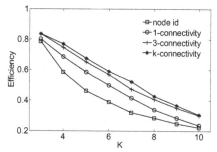

Fig. 16. Impact of the selection of clustering parameter

declare to be heads sequentially, some nodes having several potential heads may update their selections several times, and a number of notifications are sent out.

Finally, we relax some assumptions in the ideal network model in which nodes have a fixed communication range and each packet is broadcast reliably. We set links shorter than 10 meters with link error rate 10%, and the error rate increases linearly from 10% to 100% for the links with a length from 10 to 15 meters. The packet collision problem is simulated as well. In the simulation, we choose node ID, 1-hop connectivity, 3-hop connectivity, and K-hop connectivity as the clustering parameter respectively. With the generated network framework, each member node will periodically send a packet to its cluster head. We utilize the best-effort routing algorithm in [2] and measure the network efficiency on the packets received by cluster heads. The network efficiency refers to the ratio of the traffic caused by successfully received packets to all the traffic in the network. When node ID is selected as the clustering parameter, network efficiency degrades quickly as K increases as shown in Fig. 16. K-hop connectivity performs better than all the other three clustering parameters. However, calculating K-hop connectivity incurs heavy communication overhead. We recommend to use a small hop connectivity as the clustering parameter when implementing EDC, such as 3-hop connectivity for each K, when K is larger than 3.

6 Conclusions and Future Work

Aiming to evenly distribute cluster heads across the sensing field in wireless sensor networks, we propose the Evenly Distributed Clustering (EDC) algorithm. Our simulation results have shown that EDC minimizes the number of clusters, and achieves most evenly distributed clusters across the sensing field compared with other approaches. In addition, EDC converges fast with communication overhead as low as the stochastic approaches. With the clustering parameter of K-hop connectivity, EDC provides an energy-efficient network framework.

To date, we just prove the EDC algorithm to be efficient by theory and simulations. However, the real environment in wireless sensor networks may be quite different from simulation settings. For example, the link quality is rather poor and varies over time. It may cause that a node's neighborhood keeps changing even during a short period of time. Part of our future work will focus on applying EDC on real systems to investigate the performance. In addition, nodes may join or leave the network dynamically because of the deployment of new nodes or node failures. To handle the dynamics of network topology, maintaining and updating clustering in real time is an important problem we should tackle in the future. Moreover, we would like to achieve load balance among all the nodes with low cost.

Acknowledgements

This work was supported in part by the Hong Kong RGC Grant HKUST6183/05E, the Key Project of China NSFC Grant 60533110, and the National Basic Research Program of China (973 Program) under Grant No. 2006CB303000. We wish to thank the anonymous reviewers for their valuable comments on our work.

References

1. A. Mainwaring, J. Polastre, R. Szewczyk and D. Culler, "Wireless Sensor Networks for Habitat Monitoring," in ACM International Workshop on Wireless Sensor Networks and Applications (WSNA), 2002.
2. A. Woo, T. Tong and D. Culler, "Taming the Underlying Challenges of Reliable Multihop Routing in Sensor Networks," SenSys, 2003.
3. A.D. Amis, R. Prakash, T.H. Vuong and D.T. Huynh, "Max-Min D-Cluster Formation in Wireless Ad Hoc Networks," INFOCOM, 2000.
4. V.D. Park and M.S. Corson, "A Highly Adaptive Distributed Routing Algorithm for Mobile Wireless Networks," INFOCOM, 1997.
5. C.E. Perkins and P. Bhagwat, "Highly Dynamic Destination-Sequenced Distance-Vector Routing (DSDV) for Mobile Computers," SIGCOMM, 1994.
6. S. Bandyopadhyay and E.J. Coyle, "An Energy Efficient Hierarchical Clustering Algorithm for Wireless Sensor Networks," INFOCOM, 2003.
7. M. Chatterjee, S. Das and D. Turgut, "WCA: A Weighted Clustering Algorithm for Mobile Ad hoc Networks," Journal of Cluster Computing, Special issue on Mobile Ad hoc Networking, no. 5, pp. 193-204, 2002.

8. D. Baker and A. Ephremides, "The Architectural Organization of a Mobile Radio Network via a Distributed Algorithm," IEEE Transactions on Communications vol. 29, pp. 1694-1701, 1981.

9. A. Ephremides, J.E. Wieselthier and D. Baker, "A Design Concept for Reliable Mobile Radio Networks with Frequency Hopping Signaling," Proceeding of IEEE vol. 75, no. 1, pp. 56-73, 1987.

10. W. Heinzelman, A. Chandrakasan and H. Balakrishnan, "An Application-Specific Protocol Architecture for Wireless Microsensor Networks," IEEE Transactions on Wireless Communications vol. 1, no. 4, pp. 660-669, 2002.

11. A. Parekh, "Selecting Routers in Ad-hoc Wireless Networks," SBT/IEEE International Telecommunications Symposium, 1994

12. A. Cerpa and D. Estrin, "ASCENT: Addaptive Self-Configuring sEnsor Networks Topologies," INFOCOM, 2002.

13. B. Chen, K. Jamieson, H. Balakrishnan and R. Morris, "Span: An Energy-Efficient Coordination Algorithm for Topology Maintenance in Ad Hoc Wireless Networks," MobiCom, 2000.

14. Y. Xu, J. Heidemann and D. Estrin, "Geography-informed Energy Conservation for Ad Hoc Routing," MobiCom, 2001.

15. J. Wu and F. Dai, "A Distributed Formation of a Virtual Backbone in Ad Hoc Networks using Adjustable Transmission Ranges," ICDCS, 2004.

16. F. Dai and J. Wu, "On Constructing k-Connected k-Dominating Set in Wireless Networks," IPDPS, 2005.

17. J. Ma, M. Gao, Q. Zhang, L.M. Ni and W. Zhu, "Localized Low-Power Topology Control Algorithms in IEEE 802.15.4-based Sensor Networks," ICDCS, 2005.

18. P. Levis, S. Madden, D. Gay, J. Polastre, R. Szewczyk, A. Woo, E. Brewer and D. Culler, "The Emergence of Networking Abstractions and Techniques in TinyOS," NSDI, 2004.

Efficient Routing
from Multiple Sources to Multiple Sinks
in Wireless Sensor Networks

Pietro Ciciriello[1], Luca Mottola[1], and Gian Pietro Picco[1,2]

[1] Department of Electronics and Information, Politecnico di Milano, Italy
{ciciriello,mottola}@elet.polimi.it
[2] Department of Information and Communication Technology, University of Trento, Italy
picco@dit.unitn.it

Abstract. Initial deployments of wireless sensor networks (WSNs) were based on a *many-to-one* communication paradigm, where a single sink collects data from a number of data sources. Recently, however, scenarios with multiple sinks are increasingly being proposed, e.g., to deal with actuator nodes or to support high-level programming abstractions. The resulting *many-to-many* communication makes the existing solutions for single-sink scenarios inefficient.

In this paper, we propose a scheme for routing data efficiently from multiple sources to multiple sinks. We first study the problem from a theoretical standpoint, by mapping it to the multi-commodity network design problem. This allows us to derive an optimal solution that, albeit based on global knowledge and therefore impractical, provides us with a theoretical lower bound to evaluate decentralized solutions against. Then, we propose our own decentralized scheme, based on a periodic adaptation of the message routes aimed at minimizing the number of network links exploited. The resulting protocol is simple and easily implementable on WSN devices. The evaluation of our implementation shows that our protocol generates 50% less overhead than the base scheme without adaptation, a result close to the theoretical optimum we derived.

1 Introduction

Early deployments of wireless sensor networks (WSNs) were based on a *many-to-one* paradigm. For instance, in habitat monitoring [1] a single sink node collects environmental data from a large number of sensing devices. Therefore, communication protocols are geared towards the efficient and reliable transmissions to a single receiver.

Recent developments, however, increasingly call for scenarios where the sensed data must be delivered to multiple sinks. This network architecture is obviously required when the same WSN is serving multiple applications, each running on distinct devices. However, the need for multiple sinks arises also in other situations. For instance, researchers are increasingly investigating the use of actuator nodes in WSNs [2]. Different actuators are likely to need data coming from the same set of source nodes, as in the case of an emergency signal and a water sprinkler that cope with a fire scenario by basing their actions on temperature readings sensed nearby. Moreover, multiple sinks are

K. Langendoen and T. Voigt (Eds.): EWSN 2007, LNCS 4373, pp. 34–50, 2007.

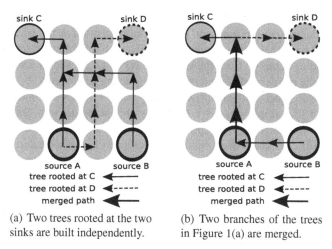

(a) Two trees rooted at the two sinks are built independently.

(b) Two branches of the trees in Figure 1(a) are merged.

Fig. 1. A sample multi-source to multi-sink scenario

increasingly and inherently required to implement advanced applications and programming abstractions. For instance, data collection is evolving into complex in-network data mining [3]. In these applications, the mining process is distributed across the nodes in the system, each collecting readings from different sets of data sources. Analogously, to support high-level programming constructs (e.g., the proposals in [4,5]), the physical nodes in the system need to communicate their data to multiple receivers, where a different processing is performed.

The aforementioned scenarios naturally call for a *many-to-many* communication paradigm. Unfortunately, existing protocols and algorithms for many-to-one communication are inherently ill-suited to cope efficiently with scenarios where the data needs to be reported to multiple sinks. Indeed, available solutions deal with multi-sink scenarios by simply *replicating* the routing infrastructure. For instance, the well-known Directed Diffusion protocol [6] sets up a tree along which sources report their data to the single sink. Dealing with multiple sinks involves setting up a separate, independent tree for each sink—a rather inefficient solution.

To see why this is a problem, consider the sample scenario with two sources and two sinks illustrated in Figure 1(a). Node A reports data to both sinks, whereas node B only transmits to sink C. To achieve multi-hop communication, two trees rooted at the two sinks have been built *independently* (e.g., by flooding a control message from each sink and having each node remember the reverse path to the sink, as in [6]). This base solution exploits 13 networks links and 13 nodes for message routing. Moreover, to report to the two sinks node A is forced to duplicate its data right at the first hop.

Figure 1(b) illustrates a better solution for the same scenario, based on the scheme we describe in the rest of the paper, obtained by maximizing the overlapping between the two sink-rooted trees. The two parallel branches starting from node A have been merged in a single one, and node B leverages off this merged path instead of relying on an independent one. As a consequence, the resulting topology now exploits only 8 network links and 9 nodes. By reducing the number of links exploited, we decrease the amount of redundant information flowing in the network, and duplicate data only if and when strictly necessary. Moreover, less nodes are involved in routing messages. This increases the system life-time, and reduces the contention on the wireless medium and packet collisions, therefore ultimately increasing the reliability of communication. Finally, the readings coming from the two sources can be packed in a single physical message along the merged path, reducing the per-reading header cost.

Our goal in this paper is to support efficiently many-to-many communication from multiple sources to multiple sinks. We do this by enhancing the well-established tree-based solution, thus enabling easy integration of our solution into existing routing schemes, e.g., [6]. Therefore, we assume the presence of a very basic routing infrastructure made of separate trees connecting the sources to the corresponding sinks. In this case, a *single path* connecting a given source to each sink is always established. This is a commonly adopted approach in WSNs, motivated by the reduction in network traffic w.r.t. a solution exploiting multiple paths from a source to the same sink. Furthermore, we do not make any assumption about the pairing of sources and sinks, as it is indeed determined by the initial tree structure. Given this setting, our objective is *to enable efficient routing of messages from the sources to the corresponding sinks by minimizing the number of network links exploited.*

To achieve our goal, we put forth two main contributions:

1. We present a theoretical model of the problem, derived as a particular instance of the multi-commodity network design problem [7, 8]. Thanks to this formulation, we reuse available results and tools for integer programming to easily compute the the theoretical optimal solution to our problem. The model and optimal solution are illustrated in Section 2. The technique we use, however, assumes global knowledge and is therefore derived in an off-line, centralized fashion, impractical for real WSN deployments. Nevertheless, this theoretical result is valuable for providing a lower bound against which to compare more efficient and decentralized solutions.

2. We present and evaluate our own decentralized solution, based on a periodic adaptation of sink-rooted trees. The adaptation consists of selecting a different neighbor as the parent towards a given sink. The decision to adapt is taken locally by a node and is based on the evaluation of a *quality metric* that aggregates into a single value information disseminated by the node's neighbors. Our adaptive protocol, whose details are illustrated in Section 3, is simple enough to be easily implemented on resource-scarce WSN devices. At the same time, as shown in Section 4, the evaluation of our implementation shows that it is able to reduce the network overhead of about 50% w.r.t. the base solution with independent trees, a result close to the theoretical optimum we derive in Section 2.

The paper is concluded by a survey of related efforts in Section 5 and by brief concluding remarks in Section 6.

2   System Model and Optimal Solution

In this section we provide a mathematical characterization of our problem. Besides providing a formal foundation for the results presented in this paper, in this section we show how our model can be used to derive directly an optimal solution, using tools for mathematical programming.

System Model. We can straightforwardly model a WSN as a directed graph whose node set $\mathcal{N}$ is composed of the WSN devices, and whose arc set $\mathcal{A}$ is obtained by setting an arc (i, j) between two nodes i and j when the latter is within the communication range of the former. (Note how this accounts for asymmetric links.)

With this notion of network, the problem of routing from multiple sources to multiple sinks can easily be mapped to the multi-commodity network design problem [7]. In this problem, given a set of commodities $\mathcal{C}$, the goal is to route each *commodity* $k \in \mathcal{C}$ (e.g., a physical good) through a network (e.g., a transportation system) from a set of sources $O(k) \subseteq \mathcal{N}$ to a set of destinations $D(k) \subseteq \mathcal{N}$, by minimizing a given metric. Without loss of generality, as shown in [8], a commodity can be assumed to flow from a single source to a single destination. In this case, since commodities generated from the same source and directed to the same destination follow the same route, one can state a one-to-one mapping between the route connecting any source-sink pair $(o(k), d(k))$, and any commodity k.

Once the mapping to the multi-commodity network design problem is made, we can model our problem as follows:

– We capture message routing with a set of decision variables:

$$r_{i,j}^k = \begin{cases} 1 & \text{if the route for the source-sink pair } k \text{ contains arc } (i, j) \\ 0 & \text{otherwise} \end{cases} \tag{1}$$

A value assignment $\forall (i, j) \in \mathcal{A}$ to these variables formally represents the route messages must follow from the source $o(k)$ to the sink $d(k)$.
– A network link can be used for multiple source-sink pairs. The fact that an arc (i, j) is used to route *at least one message for a source-sink pair* can then be captured as:

$$u_{i,j} = \begin{cases} 1 & \text{if } \exists k \in \mathcal{C} \mid r_{i,j}^k = 1 \\ 0 & \text{otherwise} \end{cases} \tag{2}$$

– The overall number of links used to route messages for a given set of source-sink pairs is therefore:

$$UsedLinks(\mathcal{C}, \mathcal{A}) = \sum_{(i,j) \in \mathcal{A}} u_{i,j} \tag{3}$$

Our goal consists of finding the optimal set of routes used to deliver data messages from sources to sinks. Formally:

Goal: to find the value assignment of $r_{i,j}^k, \forall k \in \mathcal{C}, \forall (i, j) \in \mathcal{A}$ that minimizes the value of $UsedLinks(\mathcal{C}, \mathcal{A})$.

The relation between $r_{i,j}^k$ and $u_{i,j}$ defined in (2) captures the essence of the problem, as well as the rationale of our distributed solution, presented next. Indeed, to minimize *UsedLinks* one should strive for reusing as much as possible links that have already been used for other source-sink pairs, i.e., for which the cost $u_{i,j}$ is already paid. In other words, we *can minimize the number of links used by maximizing the overlapping among source-sink paths*. In Section 3 we present a protocol for achieving this goal efficiently.

Variable	Value
$r_{C,B}^{C,A}$	1
$r_{D,A}^{C,A}$	1
Remaining $r_{i,j}^{C,A}$	0

Variable	Value
$r_{C,B}^{C,A}$	1
$r_{B,A}^{C,A}$	1
Remaining $r_{i,j}^{C,A}$	0

(a) An assignment and topology representing non-consistent routes for a commodity representing the source-sink path (C, A). Node B and D do not obey to (4).

(b) An assignment and topology representing meaningful routes for a commodity representing the source-sink path (C, A). Constraint (4) holds for every node.

Fig. 2. Sample assignments for $r_{i,j}^{C,A}$

Although this formalization of the problem is simple and general, alternatives exist and are discussed in Section 5.

Finding the Optimal Solution. Based on the model we just presented, we can derive an optimal solution using techniques of mathematical programming, provided that we specify the constraints to be satisfied by a meaningful solution. We first require that $r_{i,j}^{k}$ and $u_{i,j}$ are integer, binary variables and that the following relation holds among them:

$$\forall (i, j) \in \mathcal{A}, \forall k \in \mathcal{C}, \quad r_{i,j}^{k} \le u_{i,j}$$

In our case, these constraints are satisfied by construction through (1) and (2).

Most importantly, we state the requirement that the assignment to $r_{i,j}^{k}$ contains a connected, end-to-end path for each source-sink pair k. This can be expressed by requiring every node different from the source $o(k)$ and the sink $d(k)$ to "preserve" the message, i.e.:

$$\forall i \in \mathcal{N}, \forall k \in \mathcal{C}, \quad \sum_{m:(i,m)\in\mathcal{A}} r_{i,m}^{k} - \sum_{n:(n,i)\in\mathcal{A}} r_{n,i}^{k} = \begin{cases} 1 & \text{if } i = o(k) \\ -1 & \text{if } i = d(k) \\ 0 & \text{otherwise} \end{cases} \quad (4)$$

The previous expression is similar to a network flow conservation equation, and indeed imposes the existence of a multi-hop route from each source to every sink. Figure 2 illustrates the concept in the case of a single source-sink pair. The solution in Figure 2(a) is not acceptable, as the message originated at C and directed to A is lost at node B and suddenly reappears at node D. Indeed, the constraint in (4) does not hold for node B and D, as its left-hand side evaluates to -1 when $i = B$ and to 1 for $i = D$, and neither node is an origin or destination for the source-sink pair. Conversely, the solution in Figure 2(b) is perfectly meaningful: a connected, multi-hop path from the source to the sink exists, and indeed the constraint in (4) holds for every node.

With this formulation, the problem of finding the optimal assignment that satisfies our goal can be solved straightforwardly by using well-established techniques and tools from mathematical programming. These techniques require global knowledge of the system state and are computationally expensive, and therefore impractical for WSNs. For this reason, we devised a distributed scheme that relies only on local (i.e., within the 1-hop neighborhood) knowledge, and can be implemented on resource-constrained devices. We return to the theoretical optimal solution in Section 4, where we show how it is efficiently approximated by the distributed solution, discussed next.

3   A Distributed Solution

As we discussed in Section 2, the goal of minimizing the number of links can be achieved by maximizing the overlapping of the paths along which data is routed from a given source to a given sink. In this section, we illustrate the distributed solution we devised to achieve this goal.

We assume that the initial state of the system is such that a tree exists for each sink, connecting it to all the relevant sources. These sink-rooted trees are easily built using mechanisms available in the literature, e.g., along the reverse path of interest propagation as in Directed Diffusion [6]. Clearly, these mechanisms are designed to build each tree independent of the others, and therefore do not guarantee any property regarding their overlapping.

To guarantee a high degree of overlapping among source-sink paths, our protocol relies on a simple adaptive scheme. Each node can decide to locally manipulate a source-sink path by changing the neighbor serving as its parent along a path towards a given sink. The decision is based on information about the neighbor nodes, piggybacked on application messages and overheard during transmission. This control information is fed into a quality metric $q(n, s)$ that yields a measure of the quality of a neighbor n as the parent towards a sink s, and is periodically evaluated for each neighbor n and sink s. Changing the current parent to a different neighbor n occurs when the value of $q(n, s)$ becomes the maximum value of q among all neighbors for sink s. In this case, the node simply begins forwarding data to the new parent. The switch can be managed without additional control messages by using a timeout.

In principle, the quality metric q can be designed to rely on various quantities. In this paper, we present and evaluate an instantiation of our protocol where our quality metric relies on:

1. $dist(j, s)$, the distance (in hops) from a node j to a given sink s, as determined by the initial interest propagation;
2. $paths(j)$, the number of source-sink paths passing through a given node j, i.e., using the notation in Section 2:

$$paths(j) = \sum_{k \in C} r_{i,j}^k \quad (i, j) \in \mathcal{A}$$

3. $sinks(j)$, the number of sinks a given node j currently serves.

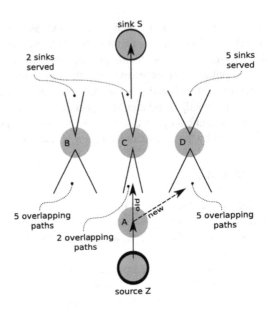

Fig. 3. An abstract view of a WSN with multiple sources and multiple sinks. Source Z generates data to be delivered to sink S, routed through node A. Besides Z, node A is a neighbor of B, C, and D. At node A, the current parent towards S is C. However, a better choice is represented by D, since it enjoys the highest number of overlapping paths and served sinks among A's neighbors.

The distance between a neighbor and a sink is of fundamental importance in increasing reliability and reducing overhead. Indeed, the higher the number of nodes traversed by a message, the higher the probability to lose a message due to unreliable transmission, and the higher the overall computational and communication cost paid to deliver the message end-to-end. The rationale behind the choice of the other two quantities can be visualized with the help of Figure 3. In the network shown, a source Z needs to send data to the sink S, and to do so routes messages upstream through its neighbor A. Node A, in turn, has three neighbors B, C, and D, with C being the current parent in the tree rooted at S. Nevertheless, the figure also shows how both B and D are currently traversed by more source-sink paths than node C. Therefore, if A were to choose either of these neighbors as the new parent towards S, there would be more *overlapping paths* passing through either B or D than in the current situation—which is exactly our goal. Finally, the figure also shows that D is serving more sinks than node B. Therefore, with respect to B, D is more likely[1] to be already reporting readings to S, possibly on behalf of other sources. If this is actually the case, choosing D leads to reusing an "already open" path towards S, therefore further increasing the overlapping of source-sink paths at no additional cost. Therefore, node D is the best choice among A's neighbors, and A will eventually switch to D as its parent towards the sink S.

---

[1] As we know only the *number sinks*(j) of sinks served by j we cannot be sure that S is really among them. To obviate to the problem, we could propagate the *identifier* of the sinks served instead of their number. However, as shown in Section 4, the latter already yields good performance and generates much less overhead.

Field Name	Description
neighborId	The identifier of the neighbor relative to this entry.
dist	An associative array containing, for each sink in the system, its distance from *neighborId*.
paths	The number of different source-sink paths currently passing through *neighborId*.
sinks	The number of sinks served through *neighborId*, possibly along a multi-hop path.

Fig. 4. Information used to compute the quality metric for a neighbor node

As we already mentioned, the actual decision to switch to a different parent is determined by a quality metric q, an estimate of how "beneficial" this decision would be. In this paper, we designed q to be a linear combination of the three quantities above:

$$q(n, s) ::= \delta \cdot dist(n, s) + \alpha_1 \cdot paths(n) + \alpha_2 \cdot sinks(n) \tag{5}$$

where $\delta, \alpha_1, \alpha_2$ are tuning parameters of the protocol. Again, the shape of the function q and its constituents can in principle be different. For instance, one could take the node remaining energy into account and rely on our solution to automatically alternate among different parents, therefore achieving load balancing among the possible parents in a given tree. Although the results presented in Section 4 with the quality metric in (5) are already very positive, investigating the impact of alternative definitions of q is in our immediate research agenda.

To compute $q(n, s)$ for a given neighbor n and sink s, a node must first determine the three constituents $dist(n, s)$, $paths(n)$, and $sinks(n)$. These are evaluated by relying on a data structure maintained by each node. Figure 4 shows the data structure fields for a single neighbor. Note how the various fields are maintained differently. The value of the field *neighborId* is clearly determined locally based on information from the lower layers, and serves as the key to index the data structure. The content of *dist* is determined from the messages flooded by the sink either during the tree setup phase, or in successive flooding operations performed to keep this information up-to-date with respect to nodes joining or failing. The values of $paths(n)$ and $sinks(n)$ are instead derived by the node through overhearing of messages sent by n. Indeed, these messages piggyback the control information above, which can then be used to update the data structure in Figure 4. Note how the overhead due to this additional control information is very small: only two integer values are needed.

Figure 5 illustrates a sample adaptation process. For the sake of the example, we focus on node E and sink C, and we assume $\delta = \alpha_1 = \alpha_2 = 1$ in (5). With these parameters, node E evaluates the quality metric q towards sink C for its two neighbors F and G. Figure 6 shows the content of the data structures in Figure 4 for F and G. The evaluation returns $q(G, C) = 2 + 1 + 1 = 4$ and $q(F, C) = 2 + 2 + 2 = 6$. Therefore, E recognizes F as the best next-hop towards C, and changes its parent accordingly, as depicted in Figure 5(b). The benefit of this change can be easily seen by computing the number of links and nodes involved: the

Field Name	Value
neighborId	**G**
dist	$\{C = 2, D = 4\}$
paths	1
sinks	1
neighborId	**F**
dist	$\{C = 2, D = 4\}$
paths	2
sinks	2

Fig. 6. Data stored at node E in the situation depicted in Figure 5(a)

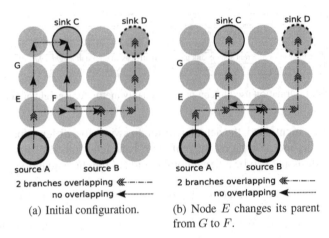

(a) Initial configuration.

(b) Node E changes its parent from G to F.

Fig. 5. A sample adaptation process

network in Figure 5(a) uses 13 network links and 12 nodes, against the 10 links and 10 nodes of Figure 5(b).

To break ties between the current parent and a new one, a node always selects the latter, as it is guaranteed to enjoy a higher value of q after becoming a parent. Indeed, at least the number of source-sink paths passing through it increases by one. In selecting the new parent, the only additional constraint is to not select as a new parent a neighbor whose distance from a sink is greater than that of the selecting node. Without this constraint, a node could potentially select one of its children as the new parent, hence creating a routing loop.

Finally, our distributed protocol is complemented by a simple scheme for packing multiple readings in the same network message. To this end, each node maintains a buffer for each neighbor, limited by the number of readings allowed in a message. Upon receiving a reading from another node, the reading is inserted in the buffer for the neighbor on the route to the target sink. When the buffer for a given neighbor is full (or upon expiration of a timeout) a message is created and actually forwarded to the neighbor. This simple scheme decreases the per-reading header cost and helps reducing collisions, since buffers are likely to become full at different times and therefore messages are going to be reasonably spread in time. In principle, the same packing scheme can be used without our adaptation protocol. However, its impact is greater in the presence of adaptation, since the latter guarantees a higher degree of overlapping among trees, with more readings being funneled through the same links.

4   Evaluation

In this section, we report about simulation results comparing the performance of our solution against a base mechanism without adaptation as well as the optimal solution identified in Section 2. These solutions provide the two extremes for our evaluation: we indeed demonstrate that our adaptation strategy provides remarkable benefits, and that its effectiveness approaches the theoretical optimum. In our evaluation, we also show that our solution converges rapidly, and investigate the impact of the various constituents of our quality metric q, as introduced in Section 3. We are currently investigating alternative definitions of q (e.g., including the remaining node energy for achieving load balancing, as mentioned earlier).

Simulation Settings and Metrics. We implemented our distributed scheme on top of TinyOS [9], and evaluated its performance using the TOSSIM [10] simulator. As for the theoretical optimum discussed in Section 2, we used the CPLEX [11] solver to compute the ideal topology' connecting sources to sinks, given their respective placement in the system and the constraints defined in Section 2.

We first report about simulated deployments in a regular grid, where each node can communicate with its four neighbors. This choice simplifies the interpretation of results by removing the bias induced by random deployments, while also well modeling some of the settings we target, e.g., indoor WSN deployments for control and monitoring [12]. To this end, the nodes are placed 35 ft. apart with a communication range[2] of 50 ft. Moreover, we also evaluated the performance of our protocol in deployments with a random topology, characterized by a pre-specified average number of neighbors for each node. With respect to the fixed grid above, these scenarios allow us to assess the impact of the connectivity degree on our results, as well as evaluate our protocol in more unstructured scenarios (e.g., modeling outdoor WSNs deployments).

As for the modeling of sources and sinks, each scenario is set so that 10% of the nodes are data sources. These send data to a number of sinks that varies according to the scenario, at the rate of one reading per minute. Hereafter, the time period between two successive readings generated from the same source is termed *epoch*. Also, note that sources are not synchronized in generating these readings. The placement of sources and sinks in the network is determined randomly. A single sensor reading is represented by a 16-bit integer value, while the message size at the MAC layer is 46 bytes. In all our implementations, messages are always sent when there are sufficiently many readings to fill the physical message completely. Each simulation lasted 2000 s, and was repeated 5 times.

The initial tree is built by flooding the system with a "tree construction" message sent by every sink. Each node keeps track of the messages received from the same sink, and stores the identifier of the neighbor along which the message was received with the least number of traversed hops. This way, the initial tree is built by minimizing the length of the path connecting each source to every sink. In the chart, this *base* tree is also used, without any additional modification, as the point of comparison against our solution. Indeed, it essentially provides a baseline, representative of protocols that build independent trees (e.g., Directed Diffusion [6]), against which we show the benefits of our adaptive scheme.

For what concerns the protocol parameters, we evaluate independently the impact of the number of overlapping paths and the number of served sinks by simulating scenarios with $\langle \alpha_1 = 1, \alpha_2 = 0 \rangle$ and $\langle \alpha_1 = 0, \alpha_2 = 1 \rangle$. Moreover, we also evaluate the combined contribution of these quantities using $\langle \alpha_1 = 1, \alpha_2 = 1 \rangle$. As for the distance from sinks, we discussed in Section 3 how its contribution is key in achieving a good

---

[2] We used TinyOS' `LossyBuilder` to generate topology files with transmission error probabilities taken from real testbeds.

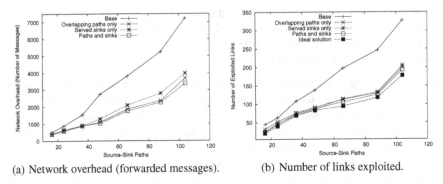

(a) Network overhead (forwarded messages).   (b) Number of links exploited.

Fig. 7. Grid topology: performance metrics vs. number of source-sink paths

ratio of delivered readings. Differently from the two quantities above, the lower is this value, the better (closer) is the neighbor located w.r.t. a given sink. For this reason, we always set $\delta = -2$ throughout all the simulation runs, so that neighbors at a few hops from the considered sink are preferred over neighbors farther away. As we verified experimentally, this value provides a good trade-off w.r.t. the other parameters.

The main quantities we measured are:

- the *ratio of readings delivered* to the sinks over those sent;
- the *network overhead* as the number of messages sent at the MAC layer—being communication the most prominent source of energy drain in WSNs, this measure can be considered as proportional to the system lifetime;
- the *number of links exploited*, i.e., the number of physical links used to route messages—the fundamental metric we strive to minimize[3].

Moreover, to provide further insights on the behavior of our protocol we analyzed the number τ of trees insisting on each physical link, showing the ratio $\tau_{adaptive}/\tau_{base}$ in different scenarios. Finally, to analyze the dynamics of our protocol we measured the *number of topological changes* against the epoch number, showing the time needed for our solution to stabilize.

Results. We first focus on a grid topology. The comparison of the charts in Figure 7 captures the essence of our approach. Figure 7(a) plots the network overhead against the number of source-sink paths, and shows how our adaptive scheme exhibits only about 50% the overhead of the base solution, on the average. On the other hand, Figure 7(b) shows that our distributed scheme relies on only about 50% of the links used by the base solution. Remarkably, the number of network links exploited in Figure 7(b) exhibits the same trend of the overhead in Figure 7(a), therefore evidencing that the gains in network overhead are made possible by the reduction in the number of links exploited. Indeed, in our approach messages are duplicated only where it is really necessary, whereas the base solution often duplicates messages too early, as they are routed independently. Furthermore, Figure 7(b) shows also a curve for the theoretical optimum we computed

---

[3] Notice we count multiple links also when different sinks can be reached with a single broadcast message at the physical level.

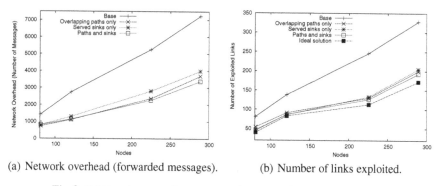

(a) Network overhead (forwarded messages).　　(b) Number of links exploited.

Fig. 8. Grid topology: performance metrics vs. number of nodes (4 sinks)

in Section 2. Remarkably, our solution always achieves a performance very close to the optimum—at most 10% in the worst case—but *without* requiring global knowledge. Note how these significant improvements in overhead are obtained without impacting message delivery: actually, the ratio of delivered readings improves of about 10% in our adaptive scheme[4].

Figure 7 also evidences that considering only the number of served sinks in our quality metric q yields the worst results in the adaptive solution—although still significantly better than the base scheme. The combination of the two metrics provides the best results in scenarios with a high number of source-sink paths, exhibiting a gain around 10% w.r.t. the number of overlapping paths alone. Conversely, little or no improvement is obtained by $\langle \alpha_1 = 1, \alpha_2 = 1 \rangle$ in settings with less sources and sinks. A closer look at our simulation logs revealed that in these scenarios the combination of overlapping paths and served sinks simply amplifies the differences in the value of q for different neighbors, only seldom changing the decision on the parent to be selected. This is partially expected, as in the aforementioned settings more overlapping paths easily correspond to more served sinks and vice versa.

Thus far, we analyzed the performance of our protocol only w.r.t. the number of source-sink paths. Indeed, we noted the performance of our approach is affected more directly by this parameter than by the number of nodes in the system. For instance, we obtained comparable performance in a scenario with 81 nodes (8 sources) and 4 sinks, w.r.t. a setting with 121 nodes (12 sources) and 3 sinks. The settings shown thus far were obtained with different system sizes, starting from 2 sinks in a system of 81 nodes, up to 4 sinks among 289 nodes. Nevertheless, to investigate the scalability properties of our solution, Figure 8 illustrates the same trends discussed above, this time against the number of nodes in the system in a scenario with 4 sinks. The adaptive scheme scales fairly well w.r.t. system size and, again, much better than the base solution with no adaptation, and very close to the theoretical optimum. Moreover, once more the trend of network overhead (Figure 8(a)) is mirrored by the one for the number of exploited links (Figure 8(b)).

A finer-grained analysis is shown Figure 9, where we show the ratio $\tau_{adaptive}/\tau_{base}$ of overlapping trees per physical link using $\langle \alpha_1 = 1, \alpha_2 = 1 \rangle$. As expected, based on

---

[4] Due to space limitations we do not show the corresponding charts here.

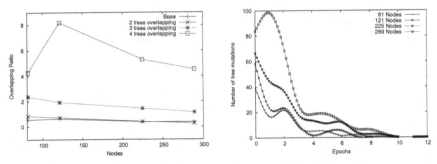

Fig. 9. Ratio of overlapping source-sink paths per physical link vs. number of nodes

Fig. 11. Convergence time, in a system with 4 sinks

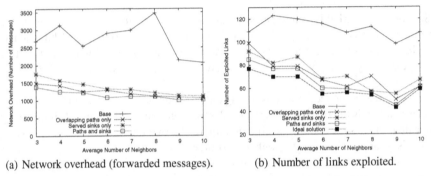

(a) Network overhead (forwarded messages).   (b) Number of links exploited.

Fig. 10. Random topology: performance metrics vs. average number of neighbors per node

the previous considerations about network overhead and number of exploited links, our adaptive scheme sensibly increments the number of source-sink paths overlapping on the same link. For instance, in a scenario with 121 nodes, the number of links shared among 4 trees is about 8 times the one for the base scheme. However, as the number of nodes increases with a fixed number of sinks, this ratio decreases since the different source-sink paths may become too far from each other to be merged effectively.

The impact of connectivity is considered in Figure 10, with a random deployment of the nodes. The charts show the network overhead and number of used links against the average number of neighbors per node in a system with 150 nodes, 4 of which are sinks. The trends are more irregular in this case, because of the bias introduced by the random topology. However, Figure 10(a) shows that our solution always outperforms the base scheme, achieving improvements from 40% to 60% in network overhead. As for the number of physical links exploited, shown in Figure 10(b), it is interesting to notice that, as connectivity increases, the gap between our solution and the theoretical optimum is reduced. Indeed, the more the system is globally connected, the more information the nodes collect by overhearing messages, and the more options they enjoy when selecting a parent for a given tree. Our distributed scheme should converge to the optimal solution as the system becomes more and more connected. Incidentally, the trend in Figure 10(b) also highlights how our previous choice of 4 neighbors per node in the grid topology was fairly conservative.

Finally, as our solution is based on successive rounds of adaptation, we also analyzed the time needed to converge to a stable configuration. Figure 11 shows the number of topological changes against the epoch number. Results are obtained in network of various sizes with 4 sinks. The chart shows that the higher is the number of nodes in the system, the higher is the number of topological changes and the time needed to converge. However, in the worst case 10 epochs are sufficient to reach a stable configuration, with most of the changes concentrated in the first few epochs. Therefore, in stable deployment scenarios there is no need to run continuously the adaptation process, which instead can be triggered with a large period or only upon detecting topology changes.

5   Related Work

The model we presented in Section 2 is derived from the large body of literature in operational research and network design. Our choice of the multi-commodity network design problem as a modeling framework is motivated by the generality it allows in pairing sources and sinks. In contrast, modeling the same problem as a p-source minimum routing cost spanning tree [13] or a Steiner minimal tree [14] would force us to consider *every* node (or source, respectively) to be a sink as well. At the same time, the model we presented here is a simple instance of the multi-commodity network design problem. More sophisticated formulations exist, e.g., taking into account the capacity of network links [15]. In this case, when the capacities along a path are exhausted, alternative, parallel paths are used to share the traffic load, therefore activating more links. However, in WSNs it is difficult to evaluate precisely the actual bandwidth available, due to contention of the wireless medium, collisions and unreliable transmissions [16]. Moreover, these issues are amplified as the number of links used to route messages increase. Therefore, we believe these formulations are not suited for the wireless setting.

For what concerns distributed solutions, it is safe to say that most research work in sensor network focuses on optimizing communication from multiple sources to a single sink, as witnessed by the vast amount of literature on the subject [17]. As we already mentioned, these approaches cannot provide efficient solutions to more decentralized scenarios like sensor and actuator networks [2], which inherently call for routing solutions to report to multiple receivers.

In [18] the authors propose mechanisms to build sink-rooted trees incrementally, to perform data aggregation and in-network processing. A path from a single source to the sink is first built, and then shared by other, nearby sources. In this sense, their approach resembles our rational of minimizing the number of network links exploited to reduce the network traffic. However, their solution is geared to single-sink scenarios, and the results barely comparable to ours, as they are obtained in simulation using a MAC layer derived from IEEE 802.11. Devising mechanisms to combine the two techniques could provide further benefits, and is a topic worth further investigation.

The work in [19] addresses the problem of routing from a single source to multiple sinks. Common to our approach is the use of broadcast transmissions to let nodes collect information on alternative routes. However, the adaptation in [19] is performed based on *long-range* information (e.g., the number of hops from a node to the different sinks). As this information may not be immediately available, the algorithm starts with a worst case estimation and randomly tries different routes, including those deemed less favorable. When the information gathered during this exploration phase is not modified for a given number of iterations, the algorithm switches to a stable phase where the discovered routes are used. The adaptation mechanism we proposed in this work is instead based mainly on *local* information that is immediately available (e.g., the number of source-sink paths passing through a node), Moreover, our algorithm is basically self-stabilizing, and does not require distinct phases of operation.

Some researchers addressed the problem of routing from multiple sensors to mobile sinks, focusing on mechanisms to deal with frequent location updates. To this end, in [20] a two-level grid structure is proactively built by the sources. This identifies a reduced subset of nodes responsible for storing information about the sink position, and to which location updates are sent. Conversely, in [21] a stationary sensor node builds a tree on behalf of one or more mobile sinks. These remain linked to this node until they move too far away, at which point they are forced to select a different stationary node. In-network data processing in the presence of mobile sinks is also considered in [22], where a tree is built by a master sink and then shared by slave sinks. Local repair strategies are employed to adjust the tree according to sink mobility. Differently from our approach, in these works sink mobility is the distinctive feature of the target scenario, and the proposed solutions are aimed at reducing the overhead induced by it. In contrast, we concentrate on optimizing the source-sink paths, as this is key to improve the system lifetime in our target scenarios, actually less dynamic. In doing so we make only minimal assumptions about the node capabilities (i.e., the ability to overhear messages sent by neighbors), while all the aforementioned proposals require nodes to be aware of their geographical position, exploited for routing.

Instead, the work in [23] introduces an algorithm targeting monitoring applications for achieving energy-efficient routing to multiple sinks. The optimizations proposed are centered around the ability to adjust the sensing rate at different nodes, eliminating the redundancy in the data gathered while preserving the ability to reconstruct the corresponding phenomenon. Instead, we do not assume the ability to influence the source behaviors. Conversely, common to our approach is the problem formulation based on integer linear programming. The authors then map this formulation to a distributed search algorithm based on subgradient optimization, executed in a decentralized fashion. However, they do not provide any insights on the processing overhead this solution would impose on real, resource constrained nodes. We use instead the model presented in Section 2 as a theoretical bound for careful analysis of a lightweight, distributed solution straightforwardly implementable on WSN devices.

Finally, other works have focused on the opportunity to employ multiple sinks not to meet an application requirement, but as a mechanism to increase the system lifetime. For instance, the work in [24] investigates the design problem related to optimally locating multiple sinks in the sensor field, so as to achieve a pre-specified operational time. In this case, even if multiple sinks are present, these simply act as cluster-heads, with each sensor node reporting to only one of them. Similarly, the proposal in [25] studies the problem of selecting, at each node, one of the many sinks present in the system to minimize the overall energy expenditures. Clearly, this is a different problem w.r.t. ours, where the multiple sinks actually represent different system actors, that need to *simultaneously* gather sensor data for potentially different tasks.

6   Conclusions and Future Work

This paper addressed the problem of efficiently routing data from multiple sources to multiple sinks. We defined a model based on mathematical programming that, albeit relying on global knowledge, can be easily used to derive an optimal solution. Then, we illustrated a novel decentralized scheme that adapts the topology by maximizing the overlapping among source-sink paths, therefore minimizing the overall number of network links exploited. This results in reduced overhead, increases the system life-time, and makes communication more reliable. The approach is simple enough to be implemented on resource-scarce WSN devices, and we showed that achieves a 50% improvement in network overhead. Additionally, we illustrated how the quality of the routes obtained is close to the theoretical lower bound.

Our immediate research agenda includes an assessment of the impact of our adaptive strategy on the processing load at each node, and the design of techniques for balancing such load using alternative definitions of the quality metric we introduced in this paper. A formal proof of the convergence properties of our distributed scheme is also among our future research goals.

Acknowledgements. The authors wish to thank Roberto Cordone and Marco Trubian for their insightful suggestions on modeling the multiple sources to multiple sinks routing problem, and Kay Römer for providing suggestions and comments on early versions of this paper. The work described here is partially supported by the European Union under the IST-004536 RUNES project.

References

1. Mainwaring, A., Culler, D., Polastre, J., Szewczyk, R., Anderson, J.: Wireless sensor networks for habitat monitoring. In: Proc. of the 1st ACM Int. Workshop on Wireless sensor networks and applications. (2002) 88–97
2. Akyildiz, I.F., Kasimoglu, I.H.: Wireless sensor and actor networks: Research challenges. Ad Hoc Networks Journal **2**(4) (2004) 351–367
3. Roemer, K.: Distributed mining of spatio-temporal event patterns in sensor networks. In: Proc. of the 1st Euro-American Wkshp. on Middleware for Sensor Networks (EAWMS). (2006)
4. Bakshi, A., Prasanna, V.K., Reich, J., Larner, D.: The abstract task graph: a methodology for architecture-independent programming of networked sensor systems. In: Proc. of the 2005 Wkshp. on End-to-end, sense-and-respond systems, applications and services (EESR), Berkeley, CA, USA, USENIX Association (2005) 19–24
5. Ciriciello, P., Mottola, L., Picco, G.P.: Building Virtual Sensors and Actuator over Logical Neighborhoods. In: Proc. of the 1st ACM Int. Wkshp. on Middleware for Sensor Networks (MidSens06 - colocated with ACM/USENIX Middleware). (2006)
6. Intanagonwiwat, C., Govindan, R., Estrin, D., Heidemann, J., Silva, F.: Directed diffusion for wireless sensor networking. IEEE/ACM Trans. Networking **11**(1) (2003) 2–16
7. Wu, B.Y., Chao, K.M.: Spanning Trees and Optimization Problems. Chapman & Hall (2004)
8. Holmberg, K., Hellstrand, J.: Solving the uncapacitated network design problem by a lagrangean heuristic and branch-and-bound. Oper. Res. **46**(2) (1998) 247–259
9. Hill, J., Szewczyk, R., Woo, A., Hollar, S., Culler, D., Pister, K.: System architecture directions for networked sensors. In: ASPLOS-IX: Proc. of the 9^{nt} Int. Conf. on Architectural Support for Programming Languages and Operating Systems. (2000) 93–104

10. Levis, P., Lee, N., Welsh, M., Culler, D.: TOSSIM: accurate and scalable simulation of entire TinyOS applications. In: Proc. of the 5th Symp. on Operating Systems Design and Implementation (OSDI). (2002) 131–146

11. I-Log: CPLEX Home Page. (www.ilog.com/products/cplex/)

12. Stoleru, R., J.A. Stankovic: Probability grid: A location estimation scheme for wireless sensor networks. In: Proc. of the 1st Int. Conf. on Sensor and Ad-Hoc Communication and Networks (SECON). (2004)

13. Wu, B.Y., Lancia, G., Bafna, V., Chao, K.M., Ravi, R., Tang, C.Y.: A polynomial-time approximation scheme for minimum routing cost spanning trees. SIAM J. Comput. **29**(3) (2000) 761–778

14. Hwang, F.K., Richards, D.S., Winter, P.: The Steiner Tree Problem. North-Holland (1992)

15. Gendron, B., Crainic, T.G., Frangioni, A.: Multicommodity capacitated network design. Telecommunications Network Planning (1998) 1–19

16. Pottie, G.J., Kaiser, W.J.: Wireless integrated network sensors. Commun. ACM **43**(5) (2000) 51–58

17. Al-Karaki, J., Kamal, A.E.: Routing techiniques in wireless sensor networks: a survey. (To appear in IEEE Wireless Communications)

18. Intanagonwiwat, C., Estrin, D., Govindan, R., Heidemann, J.: Impact of network density on data aggregation in wireless sensor networks. In: Proc. of the $22th$ Int. Conf. on Distributed Computing Systems (ICDCS), Washington, DC, USA, IEEE Computer Society (2002) 457

19. Egorova-Förster, A., Murphy, A.L.: A Feedback Enhanced Learning Approach for Routing in WSN. Technical report, University of Lugano (2006) Available at www.inf.unisi.ch/phd/foerster/publications/foerster06.pdf.

20. Luo, H., Ye, F., Cheng, J., Lu, S., Zhang, L.: Ttdd: Two-tier data dissemination in large-scale wireless sensor networks. Wireless Networks (11) (2005) 161–175

21. Kim, H.S., Abdelzaher, T.F., Kwon, W.H.: Minimum-energy asynchronous dissemination to mobile sinks in wireless sensor networks. In: Proc. of the 1st Int. Conf. on Embedded networked sensor systems (SENSYS). (2003) 193–204

22. Hwang, K., In, J., Eom, D.: Distributed dynamic shared tree for minimum energy data aggregation of multiple mobile sinks in wireless sensor networks. In: Proc. of 3rd European Wkshp. on Wireless Sensor Networks (EWSN). (2006)

23. Yuen, K., Li, B., Liang, B.: Distributed data gathering in multi-sink sensor networks with correlated sources. In: Proc. of 5th Int. IFIP-TC6 Networking Conf. (2006) 868–879

24. Oyman, E.I., Ersoy, C.: Multiple sink network design problem in large scale wireless sensor networks. In: Proc. of 1st Int. Conf. on Communications (ICC). (2004)

25. Das, A., Dutta, D.: Data acquisition in multiple-sink sensor networks. Mobile Computing and Communications Review **9**(3) (2005) 82–85

inTrack: High Precision Tracking of Mobile Sensor Nodes

Branislav Kusý[1], György Balogh[1], János Sallai[1], Ákos Lédeczi[1],
and Miklós Maróti[2]

[1] Institute for Software Integrated Systems,
Vanderbilt University, Nashville, TN, USA
akos.ledeczi@vanderbilt.edu
http://www.isis.vanderbilt.edu
[2] Department of Mathematics,
University of Szeged, Hungary
mmaroti@gmail.com

Abstract. Radio-interferometric ranging is a novel technique that allows for fine-grained node localization in networks of inexpensive COTS nodes. In this paper, we show that the approach can also be applied to precision tracking of mobile sensor nodes. We introduce inTrack, a cooperative tracking system based on radio-interferometry that features high accuracy, long range and low-power operation. The system utilizes a set of nodes placed at known locations to track a mobile sensor. We analyze how target speed and measurement errors affect the accuracy of the computed locations. To demonstrate the feasibility of our approach, we describe our prototype implementation using Berkeley motes. We evaluate the system using data from both simulations and field tests.

1 Introduction

Node localization is an important service for sensor network applications because in order to correlate the observations of a physical phenomenon made by different sensor nodes, their precise locations need to be known. When some of the sensors are mobile, they need to be tracked continuously. Alternatively, one can envision applications where the whole purpose of the sensor network is to track some objects, for instance, vehicles, people or animals, and a node is mounted on each object for this purpose. The location data may be used locally for navigation, for example, but it is typically transmitted to a remote computer and used, for instance, to display the position of the object on a map in real-time. GPS navigation systems and tracking services are examples of such applications outside of the sensor network realm. However, when low-cost, low-power and/or high precision are required and the area of interest is relatively constrained in size, a wireless sensor network can provide an ideal platform.

In this work, we concentrate on cooperative tracking, in which the tracked object works together with the tracking system to determine its location. We envision a fixed set of resource constrained wireless devices deployed at known

K. Langendoen and T. Voigt (Eds.): EWSN 2007, LNCS 4373, pp. 51–66, 2007.

locations forming the infrastructure of the tracking service. Their function is the same as that of the GPS satellites: they act as RF sources for the purpose of locating objects relative to their known positions.

Low-power, low-cost devices typically offer only limited computational power, memory and radio range. Despite these limitations, it has been shown that it is possible to measure highly accurate ranges over large distances [1]. The radio-interferometric positioning system presented in [1] was further improved in [2] to achieve a demonstrated localization error of less than 10 cm at a remarkably low node density of 650 nodes/km^2.

Previous work on radio-interferometric positioning in sensor networks focused exclusively on networks with stationary nodes. The single limiting factor making tracking a more challenging problem than node localization is the non-zero time required to measure the ranges, constraining both the real-time availability of the location estimates and the maximum allowable speed of the tracked object. On one hand, localization accuracy depends on the amount of ranging data available. Increasing the number of ranging measurements, however, limits the refresh rate. On the other hand, if the speed of the tracked object is high, the range changes significantly during the measurement and inconsistent ranging data is obtained. Radio-interferometric ranging is especially prone to these errors, because a single range measurement takes anywhere between 100 ms and 1 sec, depending on the required ranging accuracy and also on the capabilities of the hardware platform.

The objectives for a practical and effective tracking system are:

Accuracy: location errors are less than a meter error on average.

Large scale: the node density is less than 1000 nodes/km^2.

Real-time tracking: refresh rate and latency are adequate for tracking a walking person.

Resilience to multipath: the approach should work in moderate multipath environments, meaning outdoor deployments with buildings, cars, trees and people close by.

Low-power, low-cost: the range measurements can be collected using standard sensor network devices with resource constraints such as 8 MHz microcontroller, 9 kHz ADC sampling, 4 kB of RAM memory, 56 kbps radio and no additional specialized hardware.

In this paper, we show how to improve the time effectiveness of radio-interferometric ranging to allow for real-time refresh rates with sufficient ranging accuracy. First, frequent calibration of radio hardware is required to achieve the desired beat frequency, because manufacturing differences coupled with environmental effects may cause up to 50 ppm errors in the emitted frequency. We show that it is possible to completely eliminate time consuming recalibration by measuring the frequency of the interference signal and adjusting the radio settings on-the-fly. As a result, the improved algorithm carries out the calibration in parallel with ranging. Second, we observe that certain types of measurement errors cannot be eliminated at the ranging level and propose a novel technique that outputs a set of possible ranges, the true range being one of them with high probability. In turn, our tracking algorithm uses the fact that the true ranges from different nodes correlate and it is able to reject the erroneous measurements. We implement this algorithm on a centralized node (a PC laptop) where all ranging measurements from the individual sensors are routed. We show that this process is superior to the previously described localization algorithm, improving the time required to compute the location by an order of magnitude.

2   Radio-Interferometric Ranging

Our tracking algorithm builds on the radio-interferometric ranging technique introduced in [1] which was shown to provide accurate ranges over large distances using low-cost COTS hardware. The unique feature of this work is that two transmitters A and B transmit unmodulated high frequency sine waves at slightly different frequencies concurrently. The resulting composite interference signal has a low beat frequency and can be analyzed on resource-limited hardware using the received signal strength indicator (RSSI) signal. The phase of the composite signal, when measured at receiver C, depends on the phase difference of the two transmitters and their distances from C. Typical low-cost hardware does not allow for phase control at the transmitters, therefore, one more receiver D is used to analyze the same composite signal. The relative phase offset of C and D depends only on the distances between the four nodes and can be expressed as follows (see [1] for the formal proof):

$$d_{ABCD} \bmod \lambda \; = \; \varphi_{CD} \frac{\lambda}{2\pi}, \tag{1}$$

where λ is the wavelength corresponding to the carrier frequency, φ_{CD} is the relative phase offset of C, D, and d_{ABCD} is the interferometric range (q-range) given by the equation $d_{ABCD} = d_{AD} + d_{BC} - d_{AC} - d_{BD}$, d_{XY} being the Euclidean distance between X and Y.

Therefore, radio-interferometric ranging measures q-ranges, rather than pairwise ranges. Furthermore, the wavelength λ is typically much smaller than the actual distances between the nodes, so Eq. (1) can have many solutions. This ambiguity of the q-range solution can be resolved by measuring phase differences φ_{CD_i} at multiple frequencies with wavelengths λ_i, resulting in a system of Diophantine equations with unknowns d_{ABCD} and $n_i \in \mathbb{N}$:

$$d_{ABCD} \; = \; \varphi_{CD_i} \frac{\lambda}{2\pi} + n_i \lambda_i \quad (i = 1, \ldots, m) \,. \tag{2}$$

The q-ranging algorithm proposed in [1] first instruments two nodes to transmit at multiple radio channels, collects the phase readings from the receivers and then solves (2) for each pair of receivers. The prototype implementation achieved an average localization error of 4 cm for 16 stationary Mica2 nodes covering a 120×120 m area.

2.1   Radio-Interferometric Ranging and Tracking

In tracking, we can assume that we only measure q-ranges d_{ABCD} for which we know locations of three out of the four nodes. The q-range equation then reduces to the equation defining a hyperboloid in 3D space with the tracked node being located on the surface of the hyperboloid. If the target node is one of the transmitters, for example A, then both distances d_{BD} and d_{BC} are known and the q-range defines the following hyperboloid with foci C and D:

$$d_{AD} - d_{AC} = d_{BD} - d_{BC} - d_{ABCD} \ . \tag{3}$$

Similarly, if the target is one of the receivers, for example C, the q-range defines the following hyperboloid with foci A and B:

$$d_{BC} - d_{AC} = d_{BD} - d_{AD} - d_{ABCD} \ . \tag{4}$$

For a set of n nodes, a single measurement round (i.e. two nodes are transmitting and the remaining $n - 2$ nodes are measuring the phase) yields $\binom{n-2}{2}$ pairwise phase differences, and thus $\binom{n-2}{2}$ q-ranges.

It is easy to see that if the tracked node is one of the transmitters, its location can be found at an intersection of $\binom{n-2}{2}$ hyperboloids defined by these q-ranges. Moreover, the receivers (that is, the foci of the hyperboloid) are presumably located at different points in space, so each pair of receivers defines a unique hyperboloid (see Eq. (3)).

In contrast, if the tracked node is a receiver C, only $n - 3$ of these q-ranges are relevant for its localization–those defined by the receiver pairs in which C participates. More significantly, each of the hyperboloids corresponding to the $n - 3$ q-ranges is uniquely defined by the two fixed foci, transmitters A and B, and the target C. Therefore, all $n - 3$ q-ranges define a single hyperboloid. In order to obtain a unique solution for C, multiple measurement rounds with different transmitter pairs are thus required.

We choose the tracked node to be a transmitter because it provides better ranging data per ranging measurement. A drawback of this approach relates to its extension to multiple tracked targets. Such extension would require serialized access to the radio channel by the targets which would decrease the refresh rate proportionally to the number of targets.

3   Approach

The overall approach of inTrack, as shown in Fig. 1, is as follows.

1. The target requests the location calculation on demand. The second transmitter is chosen from the infrastructure nodes and all nodes involved in the measurement time-synchronize using the estimated time on arrival (ETA) primitive [19] to coordinate their transmissions and receptions.
2. For each radio channel, receivers measure frequency and phase of the periodic interference signal by analyzing the signal at the RSSI pin of the radio chip. Each receiver then routes all measured data to a PC-class server. After the routing task is completed, the target requests another localization round.
3. For each pair of receivers, the phase differences are computed for all channels. Consequently, the q-ranging algorithm is executed on the server to calculate q-range for each receiver pair.

4. The location of the tracked node is computed. This algorithm is executed on the server and makes the computed location available remotely on the web.
5. Both Google Earth (see Fig. 7) and our proprietary GUI show the location and the track of the target node on the map in real-time.

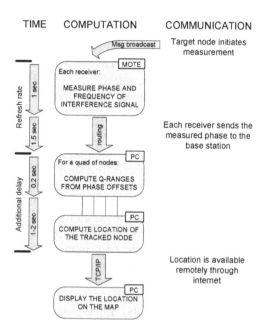

Fig. 1. A block diagram of the tracking algorithm illustrating the timing, computation and communication components of the algorithm. The time requirements consist of the refresh rate portion (2.5 sec) which is the time needed to measure and route ranging data from the nodes to the base station, and the additional delay (2 sec) needed for the location computation. Only the phase measurement is currently implemented on the nodes, all other computation is done on a PC.

3.1   Frequency and Phase Analysis

Probably the most time consuming operation in the process of acquiring the frequency and phase of the interference signal is frequent calibration (see [1]). This is required because the frequency at which the transceivers transmit is dependent on the hardware differences and the temperature and voltage variations observed in a real-world deployment of the sensors. The time required for the calibration is unacceptably long and would decrease the refresh rate of tracking. We have enhanced our approach eliminating the re-calibration completely and hence, significantly decreasing the measurement time.

VCO and PLL Self-Calibration. To compensate for changes in supply voltage and temperature, the VCO and PLL of the radio transceiver (CC1000 from Texas Instruments, formerly Chipcon) [17]) need to be calibrated. This self-calibration takes 34ms for the transceiver to complete, and has to be repeated every time when a new operating frequency is set.

We found that the calibrated settings for the VCO and PLL do not change significantly for a few hours of continuous operation. Therefore, we self-calibrate the radio chip for all radio channels at start-up, store the calibration values in local memory, and use the recorded values to rapidly set up the radio for consequent radio-interferometric measurements at different frequencies. The price we pay is a) larger initialization time of the node (up to two seconds) and b) a dedicated memory buffer at each node to hold calibration values (up to a hundred bytes to cover the frequency band from 400MHz to 460MHz). This is, however, well worth the achieved 50 % improvement of the channel measurement time.

Beat Frequency Calibration (tuning). The algorithm that calculates the phase and the frequency of the interference signal (see [1]) can only analyze signals with frequencies in a relatively narrow range (i.e. 250–450 Hz), due to the resource limitations on the motes. Therefore, it is essential that we can set the frequency difference of the two transmitters with a very fine grained resolution.

However, the errors of up to 50 ppm in the transmit frequency can be expected when using low-cost hardware, which results in an interference frequency out of the analyzable range. Previously, we have proposed a tuning algorithm [1] that is executed before every ranging measurement to compensate for these deviations. As the tuning procedure for a given pair of transmitters takes approximately 3 seconds to finish, this conflicts with the real-time requirements of our tracking service.

Since the output frequency of the radio transceiver is highly sensitive to conditions such as supply voltage and temperature, it is not sufficient to execute the tuning algorithm at application startup only. Instead of time consuming periodic tunings we inserted the following control loop in our algorithm: we monitor the beat frequencies measured by the receivers during q-range measurements and optionally update the tuning values of the transmitters. If the observed frequency is too low (< 300 Hz) or too high (> 400 Hz), the receivers notify the transmitters to update their tuning values accordingly. Consequently, the transmitters are being constantly adjusted and there is no need for the tuning procedure (provided the q-range measurement is initiated frequently enough). The tracking algorithm calculates a new location every few seconds assuring the constant flow of q-range measurements as well as the constant update of the transmit frequencies.

3.2   q-Range Computation

The algorithm published in [1] solves the system of Diophantine equations (2) in the following way: it defines a phase offset discrepancy function f for a q-range q as the root mean square error (RMSE) of the measured phase offsets φ_{CD_i} from their expected value at q:

$$f(q) = \sqrt{\sum_i (\varphi_{CD_i} - \mathbf{mod}(q, \lambda_i))^2} \ .$$

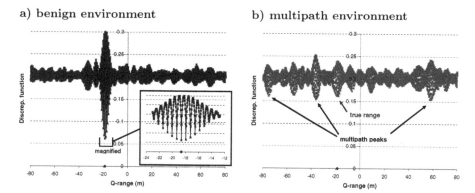

Fig. 2. a) The global minimum of the discrepancy function f is at the true range. The magnified interval shows that the values of f are close to the global minimum at certain points around the true range (multiples of $\overline{\lambda} = 70$ cm). b) Multipath introduces additional phase measurement errors, resulting in multiple local minima with almost the same value. Global minimum may no longer be at the true range.

q-range d_{ABCD} is then defined as the point where f has the global minimum (see Fig. 2a). It has been observed in [2] that the phase measurement errors and the relatively small bandwidth the radio circuitry allows (difference between the maximum and minimum wavelengths is 10 cm) have negative effects on the error distribution of the calculated q-ranges. In particular, the value of the function f is close to the global minimum at small integer multiples of the average wavelength $\overline{\lambda}$ from d_{ABCD} (see magnification in Fig. 2a). Therefore, the distribution of q-ranging errors is not Gaussian, but it exhibits increased error probabilities at small integer multiples of $\overline{\lambda}$ from the mean. The q-ranging error is further influenced by multipath as shown in Fig. 2b. Even though the discrepancy function has a local minimum at the true q-range d_{ABCD}, the global minimum of f can be located far away.

In this paper, we aim to eliminate both the wavelength and multipath related portions of the ranging error (shown in Fig. 2). Since the global minimum of the discrepancy function might be a false solution and hence the true solution might be at a local minimum, we define the output of our ranging algorithm as a set of possible q-ranges rather than a single value. The task of choosing the correct q-range from this set is left to the tracking algorithm. Formally, we define the **q-set** S_{ABCD} as:

$$S_{ABCD} = \{q \in \mathbb{R}, \forall i : |q \bmod \lambda_i - \varphi_{CD_i}| < \textbf{windowSize}\}, \tag{5}$$

where A, B are transmitters, C, D are receivers, φ_{CD_i} is the relative phase offset of C, D measured at channel with wavelength λ_i, for $i = 1, \ldots, \textbf{m}$ and **windowSize** specifies how much discrepancy in the phase offset measurements is tolerated.

We would like to point out that if the tracked object is moving during a measurement round, q is not constant in Eq. (5). If the speed of the tracked object is large, or the measurement takes too long (large **m**), the observed variance of q becomes larger than **windowSize**, resulting in $S_{ABCD} = \emptyset$. One could argue that this could be resolved by setting **windowSize** large enough. However, increasing the window size above $\overline{\lambda}/2$ would mean that every range q would satisfy the constraints of Eq. (5). Therefore, we needed to constrain the window size and consequently, the maximum speed of the tracked object as well.

The tradeoff between accuracy and real-time requirements also needs to be considered: using more phase offset measurements to constrain the q-range set (larger **m**) results in smaller q-set S_{ABCD} which requires less computation in the subsequent location calculation and allows for more accurate location estimation. Using less phase measurements, on the other hand, decreases the measurement time resulting in better refresh rate and higher maximum speed.

The choice of parameters **windowSize** and **m** is therefore influenced by the objectives of the tracking algorithm. We wanted to track targets of up to 2 m/s with 2–3 sec update rate with a reasonable accuracy. Our measurements (see Fig. 3) have shown that good accuracy can be achieved using **m** = 11 channels. On the other hand, to keep the size of the calculated q-sets reasonably small, we had to limit **windowSize** to 25 cm. These two parameters are in sharp contrast: since the measurement time is 40 ms for a single channel, the q-range can change by almost 1 m during the 11-channel measurement for a target moving 2 m/s. This is significantly more than the allowed **windowSize** limit and so the calculated q-set will be empty. We solved this problem by calculating q-sets using small subsets of consecutively measured channels, called *frames*, instead of using the full set of eleven channels. The small number of channels in a frame allows to compute q-ranges for a moving target, and multiple frames together can utilize information measured at all 11 channels, allowing for high accuracy. In practice, we used 4 frames that utilized each of the 11 measured channels. The q-ranges, calculated for different frames, can still differ by up to 1 m because of the moving target. However, the localization algorithm can resolve this by considering larger regions as will be shown in the next section.

3.3   Tracking

Ranging algorithms often have to deal with multiple sources of error that distort the measurements. It is usually possible to study these error sources and calculate more information than just a range from the measured data. This extra information can help to improve the location estimates calculated from a large set of ranging data.

The study of the errors involved in the radio-interferometric ranging enables us to determine q-sets from the measured data. Q-sets are relatively small sets of q-range candidates, the true range being one of them with a high probability. We have shown in Sect. 2.1 that each q-range corresponds to a hyperboloid in 3D and that a single ranging measurement results in multiple q-sets (one for each receiver pair). Our localization algorithm then uses the fact that there is at least one hyperboloid in each of the q-sets that intersects the location of the target. In contrast, it is very improbable that a significant number incorrect

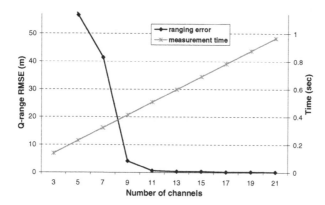

Fig. 3. Radio-interferometric ranging measures the relative phase offsets of two receivers at multiple radio channels. The root mean square error (RMSE) of q-range improves as the number of channels is increased, whereas the time required to measure and transfer the data to the base station grows. The figure shows simulated data with typical measurement noise.

hyperboloids intersect at a single point. Consequently, even though the majority of the ranging data is incorrect, the localization algorithm can find the position of the tracked node by finding a region where most hyperboloids intersect.

This is basically a search problem which can be solved algorithmically. Let $S_D = \bigcup S_{ABCD}$ be the set of all q-ranges computed by the ranging algorithm for a target node A. Let $\mathcal{X}$ be a box in 3D space. We define the consistency function $C(\mathcal{X})$ as the number of q-ranges from S_D such that their corresponding hyperboloids intersect box $\mathcal{X}$:

$$C(\mathcal{X}) = \left|\{d_{ABCD} \in S_D : d_{ABCD} = d_{XBCD} \text{ for some point } X \in \mathcal{X}\}\right|$$

The General Bisection method based on interval arithmetic [18] was shown to find global maxima of nonlinear functions in a computationally efficient way [3]. The algorithm maintains a list of boxes along with the values of the consistency function for each of the boxes. It is initialized with a box that corresponds to the whole search space, the consistency value of which is the number of all q-ranges $|S_D|$. At subsequent steps, the algorithm removes the box with the largest value, splits the box along the longest dimension into two equal boxes, recalculates the consistency function of the two boxes and inserts the new boxes back to the list. As the sizes of the boxes decrease, the consistency value is also decreasing. The algorithm stops, if the consistency function falls under a certain threshold and the center of the smallest box is returned as the location estimate. We allowed for 5% overlap of the boxes to reduce the risk of splitting a large box at the target location, resulting in two smaller boxes containing half of the good data each.

The value of the consistency function for the resulting box is ideally $\binom{n-2}{2}$ times number of frames calculated per receiver pair (which was 4 as discussed in the previous section). In practice, we used 60% of this ideal value as the consistency function threshold. Further, we accepted the computed box as a valid solution, only if all its sides were smaller than 2 m.

3.4   Tradeoffs

Tracking algorithms approximate continuous change of the location of the tracked object with discrete location measurements. Therefore, the design of these algorithms needs to balance the frequency of the location estimates with the amount of collected localization data and the computational power of available hardware. In other words, real-time can be traded off with the location accuracy and the price of the system. This tradeoff is especially important in the resource constrained domain of wireless sensor networks.

The accuracy of the radio-interferometric ranging depends on the number of channel measurements made for a fixed pair of transmitters. Simulation results in Fig. 3 show, that the ranging error can be significantly improved if more channels are measured. However, it requires more time to measure more channels.

More powerful hardware allows for faster sampling, computation, and radio transmission of the data. Therefore, more data can be measured at the same or even shorter time improving both accuracy and refresh rate. However, more powerful hardware is typically more expensive and consumes more power, increasing the cost and decreasing lifetime of the tracking system.

Lower speed of the tracked object means more stable q-range during the measurement resulting in higher accuracy. However, if the speed goes over a certain limit, the tracking algorithm fails to return a location at all (see Sect. 3.2).

4   Results

4.1   Simulation Results

In this section, we present simulation results to evaluate the tracking algorithm. In particular, we investigate the effects of target speed, as well as the sensitivity of the calculated positions to measurement noise.

Parameters. The simulator generates phase and beat frequency measurements emulating the target node moving along a trajectory being tracked by a set of infrastructure nodes. The inputs of the simulator are the infrastructure node locations, target speed, trajectory of the target, noise pattern, transmitter pairs, channel frequencies and channel measurement time.

Assumptions. The trajectory of the target is defined by a sequence of waypoints, the simulated trajectory between waypoints is a line. The target speed is assumed to be constant. These assumptions allow for easy implementation and provide a sufficiently detailed model for our purposes.

The simulator assumes that a phase measurement at given radio channel is instantaneous, that is, the phase does not change during the measurement. In practice, measuring one channel takes about 40 ms which corresponds to 8 cm position change at a speed of 2 m/s, hence the above assumption is justifiable.

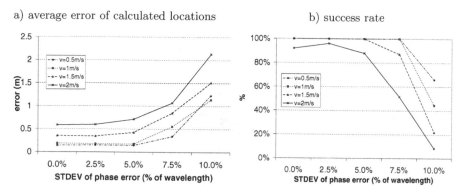

Fig. 4. Target locations are calculated for randomly generated set of 250 target positions and velocity vectors for each pair of speed and phase error deviation. a) shows the average error of the calculated locations and b) shows the percentage of simulated target locations where the tracking algorithm returned a location.

For simplicity, the simulator uses a Gaussian noise model. The noise is added to the generated phase measurement data, is assumed to have zero mean and its variance is a parameter. Our experimental observations show that these are reasonable assumptions.

In practice, message loss and communication delays do influence the results computed by the tracking algorithm. Evaluating the effects of data loss is beyond the scope of this paper, so we assume no data loss in the simulation.

Approach. To generate simulated phase measurements, we use Eq. (1), a formula that relates a distance aggregate for a quad of nodes and the difference of phases measured at two receivers. We evaluate Eq. (1), where A is the instantaneous position of the target at the time of the measurement, point B is the position of the second transmitter, point C is the infrastructure node that is measuring the phase offset and point D is a dedicated reference infrastructure node. This way, the simulated phase measurement is a phase offset between node C and the reference node. Since the phase values are never used directly in the tracking algorithm, just pairwise phase differences, having the same additive constant (the phase measured by the reference node D) in all phase measurements is indifferent. Therefore, the simulated values are valid.

To calculate the target position, the tracking algorithm uses phase data measured at different frequencies, and thus at different time instances. Therefore, there are multiple ground truth positions belonging to a calculated target position. In order to relate the output of the tracking algorithm to a single reference position, we consider the centroid of the positions at which the phase measurement data was collected as the ground truth.

The generated phase and frequency measurement are input to the tracking algorithm. The calculated target positions are compared to the ground truth and the average error is calculated.

Fig. 5. Our experimental setup at the Vanderbilt football stadium. 12 infrastructure nodes (visible ones are circled on the picture), were positioned on the tripods on the field and on the bleachers in the stands.

Results. We ran the simulation in a 80×90 m area covered by 12 infrastructure nodes, which is identical to our experimental setup described in the next section. The phase measurement time was set to 40 ms. The phases were measured at 11 channels in the 400–460 MHz frequency range. We used a 4-second position refresh period. For a particular set of simulation parameters, we used the same trajectory defined by randomly generated waypoints within the area of interest. We varied the standard deviation of the Gaussian phase measurement error between 0% and 10% of the wavelength and the target speed between 0 and 2 m/s. A typical standard deviation of the phase error measured by our hardware varies between 3 and 5%, depending on the environment.

The simulation results are shown in Fig. 4. As expected, position errors increase as the speed or the phase measurement errors increase. When the target speed is smaller than 2m/s and there are no significant phase errors present, the position errors are below half a meter. The average position errors exceed one meter only for a large (10%) phase error. The negative effect of large noise combined with large speed is that the tracking algorithm is not able to compute any location for a significant number of measurements, as discussed in Sect. 3.3.

It is interesting to see that for speeds less than 1.5 m/s, the effect of phase measurement error of 5% and under is very similar. The implications of this finding are twofold. First, this means that our tracking algorithm is resilient to errors up to 5% of the wavelength. Second, this result tells us that increasing the precision of the phase measurement, or using a more precise numerical representation of the phase data such that the errors are bounded by 5% of the wavelength would yield no improvement in the tracking results.

4.2   Experimental Results

We have tested our system at the Vanderbilt football stadium using XSM motes by Crossbow [16] (a version of the Berkeley Mica2 mote in a weatherproof

a) test results

b)   histogram   of   errors

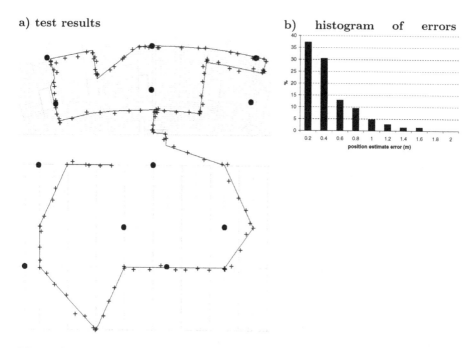

Fig. 6. a) shows a test run in which the target moves along the line segments, 12 black circles show the infrastructure nodes and the crosses show the calculated locations. b) shows the histogram of distances of the calculated locations from the trajectory: the average is 37 cm, the maximum is 1.5 m and the dataset size is 148.

package), running TinyOS [9]. 12 infrastructure nodes were placed at known locations, 6 of them on the field and the other 6 in the stands on one side of the stadium. The trajectory, spanning the whole area, was defined by a series of waypoints. We assume that between the points, the tracked object travelled approximately along a straight line at a constant speed between 1.5 to 2 m/s. The test area that we covered was approximately 80×90 m. We achieved a location refresh rate of 3 seconds with an additional 2 second latency. The calculated location and trajectory of the target were available on the internet through Google Earth in real-time. Fig. 5 shows the photo of our experimental setup, Fig. 6 presents the results of one of the test runs in our Java tool and Fig. 7 shows a snapshot of Google Earth.

The elevation map of the area was available to us, so we were only interested in the 2-dimensional location error. For every calculated position, we computed its distance from the closest point on the trajectory and show the corresponding histogram in Fig. 6b.

This evaluation metric, however, underestimates the actual 2-dimensional location error as we do not have any information on *where* on the trajectory the target was at the moment of the corresponding measurement. By simulation, we found that the distance from the trajectory is typically 65% more than the

Fig. 7. The current location and trajectory of the tracked node could be accessed through Google Earth in real-time. A large balloon shows the locations of the tracked node while smaller ones indicate the twelve infrastructure nodes.

actual location error: therefore, we estimate that the average location error was 0.61m in our experiment. This result aligns well with the simulated data: if the standard deviation of the phase errors is between 2.5% and 5% of the wavelength, and the target speed is 1.5 m/s to 2 m/s, the location errors range from 0.34 m to 0.71 m.

5 Related Work

Both node localization and tracking are well established areas in sensor networks research. These algorithms typically rely on distance measurements to estimate the range between neighboring nodes. Several techniques can be used to generate these measurements, including time-of-flight, time difference of arrival, angle of arrival, phase and/or signal strength measurements, and others. A comprehensive survey of different approaches can be found in [7].

The Global Positioning System is perhaps the most widely published localization system [10]. GPS provides reliable worldwide coverage, but is considered to be a coarse-grained, high-cost and power inefficient solution in sensor networks. State of the art low-power GPS receiver ICs cost around $50, have an accuracy of 3–5m and power consumption in the 50-100mW range.

Among the typical sensor network solutions, time-of-flight ranging that combines acoustic and RF signals tends to give much better results than RF received signal strength (RSSI) because of the high variance of RSSI [8,14]. Ultrasound and more recently broad ultrasound measurements have become popular, especially for fine-grained indoors localization and tracking [4,13,6]. The system presented in [5] avoids using range measurements by using only connectivity between nodes at the price of decreased accuracy.

Few of the published tracking algorithms have been demonstrated at scale. The system published in [11] is capable of 1 Hz location update rate with a few centimeter average error, but the experimental setup uses 6 anchor nodes to track the target within a 1.5 × 2 m area. The connectivity-based algorithm in [5] covers a somewhat larger area (10 × 10 m) with 4 anchor nodes and achieves a 2-second update rate and an accuracy of 1.83 m.

Most tracking algorithms assume the existence of fixed nodes with known locations. The errors of these locations can significantly degrade the accuracy of the calculated target location. Pathirana et al. [12] have shown that the known trajectory of the target can be used to discover and improve the location estimates of the fixed nodes. Taylor [15] have improved this to the point where they perform localization and tracking simultaneously, without the knowledge of the mobile node's trajectory. However, their system relies on acoustic ranging and hence, it requires a fairly dense network.

6   Discussion

We have introduced inTrack, a cooperative tracking system that is able to locate a moving sensor node with high accuracy over large areas. The system can tolerate measurement errors typical in moderate multipath environments. Moreover, inTrack has been implemented on COTS mote hardware, making its deployment economically viable.

The experimental evaluation shows $2-3$ second update rate and 0.6 m average error of the location estimates with the target moving up to 2 m/s within a 80×90 m area. We have generated a large number of random positions, speeds and directions in our simulator and verified the performance of inTrack in much larger scale than was experimentally feasible.

One weakness of inTrack is that it can track only a single target in its current implementation. Multiple targets would have to serialize their access to the inTrack system and the update rate of the locations would decrease. One possible solution is to make the target node a receiver rather than a transmitter. While our prototype uses the XSM motes that cost several hundred dollars, we envision that such a tracking system, assuming mass production of specialized hardware, can work as a cheaper and more accurate version of GPS in such geographically constrained areas as sports stadiums or amusement parks.

Currently a significant portion of our code runs on a PC, namely the computationally expensive search that finds intersections of hyperboloids. A solution could be to find these intersections analytically, enabling the implementation of the algorithm on resource constrained hardware. Finally, we plan to improve the current speed limitation of the inTrack system.

Acknowledgments. We would like to thank Peter Volgyesi and Andras Nadas for their help with the experimental evaluation and Dr. Vladimir Protopopescu for his helpful comments and suggestions.

References

1. M. Maróti (et al.): Radio-interferometric geolocation. *In Proc. ACM 3rd Conference on Embedded Networked Sensor Systems (SenSys)*, San Diego, CA, USA, 2005.
2. B. Kusý, A. Lédeczi, M. Maróti, and L. Meertens: Node-density independent localization. *In Proc. of 5th Int'l Symposium on Information Processing in Sensor Networks (IPSN SPOTS)*, Nashville, TN, USA (2006).
3. A. Lédeczi (et. al): Countersniper System for Urban Warfare. *ACM Transactions on Sensor Networks*, Vol. 1 (2005), 153–177.
4. M. Addlesee (et al.): Implementing a Sentient Computing System. *Computer*, vol. 34, no. 8, pp. 50–56, Aug. 2001.
5. N. Bulusu, J. Heidemann, and D. Estrin: GPS-less low-cost outdoor localization for very small devices. *IEEE Personal Communications*, 7(5):28-34, Oct 2000.
6. M. Hazas and A. Hopper. Broadband Ultrasonic Location Systems for Improved Indoor Positioning. *IEEE Transactions on Mobile Computing*, volume 5, number 5, pages 536-547, May 2006.
7. J. Hightower and G. Borriello: Location Systems for Ubiquitous Computing. *Computer*, vol. 34, no. 8, pp. 57-66, Aug. 2001.
8. J. Hightower, R.Want, and G. Borriello: SpotON: An indoor 3D location sensing technology based on RF signal strength. UW CSE 00-02-02, University of Washington, Department of Computer Science and Engineering, Seattle, WA, feb 2000.
9. J. Hill and R. Szewczyk and A. Woo and S. Hollar and D. Culler and K. Pister: System architecture directions for networked sensors. *in Proc. of ASPLOS 2000*, Cambridge, MA (2000).
10. B. Hofmann-Wellenhof, H. Lichtenegger, and J. Collins: Global Positioning System: Theory and Practice, 4th ed. *Springer Verlag*, 1997.
11. D. Moore, J. Leonard, D. Rus, and S. Teller. Robust distributed network localization with noisy range measurements. *in Proceedings of ACM Sensys*, Nov 2004.
12. P. Pathirana, N. Bulusu, S. Jha, and A. Savkin Node localization using mobile robots in delay-tolerant sensor networks. *IEEE Transactions on Mobile Computing*, vol. 4, no. 4, Jul/Aug 2005.
13. N.B. Priyantha, A. Chakraborty, and H. Balakrishnan: Cricket Location-Support System. *Proc. Sixth Intl Conf. Mobile Computing and Networking (MobiCom)*, 2000.
14. A. Savvides, CC. Han, and M. Srivastava: Dynamic finegrained localization in ad-hoc networks of sensors. *In 7th ACM Int. Conf. on Mobile Computing and Networking (Mobicom)*, pages 166-179, Rome, Italy, July 2001.
15. C. Taylor, A. Rahimi, J. Bachrach, H. Shrobe, and A. Grue: Simultaneous Localization, Calibration and Tracking in an Ad Hoc Sensor Network. *Proc. 5th Int'l Symposium on Information Processing in Sensor Networks (IPSN)*, Nashville, TN, USA (2006).
16. P. Dutta, M. Grimmer, A. Arora, S. Bibyk, and D. Culler. Design of a wireless sensor network platform for detecting rare, random, and ephemeral events. *In Proc. of 4th Int'l Conference on Information Processing in Sensor Networks (IPSN SPOTS)*, April 2005.
17. Chipcon: CC1000 Product Information. 2004, http://www.chipcon.com.
18. C. Hu, S. Xu, X. Yang: A Review on Interval Computation – Software and Applications. *Int. J. of Computational and Numerical Analysis and Applications*, Vol. 1, No. 2, pp. 149–162, 2002.
19. B. Kusy, P. Dutta, P. Levis, M. Maroti, A. Ledeczi, and D. Culler: Elapsed Time on Arrival: A simple and versatile primitive for canonical time synchronization services. *International Journal of Ad Hoc and Ubiquitous Computing*, January 1, 2006.

Approximate Initialization of Camera Sensor Networks*

Purushottam Kulkarni, Prashant Shenoy, and Deepak Ganesan

Department of Computer Science
University of Massachusetts, Amherst, MA 01003
{purukulk, shenoy, dganesan}@cs.umass.edu

Abstract. Camera sensor networks—wireless networks of low-power imaging sensors—have become popular recently for monitoring applications. In this paper, we argue that traditional vision-based techniques for calibrating cameras are not directly suitable for low-power sensors deployed in remote locations. We propose approximate techniques to determine the relative locations and orientations of camera sensors without any use of landmarks or positioning technologies. Our techniques determine the degree and range of overlap for each camera and show this information can be exploited for duty cycling and triggered wakeups. We implement our techniques on a Mote testbed and conduct a detailed experimental evaluation. Our results show that our approximate techniques can estimate the degree and region of overlaps to within 10% of their actual values and this error is tolerable at the application-level for effective duty-cycling and wakeups.

1 Introduction

1.1 Motivation

Wireless sensor networks have received considerable research attention over the past decade, and rapid advances in technology have led to a spectrum of choices of image sensors, embedded platforms, and communication capabilities. Consequently, camera sensor networks— networks consisting of low-power imaging sensors [18,19]—have become popular for applications such as environmental monitoring and surveillance.

Regardless of the end-application, camera sensor networks perform several common tasks such as object detection, recognition, and tracking. While object detection involves determining when a new object appears in range of the camera sensors, recognition involves determining the type of the object, and tracking involves using multiple camera sensors to continuously monitor the object as it moves through the environment. To effectively perform these tasks, the camera sensor network needs to be *calibrated* at setup time. Calibration involves determining the location and orientation of each camera sensor. The location of a camera is its position (3D coordinates) in a reference coordinate system, while orientation is the direction in which the camera points. By determining these parameters for all sensors, it is possible to determine the viewable range of each camera and what portion of the environment is covered by one or more cameras. The relationship with other nearby cameras, in particular, the overlap in the

---

* This work was supported in part by National Science Foundation grants EEC-0313747, CNS-0219520, CNS-052072 and EIA-0098060.

K. Langendoen and T. Voigt (Eds.): EWSN 2007, LNCS 4373, pp. 67–82, 2007.

viewable ranges of neighboring cameras can be determined. This information can be used by applications to determine which camera should be used to sense an object at a certain location, to triangulate the position of an object using overlapping cameras, and to handoff tracking responsibilities from one camera to another as the object moves.

Calibration of camera sensors is well-studied in the computer vision community and a number of techniques to accurately estimate the location and orientation of cameras have been proposed [8,22,24]. These techniques assume coordinates of few landmarks are known a priori and use the projection of these landmarks on the camera's image plane, in conjunction with principles of optics, to determine a camera's coordinates and orientation.[1] In certain cases locations of landmarks are themselves determined using range estimates from known locations; for instance, a positioning technology such as Cricket can be used to determine the coordinates of landmarks from known beacon locations. However, these techniques are not feasible for deployments of ad-hoc low power camera sensors for the following reasons: (i) **Resource constraints:** Vision-based techniques for accurate calibration of cameras are compute intensive. Low-power cameras do not have the computation capabilities to execute these complex mathematical tasks. Further, images of low-power cameras are often of low fidelity and not well suited for high precision calibration, (ii) **Availability of landmarks:** In many scenarios, ad-hoc camera sensor networks are deployed in remote locations for monitoring mountainous and forest habitats or for monitoring natural disasters such as floods or forest fires. No landmarks may be available in remote inhabited locations, and infrastructure support such as positioning technologies may be unavailable or destroyed, making it difficult to define new landmarks.

One solution that eliminates the need to use landmarks is it to equip each camera sensor with a positioning device such as GPS [4] and a directional digital compass [6], which enable direct determination of the node location and orientation. However, today's GPS technology has far too much error to be practical for calibration purposes (GPS can localize an object to within 5-15m of its actual position). Ultrasound-based positioning and ranging technology [16] is an alternative which provides greater accuracy. But use of additional hardware with low-power cameras both consumes more energy and in some cases, can be prohibitive due to its cost. As a result, accurate calibration is not always feasible for initialization of resource-constrained camera sensor networks with limited or no infrastructure support.

Due to these constraints, in this paper we ask a fundamental question: *is it possible to initialize camera sensors without the use of known landmarks or without using any positioning technology?* In scenarios where accurate camera calibration may not always be feasible, determining relative relationships between nearby sensor nodes may be the only available option. This raises the following questions:

- How can we determine relative locations and orientations of camera sensors without use of known landmarks or positioning infrastructure?
- What kind of accuracy can these approximate initialization techniques provide?
- What is the performance of applications based on approximate initialization?

---

[1] Vision-based calibration techniques can also determine a camera's internal parameters such as the camera focal length and lens distortion, in addition to external parameters such as location and orientation.

1.2   Research Contributions

To address the above challenges, in this paper, we propose novel *approximate initialization* techniques for camera sensors. Our techniques rely only on the inherent picture-taking ability of cameras and judicious use of on-board computational resources to initialize each camera relative to other cameras in the system. No infrastructure support for beaconing, range estimation or triangulation is assumed. Our initialization techniques are computationally lightweight and easily instantable in environments with little or no infrastructure support and are well suited for resource-constrained camera sensors.

Our techniques rely on two key parameters—the *degree of overlap* of a camera with other cameras, and the *region of overlap* for each camera. We present approximate techniques to estimate these parameters by taking pictures of a randomly placed reference object. To quantify the accuracy of our methods, we implement two techniques—duty-cycling and triggered wakeup—that exploit this initialization information.

We have implemented our initialization techniques on a testbed of Cyclops [18] cameras and Intel Crossbow Motes [14] and have conducted a detailed evaluation using the testbed and simulations. Our experiments yield the following results:

- Our approximate initialization techniques can estimate both k-overlap and region of overlap to within 10% of the actual values.
- The approximation techniques can handle and correct for skews in the distribution of reference point locations.
- The application-level accuracy using our techniques is 95-100% for determining the duty-cycle parameter and 80% for a triggered wakeup application.

2   Problem Formulation

We consider a wireless network of camera sensors deployed in an ad-hoc fashion with no a priori planning. Each sensor node is assumed to consist of a low-power imaging sensor such as the Cyclops [18] or the CMUCam [19] connected to an embedded sensor platform such as the Crossbow Mote [14] or the Telos [15]. No positioning hardware is assumed to be present on the nodes or in the environment. Given such an ad-hoc camera sensor network, our goal is to determine the following parameters for each sensor node:

- *Degree of overlap*, which is the fraction of the viewable range that overlaps with other nearby cameras; specifically we are interested in the *k-overlap*, which is the fraction of the viewable region that overlaps with exactly k other cameras.
- *Region of overlap*, which is the spatial volume within the viewable region that overlaps with another camera. While the degree of overlap indicates the extent of the viewable region that overlaps with another camera, it does not indicate *which* portion of the viewable range is covered by another camera. The region of overlap captures this spatial overlap and is defined as the 3D intersection of the viewable regions of any pair of cameras.

Our goal is to estimate these parameters using the inherent picture-taking capability of cameras. We assume the presence of a reference object that can be manually placed at different locations in the environment; while the coordinates of the reference object are *unknown*, the sensors can take pictures to determine if the object can be viewed simultaneously by two or more cameras from a particular location. Our goal is to design techniques that use this information to determine the degree and region of overlap for the various nodes. The physical dimensions of the reference object as well as the focal length f of each camera is assumed to be known a priori.

3   Approximate Initialization

In this section, we describe approximate techniques to determine the *degree of overlap* and *region of overlap* for camera sensors.

3.1   Determining the Degree of Overlap

As indicated earlier, degree of overlap is defined by the *k-overlap*, which is the fraction of the viewing area simultaneously covered by *exactly* k cameras. Thus, 1-overlap is the fraction of a camera's viewable region that does not overlap with any other sensor; 2-overlap is the fraction of region viewable to itself and one other camera, and so on. This is illustrated in Figure 1 where k_1 denotes the region covered by a single camera, k_2 and k_3 denote the regions covered by two and three cameras, respectively. It follows that the union of the k-overlap regions of a camera is exactly the total viewable range of that camera (i.e., the sum of the k-overlap fractions is 1). Our goal is to determine the k-overlap for each camera, $k = 1 \ldots n$, where n is the total number of sensors in the system.

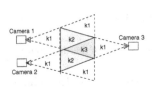

Fig. 1. Different degrees of overlap (k-overlap) for a camera

Estimating k-overlap. Our approximate technique employs random sampling of the three-dimensional space to determine the k-overlap for each camera sensor. This is done by placing an easily identifiable reference object at randomly chosen locations and by having the camera sensors take pictures of the object. Let each object location be denoted as a reference point (with unknown coordinates). Each camera then processes its pictures to determine which reference points are visible to it. By determining the subset of the reference points that are visible to multiple cameras, we can estimate the k-overlap fractions for various sensors. Suppose that r_i reference points from the total set are visible to camera i. From these r_i reference points, let r_i^k denote the reference points that are simultaneously visible to exactly k cameras. Assuming an uniform distribution of reference points in the environments, the k-overlap for camera i is given by

$$O_i^k = \frac{r_i^k}{r_i} \tag{1}$$

Depending on the density of reference points, error in the estimate of O_i^K can be controlled. The procedure is illustrated in Figure 2(a), where there are 16 reference points visible to camera 1, of which 8 are visible only to itself, 4 are visible to cameras 1 and 3 and another 4 to cameras 1, 2, and 3. This yields a 1-overlap of 0.5, 2-overlap and 3-overlap of 0.25 for camera 1. k-overlaps for other cameras can be similarly determined.

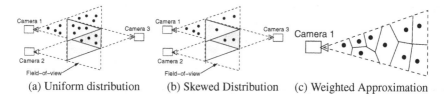

(a) Uniform distribution   (b) Skewed Distribution   (c) Weighted Approximation

Fig. 2. k-overlap estimation with distribution of reference points

Handling skewed reference point distributions. The *k-overlap* estimation technique presented above assumes uniform distribution of reference points in the environment. In reality, due to the ad-hoc nature of the deployment and the need to calibrate the system online in the field, the placement of reference objects at randomly chosen locations will not be uniform. The resulting error due to a non-uniform distribution is illustrated in Figure 2(b), where our technique estimates the 1-, 2- and 3-overlap for camera 1 as $\frac{2}{3}, \frac{2}{9}, \frac{1}{9}$ as opposed to the true values of $\frac{1}{2}, \frac{1}{4} and \frac{1}{4}$ respectively. Thus, we need to enhance our technique to correct for skews in the reference point distribution.

The basic idea behind our enhancement is to assign a weight to each reference point, where the weight denotes the volume that it represents. Specifically, points in dense populated region are given smaller weights and those in sparely populated regions are given higher weights. Since *a higher weight can compensate for the scarcity of reference points in sparely populated region*, we can correct for skewed distributions of reference points. Our enhancement is based on the computational geometry technique called ***Voronoi tessellation*** [5]. In two dimensions, a Voronoi tessellation of a set of points is the partitioning of the plane into convex polygons such that all polygons contain a single generating point and all points within a polygon are closest to the corresponding generating point. Figure 2(c) shows a skewed distribution of reference points in the 2D viewing area of a camera and the corresponding Voronoi tessellation. Each reference point in the camera is contained within a cell, with all points in a cell closest to the corresponding reference point. Given a skewed distribution of reference points, it follows that densely situated points will be contained within smaller polygons, and sparsely situated points in larger polygons. Since the size of each polygon is related to the density of the points in the neighborhood, it can be used as an approximation of the area represented by each point. Voronoi tessellations can be extended to points in three dimensions, with each point contained with a 3D cell instead of a polygon.

Using Voronoi tessellation, each reference point is assigned a weight that is approximately equal to volume of the cell that it lies in. The k-overlap is then computed as

$$O_i^k = \frac{w_i^k}{w_i} \qquad (2)$$

where w_i^k is the cumulative weight of all reference points that are simultaneously visible to exactly k cameras and w_i is the total weight of all the cells in the viewable region of camera i. Observe that when the reference points are uniformly distributed, each point gets an equal weight, and the above equation reduces to Equation 1. Note that Voronoi tessellation requires the coordinates of reference points in order to partition the viewable region into cells or polygons. Section 3.2 describes how to approximately estimate this in .

Approximate Tessellation. Since tessellation is a compute-intensive procedure that might overwhelm the limited computational resources on a sensor node, we have developed an approximation. Instead of tessellating the 3D viewing region of a camera into polyhedrons, a computationally expensive task, the viewing region is discretized into smaller cubes. For each cube, the closest viewable reference point from the center of the cube is calculated. The volume of the cube is added to the weight of that reference point. When all cubes are associated and their volumes added to the respective reference points, the weight of each reference points is in proportion to the density of points in the vicinity—points in less dense regions will have higher weights than points in less dense regions, thereby yielding an approximation of the tessellation process.

3.2   Determining the Region of Overlap

Since k-overlap only indicates the extent of overlap but does not specify *where* the overlap exists, our techniques also determine *region of overlap* for each camera. Like before, we assume a reference object placed at randomly chosen locations. Using these points, first a Voronoi tessellation of the viewing area is obtained for each camera. The *region of overlap* for any two cameras C_i and C_j is simply the the union of cells containing all reference points simultaneously visible to the two cameras. Figure 3(c) shows the Voronoi tessellation of the 2D viewing region of camera 1, the reference points viewable by cameras 1 and 2, and the approximate *region of overlap* (shaded region) for (C_1, C_2). Thus, our approximate tessellation (described in Section 3.1) can be used to determine the region of overlap for all pairs of cameras in the system.

Estimating reference point locations. As indicated before, the tessellation process requires the locations of reference points. Since no infrastructure is available, we present a technique to estimate these locations using principles of optics. A key insight is that *if each camera can determine the coordinates of visible reference points relative to itself, then tessellation is feasible—absolute coordinates are not required.* Assuming the origin lies at the center of the lens, the relative coordinates of a point are defined as (d_r, v_r), where d_r is its distance from the origin, and v_r is a vector from the origin in the direction of the reference point that defines its orientation in 3D space.

We illustrate how to determine the distance d_r from the camera in 2-dimensions. We have assumed that the size of the reference object is known a prior, say s. The focal length f is also known. Then the camera first estimates the size of the image projected by the object—this is done by computing the bounding box around the image, determining the size in pixels and using the size of the CMOS sensor to determine the

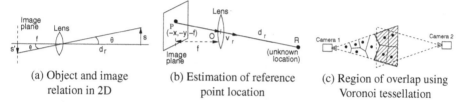

Fig. 3. Region of overlap estimation using reference points and Voronoi tessellation

size of those many pixels. If s' denotes the size of the image projected by the reference object on the camera, then from Figure 3(a) , the following condition holds

$$tan\theta = \frac{s}{d_r} = \frac{s'}{f} \tag{3}$$

Since s, s' and f are known, d_r can be computed. A similar idea holds in 3D space where instead of size, area of the object has to be considered.

Next, to determine the orientation of the reference point relative to the camera, assume that the reference object projects an image at pixel coordinates (x, y) on the image plane of the camera. Then the vector v_r has the same orientation as the vector that joins the centroid of the image to center of the lens (i.e., the origin). As shown in Figure 3(b), the vector $PO = (x, y, f)$ has the same orientation as v_r, where O is the origin and P is the centroid of the image with coordinates $(-x, -y, -f)$. Since (x, y) can be determined by processing the image and f is known, the relative orientation of the reference point can be determined.

4   Applications

In this section, we describe how camera that are initialized approximately can satisfy application requirements.

4.1   Duty-Cycling

Duty-cycling is a technique to operate sensors in cycles of ON and OFF durations to increase lifetime while providing the desired event-detection reliability and also to bound the maximum time to detect an event. The duty-cycling parameter d is commonly defined as the fraction of time a sensor is ON. An important criteria in deciding the duty-cycle parameter is the degree of overlap. Sensors with high coverage redundancy can be operated at low duty cycles to provide desired event detection probability, whereas those with lower redundancy will require higher duty cycles. One of the several techniques to estimate the duty-cycle parameter based on degree of overlap is as follows,

$$d_i = \sum_{k=1}^{n} O_i^k \times \frac{1}{k} \tag{4}$$

where, d_i is the duty-cycle parameter of camera i, O_i^k the fraction of k-overlap with the neighboring cameras and n the total number of cameras. The intuition is to duty-cycle each camera in proportion to its degree of overlap with neighboring cameras.

4.2 Triggered Wakeup

Object tracking involves continuous monitoring of an object—as the object moves from the range of one camera to another, tracking responsibilities are transferred via a handoff. Since cameras may be duty-cycled, such a handoff involves a triggered wakeup to ensure that the destination camera is awake. A naive solution is to send triggered wakeups to all overlapping cameras and have one of them take over the tracking. While doing so ensures seamless handoffs, it is extremely wasteful in terms of energy by triggering unnecessary wakeups. A more intelligent technique is to determine the trajectory of the object and using the region of overlap determine which camera is best positioned to take over tracking duties and only wake it up. However, since the object's location cannot be calculated without knowledge of accurate camera parameters, its trajectory can not be accurately determined. The only known information about the object is its image on the camera's image plane—the object is known to lie along a line that connects the image to the center of the lens. As shown in Figure 4, we refer to this line as the *projection line*, the line on which the object must lie. We can exploit this information to design an intelligent triggered wakeup technique. Any camera whose region of overlap intersects with the projection line can potentially view the object and is a candidate for a handoff. To determine all such cameras, we first determine the set of reference points within a specific *distance threshold* of the line (see Figure 4). To determine these reference points, equidistant points along the length of the projection line are chosen and reference points within the distance threshold are identified. Next, the set of neighboring cameras that can view these reference points is determined (using information gathered during our initialization process). One or more of these camera can then be woken up. Depending on the extent of overlap with the projection line, candidate cameras are prioritized and woken up in priority order—the camera with highest overlap has the highest probability of detecting the object on wakeup and is woken up first. Two important parameters of the scheme are the *distance threshold* and the *maximum number of cameras* to be woken up. A large distance threshold will capture many reference points and yield many candidates for wakeup, while a small threshold will ignore overlapping cameras. The maximum number of cameras to be woken up bounds the redundancy in viewing the same object by multiple cameras—a small limit may miss the object whereas a large limit may result in wasteful wakeups. We discuss the effect of these parameters as part of the experimental evaluation.

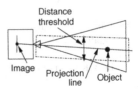

Fig. 4. Region of overlap for triggered wakeup

5 Prototype Implementation

System Design. The approximate initialization procedure involves taking pictures of reference points (or objects). Reference points are objects like a ball with a unique color or a light source, that can be easily identified by processing images at each camera. Each camera after taking a picture, processes the image to determine if it can view a reference point. If a reference point is visible, it calculates the location of the reference point on its

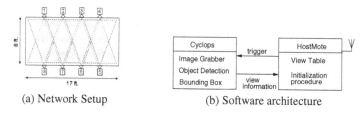

(a) Network Setup	(b) Software architecture

Fig. 5. Setup and software architecture of prototype implementation

image plane and if possible estimates the location of the reference point. The location can be estimated using an approximation of the distance of the reference point from the camera. The distance can be determined if dimensions of the reference object are known a priori along with the size of it's image on the camera's image plane. The image location and distance of object information is exchanged with all other cameras in the network. The data recorded at each camera can be stored as table of tuples,

$$< R_k : C_i, u_i, v_i, d_i, C_j, u_j, v_j, d_j... >$$

where, R_k is the kth reference point visible to camera i, (u_i, v_i) is the projection location of the reference point in the image plane and d_i is the distance of the reference point from the camera. The tuple also stores information from each camera that can view the reference point simultaneously. Multiple reference points are generated by placing the reference object at several locations.

The network setup for our prototype implementation is shown in Figure 5(a). The network consists of 8 cameras covering a region of $8ft \times 6ft \times 17ft$. The camera are equidistantly placed on the longest side, each at a height of $3ft$ facing each other and viewing inside the cubical volume. The depth-of-view for each camera is $8ft$ and the horizontal and vertical viewing regions are $7ft$ and $6ft$ respectively. The setup is used to estimate and compare k-overlap and region of overlap for each camera.

Hardware Components. We used the Cyclops [18] camera sensor in our prototype implementation to evaluate the approximate initialization techniques. The Cyclops camera sensor consists of a ADCM 1700 CMOS camera module, and supports image resolutions of 32x32, 64x64 and 128x128. Image resolution of 128x128 is used in the experimental evaluation. The Cyclops node also has an on-board ATMEL ATmega128L micro-controller, 512 KB external SRAM and 512 KB Flash memory. The on-board processing capabilities of the Cyclops are used for object detection and to detect the size of object's image. Each Cyclops sensor is connected to a Crossbow Mote (referred to as the HostMote) and they communicate via the I2C interface. The HostMote is also used to receive and send wireless messages and store initialization information on behalf of the Cyclops. A mote is also used as a remote control to send synchronized sampling triggers to detect reference points during the initialization process. A glowing ball (a translucent ball fitted on a light bulb) is used as a reference object and is manually placed at several locations to generate reference points for initialization.

Software Components. Both the Cyclops sensors and the Motes run TinyOS [21]. Each Cyclops communicates with it's attached mote using the I2C interface and the motes communicate with each other via their wireless interface (see Figure 5(b)).

Cyclops Onboard Tasks: Each Cyclops is responsible for taking images and processing them locally to detect the reference objects. On receiving a trigger from the HostMote each Cyclops takes a picture and processes it to detect and recognize reference objects. The results are communicated back to the HostMote.

HostMote Tasks: The HostMote drives each Cyclops to detect reference objects and stores all the initialization information for each camera. Once an reference object is detected, the HostMote estimates the distance of the object from the camera and transmits a broadcast message indicating visibility of the reference object, coordinates of the object on it's image plane and distance of object from the camera. Further, the HostMote receives similar broadcasts from other nodes and maintains the *ViewTable*, a table of tuples representing viewability information of each reference point.

Trigger Mote Tasks: The trigger mote is used as a remote control for synchronized detection of the reference object. Once a reference object is placed in a location, the trigger mote sends a wireless broadcast trigger to all HostMotes, which in turn trigger the attached Cyclops sensors.

6   Experimental Evaluation

In this section we present a detailed experimental evaluation of the approximate initialization techniques using both simulation and implementation based experiments. Specifically, we evaluate the accuracy of the approximate initialization procedure in estimating the *degree of overlap* and *region of overlap* of camera sensors. In addition, we evaluate the effect of skew in location of reference points on the accuracy of estimation. Further, we also evaluate the performance of an triggered wakeup application which demonstrates effective use of the region of overlap information.

6.1   Simulation Setup

The simulation setup used for evaluation consisted of a cubical region with dimensions 150x150x150. Two cases, one with 4 cameras and the other with 12 cameras are used. In the first case, 4 cameras are placed at locations (75,0,75), (75,150,75), (0,75,75), (150,75,75), oriented perpendicular to the side plane looking inwards. The k-overlap at each camera is as follows: 1-overlap: 0.54, 2-overlap: 0.23, 3-overlap: 0.07 and 4-overlap: 0.16. In the second case, additional 8 cameras are placed at the 8 corners of the cube and each of them is oriented inwards with the central axis pointing towards the center of the cube.

An uniform distribution of reference points was simulated by uniformly distributing points in the cubical viewing region. To simulate a skewed distribution, a fraction of reference points were distributed in a smaller region at the center of the viewing region and the rest were distributed in the entire viewing area. For example, a region of size 25x25x25 at the center of the viewing region, in different cases, had atleast 25%, 33%, 50%, 66% and 75% of total points within its boundary. We also used restricted regions of sizes 50x50x50 and 75x75x75 with varying fractions of skew in our evaluation.

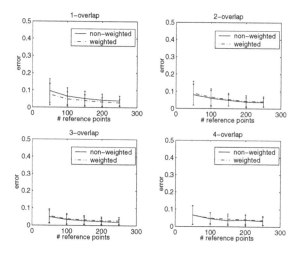

Fig. 6. Evaluation of k-overlap estimation scheme with uniform distribution of reference points

6.2 Degree of Overlap Estimation

In this section we present evaluation of the techniques used to estimate *k-overlap*, the degree of overlap metric, and its use to estimate the duty-cycling parameter.

Initialization with uniform distribution of reference points. Figure 6 plots the error in k-overlap estimation using the four camera setup with uniform distribution of reference points. The absolute difference in the approximate estimation and the exact k-overlap fraction averaged over the 4 cameras is reported as *error*. The error in k-overlap estimation using both the non-weighted and weighted techniques is similar.

Figure 6 also plots the effect of number of viewable reference points— reference points viewable by atleast a single camera— on k-overlap estimation. The error in k-overlap estimation decreases with increase in number of reference points for both the non-weighted and weighted schemes. Error in 1-overlap estimation with the weighted scheme decreases from 0.075 to 0.04 with 50 and 150 reference points respectively.

Initialization with skewed distribution of reference points. Figure 7 plots the k-overlap estimates with non-uniform distribution of reference points. The results are averaged for the different fractions of skew within a restricted region of 25x25x25. As seen from the figure, the weighted scheme accounts for skew better than the non-weighted scheme—with most benefits for 1-overlap and 4-overlap estimation. The non-weighted scheme performs poorly as it only counts the number of simultaneously viewable points, while the weighted scheme accounts for the spatial distribution of the points. Further, with increase in number of reference points, the error with the weighted scheme decrease, whereas that with the non-weighted scheme remains the same. Figure 8(a) plots the k-overlap with 150 reference points, and it shows that the weighted scheme performs better than the non-weighted scheme. The error with the non-weighted scheme for 1 and 4 overlap is worse by a factor of 4 and 6 respectively.

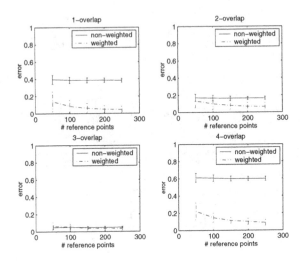

Fig. 7. Evaluation of weighted k-overlap estimation with skewed distribution of reference points

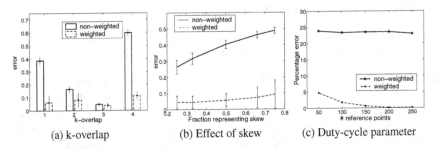

(a) k-overlap   (b) Effect of skew   (c) Duty-cycle parameter

Fig. 8. Evaluation of the weighted k-overlap estimation scheme

Figure 8(b) plots error in estimation of 1-overlap with 150 reference points and varying skew. As skew increases, so does the error in both non-weighted and weighted schemes—error with the weighted scheme being smaller than the non-weighted scheme. The increase in error is also more gradual with the weighted scheme as compared to the non-weighted scheme. The error with the non-weighted scheme increases from 0.26 to 0.49 with increase in skew fraction from 25% to 75% and the corresponding values for the weighted scheme are 0.045 and 0.09 respectively.

Duty-Cycling. The percentage error in duty-cycle parameter estimation (see Section 4.1) using the k-overlap estimates is shown in Figure 8(c). As seen from the figure, error using the non-weighted scheme is close to 24% and remains unchanged with increase in reference points. Whereas, error with the weighted scheme is 5% even with only 50 points and decreases very close to zero with more than 150 points.

From the results presented above, we conclude that the weighted k-overlap estimation scheme is well suited to estimate degree of overlap of cameras. The scheme performs identical to the non-weighted scheme with uniform distribution of reference points

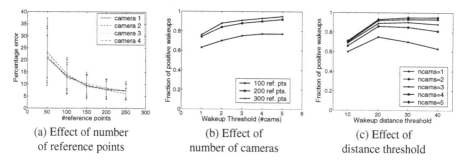

(a) Effect of number
of reference points

(b) Effect of
number of cameras

(c) Effect of
distance threshold

Fig. 9. Region of overlap estimation and wakeup heuristic performance

and significantly better with non-uniform distributions. The application-level error in determining the duty-cycle parameter using the weighted scheme is close to zero.

6.3 Region of Overlap Estimation

In this section we present evaluation of *region of overlap* estimation and the triggered wakeup heuristic that uses this estimate. Figure 9(a) plots results evaluating the effect of number of reference points on region of overlap estimation. The percentage error reported is the absolute error in estimated volume corresponding to a region of overlap and the exact volume. As seen in Figure 9(a), with uniform distribution of reference points, the percentage error of all four cameras follows a similar trend. With 50 reference points the percentage error for the four cameras is between 21-23% and with 100 reference points is 12-14%. With higher number of reference points the error decreases and so does the standard deviation. With 200 reference points the error is 7-8% and with 250 points is 6-7%. *The above results show that region of overlap between pair of cameras can be estimated with low error—6-7% with uniform distribution in our setup.*

Wakeup Heuristic. Next, we evaluate effectiveness of the wakeup heuristic based on the region of overlap estimates with the 12-camera setup. Figure 9(b) plots the effect of maximum number of cameras triggered on the fraction of positive wakeups, i.e., fraction of cases when atleast one of the triggered cameras could view the object. As seen from the figure, with increase in maximum number of cameras triggered per wakeup, the fraction of positive wakeups increases. Further, the fraction also increases with increase in total reference points in the environment. The fraction of positive wakeups with a maximum of 2 cameras to be triggered is 0.7 and 0.88 for 100 and 300 reference points respectively with a distance threshold (see Section 4.2) of 20 inches. With a maximum of 5 cameras to be triggered the corresponding fractions are 0.77 and 0.93 respectively. The fraction of positive wakeups is over 0.8 with a maximum of 2 wakeups per trigger. *The result shows that the wakeup heuristic based on region of overlap estimate can achieve high fraction of positive wakeups—close to 80% accuracy with 2 cameras woken up per trigger.*

Another parameter that influences the performance of the heuristic is the *distance threshold*—the distance along the projection of the object's image used to approximate overlapping cameras. As shown in Figure 9(c), with increase in distance threshold from

Camera	Error
1	1.5%
2	7.1%
3	4.9%
4	5.8%
5	8.7%
6	3.1%
7	7.9%
8	6.7%

(a) k-overlap error

Camera	Error
1	2.4%
2	2%
3	6.4%
4	10.8%
5	3%
6	4.7%
7	4.3%
8	0.65%

(b) Region-of-overlap error

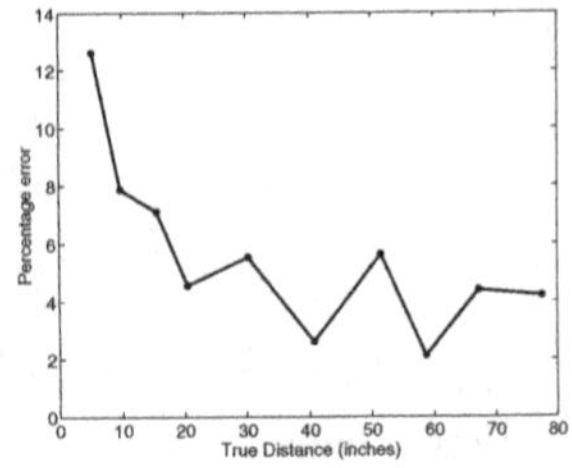

(c) Distance estimation error

Fig. 10. Initialization using prototype implementation

10 to 20 with 200 reference points, the fraction of positive wakeups increases and remains relatively constant for a maximum 2, 3, 4 and 5 triggered cameras. With just one camera to be woken up for each trigger, the fraction of positive wakeups decreases with further increase (beyond 20) in distance threshold. This indicates that the distance threshold is an important factor affecting the performance of the heuristic and for our setup a threshold of 20 yields best performance.

6.4 Implementation Results

In this section, we evaluate the estimation of k-overlap and region of overlap using our prototype implementation. As described in Section 5, we used 8 cameras in our setup and a glowing ball(1.5 inches in diameter) as a reference object. The object was manually placed at several locations to approximate an uniform distribution of reference points. Table 10(a) shows the average k-overlap percentage error at each camera. The percentage error in k-overlap estimation over all cameras is 2-9%.

We also evaluate the accuracy of region of overlap estimate between pairs of cameras in the 8-camera setup. Figure 10(b) tabulates the average percentage error estimating the region of overlap between pairs of cameras. The average error in estimating the region of overlap between pairs of cameras varies form 1-11% for our setup. An important factor that affects the region of overlap estimate is the distance estimate of the object from the camera. Figure 10(c) plots the percentage error in estimating the distance of the object from the camera based on its image size. As can been from the figure, the error is varies from 2-12%. For our setup, the region of overlap estimates show that the error is below 11% inspite of the error in distance estimation of the object.

Our results show that the approximate initialization techniques are feasible in real-world deployments and for our setup had errors close to 10%.

7   Related Work

Several techniques have been developed by the vision community for accurate camera calibration that use a set of reference points with known locations [22,24]. In sensor networks, techniques like [9,10,23] are specialized to estimate only the extrinsic parameters of cameras in an exact manner, typically using additional infrastructure or hardware. Further, distributed techniques proposed in [20,13] are suited to calibrate networked cameras. In [20], cameras collaborate to track an object and reason about consistent camera location and orientations for observed images. The technique simultaneously solves both the object tracking and camera calibration problem. Examples of systems that use accurately calibrated cameras for video surveillance and tracking are [12,17]. All the above techniques estimate exact parameters of camera, whereas our work focuses on approximate initialization of camera networks with no or limited infrastructure support and camera nodes with limited resources.

Positioning and locationing techniques for sensor nodes other than cameras have also been well studied. These techniques depend on a beaconing infrastructure and use several modalities—Active Badge [1] uses IR signals, Active Bat [2] and Cricket [16] use ultrasound signals and RADAR [3] uses RF signals. Further, GPS [4] is an example of an outdoor localization system, which can localize object to within 5–15 meters of their actual location. While these methods can be used to localize cameras and in some cases to estimate their orientation, they either have high error or are not suitable for low-power resource constrained camera sensor networks.

There exist several types of camera sensor nodes, each with different resources and capabilities. The Cyclops [18] and CMUCam [19] are examples of low-power nodes capturing low-resolution images with limited computation capabilities. XYZ [11] is a power-aware sensor platform which can be equipped with image sensors. Panoptes [7] is a camera sensor node comprising of a webcam capturing high-resolution images and a Intel StrongARM PDA processor for reasonably high computation resources. Even more sophisticated camera nodes are those with pan-tilt-zoom capabilities connected to PDA or laptop-class devices. In this work, we are interested in developing techniques for low-power resource constrained camera nodes, and our solutions can be applied to more powerful nodes as well.

8 Conclusions

In this paper, we argued that traditional vision-based techniques for accurately calibrating cameras are not directly suitable for ad-hoc deployments of sensors networks in remote locations. We proposed approximate techniques to determine the relative locations and orientations of camera sensors without any use of landmarks or positioning technology. By randomly sampling the environment with a reference object, we showed how to determine the degree and range of overlap for each camera and how this information can be exploited for duty cycling and triggered wakeups. We implemented our techniques on a Mote testbed. Our experimental results showed that our approximate techniques can estimate the degree and region of overlaps to within 10% of their actual values and this error is tolerable at the application-level for effective duty-cycling and wakeups.

References

1. Andy Harter and Andy Hopper. A Distributed Location System for the Active Office. *IEEE Network*, 8(1), January 1994.
2. Andy Ward and Alan Jones and Andy Hopper. A New Location Technique for the Active Office. *IEEE Personal Communications*, 4(5):42–47, October 1997.

3. P. Bahl and V. N. Padmanabhan. RADAR: An In-building RF-based User Location and Tracking System. In *IEEE INFOCOM* , Volume 2, pages 775–784, March 2000.
4. R. Bajaj, S. L. Ranaweera, and D. P. Agrawal. GPS: Location-tracking Technology . *Computer*, 35(4):92–94, March 2002.
5. M. Berg, M. Kreveld, M. Overmars, and O. Schwarzkopf. *Computational Geometry*. Springer, Second edition, 2000.
6. Sparton SP3003D Digital Compass. http://www.sparton.com/.
7. W. Feng, B. Code, E. Kaiser, M. Shea, W. Feng, and L. Bavoil. Panoptes: A Scalable Architecture for Video Sensor Networking Applications. In *ACM Multimedia*, 2003.
8. B. K. P. Horn. *Robot Vision* . The MIT Press , First edition, 1986.
9. X. Liu, P. Kulkarni, P. Shenoy, and D. Ganesan. Snapshot: A Self-Calibration Protocol for Camera Sensor Networks. In *IEEE/CreateNet BASENETS*, October 2006.
10. D. Lymberopoulos, A. Barton-Sweeny, and A. Savvides. Sensor Localization and Camera Calibration using Low Power Cameras. Technical Report, Yale University, 2005.
11. D. Lymberopoulos and A. Savvides. XYZ: A Motion-Enabled, Power Aware Sensor Node Platform for Distributed Sensor Network Applications. In *IPSN*, April 2005.
12. M. Chu and J. E. Reich and F. Zhao. Distributed Attention for Large Video Sensor Networks. In *Intelligent Distributed Surveillance Systems*, 2004.
13. W. Mantzel, H. Choi, and R. Baraniuk. Distributed Camera Network Localization. In *Asilomar Conference on Signals, Systems, and Computers*, volume 2, November 2004.
14. Crossbow Wireless Sensor Platform. http://www.xbow.com/
15. J. Polastre, R. Szewczyk, and D. Culler. Telos: Enabling Ultra-Low Power Wireless Research. In *IPSN/SPOTS*, April 2005.
16. N. B. Priyantha, A. Chakraborty, and H. Balakrishnan. The Cricket Location-Support System. In *ACM MOBICOM*, pages 32–43, August 2000.
17. R. Collins and A Lipton and T. Kanade. A System for Video Surveillance and Monitoring. In *American Nuclear Society (ANS) Eighth International Topical Meeting on Robotics and Remote Systems*, 1999.
18. M. Rahimi, R. Baer, O. I. Iroezi, J. C. Garcia, J. Warrior, D. Estrin, and M. Srivastava. Cyclops: In Situ Image Sensing and Interpretation in Wireless Sensor Networks. In *ACM SENSYS*, pages 192–204, November 2005.
19. A. Rowe, C. Rosenberg, and I. Nourbakhsh. A Low Cost Embedded Color Vision System. In *International Conference on Intelligent Robots and Systems*, 2002.
20. S. Funiak and C. Guestrin and M. Paskin and R. Suthankar. Distributed Localization of Networked Cameras. In *IPSN*, April 2006.
21. TinyOS Website. http://www.tinyos.net/.
22. R. Y. Tsai. A Versatile Camera Calibration Technique for High-Accuracy 3D Machine Vision Metrology Using Off-the-Shelf TV Cameras and Lenses. *IEEE Journal of Robotics and Automation*, RA-3(4):323–344, August 1987.
23. F. Y. Wang. A Simple and Analytical Procedure for Calibrating Extrinsic Camera Parameters. *IEEE Transactions on Robotics and Automation*, 20(1):121–124, February 2004.
24. Z. Y. Zhang. A Flexible New Technique for Camera Calibration. *IEEE Transactions on Pattern Analysis and Machine Intelligence*, 22(11):1330–1334, November 2000.

Trail: A Distance Sensitive WSN Service for Distributed Object Tracking

Vinodkrishnan Kulathumani[1], Anish Arora[1],
Murat Demirbas[2], and Mukundan Sridharan[1]

[1] Dept. of Computer Science and Engineering, The Ohio State University
{vinodkri,anish,sridhara}@cse.ohio-state.edu
[2] Dept. of Computer Science and Engineering, SUNY at Buffalo
demirbas@cse.buffalo.edu

Abstract. Distributed observation and control of mobile objects via static wireless sensors demands timely information in a *distance sensitive* manner: information about closer objects is required more often and more quickly than that of farther objects. In this paper, we present a wireless sensor network protocol, *Trail*, that supports distance sensitive tracking of mobile object by in-network subscribers upon demand. *Trail* achieves a *find* time that is linear in the distance from the subscriber to the object, via a distributed data structure that is updated only locally when objects move. *Trail* seeks to minimize the size of the data structure. Moreover, *Trail* is reliable, fault-tolerant and energy-efficient, despite the network dynamics that are typical of wireless sensor networks. We evaluate the performance of *Trail* by simulations in a 90-by-90 sensor network and report on 105 node experiments in the context of a pursuer-evader control application.

1 Introduction

Tracking of mobile objects has received significant attention in the context of cellular telephony, mobile computing, and military applications [1,2,3,4]. In this paper, we focus on the tracking of mobile objects using a network of static wireless sensors. Examples of such applications include those that monitor objects [5,6,7], as well as applications that "close the loop" by performing tracking-based control; an example is a pursuer-evader tracking application, where a controller's objective is to minimize the catch time of evaders.

We are particularly interested in large scale WSN deployments. Large networks motivate several tracking requirements. First, queries for locations of objects in a large network should not be answered from central locations as the querier may be close to the object but still have to communicate all the way to a central location. Such a solution not only increases the latency but also depletes the intermediate nodes of their energy. Plus, answering queries locally may also be important for preserving the correctness of applications deployed in large WSNs. As a specific example, consider an intruder-interceptor application, where a large number of sensor nodes lie along the perimeter that surrounds a

K. Langendoen and T. Voigt (Eds.): EWSN 2007, LNCS 4373, pp. 83–100, 2007.

valuable asset. Intruders enter the perimeter with the intention of crossing over to the asset and the objective of the interceptors is to "catch" the intruders as far from the asset as possible. In this case, it has been shown [8] that there exist Nash equilibrium conditions which imply that, for satisfying optimality constraints, the latency with which an interceptor requires information about the intruder it is tracking depends on the relative locations of the two: the closer the distance, the smaller the latency. This requirement is formalized by the property of *distance sensitivity* for querying, i.e, the cost in terms of latency and number of messages for returning the location of a mobile object grows linearly in terms of the distance between the object and the querier.

Second, tracking services for large networks must eschew solutions with disproportionate update costs that update object locations across the network even when the object moves only by a small distance. This requirement is formalized by the property of *distance sensitivity* for updates, i.e., the cost of an update is proportional to the distance moved by the object.

Third, for large networks it is critical that object locations or pointers to the objects be maintained across only a minimum set of nodes across the network. Longer tracks have a higher cost of initialization and given that network nodes may fail due to energy depletion or hardware faults, longer tracks increase the probability of a failed node along a track as well as increase the cost of detecting and correcting failures in the track. This requirement motivates us to eschew solutions that hierarchically partition the network into a fixed number of levels [3,4,1] Hierarchical partitions not only yield longer track lengths, these solutions also tend to be sensitive to the failures of nodes higher up in the hierarchy.

Finally, even though solutions should designed to accommodate large networks, they should also be simple, energy-efficient and robust for use in small or medium networks.

Contributions: In this paper, we use geometric ideas to design an energy-efficient, fault-tolerant and hierarchy-free WSN service, *Trail*, that supports tracking-based WSN applications. The specification of *Trail* is to return the location of a particular object in response to an in-network subscriber issuing a *find* query regarding that object. To this end, *Trail* maintains a tracking data structure by propagating mobile object information only locally, and satisfying the distance sensitivity requirement. *Trail* avoids the need for hierarchies by determining anchors for the tracking paths on-the-fly based on the motion of objects; this allows for minimizing the length of tracking paths. *Trail* maintains tracks from each object to only one well-known point, namely, the center of the network; these tracks are *almost* straight to the center, with a stretch factor close to 1. We analytically compare the performance of *Trail* with that of other hierarchy based solutions for tracking objects and as seen in Fig. 11 in Section 7, *Trail* is more efficient than other solutions. *Trail* has about 7 times lower updates costs at almost equal *find* costs. By using a tighter tracking structure, we are also able to decrease the upper bound *find* costs at larger distances and thereby decrease the average find cost across the network. By not relying on hierarchies *Trail* can tolerate faults more locally as well.

Trail is a family of protocols. Refinements of a basic *Trail* protocol are well suited for different network sizes and *find/update* frequency settings: One refinement is to tighten its tracks by progressively increasing the rate at which the tracking structure is updated; while this results in updating a large part of the tracking structure per unit move, which is for large networks still *update* distance sensitive, it significantly lowers the *find* costs for objects at larger distances. Another refinement increases the number of points along a track, i.e, progressively loosens the tracking structure in order to decrease the *find* costs and be more $find - centric$ when object *updates* are less frequent or objects are static; as an extreme case, the *find* can simply follow a straight line to the center. Moreover, *Trail* increasingly centralizes *update* and *find* as the network size decreases.

Organization of the paper: In Section 2, we describe the system model and problem specification. In Section 3, we design a basic *Trail* for a 2-d real plane. Then, in Section 4, we present an implementation of the basic *Trail* protocol for a 2-d sensor network grid. In Section 5, we discuss refinements of the basic *Trail* protocol. In Section 6, we present results of our performance evaluation. In Section 7, we discuss related work and, in Section 8, we make concluding remarks and discuss future work.

2   Model and Specification

The system consists of a set of *mobile objects*, and a network of static *nodes* that each consist of a sensing component and a radio component. Tracking applications execute on the mobile objects and use the sensor network to track desired mobile objects. Object detection and association services execute on the nodes, as does the desired *Trail* network tracking service. The object detection service is an orthogonal service to object tracking. The object detection service assigns a unique id, P, to every object detected by nodes in the network and stores the state of P at the node j that is closest to the object P. This node is called the *agent* for P and can be regarded as the node where P resides. The association service can be implemented in a centralized [9] or distributed [10] fashion; the latter approach would suit integration with *Trail*.

Trail Network Service: *Trail* maintains an in-network tracking structure, $trail_P$, for every object P. *Trail* supports two functions: *find(P, Q)*, that returns the state of the object P, including its location at the current location of the object Q issuing the query and *move(P, p', p)* that updates the tracking structure when object P moves from location p' to location p.

Definition 1 (*find(P, Q)* Cost). *The cost of the* find(P, Q) *function is the total communication cost of reaching the current location of* P *starting from the current location of* Q.

Definition 2 (*move(P, p', p)* Cost). *The cost of the* move(P, p', p) *function is the total communication cost of updating* $trail_P$ *to the new location* p *and deleting the tracking structure to the old location* p'.

To simplify our presentation, we first describe *Trail* in a 2-d real plane. We then refine the *Trail* protocol to suitably implement in a dense connected grid model of a WSN. We describe this model in Section 4.

3   Trail

In this section, we use geometric ideas to design *Trail* for a bounded 2-d real plane. Let C denote the center of this bounded plane.

3.1   Tracking Data Structure

We maintain a tracking data structure for each object in the network. Let P be an object being tracked, and p denote its location on the plane. Let d_{pC} be the distance of p from the center C. We denote the tracking data structure for object P as $trail_P$. Before we formally define this tracking structure, we give a brief overview.

Overview: If $trail_P$ is defined as a straight line from C to P, then every time the object moves, $trail_P$ has to be updated starting from C. This would not be a distance sensitive approach. Hence we form $trail_P$ as a set of *trail segments* and update only a portion of the structure depending upon the distance moved. The number of *trail segments* in $trail_P$ increases as d_{pC} increases. Note that we do not partition the network into a hierarchy and assign roles to specific nodes in the network. Rather, the end points of the *trail segments* serve as marker points to update the tracking structure when an object moves. The point from where the update is started depends on the distance moved. Only, when P moves a sufficiently large distance, $trail_P$ is updated all the way from C. We now formally define $trail_P$.

Definition 3 ($trail_P$). *The tracking data structure for object P, $trail_P$, for $d_{pC} \geq 1$ is a path obtained by connecting any sequence of points $(C, N_{max}, ..., N_k, ..., N_1, p)$ by line segments, where $max \geq 1$, and there exist auxiliary points $c_1..c_{max}$ that satisfy the properties (P1) to (P4) below.*

For brevity, let N_k be the level k vertex in $trail_P$; let the level k trail segment in $trail_P$ be the segment between N_k and N_{k-1}; let $Seg(x, y)$ be any line segment between points x and y in the network.

- *(P1): $dist(c_k, N_k) = 2^k$, ($max \geq k \geq 1$).*
- *(P2): N_{k-1}, ($max \geq k \geq 1$), lies on $Seg(N_k, c_{k-1})$; N_{max} lies on $Seg(C, c_{max})$.*
- *(P3): $dist(p, c_k) < 2^{k-b}$, ($max \geq k \geq 1$) and $b \geq 1$ is a constant.*
- *(P4): $max = \lceil (log_2(dist(C, c_{max}))) \rceil - 1$.*

If $(d_{pC} = 0)$, $trail_P$ is C; and if $(0 \leq d_{pC} < 1)$, $trail_P$ is $Seg(C, p)$.   □

Observations about $trail_P$**:** From the definition of $trail_P$, we note that the auxiliary points $c_1..c_{max}$ are used to mark vertices $N_1..N_{max}$ of $trail_P$. P1 and P2 describe the relation between the auxiliary points and the vertices of $trail_P$. Given $trail_P$, points $c_1..c_{max}$ are uniquely determined using P1 and P2. Similarly given p and $c_1, ..c_{max}$, $trail_P$ is uniquely determined. By property P3, the

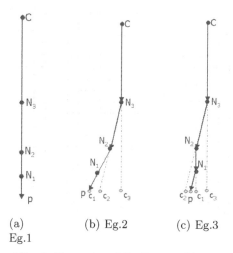

(a)   (b) Eg.2   (c) Eg.3
Eg.1

Fig. 1. Examples of Trail to an Object P

maximum separation between p and any auxiliary point c_k decreases exponentially as k decreases from max to 1. By changing parameter b in property $P3$, we can tune the rate at which the tracking structure is updated. We discuss these refinements in Section 5. Note that we do not partition the network into a fixed number of levels. Rather, the value of max which denotes the number of *trail segments* in $trail_P$, depends on the distance of P from C.

We now show 3 examples of the tracking structure in Fig. 1. In this figure, $b = 1$. Fig. 1(a) shows $trail_P$ when $c_3, ..c_1$ are collocated. When P moves away from this location, $trail_P$ is updated and Fig. 1(b) shows an example of $trail_P$ where $c_2, ..c_1$ are displaced from c_3. In Fig. 1(b), $dist(c_3, c_2) = 2$ units, $dist(c_2, c_1) = 1$ unit, $dist(p, c_1) < 1$ units. Moreover, N_3 lies on $Seg(C, c_3)$, N_2 lies on $Seg(N_3, c_2)$ and so on. In Fig. 1(c) we show an example of a zig zag trail to an object P, when P moves away from c_3 and then moves back in the opposite direction.

3.2   Updating the Trail

We now describe a procedure to update the tracking structure when object P moves from location p' to p such that the properties of the tracking structure are maintained and the cost of update is distance sensitive.

Overview: When an object moves distance d away, if the distance $dist(c_1, p)$ is less than 1, then the trail is updated by replacing $segment(N_1, p')$ with $segment(N_1, p)$. Otherwise, we find the minimal index m, along $trail_P$ such that $dist(p, c_j) < 2^{j-b}$ for all j such that $max \geq j \geq m$ and $trail_P$ is updated starting from N_m. In order to update $trail_P$ starting from N_m, we find new vertices $N_{m-1}...N_1$ and a new set of auxiliary points $c_{m-1}...c_1$. Let $N'_{m-1}...N'_0$ and $c'_{m-1}...c'_1$ denote the old vertices and old auxiliary points respectively. Starting from N_m, we follow a recursive procedure to update $trail_P$. This procedure is stated below:

Update **Algorithm:**

1. If $dist(p, c_1) \geq 1$, then let m be the minimal index on the trail such that $dist(p, c_j) < 2^{j-b}$ for all j such that $max \geq j \geq m$.
2. $k = m$
3. while $k > 1$
   (a) $c_{k-1} = p$; Now obtain N_{k-1} using property $P2$ as follows: the point on segment N_k, c_{k-1}, that is 2^{k-1} away from c_{k-1}.
   (b) $k = k - 1$
   If no indices exist such that $dist(c_k, p) < 2^{k-1}$, then the trail is created starting from C. This could happen if the object is new or if the object has moved a sufficiently large distance from its original position. In this case, max is set to $(\lceil log_2(d_p) \rceil) - 1$. c_{max} is set to p. N_{max} is marked on $segment(C, p)$ at distance 2^{max} from c_{max}. Step 1 is executed with $k = max$. $\qquad\square$

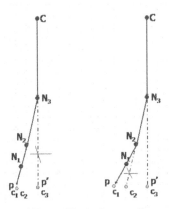

Fig. 2. Updating $trail_P$

Fig. 2 illustrates an update operation, when $b = 1$. In Fig. 2a, $dist(p, p')$ is 2 units. Hence update starts at N_3. Initially c_3, c'_2, c'_1 are at p'. We use the *update* algorithm to determine new c_2, c_1 and thereby the new N_2, N_1. Using step $(3a)$ of the update algorithm, the new c_2 and c_1 lie at p. The vertex N_2 then lies on $segment(N_3, c_2)$ and N_1 lies on $segment(N_2, c_1)$. In Fig. 2b, P moves further one unit. Hence update now starts at N_2. Using step $(3a)$ of the update algorithm, the new c_1 lies at p and N_1 lies on $segment(N_2, c_1)$.

Lemma 1. *The update algorithm for* Trail *yields a path that satisfies* $trail_P$.

Proof. 1. Let m be the index at which *update* starts. By the condition in step 1, $dist(c_j, p) < 2^{j-b}$ for all $max \geq j \geq m$. Now, for $m > j \geq 1$, $c_j = p$. Therefore for $m > j \geq 1$, $dist(c_j, p) < 2^{j-b}$. Thus property $P3$ is satisfied.
2. Properties $P2$ and $P1$ are satisfied because $m \geq k > 1$, we obtain N_{k-1} as the point on $Seg(N_k, c_{k-1})$, that is 2^{k-1} away from c_{k-1}.
3. max is defined for $trail_P$, when $trail_P$ is created or updated starting from C. When max is (re)defined for $trail_P$, c_{max} is the position of the object and max is set to $(\lceil log_2(d_p) \rceil) - 1$. Thus the update algorithm satisfies property $P4$.
$\qquad\qquad\qquad\qquad\qquad\qquad\qquad\qquad\qquad\qquad\qquad\qquad\qquad\square$

Definition 4 (Trail Stretch Factor). *Given* $trail_P$ *to an object* p, *we define the trail stretch factor for any point* x *on* $trail_P$ *as the ratio of the length along* $trail_P$ *from* x *to* p, *to the Euclidean distance* $dist(x, p)$.

Lemma 2. *The maximum* Trail Stretch Factor *for any point along* $trail_P$, *denoted as* TS_p *is* $sec(\alpha) * sec(\frac{\alpha}{2})$ *where* $\alpha = arcsin(\frac{1}{2^b})$.

Proof Sketch: We first show that the maximum *Trail Stretch Factor* occurs when point $N_{max}..N_1$ lie on a logarithmic spiral with origin p and the angle between the radius of the spiral and tangent to any point on the spiral being equal to

$\alpha = arcsin(\frac{1}{2^b})$ [11]. We then use the property of logarithmic spirals that the ratio of length along spiral from any point on the spiral to the origin over the Euclidean distance of that point to the origin is $sec(\alpha)$.   □

Lemma 3. *The length of $trail_P$ for an object P starting from a level $k(0 < k \le max)$ vertex, denoted as L_k is bounded by $(2^k + 2^{k-b}) * TS_p$.*

Proof Sketch: $dist(c_k, p) < 2^{k-b}$. Therefore, $dist(N_k, p) < 2^k + 2^{k-b}$. Then using lemma 2, the result follows.   □

Theorem 1. *The upper bound on the amortized cost of updating $trail_P$ when object P moves distance $d_m(d_m > 1)$ is $4 * (2^b + 1) * TS_p * d_m * log(d_m)$.*

Proof. Note that in *update* whenever $trail_P$ is updated starting at the level k vertex, we set $c_{k-1} = p$. P can now move a distance of 2^{k-1-b} before another update starting at the level k vertex. Thus, between any two successive updates starting from a level k vertex, the object must have moved at least a distance of 2^{k-1-b}. The total cost to create a new path and delete the old path starting from a level k vertex costs at most $2 * L_k$.

Note that over a distance d_m where $d_m > 1$, the *update* can start at level $(\lfloor log_2(d_m) \rfloor + b + 1)$ vertex at most once. This is because, update starts at level $(\lfloor log_2(d_m) \rfloor + b + 1)$ vertex, only when P has moved at least d_m distance. Similarly, update can start at level $(b + 1)$ vertex atmost d_m times, update can start at level $(b + 2)$ vertex can at most $\lfloor d_m/2 \rfloor$ times, and so on. Adding the total cost, Theorem 1 follows.   □

For illustration, we summarize the *Trail Stretch factor* and *update* costs for different values of b in Fig. 3. We explain the significance of the refinement of *Trail* by varying b in Section 5.

b	Trail Stretch	$Update$ Cost
1	1.2	$14 * d_m * log d_m$
2	1.05	$20 * d_m * log d_m$
> 3	Approaches 1	$4 * (2^b + 1) * d_m * log d_m$

Fig. 3. Effect of b on $Update$ Cost

3.3 Basic Find Algorithm

Given $trail_P$ exists for an object P in the network, we now describe a basic *find* algorithm that is initiated by object Q at point q on the plane. We use a basic ring search algorithm to intersect $trail_P$ starting from Q in a distance sensitive manner. We then show from the properties of the *Trail* tracking structure that starting from this intersection point, the current location of P is reached in a distance sensitive manner.

Basic *find* Algorithm:

1. With center q, successively draw circles of radius $2^0, 2^1, ...2^{\lfloor log(d_qC) \rfloor - 1}$, until $trail_P$ is intersected.
2. If $trail_P$ is intersected, follow it to reach object P; else follow $trail_P$ from C (note that if object exists, $trail_P$ will start from C).

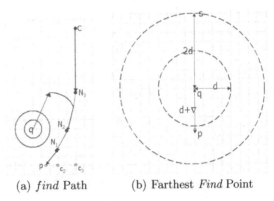

(a) *find* Path   (b) Farthest *Find* Point

Fig. 4. Basic Find Algorithm in *Trail*

Theorem 2. *The cost of finding an object P at point p from object Q at point q is $O(d_f)$ where d_f is $dist(p,q)$.*

Proof. Note that as q is distance d_f away from p, a circle of radius $2^{\lceil log(d_f) \rceil}$ will intersect $trail_P$. Hence the total length traveled along the circles before intersecting $trail_P$ at point s is bounded by $2 * \pi * \sum_{j=1}^{\lceil log(d_f) \rceil} 2^j$, i.e., $8 * \pi * d_f$. The total cost of connecting segments between the circles is bounded by $2 * d_f$.

Now, when the trail is intersected by the circle of radius $2^{\lceil log(d_f) \rceil}$, the point s at which the trail is intersected can be at most $3 * d_f$ away from the object p. This is illustrated in Fig. 4(b). In this figure, q is $d_f + \nabla$ away from p. Hence the trail can be missed by circle of radius 2^{d_f}. From lemma 3, we have that distance along the trail from s to p is at most $3 * TS_p * d_f$. Thus, the cost of finding an object P at point p from object Q at point q is $O(d_f)$ where d_f is $dist(p,q)$.   □

4   Implementing Trail in a WSN

In this section, we describe how to implement the *Trail* protocol in a WSN, that is a discrete plane as opposed to a continuous plane as described in the previous section. *Trail* can be implemented under any random deployment of a WSN aided by some approximation for routing along a circle. For reasons of exposition, in this section we describe the implementation of *Trail* specifically in a WSN grid. In this model, each node is assigned some grid location x, y and is aware of that location. We refer to unit distance as the one hop communication distance. $dist(i, j)$ now stands for distance between motes i and j in these units. We also assume the existence of an underlying geographic routing protocol such as GPSR [12], aided by an underlying neighborhood service that maintains a list of neighbors at each mote. In the WSN grid, we assume that nodes in the network can fail due to energy depletion or hardware faults and there can be a bounded error in the placement of motes with respect to their ideal grid locations, thus leading to *holes* in the network. However, we assume that the network may not be partitioned; there exists a path between every pair of nodes in the network.

When implementing on a WSN grid, *Trail* is affected by the following factors: (1) discretization of points to nearest grid location; (2) Overhead of routing between any two points on the grid; and (3) *holes* in the network. We discuss these issues in this section.

Routing Stretch Factor: When using geographic routing to route on a grid, the number of hops to communicate across a distance of d units will be more than d. We measure this stretch in terms of the routing stretch factor, defined as the ratio of the communication cost (number of transmissions) between any two grid locations, to the euclidean distance d between two grid locations. It can be shown that the upper bound on the routing stretch factor for the WSN unit grid is $\sqrt{2}$. The routing stretch factor will decrease in the denser grids because there are more nodes and routes will be increasingly closer to the segment between two grid points.

4.1 Implementing *find* on WSN Grid

We now describe how to implement the *find* algorithm in the WSN grid. As seen in Section 3, during a find, exploration is performed using circles of increasing radii around the finder. However, in the grid model, we approximate this procedure and instead of exploring around a circle of radius r, we explore along a square of side $2 * r$. The perimeter of the square spans a distance $8 * r$ instead of $2 * \pi * r$. We could use tighter approximations of the circle, but approximating with a square is simple for a grid.

Lemma 4. *The upper bound on the cost of finding an object P at point p from object Q at point q is $38 * d$ where d is $dist(p, q)$.*

4.2 Implementing *Update* on WSN Grid

We use three types of messages in the update actions. Initially, when an object is detected at a node, it sends an *explore* message that travels in around the square perimeters of increasing levels until it meets $trail_P$ or it reaches the center. Note that if the object is updated continuously as it moves, then the *explore* message will intersect the trail within a 1 hop distance. As before, the trail update is started from the level m vertex node where m is the minimal index such that $dist(c_m, p) < 2^{m-1}$ for all j such that $max \geq j \geq m$.

Starting from the level m node where update is started, a new path is created by sending a *grow* message towards c_{m-1}. Geographic routing is used to route the message towards c_{m-1}. On this route, the node closest to, but outside a circle of radius 2^{m-1} around c_{m-1} is marked as N_{m-1}. This procedure is then repeated at subsequent vertex motes and the path is updated. Fig. 5(b) shows how a trail is updated in the grid model with the grid spacing set equal to the unit communication distance. The vertex pointers $N_3, ... N_1$ are shown approximated on the boundary of the respective circles. Also, starting from the level k node where update is started, a *clear* message is used to delete the old path. We formally state the *update* and *find* algorithms in guarded command notation that

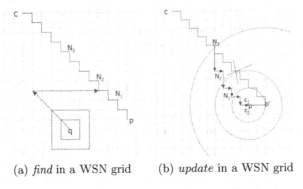

(a) *find* in a WSN grid   (b) *update* in a WSN grid

Fig. 5. Find and Update Algorithm in a WSN grid

for reasons of space have been relegated to our anonymous technical report [11]. We also implement the algorithms in *Java*, which we use in Section 6, to study the performance of *Trail*.

4.3   Fault-Tolerance

Due to energy depletion and faults, some nodes may fail leading to *holes* in the WSN grid. A hole consists of a contiguous set of nodes that have failed in the network. *Trail* uses minimal infrastructure and does not require expensive constructions such as hierarchical partitioning and in contrast to such solutions that are vulnerable to failures of nodes higher in the hierarchy, *Trail* supports a graceful degradation in performance in the presence of node failures. As the number of failures increase, there is only a proportional increase in *find* and *update* costs as the tracking data structure and the find path get distorted, as opposed to completely breaking down. We discuss the robustness of *Trail* under three scenarios: during *update*, maintaining an existing trail and during *find*.

Tolerating node failures during *update*: A *grow* message is used to update a trail starting at a level k mote and is directed towards the center of circle $k - 1$. In the presence of holes, we use a right hand rule, such as in [12], in order to route around the hole and reach the destination. As indicated in the *update* algorithm for WSN grid, during routing the node closest to, but outside a circle of radius 2^{k-1} around c_{k-1} is marked as N_{k-1}. Since we assume that the network cannot be partitioned, eventually such a node will be found. (If all nodes along the circle have failed, the network is essentially partitioned).

Maintaining an existing trail: Nodes may fail after a trail has been created. Also, in some cases, *clear* messages may fail thereby not deleting an old trail. In order to stabilize from these faulty states, we use periodic *heartbeat* actions along the trail. We state the stabilizing actions in guarded command notation and explain how they restore the invariants. For reasons of space, we have relegated this discussion to the technical report.

Tolerating failures during a *find*: We now describe how the *find* message explores in squares of increasing levels. When a *find* message comes across a hole, it is rerouted only radially outwards of the square and we do not allow back tracking. If all nodes in the forward direction of the explore have failed, then the *level* of search is incremented and routed towards a node in the next level. Thus, in the presence of larger holes, we abandon the current level and move to the next level, instead of routing around the hole back to the current level of exploration. Finally, if even that fails, the destination is marked as C and message is routed towards C. In the worst case, *find* may reach C.

5   Refinements to Trail

In this section, we discuss two techniques to refine the basic *Trail* network protocol: (1) tuning how often to update a *Trail* tracking structure, and (2) tuning the shape of a *Trail* tracking structure.

5.1   Tightness of *Trail* Tracking Structure

The frequency at which $trail_P$ is updated depends on parameter constant b in property $P3$ of $trail_P$. As seen in Section 3, for values of $b > 1$, $trail_P$ is updated more and more frequently, hence leading to larger update costs. However, $trail_P$ becomes tighter and increasingly tends to a straight line with the *trail stretch factor* approaching 1. We exploit this tightness of $trail_p$ to optimize the *find* strategy.

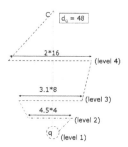

Fig. 6. Optimized *find*

The intuition behind this optimization is that since the trail to any object P originates at C, the angle formed by p with C and the higher level vertices is small and bounded. Hence as the levels of explorations increase in *find*, we can progressively decrease the size of exploration from full circles to cones of smaller angles. As an example, when $b = 2$, we prove that at the three highest levels of search, a conical pattern of search as shown in Fig. 6 is sufficient to guarantee distance sensitivity. In Fig. 6, $b = 2$, the object q is at distance 48 units from C. The levels of exploration are in the range 0..4. Exploration is along circles until level 1 and then along cones at levels 2 to 4. By increasing b, the angles formed by P with C and vertices $N_{max}..N_1$, start getting smaller. Therefore as b increases, the number of levels at which this optimization can be performed increases [11].

Impact of the Optimization: When using the optimized *find* strategy, the upper bound on $find(P, Q)$ costs remains the same when d_{pq} is small. However, we exploit the fact that trails to objects converge at C and therefore decrease the size of exploration at higher levels of search. Hence the upper bound costs for *find* decrease when d_{pq} increases. In other words, when d_{pq} is large, we mitigate the cost of Q having to explore at the lower levels. As an example, when $b = 2$ we show that the upper bound *find* costs decrease from $38 * d$ to $14 * d$ as d_{pq} increases [11]. The optimization of *find* at higher levels is thus significant in that it yields: (1) smaller upper bounds for objects that are far away from the finder; and (2) lower average cost of $find(p, q)$ over all possible locations of q and p.

We note that there are limits to tuning the frequency of updates, because for extreme values of b distance sensitivity may be violated. For example, for large values of b, that cause $dist(p, c_k) < y$ where y is a constant we end up with having to update the entire $trail_P$ when an object moves only a constant distance y. Similarly, for values of $b < 0$, the *Trail Stretch Factor* becomes unbounded with respect to distance from an object. Thus an object could be only δ away from a point on $trail_P$, yet the distance along $trail_P$ from this point to the p could travel across the network.

5.2   Modifying Trail Segments

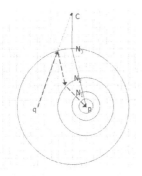

Fig. 7. Find Centric Trail

A second refinement to *Trail* is by varying the shape of the tracking structure by generalizing property $P2$ of $trail_P$. Instead of *trail segment k* between vertex N_k and N_{k-1} being a straight line, we relax the requirement on *trail segment k* to be of length at most $(2 * \pi + 1) * 2^k$. By publishing information of P along more points, the *find* path can be more straight towards C. An extreme case is when *trail segment k* is a full circle of radius 2^k centered at c_k and $segment(N_k, N_{k-1})$. We call this variation of *Trail* the *Find-centric Trail*.

Find-Centric Trail: In this refinement, the *find* procedure eschews exploring the circles (thus traversing only straight line segments) at the expense of the update procedure doing more work. This alternative data structure is used when objects are static or when object updates are less frequent than that of *find* queries in a system. Let $trail_P$ for object P consist of segments connecting $C, N_{max}, .., N_1, p$ as described before and, additionally, let all points on the circles $Circ_k$ of center c_k and radius 2^k contain pointers to their respective centers, where $max \geq k > 0$.

Starting at q, the *find* path now is a straight line towards the center. If a circle with information about object P is intersected then, starting from this point, a line is drawn towards the center of the circle. Upon intersecting the immediate inner circle (if there is one), information about its respective center is found, with which a line is drawn to this center. Object P is reached by following this procedure recursively.

Lemma 5. *In* Find Centric Trail, *when $b = 1$, the total cost of finding an object P at point p from object Q at point q is $14 * d_f$ where $d_f = dist(p, q)$.*   □

6   Performance Evaluation

In this section, we evaluate the performance of *Trail* using simulations in *JProwler* [13]. The goals of our simulation are: (1) to study the effect of routing stretch and discretization errors on the trail stretch factor, (2) to study the effect of uniform node failures on the performance of *Trail* and (3) to compare the average costs for *find* and *update*, as opposed to the upper bounds we derived earlier. Our simulation involves a 90 by 90 Mica2 mote network arranged on a grid. We implement geographic routing on a grid to route messages in the network. In the presence of failures we use a left hand rule to route around the failure [12]. We assume an underlying link maintenance layer because of which the list of *up* neighbors is known at each node.

Routing Stretch: We first study the effect of *holes* in the network on the routing stretch factor. We simulate two different density models and inject node failures from 1% to 20% that are uniformly distributed across the network. We consider a grid separation of unit distance and 0.5 unit distance. We randomly select any two points in the network and measure the average routing stretch factor to route between 300 such pairs. From Fig. 8(a), we see that the routing stretch factor is a small constant factor over the actual distance between two nodes. The stretch factor decreases as expected when density increases. As the fault percentages increase, the number of disconnections in the network increase. The average route stretch factors shown are for the instances when the network is actually connected, and in these instances the average stretch factor does not increase significantly.

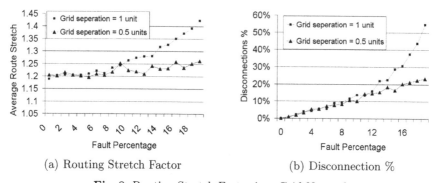

(a) Routing Stretch Factor   (b) Disconnection %

Fig. 8. Routing Stretch Factor in a Grid Network

Performance of Update Operations: We determine the number of messages exchanged for object updates over different distances when an object moves continuously in the network. We consider the unit grid separation, where each node has at most 4 communication neighbors. The number of neighbors may be lesser due to failures. We calculate the amortized cost by moving an object in different directions and then observing the cumulative number of messages exchanged up to each distance from the original position to update the tracking

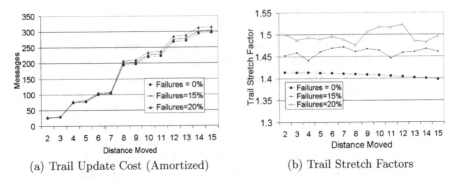

(a) Trail Update Cost (Amortized)   (b) Trail Stretch Factors

Fig. 9. Trail Update Costs and Trail Stretch

structure. The results are shown in Fig. 9(a). The jumps visible at distances 4 and 8 show the *logd* factor in the amortized cost. At these distances, the updates have to be propagated to a higher level. We also study the effect of uniform failures in the network on the increase in update costs. We consider fault percentages upto 20. We see from the figure that even with failures the average communication cost increases log linearly. This indicates that the failures are handled locally.

Trail Stretch Factor: From Section 3, we note that in the continuous model, for an object P at distance d_{pC} from C, $trail_P$ is less than $1.2 \times d_{pC}$. We now study the effect of routing overhead and the discretization factor on the length of the tracking structure that is created. We measure the trail length in terms of the number of hops along the structure. Fig. 9(b) shows the average ratio of distance from C to the length of the trail during updates over different distances from the original position. The parameter $b = 1$ in these simulations.

When the trail is first created, the trail stretch is equal to the routing stretch from C to the original location. In the absence of failures, we notice that the trail stretch increases to 1.4 at updates of smaller distances and then starts decreasing. This can be explained by the fact the trail for an object starts bending more uniformly when the update is over a large distance. Even in the presence of failures, the trail stretch factor increases to only about 1.6 times the actual distance.

Performance of *find*: We now compare the average *find* costs with upper bounds derived. We fix the finder at distance 40 units from C. We vary the distance of object being found from 2 to 16. We evaluate using the basic *find* algorithm with $b = 1$ and the optimized *find* algorithm discussed in Section 5 using $b = 2$. In the optimized *find*, at levels 2 to 4, we do not explore the entire circle.

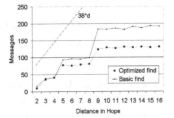

Fig. 10. Average *find* Cost

The results are shown in Fig. 10; the upper bound $38 * d$ is indicated using dotted lines and we see that the number of messages exchanged during *find* operations are significantly lower. The jumps at distances 3, 5 and 9 are due to increase in levels of exploration at these distances.

7   Related Work

In this section, we discuss related work and also compare the performance of *Trail* with other protocols designed for distance sensitive tracking and querying.

Tracking: As mentioned earlier, mobile object tracking has received significant attention [3,4,6] and we have focused our attention on WSN support for tracking. Some network tracking services [2] have nonlocal updates, where update cost to a tracking structure may depend on the network size rather than distance moved. There are also solutions such as [3,4,1] that provide distance sensitive updates and location.

Locality Aware Location Services *(LLS)* [1] is a distance sensitive location service designed for mobile adhoc networks. In LLS, the network is partitioned into hierarchies and object information is published in a spiral structure at well known locations around the object, thus resulting in larger update costs whenever an object moves. The upper bound on the update cost in LLS is $128 * d_m * log d_m$, where d_m is the distance an object moves, as opposed to the $14 * d_m * log d_m$ cost in *Trail*; the upper bounds on the *find* cost are almost equal. Moreover, as seen in Section 5, we can further reduce the upper bound on the *find* cost at higher levels in *Trail*.

The Stalk protocol [4] uses hierarchical partitioning of the network to track objects in a distance sensitive manner. The hierarchical partitioning can be created with different dilation factors $(r \geq 3)$. For $r = 3$ and 8 neighbors at each level, at almost equal *find* costs, *Stalk* has an

	Update Cost	Find Cost	Size
Trail	14*d*logd	38*d	1.2*d_c
LLS	128*d*logd	36*d	16*D
Stalk	96*d*logd	39*d	3*D
Awerbuch Peleg	O(d*logd*logN)	16*d*log(2N)	4*D

D – n/w Diameter ; N – No. of Nodes ; d_c – Distance from C

Fig. 11. Trail: Analytical Comparison

upper bound update cost of $96 * d * log d$ and this increase occurs because of having to query neighbors at increasing levels of the partition in order to establish *lateral* links for distance sensitivity [4].

Both *Stalk* and *LLS* use a partitioning of the network into hierarchical clusters which can be complex to implement in a WSN, whereas *Trail* is cluster-free. Moreover, in *Stalk*, the length of the tracking structure can span the entire network as the object keeps moving and, in *LLS*, the information about each object is published in a spiral structure across the network. In comparison, *Trail* maintains a tighter tracking structure (i.e., with more direct paths to the center) and is thus more efficient and locally fault-tolerant.

In [3], a hierarchy of regional directories is constructed and the communication cost of a find for an object d_f away is $O(d_f * log 2N)$ and that of a move of distance d_m is $O(d_m * logD * logN)$ (where N is the number of nodes and D is the network diameter). A topology change, such as a node failure, however, necessitates a global reset of the system since the regional directories depend on a non-local clustering program that constructs sparse covers.

Querying and storage: Querying for events of interest in WSNs has also received significant attention [14, 15, 16] and some of them focus on distance sensitive querying. We note that *Trail*, specifically the *Find-centric* approach can also be used in the context of static events.

Distance Sensitive Information Brokerage [17] protocol performs a hierarchical clustering of the network and information about an event is published to neighboring clusters at each level. DSIB has a querying cost of $4 * d$ to reach information about an event at distance d away. Using *Find-centric Trail* we can query information about a static event at a cost of $2 * d$. We also note that when events are static, the publish strategy can be further optimized and we study this in a recent work.

Geographic Hash tables [15] is a lightweight solution for the in-network-querying problem of static events. The basic *GHT* is not distance sensitive since it can hash the event information to a broker that is far away from a subscriber. The distance sensitivity problem of GHT can be alleviated to an extent by using geographically bounded hash functions at increasing levels of a hierarchical partitioning as used in DIFS protocol. Still, attempting such a solution suffers from a multi-level partitioning problem: a query event pair nearby in the network might be arbitrarily far away in the hierarchy. However, we do note that *GHT* provides load balancing across the network, especially when the types of events are known and this is not the goal of *Trail*.

In [16], a balanced push-pull strategy is proposed that depends on the query frequency and event frequency; given a required query cost, the advertise operation is tuned to do as much work as required to satisfy the querying cost. In contrast, *Trail* assumes that query rates depend on each subscriber (and potentially on the relative locations of the publisher and subscriber), and it also provides distance sensitivity during find and move operations, which is not a goal of [16]. In directed diffusion [14], a tree of paths is created from all objects of interest to the tracker. All these paths are updated when any of the objects move. Also, a controller initiated change in assignment would require changing the paths. By way of contrast, in *Trail*, we impose a fixed tracking structure, and tracks to all objects are rooted at one point. Thus, updates to the structure are local and any object can find the state of any other object by following the same tracking structure. Rumor routing [18] is a probabilistic algorithm to provide query times proportional to distance; the goal of this work is not to prove a deterministic upper bound. Moreover, its algorithm does not describe how to update existing tracks locally and yet retain distance sensitive query time when objects move.

8   Conclusions and Future Work

We have presented *Trail*, a family of protocols for distance sensitive distributed object tracking in WSNs. *Trail* avoids the need for hierarchical partitioning by determining anchors for the tracking paths on-the-fly, and is more efficient than other hierarchy based solutions for tracking objects: it allows 7 times lower updates costs at almost equal *find* costs and can tolerate faults more locally as well.

Importantly, *Trail* maintains tracks from object locations to only one well-known point, the center of the network, which we claim is necessary to minimize the total track length for objects. Well-known points are necessary for distance sensitive tracking and, as we prove in the associated technical report of this paper [11], multiple well-known points cannot yield shorter total track length of objects. Moreover, since its tracks are *almost* straight to the center with a stretch factor close to 1, *Trail* tends to achieve the lower bound on the total track length. By using a tight tracking structure, *Trail* also able to decrease the upper bound *find* costs at larger distances and thereby decrease the average find cost across the network.

We have shown that refinements of the basic *Trail* protocol are well suited for different network sizes and query frequency settings. We have validated the distance sensitivity and fault tolerance properties of *Trail* in a simulation of 90 by 90 network using *JProwler*. We have also succesfully implemented a *Trail* protocol in the context of a pursuer evader application for a medium size (over 100 node) mote network.

Trail operates in an environment where objects can generate updates and queries asynchronously. We note that in such an environment, due to the occurrence of collisions, there can be an increase in the message complexity for querying and updates especially when the objects are densely located in the network. As future work, we are considering a *push* version of the network tracking service where snapshots of objects are published to subscribers in a distance sensitive manner, both in time and information, in order to increase the reliability and energy efficiency of the service when the density of objects in the network is high.

References

1. I. Abraham, D. Dolev, and D. Malkhi. LLS: A locality aware location service for mobile ad hoc networks. *DIALM-POMC*, 2004.
2. S. Dolev, D. Pradhan, and J. Welch. Modified tree structure for location management in mobile environments. In *INFOCOM*, pages 530–537, 1995.
3. B. Awerbuch and D. Peleg. Online tracking of mobile users. *Journal of the Association for Computing Machinery*, 42:1021–1058, 1995.
4. M. Demirbas, A. Arora, T. Nolte, and N. Lynch. A hierarchy-based fault-local stabilizing algorithm for tracking in sensor networks. In *OPODIS*, 2004.
5. A. Arora, P. Dutta, and S. Bapat et al. A line in the sand: A wireless sensor network for target detection, classification, and tracking. *Computer Networks, Special Issue on Military Communications Systems and Technologies*, 46(5):605–634, July 2004.

6. T. He, S. Krishnamurthy, and J. Stankovic et al. Vigilnet:an integrated sensor network system for energy-efficient surveillance. *ACM Transactions on Sensor Networks*, 2004.

7. A. Arora and R. Ramnath et al. Exscal: Elements of an extreme wireless sensor network". In *The 11th International Conference on Embedded and Real-Time Computing Systems and Applications*, 2004.

8. H. Cao, E. Ertin, and V. Kulathumani et al. Differential games in large scale sensor actuator networks. In *Information Processing in Sensor Networks (IPSN)*, 2006.

9. B. Sinopoli and C. Sharp et al. Distributed control applications within sensor networks. In *Proceedings of the IEEE*, volume 91, pages 1235–46, Aug 2003.

10. J. Shin, L. Guibas, and F. Zhao. A distributed algorithm for managing multi-target indentities in wireless ad hoc networks. In *IPSN*, 2003.

11. V. Kulathumani, A. Arora, and M. Demirbas. Trail: A distance sensitive WSN service for distributed object tracking. Technical Report OSU-CISRC-7/06-TR67, The Ohio State University, 2006.

12. B. Karp and H. T. Kung. Greedy perimeter stateless routing for wireless networks. In *Proceedings of MobiCom*, 2000.

13. Vanderbilt University. JProwler. http://www.isis.vanderbilt.edu/Projects/nest/jprowler/index.html.

14. C. Intanogonwiwat and R. Govindan et al. Directed diffusion for wireless sensor networking. *IEEE Transactions on Networking*, 11(1):2–16, 2003.

15. S. Ratnasamy and B. Karp et al. GHT: A geographic hash table for data-centric storage. In *Wireless Sensor Networks and Applications (WSNA)*, 2002.

16. X. Liu, Q. Huang, and Y. Zhang. Combs, needles, haystacks: Balancing push and pull for discovery in large-scale sensor networks. In *ACM Sensys*, 2004.

17. S. Funke and L. Guibas et al. Distance sensitive information brokerage in sensor networks. In *DCOSS*, 2006.

18. D. Braginsky and D. Estrin. Rumor routing algorithm for sensor networks. In *ICDCS*, 2002.

Towards Energy-Efficient Skyline Monitoring in Wireless Sensor Networks*

Hekang Chen[1], Shuigeng Zhou[1,2], and Jihong Guan[3]

[1] Dept. of Computer Sci. and Eng., Fudan University, Shanghai 200433, China
[2] Shanghai Key Lab of Intelligent Information Processing, Shanghai 200433, China
{hkchen, sgzhou}@fudan.edu.cn
[3] Dept. of Computer Sci. and Tech., Tongji University, Shanghai 200092, China
jhguan@mail.tongji.edu.cn

Abstract. Skyline computation is a hot topic in database community due to its promising application in multi-criteria decision making. In sensor network application scenarios, skyline is still useful and important in environment monitoring, industry control, etc. To support energy-efficient skyline monitoring in sensor networks, this paper first presents a naïve approach as baseline, and then proposes an advanced approach that employs hierarchical thresholds at the nodes. The threshold-based approach focuses on minimizing the transmission traffic in the network to save the energy consumption. Finally, we conduct extensive experiments to evaluate the proposed approaches on simulated data sets, and compare the threshold-based approach with the naïve approach. Experimental results show that the proposed threshold-based approach outperforms the naïve approach substantially in energy saving.

1   Introduction

Wireless Sensor Networks (WSN) [1] have become a fundamental research subject due to its wide applications such as environment monitoring, industry control, civilian and military surveillance, etc. In a WSN, a large number of sensor nodes self-organize and collaborate with each other to send the sensed data to the base station, from which users retrieve useful information. To support data query processing in WSNs, some experimental systems have been developed, including TinyDB [2], Cougar [3], etc. Due to the hardware constraints (e.g. low CPU, memory capability and power supply), these systems only support some basic database operators such as selection, projection, groupby. As the development of hardware techniques and the deployment of advanced WSN applications, it is urgent for the WSN systems to support more complicated queries, such as join [4], outliers [5], complex aggregations, and skyline [6,7,8].

Skyline operator has received much concern in database community in recent years because of its important use of multi-criteria decision making. Point

* This work was supported by National Natural Science Foundation under grants 60373019, 60573183 and 90612007, and the Shuguang Scholar Program of Shanghai Municipal Education Committee.

K. Langendoen and T. Voigt (Eds.): EWSN 2007, LNCS 4373, pp. 101–116, 2007.

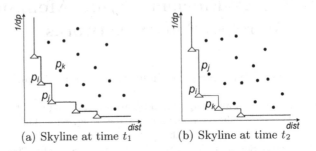

(a) Skyline at time t_1 (b) Skyline at time t_2

Fig. 1. Skylines in WSN pollution monitoring application ($\triangle$ indicates skyline point)

p dominates another point q only if p is better (according to a certain user defined preference) than q on at least one dimension and not worse than q on the other dimensions. A skyline query on a d-dimensional database returns a set of points that are not dominated by any other point. Skyline operator has been extensively studied over centralized databases and many approaches have been proposed such as BNL [6], D&C [6], NN [7], BBS [8] etc. Motivated by the requirement of the online web applications, current research concern of skyline operator is focusing on more complex and dynamic contexts, such as distributed databases [9,10,11,12] and data stream [13].

Imagine the following application scenario. We use sensor network to monitor the pollution situation in a large-scale area. The sensor nodes are deployed at the potential pollution sources (e.g. nuclear electricity plants and chemical factories). For simplicity, a sensor node corresponds to a potential pollution source. Two values are used to represent each sensor: the *degree of pollution* (simply dp) at the sensed point that measures how serious the pollution situation is at that point, and the *distance* (simply *dist*) from the sensor point to the nearest resident area. Thus a sensor u_i is equal to a 2-dimensional point $p_i(dp_i, dist_i)$. In such a context, what we concern most are those sensed points that have smaller *dist* values (i.e., nearer to the resident points) and larger dp values (i.e., more seriously polluted). This is actually a *skyline query* to the sensor network.

We illustrate the skyline at time t_1 of the application mentioned above as in Fig. 1(a). Here the horizontal axis and vertical axis correspond to *dist* and $1/dp$ (the inversion of pollution degree dp) values respectively. Point p_k is not a skyline point because it is dominated by p_i and p_j, i.e., p_k have larger *dist* and $1/dp$ (or smaller dp) values than p_i and p_j. Points p_i and p_j are skyline points because they are not dominated by each other and any other point. p_i has smaller *dist* than p_j, while p_j has smaller $1/dp$ (or larger dp) than p_i. Note that the skyline changes from time to time, thus queries in WSN should be continuous. At time t_2, the skyline is illustrated as in Fig. 1(b). With such skyline processing facility to the sensor network, we can monitor in real time all the most dangerous sites in terms of pollution degree and the distance to the nearest resident area.

In this paper, we formally address the problem of continuous skyline monitoring in sensor networks. To the best of our knowledge, this is the first of such work. We aim to minimize the transmission traffic of the entire network, which dominates the energy consumption [14]. Two approaches: naïve approach and hierarchical threshold-based approach are proposed. In the naïve approach proposed as baseline, each node actively reports to its parent the local skyline points that are evaluated based on the local points and points from its subtree. Finally, root computes the skyline after receiving reports from all its children.

The hierarchical threshold-based approach exploits the temporal correlation of the nodes. Note that the sensed data by the same node in two consecutive rounds does not deviate from each other obviously. According to this observation, skyline computation can be efficiently achieved by setting hierarchical thresholds at the nodes. We first describe the basic design of hierarchical threshold-based approach that consists of two phases: *up report* and *down query*. In the first phase, each node computes the local skyline among the points from itself and its children and then reports the points not dominated by the local threshold to its parent. The root node will obtain the reported points P with high probability being included in the skyline. The second phase is to issue a query by the root node to fetch the final skyline. The query is only sent to the nodes whose thresholds are not dominated by any point in P. By setting thresholds, both phases are able to suppress an amount of unnecessary transmissions. Based on this basic design, we further propose sophisticated *MinMax-Threshold approach* (simply MINMAX), which greatly cuts down the cost of the second phase by minimizing the size of the query message. MINMAX also deals with the issue of threshold maintenance in accordance with ever-changing data.

Extensive simulated experiments are conducted to evaluate both the naïve approach and MINMAX in terms of the average energy consumption per node. Results show that MINMAX outperforms the naïve approach significantly under all tested situations.

The rest of this paper is organized as follows. Section 2 surveys the related work. Section 3 formally states the skyline computation problem. Section 4 presents approaches to in-network skyline computation. Section 5 reports experimental evaluation of the proposed approaches. Section 6 offers the conclusion.

2   Related Work

This section reviews the related work on both skyline operator in database and data processing in sensor networks.

2.1   Skyline Operator in Database

Skyline operator [6] has received much concern in database field. Both centralized and distributed algorithms have been proposed in the literature.

Centralized Algorithms. [6] proposes two centralized algorithms, namely Block Nested Loops (BNL) and Divide-and-Conquer (D&C). BNL compares each point with a list of skyline candidates kept in the main memory. Dominated points are pruned after comparison. D&C first divides the data set into several partitions that can fit into memory. Skyline points for each partition are then computed, and the final skyline can be obtained by merging these skyline points. NN [7] and BBS [8] are index-based algorithms. NN recursively searches for the nearest neighbor in the current region (full data space at first) and divides the region into smaller subregions. The nearest neighbor can be immediately output as it must be a skyline point. BBS [8] is known as the best centralized skyline algorithm up to now. It only traverses the R-tree once and processes the entries in ascending order of their minimum distances to the origin of the data space. Similar to our work, Lin et al. [13] address continuous skyline monitoring on data streams. The main idea is to map dominance relationships of the incoming points to an interval tree, on which stabbing query is executed. However, we focus on the sensor network scenario. Thus, the essential task is to save the energy consumption of the network.

Distributed Algorithms. W. Balke et al. [9,10] propose the first distributed skyline algorithm, in which a d-dimensional database is vertically partitioned into d subsets. The algorithm accesses all subsets via round-robin strategy until obtaining a point with values on all dimensions fetched. The points that have been partially obtained are skyline candidates whereas the other points can be pruned as they cannot be qualified to be skyline points. Thus, the remaining steps are to access the subsets to fill in the blank values of each incomplete point and find the skyline points after comparisons between each pair of points. [11] addresses skyline queries processing in P2P systems. Dealing with the peculiarities of P2P systems (e.g. dynamics and limited knowledge), this paper focuses on minimizing the number of queried peers and pruning query paths that are not likely to lead to peers possessing relevant data. Our work differs from the skyline computation on distributed databases because senor networks are dynamic network environment and skyline computation is continuous.

2.2   Data Processing in Sensor Networks

Data processing is a key issue in WSN. Due to its application-oriented characteristics, we classify the applications into two types: *entire-network data collection* and *partial-network data collection*.

Entire-Network Data Collection. The applications of this type need to keep in database the sensed data from all nodes without aggregation for later analysis. TinyDB [2] and Gougar [3] support data gathering of entire network by setting an empty WHERE clause. CONCH (CONstraint CHaining) [15], focusing on one-dimensional data collection, monitors the network by tracking the value updating of the nodes and edges. Reports of these monitored nodes and edges can reconstruct the values of all nodes. [16] addresses the problem of approximate multi-dimensional data monitoring. The data of each node is modeled as an $N \times M$ matrix, in which N is dimensionality and M is the number of recorded values on each dimension. The algorithm conjoins the rows of the matrix and extracts a piece of values called *base signal* to approximate other pieces via linear regression. [17] exploits both intra-node and inter-node data correlation and proposes Distributed Regression algorithm, which is formalized to be a set of linear equations and can be solved by Gaussian Elimination.

Partial-Network Data Collection. This kind of applications are only interested in the data from some nodes. In industrial applications, for example, reporting values that exceed the threshold just suffice for manufacture environment monitoring. TinyDB and Cougar also support partial-network reports by designating query conditions. [18,19] address continuous monitoring of the maximum values. [18] stores at each node a value range that is also kept at the root. To find the maximum value, the root queries each node in descending order of the upper bound until the upper bounds of the remaining nodes are below the current maximum value. [19] sets hierarchical thresholds at the nodes, which is similar to our approaches. The threshold of each node should be smaller than that of its parent. The processing consists of two steps: *node-initiated reporting* and *root-initiated querying*. In the first step, each node reports its value if it exceeds the threshold. In the second step, the root queries the nodes whose thresholds are larger than current maximum value. [5] addresses in-network outlier detection in sensor networks and proposes an algorithm that works in-network with communication cost proportional to the outcome.

In this paper, we combine the skyline computation problem with the sensor network application context, which leads to a new unsolved problem. The current data processing methods in sensor networks cannot be applied to skyline computation. Thus, new solutions to this problem are expected.

3 Problem Statement and Preliminaries

In a sensor network containing n fixed-location sensor nodes, each sensor node collects a single data point at a time interval (we call it *round* in the rest of this paper). A sensed point contains several attributes such as temperature, humidity, pressure, etc. In every round, each node u_i can be regarded as a multidimensional *point* $p_i = (p_i[1], p_i[2], ..., p_i[d])$, where d is the number of attributes or dimensionality. As a result, the entire sensor network forms a set of points. The skyline query is a continuous query, which returns the skyline points that are not dominated by any other point in every round[1].

The base station, point collector of the network, has full computing capabilities. All sensor nodes can communicate with the base station via one or multiple hops to report their sensed points. In most cases, the entire network is deployed as a tree-based infrastructure rooted at the base station, so that messages of each node are routed via its ancestors to root. Our goal is to minimize the total energy consumption of entire network, which can be simplified to measure the communication cost since it dominates the total energy consumption [14]. Generally, transmitting a message with k bytes by MICA2 [20] costs $\sigma_t + \delta_t k$, where $\sigma_t = 0.645J$ and $\delta_t = 0.0144J$. Receiving cost is defined similarly with σ_r and δ_r being 60% less than σ_t and δ_t respectively. According to the above formulas,

---

[1] Assume that each round is long enough to finish the skyline computation.

the main design of approaches should focus on minimizing the number and size of transmission messages.

Table 1 lists the notation used in the rest of the paper.

Table 1. Notation

Symbol	Description
p_i	The point of node u_i in the current round
$p_i(j)$	The point of node u_i in the jth round
P	A set of points
τ_i	The threshold of node u_i
$\tau_i(j)$	The threshold of node u_i in the jth round
LS_i	The local skyline of node u_i
$p_i \prec p_j$	Point p_j is dominated by point p_i
$p_i \prec P$	Each point in P is dominated by p_i
$p_i \preceq p_j$	p_j is dominated by or equals to p_i
$P \preceq p_j$	p_j is dominated by or equals to at least one point in P

4 In-Network Continuous Skyline Computation

This section presents approaches to in-network continuous skyline computation: the naïve approach and the hierarchical threshold-based approach. We first present the naïve approach as baseline. Then, we describe basic design of hierarchical threshold-based approach and prove its correctness, based on which we propose the MINMAX approach by introducing the MinMax operator that is used to set and maintain thresholds. At the end of this section, we fucus on dealing with network failures caused by the dynamic environment.

4.1 Naïve Approach

Naïve approach to skyline computation is to send points of all nodes to root so that root just computes skyline among these points. However, if each report forms a message and is routed individually without aggregation, a large amount of messages will be produced, resulting in massive collisions and retransmissions. Fortunately, a tree-based infrastructure can easily deal with this problem. Each node does not issue reports until receiving all points from its children so that it can combine points into one message. In this case, both the volume of messages and the number of collisions are reduced. Note that all the points in the network should be reported. However, this is not necessary because most points are not skyline points and can be pruned as early as possible during routing. Thus, a straightforward optimization is for each internal node to compute local skyline (LS) and prune the dominated points, instead of processing immediate combination. Obviously, it can reduce the size of message, only including LS. Based on this optimization, we formally present our naïve approach as follows.

In each round, the leaf nodes first report their collected points to their parents. Each parent node then collects its own point and the points from its children, computes the LS among these points and reports the LS to its parent. This process continues on each internal node until the root receives all reports from its children. Finally, the root computes the final skyline and returns the result to the users.

4.2   Basic Design of Hierarchical Threshold-Based Approach

Naïve approach prunes dominated points at internal nodes and thus reduces message size. However, every node in the network still has to report its point or LS to its parent no matter whether they are final skyline points or not. If a node can know that its collected points will be dominated at some ancestor, then its report can be suppressed. Obverse that the points sensed at each node between two consecutive rounds will not deviate much from each other. We call this property *temporal data correlation*. It implicates that a skyline node in the previous round belongs to the current-round skyline at a high probability. Meanwhile, most of the non-skyline nodes will still be dominated this round. Temporal data correlation property of sensor network motivates our hierarchical threshold-based approach.

In hierarchical threshold-based approach, every node installs a threshold that is a d-dimensional point, with the same dimensionality as sensed points. Our approach works when *hierarchical thresholds* are set up in the network, which follow Rule 1 and Rule 2.

Rule 1. *The threshold of each node u_i should be dominated by or equal to that of its parent u_p, that is $\tau_p \preceq \tau_i$.*

Rule 2. *Each node u_i also maintains the thresholds of its children besides the local threshold τ_i.*

The meaning of Rule 1 is simple to understand as it represents *hierarchy*. The second rule is to reduce cost as you will see later in this subsection. The threshold setting is quite related to the sensed points, which will be described in detail in the next subsection. In this subsection, we focus on skyline computation in a network that has been set up with hierarchical thresholds.

The hierarchical threshold-based approach includes two phases: *up report* and *down query*. In the first phase, each node reports the points not dominated by its threshold. After pruning an amount of points by local thresholds, root node thus obtains the reported points with high probability to be skyline. However, there may still exists some skyline points that are left in the network, thus the second phase is to fetch the final skyline by querying the nodes whose thresholds are not dominated by the points gotten in the first phase.

Up Report. The progress starts from the bottom to the top of the tree, in which each node reports upward the points not dominated by its threshold.

Leaf nodes: Only if p_i is not dominated by τ_i, u_i reports p_i to its parent.

Internal nodes: Node u_i collects its own point and the reported points from its children, and then computes LS_i among them. Those dominated points are pruned since they cannot be in the final skyline. Finally, node u_i reports to its parent the points that are not dominated by τ_i, meanwhile stores the remaining points (termed *non-reported points*) in its local memory for the second phase use.

Down Query. This phase is to obtain all skyline points. Root u_r first computes LS_r among its own point and the reported points. Then, it issues a query containing LS_r to fetch all possible points that may be included in the final skyline. This can be efficiently implemented with hierarchical thresholds following Rule 1 and Rule 2. Root u_r sends the query to each child u_i that satisfies $LS_r \npreceq \tau_i$. Note that if $LS_r \preceq \tau_i$, the subtree rooted at u_i can discard the query since there cannot exist any point qualified to be a skyline point.

Internal nodes: Once node u_i receives query LS_p from its parent u_p, it computes LS_i among LS_p and non-reported points. Then u_i sends LS_i to each of its children u_j that satisfies $LS_i \npreceq \tau_j$ and waits for the reply with new points not dominated by LS_i. After all children have replied, u_i updates the local skyline points. Note that the local skyline points will no longer be updated in the current round, thus we title it *final local skyline*, simply *FLS*. Finally, u_i replies its parent u_p with new points $P_{reply} = \{p | p \in FLS_i \cap \neg p \in LS_p\}$. If u_i is the root node, then FLS_i is just the final skyline.

Leaf nodes: If node u_i has reported p_i in the first phase or satisfies $LS_p \prec p_i$, it reports nothing. Otherwise, it reports p_i.

Lemma 1. *Hierarchical thresholds can guarantee the basic approach obtain correct skyline.*

Proof. Suppose the real final skyline is denoted as *Skyline* and the obtained skyline by basic hierarchical threshold-based approach is denoted as *Skyline'*.

We first prove *Skyline* $\subseteq$ *Skyline'*, that is $\forall p_i \in$ *Skyline*, $p_i \in$ *Skyline'*. We denote $Pre(u_i)$ as a set of nodes that contain u_i and its ancestors. If $\forall u_a \in Pre(u_i)$, $\tau_a \nprec p_i$, then p_i will be reported to root in the first phase. In this case, it will finally be included in *Skyline'*. If $\exists u_a$ satisfying $\tau_a \prec p_i$, then p_i will not reach root at the end of the first phase. In the second phase, root will issue a query down. Due to Rule 1 of hierarchical thresholds and *query* $\nprec p_i$, $\forall u'_a \in Pre(u_a)$ *query* $\nprec \tau'_a$. Thus, u_i will be queried and report p_i. As a result, p_i will be contained in the final skyline.

Now that *Skyline* $\subseteq$ *Skyline'*, it is certainly satisfied that *Skyline=Skyline'*, because if there is a point within *Skyline'* but not in *Skyline*, it must be dominated by some other point. Otherwise, *Skyline* is not correct. ∎

The correctness of basic approach is guaranteed by Lemma 1. It is also of efficiency by suppressing unnecessary transmissions of both phases. Fig. 2 illustrates the processing of these two phases. Fig. 2(a) shows the sensed points and the thresholds of the current round. Nodes u_3, u_5 and u_6 send reports in the first phase because they are not dominated by thresholds. Note that p_6 is pruned by p_5 at node u_3. Thus, only p_3 and p_5 reach the root as in Fig. 2(b). Fig. 2(c) and Fig. 2(d) show the second phase. The root node issues a query containing p_3 and p_5 to its child u_1. Node u_2, however, is not queried since its threshold is

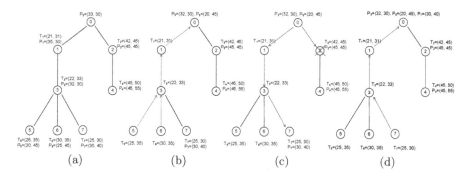

Fig. 2. An example of the basic approach

dominated by p_3. The query is finally sent to u_7. Since p_7 is not dominated by the query, it must be reported. Ultimately, the current-round skyline includes p_3, p_4, and p_7. Notice that during both phases, node u_2 and u_4 do not need to transmit any point.

4.3 MINMAX

The previous subsection presents the basic hierarchical threshold-based approach to compute single-round skyline. Note that the approach only works when it is paired with the method of setting and updating hierarchial thresholds. In this subsection, we first introduce MinMax operator and extract a few useful properties. Then we specify the basic approach to a more efficient one named MINMAX approach according to the extracted properties. Finally, we present method of threshold maintenance by using the MinMax operator.

First, we give the definition of the MinMax operator, in which the input is a point set with the same dimensionality and the output is a single point. Suppose data set[2] $P = \{p_1, p_2, ..., p_n\}$, $MinMax(P)$ is defined as follows.

$$max_i = \text{MAX}_{k=1}^d p_i[k] \ (1 \le i \le n)$$
$$minmax = \text{MIN}_{i=1}^n max_i$$
$$MinMax(P) = \underbrace{\{minmax, minmax, ..., minmax\}}_{d} \quad (1)$$

Fig. 3 shows an example of the MinMax operator. Point set P consists of five 2-dimensional points. We observe $max_i = p_i[y]$ when $i = 1, 2$ and $max_i = p_i[x]$ when $i = 3, 4, 5$. As shown in Fig. 3, $p_3[x]$ is the smallest among $p_1[y]$, $p_2[y]$, $p_3[x]$, $p_4[x]$, $p_5[x]$, so $MIN\{p_1[y], p_2[y], p_3[x], p_4[x], p_5[x]\}$ equals to $p_3[x]$. As a result, $MinMax(P)$ returns $(p_3[x], p_3[x])$. The MinMax operator possesses the following Lemmas.

---

[2] Suppose sensed values on each dimension are always limited within a value range. Without loss of generality, we normalize values on each dimension to be within the range $[0, 1]$.

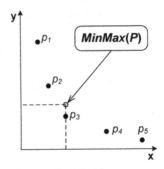

Fig. 3. The MinMax operator

Lemma 2. *Given two data sets* $P = \{p_1, p_2, ..., p_m\}$ *and* $Q = \{q_1, q_2, ..., q_n\}$, $MinMax(P \cup Q) = MinMax(P \cup MinMax(Q)) = MinMax(MinMax(P) \cup Q) = MinMax(MinMax(P) \cup MinMax(Q))$.

Proof. This lemma is obvious and we omit the proof here.   ■

Lemma 3. *Given point set* $P = \{p_1, p_2, ..., p_m\}$ *and a point* $\tau = (v_\tau, v_\tau, ..., v_\tau)$ *with the same value on all dimensions,* $P \preceq \tau \equiv MinMax(P) \preceq \tau$ *and* $P \npreceq \tau \equiv MinMax(P) \npreceq \tau$.

Proof. Suppose $max_i = MAX_{k=1}^d p_i[k]$ $(1 < i \leq m)$, and $minmax = MIN_{i=1}^m max_i$. Without loss of generality, we assume $minmax = max_1$ and thus $MinMax(P) = (max_1, max_1...max_1)$. It is obvious $p_1 \preceq (max_1, max_1, ..., max_1)$.

- Necessary Condition: If $MinMax(P) \preceq \tau$, that is $(max_1, max_1, ..., max_1) \preceq \tau$, then $p_1 \preceq \tau$ and thus $P \preceq \tau$. If $MinMax(P) \npreceq \tau$, it means $max_1 > v_\tau$ and thus $p_1 \npreceq \tau$. Note that $max_i \geq max_1$ when $i = 2, 3, ..., m$, thus $\nexists p_i$, $p_i \preceq \tau, i = 1, 2, ..., m$. Therefore, $P \npreceq \tau$.
- Sufficient Condition: If $P \preceq \tau$, then there exists at least one point $p_k \preceq \tau$. It indicates that $max_k \leq v_\tau$. Since $max_1 \leq max_k$, it can be deduced that $p_1 = MinMax(P) \preceq \tau$. If $P \npreceq \tau$, then $max_i > v_\tau, i = 1, 2, ..., m$. Thus, $MinMax(P) \npreceq \tau$.   ■

Lemma 4. *Given two point sets* $P = \{p_1, p_2, ..., p_m\}$ *and* $Q = \{q_1, q_2, ..., q_n\}$, *if* $P \preceq Q$, *then* $MinMax(P) \preceq MinMax(Q)$.

Proof. Suppose $max_{pi} = MAX_{k=1}^d p_i[k]$ and $minmax_p = MIN_{i=1}^m max_{pi}$, $(i=1, 2, ..., m)$. Without loss of generality, assume $minmax_p = max_{p1}$ and thus $MinMax(P) = (max_{p1}, max_{p1}...max_{p1})$. The same for Q, assume $minmax_q = max_{q1}$ and $MinMax(Q) = (max_{q1}, max_{q1}...max_{q1})$. Because $P \preceq Q$, there must exist $p_j (1 < j \leq m)$, $p_j \preceq q_1$. As a result, $max_{pj} \leq max_{q1}$. Note that $max_{p1} \leq max_{pj}$, thus $max_{p1} \leq max_{q1}$. Therefore, $MinMax(P) \preceq MinMax(Q)$.   ■

MINMAX Approach. Now we describe the MINMAX approach that utilizes properties of the MinMax operator, which further promotes efficiency of skyline computation.

In the first round, there is no historical information on each node, thus the naïve approach is applied. Once the naïve approach is finished, the hierarchical threshold at each node u_i is initialized as $\tau_i = MinMax(LS_i)$. Based on Lemma 4, Rule 1 is satisfied. Rule 2 also holds since LS_i is known to its parent. The first phase *Up Report* is the same as that of the basic approach and the second phase *Down Query* is revised as follows.

Root node u_r first computes the local skyline LS_r among its own point and the reported points from its children. Instead of sending LS_r, u_r just sends $MinMax(LS_r)$, denoted as $minmax_r$. According to Lemma 3, $minmax_r$ has the equivalent dominating ability to LS_r. Note that LS_r may contain a large amount of points, especially on the high-dimensional data. As a result, such transformation minimizes the query to be one-point message and thus significantly reduces the traffic cost. Then root u_r queries each of its children u_i that satisfies $minmax_r \not\prec \tau_i$.

Internal nodes: Once node u_i receives $minmax_p$ from its parent, it computes $minmax_i = MinMax$ *(non-reported points* $\cup \{minmax_p\})$. Based on Lemma 2 and 3, sending $minmax_i$ is equivalent to sending the points from u_i and the ancestors of the u_i. Thus u_i sends $minmax_i$ to each of its children u_c that satisfies $minmax_i \not\prec \tau_c$. After the children reply the query with new points that are not dominated by $minmax_i$, u_i updates the final local skyline FLS_i. Finally, u_i sends to its parent FLS_i. If u_i is the root, then FLS_i is the final skyline.

Leaf nodes: If leaf node u_i has reported p_i in the first phase or satisfies $minmax_p \prec p_i$, it does not reply. Otherwise, u_i reports p_i (p_i is just FLS_i).

MinMax-Threshold Maintenance. In the first phase, if u_i reports P_i to its parent, $\tau_i(r+1)$ is set to $MinMax$ $(\{\tau_i(r)\} \cup P_i)$. Otherwise, $\tau_i(r+1)$ is set to $\tau_i(r)$. In the second phase, if u_i receives the query from its parent u_p, $\tau_i(r+1)$ is set to $MinMax$ $(\{minmax_i\} \cup FLS_i)$. Otherwise, $\tau_i(r+1)$ keeps unchanged.

The threshold maintenance method is quite straightforward. In the first phase, P_i breaking threshold τ_i means that τ_i is set too large, so τ_i should be lowered according to P_i. In the second phase, it indicates that threshold τ_i is set too small if u_i receives the query. Thus, it is required to reset τ_i using $minmax_i$ and FLS_i that reflect the points from its subtree or even other subtrees. Such updating benefits since the most points of its subtree can be suppressed if they are dominated by another subtree in the following rounds.

Lemma 5. *The maintained MinMax-threshold follows Rule 1 and Rule 2.*

Proof. Suppose u_c is a child of u_i. In the first round, the threshold is set according to the local skyline. On one hand, $LS_i \preceq LS_c$ can deduce $MinMax(LS_i) \preceq MinMax(LS_c)$ based on Lemma 4, thus Rule 1 is satisfied. On the other hand, u_c reports LS_c to u_i, thus u_i knows threshold τ_c. We next study the threshold updating for the subsequent rounds. Suppose in the r_{th} round, both rules are satisfied, we prove that the rules still hold in the $(r+1)_{th}$ round.

In the first phase, u_c reports P_c that are not dominated by τ_c. Since both P_c and τ_c are known to u_i, u_i can compute $\tau_c(r+1)$. Therefore, Rule 2 holds. It can also be deduced that $P_i \cup \{\tau_i\} \preceq P_c$ because $\forall p \in P_c, p \prec \tau_i$ or $p \preceq P_i$. Note that

$\tau_i \preceq \tau_c$, so $P_i \cup \{\tau_i\} \preceq P_c \cup \{\tau_c\}$. According to Lemma 4, $\tau_p(r + 1) \preceq \tau_c(r + 1)$ and Rule 1 holds.

In the second phase, we discuss two situations whether $minmax_i \preceq \tau_c$ or not.

- If $minmax_i \npreceq \tau_c$, then we need to prove $\{minmax_i\} \cup FLS_i \preceq \{minmax_c\} \cup FLS_c$ according to Lemma 4. Since $FLS_i \preceq FLS_c$, it can be simplified to $\{minmax_i\} \cup FLS_i \preceq minmax_c$. Note that $minmax_c = MinMax$ (*non-reported points* $\cup \{minmax_i\}$). According to Lemma 3 and Lemma 4, it can be further transferred to prove $\{minmax_i\} \cup FLS_i \preceq$ *non-reported points* $\cup \{minmax_i\}$. It is satisfied because $\forall p \in$ *non-reported points*, $p \prec minmax_i$ or $p \preceq FLS_i$. Thus Rule 1 holds. Meanwhile, FLS_c will be reported to u_i, so Rule 2 also holds.
- If $minmax_i \preceq \tau_c$, then $\tau_c(r+1)$ keeps unchanged. Thus, Rule 2 holds. We now show the proof of $minmax_i \preceq \tau_c(r + 1)$. Note that $minmax_i$ is constructed by the points from the ancestors of u_c using the MinMax operation. It is obvious that these points dominate $\{\tau_c(r)\} \cup P_c$ that is used to set $\tau_c(r+1)$. Thus, Rule 1 is satisfied based on Lemma 4. ∎

MINMAX further reduces cost of the second phase by transforming a point set to a single point via the MinMax operator. During high dimensional skyline computation, cost saving is significant. Lemma 5 guarantee the maintained thresholds satisfy Rule 1 and 2. As a result, correct skyline will be obtained.

4.4   Failure Management

Our threshold-based approach is discussed in the ideal situation without any node or link failure. It is also scalable to handle network failures by adjusting the parent-child relationship. Once node u_i detects a failure between itself and its parent using reliable communication protocol, u_i broadcasts *recovery* message containing threshold τ_i to find a new parent among its neighbors. The nodes that are not the descendants of u_i send a reply with their thresholds. Then u_i picks up node u_j with $\tau_j \preceq \tau_i$ as its parent. If no such node exists, the parent is chosen to be node u_j with the minimum distance $|\tau_i \tau_j|$. In this case, the threshold of each ancestor u_a with $\tau_a \npreceq \tau_i$ should be reset to τ_i. However, it is possible that u_i does not receive any reply. This means that all its neighbors reside in the subtree rooted at u_i, thus it has to choose one descendant to reconnect the network and adjust hierarchical thresholds. The worst situation is that u_i may not be able to find a path to the root, which indicates the low node density. In this case, any approach is invalid to obtain data from the separated part of the network.

5   Performance Evaluation

This section evaluates the performance of proposed approaches, the naïve approach and the threshold-based approach MINMAX.

We developed a simulator for WSN, which can adjust parameters such as the number of nodes, the transmission range and the size of the network area.

The default settings of the simulated sensor network are as follows. The network area is a rectangle grid of $200m \times 200m$, where 300 sensor nodes are randomly distributed with the transmission range $r = 50m$. The routing tree is constructed using the shortest path tree.

We use synthetic data for evaluation. Two data generation policies, *random* policy and *Multi-Signal Mixture* (MSM) policy, are utilized. In the random policy, a node's value v on each dimension is initiated randomly from $[0,1]$ in the first round and varies with the maximum fluctuation value $f < 1$. Suppose value on dimension i in round t is $v(t)[i]$, in round $(t+1)$, $v(t+1)[i]$ changes to $v(t)[i]$+rand(-f, f) with guarantee of being within $[0,1]$. The second policy generates value v on each dimension by simulating the scenario where sensor nodes sense signal strength from multiple signal generators. The signal strength received at each node is the sum of attenuated strength at that position from each signal generator. Note that the default network area is $[0,200] \times [0,200]$, we distribute 50 signal generators randomly in the area[3] of $[-200,400] \times [-200,400]$. The received signal strength (RSS) can be calculated by log-normal model [21].

$$RSS(dist) = ps - pl(d_0) - 10\eta log_{10} \frac{dist}{d_0} \qquad (2)$$

ps is the generator power, $pl(d_0)$ is path loss for a reference distance of d_0, η is the path loss exponent, and $dist$ is the distance from the generator. As a result, the summed strength can be calculated as $v = \sum_{i=1}^{50}(ps_i - pl(d_0) - 10\eta log_{10}\frac{dist_i}{d_0})$, where $dist_i$ is the distance from each generator. Generator strength ps is randomly initiated from $[0,1]$ with the maximum fluctuation value $f < 1$. The MSM policy can produce data reflecting the real environment where the nearby sensor nodes always obtain the similar values. Without specific indication, the default parameter values are set to dimensionality $d = 3$, $f = 0.01$ and the number of rounds is 50.

The performance is evaluated in terms of the average energy consumption per node. We only account for the communication cost since it dominates the total energy consumption [14].

Dimensionality. Fig. 4 shows the performance results when the dimensionality varies between 2 and 5. With the increasing of the dimensionality, the average energy consumption per node increases for each approach. MINMAX is superior to the naïve approach in any dimensionality, reducing the cost about 80% and 60% on 2-dimensional random data and MSM data respectively. However, the difference shrinks with the increasing of the dimensionality because the dominance relationship between high-dimensional points is weakened. When dimensionality $d = 5$, MINMAX only achieves about 10% ~ 20% cost saving.

Data fluctuation. Fig. 5 presents the influence of data fluctuation on the performance of the proposed approaches. The data fluctuation value f varies be-

---

[3] The distribution area of the signal generators must guarantee each node be included in skyline with the same probability.

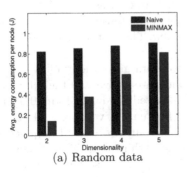
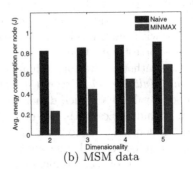

(a) Random data   (b) MSM data

Fig. 4. Performance vs. Dimensionality

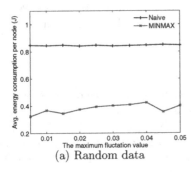
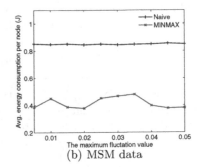

(a) Random data   (b) MSM data

Fig. 5. Performance vs. Data fluctuation

tween 0.005 and 0.05 for both the random and MSM data. The naïve approach is not affected by data varying, costing almost equally. MINMAX outperforms the naïve approach and also exhibits acceptable robustness on significantly varying data. The energy consumption fluctuates without obvious deviation. The reason is that when data is uniformly distributed, the number of the dominated points remains close for two consecutive rounds because the number of new dominated points counterbalances the number of new non-dominated points.

Network size. Fig. 6 shows the performance comparison as the network size increases from 200 to 700. To maintain the node density, the network area is enlarged proportionally to the network size. With the increasing of the network size, the energy consumption of the naïve approach rises. This is because the enlargement of the network area and size results in the growing of the routing tree. Thus, the nodes close to the root consume more energy due to more local skyline points, which increases the average energy consumption of the entire tree. The result of MINMAX is just opposite. As the network size increases, the network cost of MINMAX drops. The reason is that the heightening of the routing tree makes reports and queries be transmitted comparative less hops before pruned.

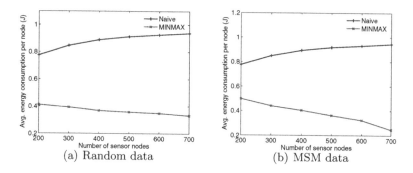

(a) Random data   (b) MSM data

Fig. 6. Performance vs. Network size

Communication range. Fig. 7 illustrates the impact of the communication range on the energy consumption. The cost of each approach is inversely proportional to the communication range. Note that the increasing of the communication range increases the degree of the node so that an internal node possesses more children. As a result, the larger broadcasting range, equivalent to stronger pruning effect, improves the efficiency of both approaches.

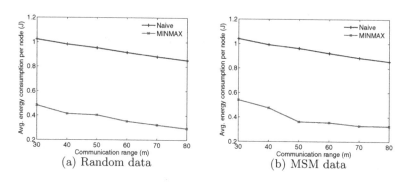

(a) Random data   (b) MSM data

Fig. 7. Performance vs. Communication range

6   Conclusion

This paper addresses a new problem of continuous skyline monitoring in sensor networks. To solve the problem in an energy-efficient way, we propose a naïve approach as baseline and a sophisticated hierarchical threshold-based approach MINMAX that is based on a basic version. The basic approach contains two phases: 1) *Up Report*: the points not dominated by thresholds are reported, 2) *Down Query*: fetching the final skyline from the nodes whose thresholds are not dominated by the query. The basic approach can obtain the correct skyline efficiently if the hierarchical thresholds are established in the network. MINMAX introduces the MinMax operator that significantly promotes the efficiency of the second phase by minimizing the size of query message. The MinMax operator is also used for hierarchical threshold maintenance, guaranteeing the correctness of MINMAX. We also present effective strategies to deal with the unexpected node or link failures in the dynamic environment. Finally, the simulated experiments demonstrate that the proposed MINMAX approach outperforms the naïva approach under all tested situations.

References

1. I. F. Akyildiz, W. Su, Y. Sankarasubramaniam, and E. Cayirci, "a survey on sensor networks," *IEEE Communications Magazine*, vol. 40, pp. 102–114, August 2002.
2. S. Madden, M. J. Franklin, J. M. Hellerstein, and W. Hong, "The design of an acquisitional query processor for sensor networks," in *Proc. of SIGMOD*, pp. 491–502, 2003.
3. Y. Yao and J. Gehrke, "Query processing in sensor networks," in *Proc. of CIDR*, 2003.
4. D. J. Abadi, S. Madden, and W. Lindner, "Reed: Robust, efficient filtering and event detection in sensor networks," in *Proc. of VLDB*, pp. 769–780, 2005.
5. J. W. Branch, B. K. Szymanski, C. Giannella, R. Wolff, and H. Kargupta, "In-network outlier detection in wireless sensor networks," in *Proc. of ICDCS*, 2006.
6. S. Borzsonyi, D. Kossmann, and K. Stocker, "The skyline operator," in *Proc. of ICDE*, pp. 421–430, 2001.
7. D. Kossmann, F. Ramsak, and S. Rost, "Shooting stars in the sky: An online algorithm for skyline queries," in *Proc. of VLDB*, pp. 275–286, 2002.
8. D. Papadias, Y. Tao, and G. Fu, "An optimal and progressive algorithm for skyline queries," in *Proc. of SIGMOD*, pp. 467–478, 2003.
9. W.-T. Balke, U. Guntzer, and J. X. Zheng, "Efficient distributed skylining for web information systems," in *Proc. of EDBT*, pp. 256–273, 2004.
10. W.-T. Balke and U. Guntzer, "Supporting skyline queries on catagorical data in web information systems," in *Proc. of IMSA*, 2004.
11. K. Hose, "Processing skyline queries in p2p systems," in *VLDB 2005 Ph.D Workshop*, pp. 36–40, 2005.
12. P. Wu, C. Zhang, and Y. Feng, "Parallelizing skyline queries for scalable distribution," in *Proc. of EDBT*, pp. 112–130, 2005.
13. X. Lin, Y. Yuan, W. Wang, and H. Lu, "Stabbing the sky: Efficient skyline computation over sliding windows," in *Proc. of ICDE*, pp. 502–513, 2005.
14. W. Pottie and W. Kaiser, "Wireless integrated network sensors," *Communications of the ACM*, vol. 43, pp. 51–58, May 2000.
15. A. Silberstein, R. Braynard, and J. Yang, "Constraint chaining: on energy-efficient continuous monitoring in sensor networks," in *Proc. of SIGMOD*, pp. 157–168, 2006.
16. A. Deligiannakis, Y. Kotidis, and N. Roussopoulos, "Compressing historical information in sensor networks," in *Proc. of SIGMOD*, pp. 527–538, 2004.
17. C. Guestrin, P. Bodk, R. Thibaux, M. A. Paskin, and S. Madden, "Distributed regression: an efficient framework for modeling sensor network data," in *Proc. of IPSN*, pp. 527–538, 2004.
18. Z. Liu, K. C. Sia, and J. Cho, "Cost-efficient processing of min/max queries over distributed sensors with uncertainty," in *Proc. of SAC*, pp. 634–641, 2005.
19. A. Silberstein, K. Munagala, and J. Yang, "Energy-efficient monitoring of extreme values in sensor networks," in *Proc. of SIGMOD*, pp. 169–180, 2006.
20. Crossbow Inc, "MPR-Mote Processor Radio Board User's Manual".
21. T. S. Rappaport, *Wireless Communications*. Principles Practice, 1999.

Secure Data Aggregation with Multiple Encryption

Melek Önen and Refik Molva

Institut Eurécom
Sophia-Antipolis, France
{melek.onen,refik.molva}@eurecom.fr

Abstract. Data aggregation has been put forward as an essential technique to achieve power efficiency in sensor networks. Data aggregation consists of processing data collected by source nodes at each intermediate node enroute to the sink in order to reduce redundancy and minimize bandwidth usage.

The deployment of sensor networks in hostile environments call for security measures such as data encryption and authentication to prevent data tampering by intruders or disclosure by compromised nodes. Aggregation of encrypted and/or integrity-protected data by intermediate nodes that are not necessarily trusted due to potential node compromise is a challenging problem. We propose a secure data aggregation scheme that ensures that sensors participating to the aggregation mechanism do not have access to the content of the data while adding their sensed values thanks to the use of an efficient homomorphic encryption scheme. We provide a layered secure aggregation mechanism and the related key attribution algorithm that limits the impact of security threats such as node compromises. We also evaluate the robustness of the scheme against node failures and show that such failures are efficiently recovered by a small subset of nodes that are at most m hops away from the failure.

1 Introduction

Wireless sensor networks (WSN) are viewed as a popular solution to various monitoring problems such as safety monitoring, wildfire tracking and traffic monitoring. A WSN consists of thousands of sensors that are in charge of both monitoring and data transmission tasks. The data collected by each sensor is transmitted via a network consisting of other sensors towards a well identified destination node called sink. In the basic setting of a WSN, each individual piece of data is thus independently transmitted over several hops towards the sink and each sensor node is involved in the forwarding of a large number of data pieces originated from other sensors. In the resource constrained WSN environment, forwarding of large amounts of data becomes the major focus of energy and bandwidth optimization efforts. Data aggregation has thus been put forward

K. Langendoen and T. Voigt (Eds.): EWSN 2007, LNCS 4373, pp. 117–132, 2007.

as an essential technique to achieve power and bandwidth efficiency in WSN. Based on the principle that the sink does not necessarily need all raw pieces of information collected by each sensor but only a summary or aggregate thereof, data aggregation consists of processing data collected by source nodes at each intermediate node enroute to the sink in order to reduce redundancy and minimize bandwidth usage. A common way to aggregate data in sensor networks is to simply sum up values as they are forwarded towards the sink. Such additive aggregations are useful for statistical measurements such as mean or variance computation.

As a distributed task achieved by several potentially compromised nodes, data aggregation raises some new security concerns in addition to the basic vulnerabilities of a WSN [1]. Data aggregation in WSN is thus exposed to various threats such as node compromise, injection of bogus aggregates, disclosure of sensed data and aggregate values to intruders or tampering with data transmitted over wireless links. In this paper, we focus on the problem of data confidentiality with a twofold objective: first to prevent intruders from accessing individual monitoring results, second to prevent any node other than the sink from accessing the aggregate values. While classical data encryption mechanisms easily meet the first objective, the second objective raises a new requirement for sensor nodes involved in the computation of intermediate aggregate values: each sensor node must be able to combine the locally monitored value that is in cleartext with the encrypted aggregate value received from adjacent nodes in order to come up with a new encrypted aggregate value. This problem typically calls for some form of homomorphic encryption technique. Existing solutions based on homomorphic encryption [2,3] either suffer from excessive computational complexity or are vulnerable to node compromise.

We suggest a secure additive data aggregation scheme based on the use of an efficient homomorphic encryption technique combined with a multiple encryption scheme using symmetric algorithms. The homomorphism of the underlying encryption technique allows sensors to aggregate their cleartext measurements with the encrypted aggregate values whereas the multiple encryption scheme assures that aggregate values and individual measurement results remain oblivious to all intermediate nodes enroute to the sink. The joint use of the homomorphism and multiple encryption assures that a secret channel is established between every sensor node and the sink without having to establish pairwise security associations or a public-key infrastructure.

We first analyze the security requirements raised by secure data aggregation and describe the need for homomorphic encryption functions. We then briefly present the CTR encryption scheme proposed by Bellare et al. in [4], and its extension in [5] for the context of multicast confidentiality. We show that CTR is homomorphic and introduce the proposed layered secure aggregation scheme based on CTR. We then evaluate the effectiveness of the proposed scheme in terms of security, safety and performance.

2 Problem Statement

2.1 Aggregation in Wireless Sensor Networks

We model a wireless sensor network (WSN) as a rooted tree $\mathcal{T} = (\mathcal{V}, \mathcal{E})$ where $\mathcal{V}$ is the set of nodes corresponding to the sensors and $\mathcal{E}$ is the set of edges between these nodes. The root S of the tree corresponds to the sink. Each other node has one or more incoming edges but a unique outgoing edge.

Aggregation techniques are used to reduce the amount of data communicated within a WSN. As measurements are recorded periodically at each sensor, one way to aggregate such information is the additive aggregation that is the addition of values as they are forwarded towards the sink. Each node receives packets from the incoming edges, aggregates them and sends the result via the outgoing edge. The sink collects the final set of aggregated packets and completes the aggregation task. Additive aggregation techniques are very useful for statistical measurements in sensor networks. Hence, once the sink receives the addition of some values, it can easily compute the mean or variance of the received values.

2.2 Security Requirements

In the context of secure data aggregation, we distinguish two confidentiality requirements:

- **generic confidentiality** whereby sensors not participating to the aggregation mechanism, should not have access to the content of the data.
- **end-to-end confidentiality** whereby sensors actively participating to the aggregation mechanism do not access the data that is already aggregated.

As to generic confidentiality, sensors need to use some cryptographic encryption algorithms in order to let only authorized sensors access the content of the data. Since sensor nodes have very limited resources, symmetric encryption algorithms are more suitable for such networks. However, with the use of classical encryption schemes such as AES [6], every sensor should first decrypt the received measurements in order to aggregate their own measured value and then re-encrypt the result in order to send it to the next sensor enroute to the sink. In this case, all sensors would have access to aggregated measurements. In order to prevent such access and thus to ensure end-to-end confidentiality, we propose a new framework that implements homomorphic encryption algorithms.

2.3 The Proposed Framework

We propose a framework whereby sensors participate to a secure aggregation mechanism without having access to the protected data. In order to ensure end-to-end confidentiality, the framework uses additive homomorphic encryption algorithms. Moreover, measurements are protected with multiple encryption layers. Sensors receiving encrypted data would be able to suppress some encryption layers, aggregate their measurements and add new encryption layers. Thanks to a new key attribution algorithm, only the sink is able to suppress all encryption layers and thus access the finally aggregated result. Since each sensor modifies the encryption of the data, the compromise of some intermediary nodes does not provide access to the protected data.

In the following section, we describe the CTR homomorphic encryption algorithm that is extended in our framework. We then introduce the new key attribution algorithm that is used in the new secure aggregation scheme that ensures both generic and end-to-end confidentiality.

3 The Proposed Encryption Algorithm

3.1 Additive Homomorphic Encryption

End-to-end confidentiality as defined in section 2.2 requires a homomorphic encryption scheme. A homomorphism is defined as a map $\phi : X \longrightarrow Y$ such that:

$$\phi(x \cdot y) = \phi(x) \circ \phi(y) \tag{1}$$

where $\cdot$ and $\circ$ respectively are the operations in X and Y. If ϕ is a homomorphic encryption algorithm, and if $\cdot$ is the aggregation operation, thanks to the homomorphism of ϕ encrypted individual measurements can be aggregated into an encrypted aggregate value. Hence, let N_i be a sensor receiving encrypted measurements $\phi(V_j)$ and $\phi(V_k)$. N_i first senses V_i, computes $\phi(V_i)$ and aggregates the three encryptions as $\phi(V_j) \circ \phi(V_k) \circ \phi(V_i)$. Thanks to the homomorphism of ϕ, this result is identical to the encrypted aggregate value: $\phi(V_j \cdot V_k \cdot V_i)$. It should be noted that N_i was able to aggregate its measurement with the received values without accessing the measurements in this example.

Let $\mathcal{M}$ be the set of plaintext messages and $\mathcal{K}$ be the set of encryption keys. In the context of secure data aggregation, we propose that the encryption function ϕ represents an additive homomorphic encryption scheme that encrypts a message $x \in \mathcal{M}$ with the encryption key $k \in \mathcal{K}$ as follows:

$$\phi : (\mathcal{M}, \mathcal{K}) \longrightarrow \mathcal{M}$$
$$\phi(x, k) = (x + k) \bmod n \tag{2}$$

n is the cardinality of $\mathcal{M}$. It is easy to show that ϕ is a homomorphic function. Hence, let x_a and x_b two different plaintext messages in $\mathcal{M}$ and k_a and k_b encryption keys in $\mathcal{K}$. We have:

$$\phi(x_a, k_a) = (x_a + k_a) \bmod n$$
$$\phi(x_b, k_b) = (x_b + k_b) \bmod n$$
$$\phi(x_a, k_a) + \phi(x_b, k_b) = (x_a + k_a + x_b + k_b) \bmod n$$
$$= \phi(x_a + x_b, k_a + k_b)$$

The security of this scheme relies on the unique utilization of the key. Hence, as one-time pads, for each message, the encryption must use a different key.

Thus, an efficient key generation algorithm is required for each encryption operation. We propose to implement the basic CTR function proposed by Bellare et al. in [4] that allows the generation of a different key for each encryption operation. Thanks to this scheme that is briefly described in the following section, sensors are able to update their encryption key without receiving any additional information from the sink.

3.2   CTR Encryption Scheme

In [4], Bellare et al. describe and analyze various cipher modes of operation. In this section, we briefly describe their proposed counter based block cipher mode of operation (CTR-mode) which we extend in our proposed scheme. We denote $\oplus$ as the binary XOR operation and define f_a as a l-bit pseudorandom permutation such as AES [6] where a is the encryption key. The CTR-mode scheme is a triplet $(\mathcal{K}, \mathcal{E}, \mathcal{D})$ defined as follows:

- $\mathcal{K}$ flips coins and outputs a random key a;
- $\mathcal{E}(ctr, x)$ splits x into n blocks of l bits $x = x_1, .., x_n$, and for each x_i returns $y_i = f_a(ctr + i) \oplus x_i$. Finally, ctr is updated by $ctr + n$;
- Symmetrically, $\mathcal{D}(ctr, y)$ first splits y into n blocks of l bits $y = y_1, .., y_n$, and for each y_i, it returns $x_i = f_a(ctr + i) \oplus y_i$. Similarly, ctr is updated by $ctr + n$.

The counter ctr is maintained by the encryption algorithm across consecutive encryptions with the same key. Thanks to this counter, the receiver that knows the key a can recompute each $f_a(ctr + i)$ and thus retrieve the original message x.

3.3   Multiple Key CTR Encryption for Secure Data Aggregation

In order to introduce the secure data aggregation, we propose an extended version of the CTR encryption with the use of multiple keys for both encryption and decryption. We first replace the XOR operation by the additive homomorphic encryption scheme defined in equation 2. In the sequel of this paper $a + b$ and $a - b$ are respectively defined as $(a + b) \bmod n$ and $(a - b) \bmod n$. The new basic encryption is again a triplet $(\mathcal{K}, \mathcal{E}, \mathcal{D})$ such that:

- $\mathcal{K}$ flips coins and outputs a random key a;
- $\mathcal{E}(ctr, x)$ splits x into n blocks of l bits and for each x_i returns $y_i = f_a(ctr + i) + x_i$. Finally ctr is updated by $ctr + n$;
- $\mathcal{D}(ctr, y)$ splits y into n blocks of l bits and for each y_i returns $x_i = y_i - f_a(ctr + i)$. Finally, ctr is updated by $ctr + n$.

Since $(\mathcal{K}, \mathcal{E}, \mathcal{D})$ is also homomorphic, we now focus on the problem of end-to-end confidentiality whereby sensors perform aggregation operations using this scheme. Since sensors are not authorized to access the content of their received aggregated information, different keys should be distributed to each sensor. In this case, we propose a triplet $(\mathcal{K}^{(r)}, \mathcal{E}^{(r)}, \mathcal{D}^{(r)})$ with r independent keys as follows:

- $\mathcal{K}^{(r)}$ chooses r random keys $a_1, .., a_r$;
- $\mathcal{E}^{(r)}(ctr_1, .., ctr_r, x)$ splits x into n blocks of l bits $x = x_1, .., x_n$, and for each x_i returns $y_i = x_i + \sum_{j=1}^{r} f_{a_j}(ctr_j + i)$;
- $\mathcal{D}^{(r)}(ctr_1, .., ctr_r, y)$ splits y into n blocks of l bits $y = y_1, .., y_n$ in order to retrieve $x_i = y_i - \sum_{j=1}^{r} f_{a_j}(ctr_j + i)$.

We recall the security property that claims that a message encrypted with multiple keys is at least secure as any individual encryptions [7]. It is obvious that $(\mathcal{K}^{(r)}, \mathcal{E}^{(r)}, \mathcal{D}^{(r)})$ is homomorphic since the encryption and decryption operations are respectively defined by additions and subtractions that are by definition homomorphic.

4   The Proposed Model: Layered Secure Aggregations

Now that we have defined the security requirements specific to the problem of data aggregation and that we have described the proposed CTR encryption algorithm, we describe the proposed layered secure aggregation scheme that allows sensors to aggregate measurements while the data remains confidential. Thanks to the addition of multiple encryption layers, the scheme remains secure against attacks such as node compromise. We first introduce a new key attribution algorithm that defines the keying material of each sensor and then present the aggregation protocol.

4.1   Notation

As described in section 2.1, a wireless sensor network is represented by a tree $\mathcal{T}$. We define the function $Depth$ that given a node identity N_i returns its depth in the tree. We set $Depth(S) = 0$. Within this tree, we also define the following relations between nodes:

- $Root(\mathcal{T})$ represents the data sink that collects and extracts the aggregated data;
- $Parent(N, m)$ is the mth parent of N if it exists or S otherwise;
- $Children(N, m)$ is the set of nodes N_i such that $\forall i, N = Parent(N_i, m)$.

In order to implement the CTR encryption algorithm with multiple encryption keys in the context of secure data aggregation, we define a key attribution algorithm that is explained in the following section. Thanks to this algorithm, any node will be able to add or suppress some encryption layers without causing any leakage of secret information.

4.2   The Proposed Key Attribution Algorithm

In this section, we describe a new key attribution algorithm for the proposed aggregation protocol. Thanks to this algorithm, the sink is able to aggregate all the measurements without leaking any secret information to any node including the sensors that participate to the aggregation mechanism.

Each node N_i shares a key $a_{i,j}$ and a counter $ctr_{i,j}$ with a node N_j where $N_j = Parent(N_i, m)$. We also define a different key and counter $(a_{l,k}, ctr_{l,k})$ shared between a leaf node N_l and $N_k = Parent(N_l, t)$, for each $0 < t < m$. The key attribution algorithm is summarized in Table 1.

Table 1. The key attribution algorithm

For each node N_i in $\mathcal{T}$:
   define $(a_{i,j}, ctr_{i,j})$ for N_i and $N_j = Parent(N_i, m)$;
   if N_i is a leaf node
   then
      for each $t < m$
         define $(a_{i,k}, ctr_{i,k})$ for N_i and $N_k = Parent(N_i, t)$;
   else
      set $t = 0$;
      while $Children(N_i, m - t) = \emptyset$
        increment t by one;
      define $(a_{i,j}, ctr_{i,j})$ for N_i and $N_j \in Children(N_i, m - t)$;

In order to illustrate this algorithm, we define a WSN with 11 nodes represented in Figure 1. In this particular network, we set $m = 2$. Following the key attribution protocol, all leaf nodes, N_5, N_6, N_9 and N_{10} share one key with their direct parent and another one with their grandparent. For example, node N_9 shares $a_{7,9}$ with node N_7 and $a_{4,9}$ with node N_4. Node N_1 which is an intermediate node, shares a different key with nodes N_5, N_6, N_7 and N_8 which are in $Children(N_1, 2)$ and with S since $Parent(N_1, 2) = S$.

4.3 The Aggregation Protocol

Now that we have defined the key attribution algorithm, each node is ready to aggregate its measurement with the received values from its children nodes. In this paper, we define the aggregation operation as a sum computation. This operation can also be a mean or variance computation. Since the encryption algorithm is homomorphic, each node adds the received values to the measured value without having to access the content of the aggregated data.

Table 2 illustrates the additive aggregation protocol. A sensor N_i first aggregates the received values and its measurement. From this value, N_i subtracts keys that it shares with its mth children nodes N_j and adds the key that it shares with its mth parent node N_k. Then, N_i sends the aggregated value denoted by A_i to its parent node.

As an example, we examine in Table 3 how the proposed additive aggregation protocol is applied on the tree of Figure 1. For the sake of clarity, we define $k_{i,j}$ as the one-time-key originating from $a_{i,j}$ and $ctr_{i,j}$.

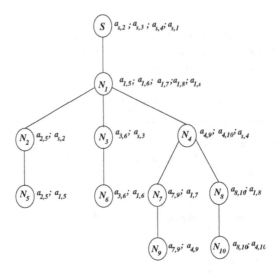

Fig. 1. Implementation of the key attribution algorithm with $m = 2$

5   Evaluation

In the following sections, we review the proposed framework with respect to:

- **confidentiality** whereby intruders and sensors should not have access to the content of the data (generic and end-to-end confidentiality);
- **robustness** whereby the impact of a node compromise or a node failure on the aggregation scheme should be minimized.

We then evaluate the performance of the scheme in terms of memory and CPU usage and in terms of communication overhead.

5.1   Security Evaluation

In this section, we first show that the proposed framework ensures generic confidentiality and then consider the node compromise scenario that could prevent the end-to-end confidentiality of the scheme.

Proposition 1. *The scheme ensures generic confidentiality.*

Proof. In a work evaluating the security of cryptosystems in the multi-user setting [8], Bellare et al. have essentially shown that if a cryptosystem is secure in the sense of indistinguishability, then the cryptosystem in the multi-user setting, where related messages are encrypted using different keys, is also secure. This result can be applied to the proposed scheme using CTR. When a message is encrypted with r keys it is at least as secure as any individual encryption. Thus, the scheme is at least as secure as a one layer encryption layer, if no node is compromised.

Table 2. The additive aggregation protocol

For each N_i with measured value V_i

    if $Children(N_i, 1) = \emptyset$ then
        Set $A_i = V_i$ and $l = 1$;
        for each $l \leq m$
            $A_i = \mathcal{E}(ctr_{i,k}, A_i)$ such that $N_k = Parent(N_i, l)$
    else
        Receive $\{A_j\}$ from $N_j \in Children(N_i, 1)$;
        Compute $S_i = \displaystyle\sum_{j, N_j \in Children(N_i, 1)} A_j$;

        for all l where $N_i = Parent(N_l, m)$
            Compute $Sd_i = D(ctr_{i,l}, S_i)$;

        Compute $A_i = \mathcal{E}(ctr_{k,i}, Sd_i + V_i)$ such that $N_k = Parent(N_i, m)$;

    Send A_i to $Parent(N_i, 1)$

Moreover the security of encryption operation that simply is a modulo n addition depends on the unique utilization of the encryption key. Thanks to the existence of a counter, at each encryption operation, the encryption key is updated and thus the operation is perfectly secure.

We now consider the node compromise scenario.

Proposition 2. *An intruder can have access to an aggregated data originating from node N_i only in two cases:*

- *Case 1: all the nodes in the subtree T^* of T whose root is N_i and depth is $m - 1$ are compromised;*
- *Case 2: all nodes N_l such that $N_l = Parent(N_i, k)$ for all $1 \leq k \leq m - 1$ are compromised;*

Proof. Let's assume that node N_i is compromised. Then the intruder has access to all keys stored by N_i, that are:

- $\{a_{i,j}\}$ shared between N_i and N_j such that $N_i = Parent(N_j, m)$;
- $a_{i,k}$ shared between N_i and N_k such that $N_k = Parent(N_i, m)$;

When N_i receives aggregated values from its children nodes, these values are still encrypted with different keys by the nodes $N_j \in Children(N_i, k)$ with $1 \leq k \leq m$. Consequently, in addition to N_i, the intruder needs to compromise all the nodes in the subtree T^* of T whose root is N_i and depth is $m - 1$. This proves the Case 1 of proposition 2.

Table 3. The Additive Aggregation Protocol: an example

Layer 4:

   Node N_9: Computes $A_9 = V_9 + k_{7,9} + k_{4,9}$
   Node N_{10}: Computes $A_{10} = V_{10} + k_{8,10} + k_{4,10}$

Layer 3:

   Node N_5: Computes $A_5 = V_5 + k_{2,5} + k_{1,5}$
   Node N_6: Computes $A_6 = V_6 + k_{3,6} + k_{1,6}$
   Node N_7: Receives $A_9 = V_9 + k_{7,9} + k_{4,9}$
   Suppresses a layer $Sd_7 = A_9 - k_{7,9}$
   Computes $V_7 + k_{1,7}$
   Adds a layer $A_7 = V_9 + V_7 + k_{4,9} + k_{1,7}$
   Node N_8: Receives $A_{10} = V_{10} + k_{8,10} + k_{4,10}$
   Suppresses a layer $Sd_8 = A_{10} - k_{8,10}$
   Computes $V_8 + k_{1,8}$
   Adds a layer $A_8 = V_{10} + V_8 + k_{4,10} + k_{1,8}$

Layer 2:

   Node N_2: Receives $A_5 = V_5 + k_{2,5} + k_{1,5}$
   Suppresses a layer $Sd_2 = A_5 - k_{2,5}$
   Computes $V_2 + k_{s,2}$
   Adds a layer $A_2 = V_5 + V_2 + k_{1,5} + k_{s,2}$
   Node N_3: Receives $A_6 = V_6 + k_{3,6} + k_{1,6}$
   Suppresses a layer $Sd_3 = A_6 - k_{3,6}$
   Computes $V_3 + k_{s,3}$
   Adds a layer $A_3 = V_6 + V_3 + k_{1,6} + k_{s,3}$
   Node N_4: Receives A_7 and A_8
   Aggregates $S_4 = A_7 + A_8$
   Suppresses two layers $Sd_4 = A_7 + A_8 - k_{4,9} - k_{4,10}$
   Computes $V_4 + k_{s,4}$
   Adds a layer $A_4 = V_{10} + V_9 + V_8 + V_7 + V_4 + k_{1,7} + k_{1,8} + k_{s,4}$

Layer 1:

   Node N_1: Receives A_2, A_3 and A_4
   Aggregates $S_1 = A_2 + A_3 + A_4$
   Suppresses four layers $Sd_1 = A_2 + A_3 + A_4 - k_{1,5} - k_{1,6} - k_{1,7} - k_{1,8}$
   Computes $V_1 + k_{s,1}$
   Adds a layer $A_1 = \sum_{i=1}^{10} V_i + k_{s,2} + k_{s,3} + k_{s,4} + k_{s,1}$

Layer 0:

   Sink S: Receives A_1
   Suppresses all layers $Sd_s = A_1 - k_{s,2} - k_{s,3} - k_{s,4} - k_{s,1}$

Furthermore, the keys used for the encryption of aggregated values by nodes N_j that construct T^* are by definition shared with nodes N_l such that $N_l = Parent(N_j, m)$. Consequently if the intruder compromises these nodes, it also can access the aggregated data originating from N_i. Since $N_i = Parent(N_j, k)$ with $1 \leq k \leq m$, the intruder needs to compromise nodes N_l such that $N_l = Parent(N_i, n)$ with $1 \leq n \leq m-1$. This result proves the Case 2 of proposition 2.

Therefore, the security of the scheme in terms of end-to-end confidentiality depends on the choice of the value m. The larger values for m imply a larger population to compromise for the intruders. However, if m is very large, the scheme becomes inefficient since the number of encryption layers decreases and the scheme tends to be vulnerable to threats such as node compromise. Hence, if m equals the depth of T denoted by h, all nodes would share one key with the sink. In this case, the advantage of the use of multiple encryption layers disappears and the proposed scheme would be similar to the secure data aggregation scheme in [2]. The scheme would still ensure end-to-end confidentiality, but a node failure would have a strong impact on the aggregation scheme since in addition to the aggregated data, sensors must include additional information about the identities of nodes participating to the aggregation. Thus m must not exceed $h - 1$. As a result, m should be as large as possible for security reasons and small enough for the sake of robustness. The ideal value for m would be the minimum depth of all leaf nodes in T.

5.2   Robustness of the Scheme

Data aggregation in WSN is exposed to the following threats:

- **node compromise** whereby intruders can have access to the security material of a sensor participating to secure data aggregation. In this case, the aggregation scheme is exposed either to the injection of bogus aggregates or to some passive behavior from the compromised node;
- **node failure** whereby the node is off and thus cannot participate to the aggregation mechanism;
- **communication failure** whereby messages enroute to the sink are lost;
- **poisoning** whereby intruders inject some bogus data and thus break the aggregation mechanism.

The impact of a node failure or a communication failure remains the same as the impact of passive behavior originating from a compromised node. Hence, in all cases, a sensor does not receive any message from some of its children nodes and thus should exclude some of its keying material from the next aggregation process. The impact of such failures should be minimized.

Poisoning attacks and the injection of bogus aggregates by compromised nodes first imply a strong need for an authentication mechanism that allows a sensor to verify the origin and the integrity of the received data. We assume that there is an underlying authentication mechanism such as digital signatures. However, compromised nodes still can inject bogus aggregates although the verification of their signature succeeds. In this particular case, since sensors do not have access to the content of aggregates, such attacks are not detected and thus bogus messages cannot be immediately discarded. We thus propose, a recovery mechanism rather than a prevention mechanism that allows the sink to react against such attacks by determining the origin of the attacks.

We thus mainly distinguish two classes of robustness problems and come up with some recovery mechanisms for each of them: **the bogus message injection** originating from compromised nodes and **the loss of messages**.

Protection against bogus message injection. We first evaluate the performance of the scheme when the intruder compromising N_i performs some bogus injection. In this case, the sink might possibly notice the attack once the aggregation protocol is complete, that is, when it decrypts the aggregated value. Therefore, the sink cannot prevent such attacks but can react against them by determining the origin of the attacks. Hence, when the sink notices such attacks due to some exaggerated values that would result from aggregation, it first contacts its children nodes and sends them the required decryption material (that is one-time) in order to let them discover the origin of the failure. This process is recursively run along the tree. Thus, the cost of discovering the compromised node is in the order of $log(N)$ where N is the number of sensors and the verification task is distributed to all nodes of the tree. The process of compromised nodes discovery is summarized in Table 4.

Protection against message losses. We now consider the case when there is a node or communication failure that imply some message loss: an error may occur during the decryption of the aggregated data. The same problem can happen when an intruder compromising a node shows a passive behavior. In this case, a node that did not receive any aggregated information from one of its children nodes, alerts nodes that are at most m distant from it about the identity of the misbehaving node. All nodes receiving this alert, will remove the keys that are related with the misbehaving node and proceed the aggregation protocol with the remaining keys. The alert messages only reach nodes that are m distant from the misbehaving node and thus have a local impact on the communication overhead.

In order to illustrate this recovery mechanism, we again refer to the WSN represented in Figure 1 and we assume that node N_{10} did not send its measurement to N_8. For the sake of simplicity, we again denote the one-time key resulting from $a_{i,j}$ and the actual $ctr_{i,j}$ by $k_{i,j}$. In this particular case, keys $k_{8,10}$ and $k_{4,10}$ should not be used during the aggregation protocol. Thus, N_8 sends an alert message with the identity of N_{10} to N_4. Since $m = 2$ and $N_4 = Parent(N_{10}, m)$, N_4 does not need to forward this alert message to its parents. Table 5 illustrates

Table 4. The discovery of compromised nodes

```
let l = 0;
at layer l, for each $N_i \in \mathcal{T}$
    verify(agg_value, expected_value)
    if OK then
        ACCEPT agg_value;
    else
        if Children($N_i$, 2) = ∅ then
            send_alert(identity(Children($N_i$)))
        else
            send (expected_value, keying_material) to Children($N_i$, 1);
```

the aggregation process for nodes that are on the path from N_{10} to the sink. While computing A_8, N_8 only includes V_8 that is encrypted with $k_{1,8}$. When N_4 receives A_8, and A_7, it does not use $k_{4,10}$ and suppresses the only encryption layer originating from node N_9 and finally adds an encryption layer with $k_{s,4}$. Once N_4 sends A_4 to N_1, there is no more modification in the aggregation process and N_1 will follow the additive aggregation protocol as defined in Table 2.

5.3 Performance Evaluation

In this section, we evaluate the performance of the scheme in terms of memory storage, computational cost and communication overhead. The computational cost and communication overhead have a direct impact on the battery usage.

First of all, the computational activity of each sensor for the encryption and decryption operations is only the sum and substraction operations modulo n. The encryption or decryption operations do not have an impact on the communication overhead. There is no additional information with respect to these two operations. The sink only receives messages from its children nodes and proceeds to the final step of aggregation.

Furthermore, thanks to the inherent key generation process provided by CTR, there is no additional overhead originating from the update of any sensor's keys.

The memory cost is related to the proposed key attribution algorithm. Sensors share one key with their mth parent node and one key with each of their mth child nodes. Furthermore, if a sensor is a leaf node of $\mathcal{T}$, this sensor shares one key with each of its kth parent with $1 \leq k \leq m$. Thus, the memory cost for each sensor equals to:

- $(|Children(N, m)| + 1)$ if $Children(N, m) \neq \emptyset$,
- $(|Children(N, k)| + 1)$ if $Children(N, k) \neq \emptyset$ and $Children(N, k + 1) = \emptyset$.

Table 5. Failure recovery of N_{10} in the path from N_{10} to S

Layer 3

Node N_8 Does not receive A_{10}
mark $k_{8,10}$ as invalid
Computes $A_8 = V_8 + k_{1,8}$
Sends A_8 and $failure\_alert(N_{10})$

Layer 2

Node N_4 Receives, A_7, A_8 and $failure\_alert(N_{10})$
mark $k_{4,10}$ as invalid
Aggregates $S_4 = A_7 + A_8$
Suppresses **one** layer $Sd_4 = A_7 + A_8 - k_{4,9}$
Computes $V_4 + k_{s,4}$
Adds a layer $A_4 = V_9 + V_8 + V_7 + V_4 + k_{1,7} + k_{1,8} + k_{s,4}$

Layer 1

Node N_1 Receives A_2, A_3 and A_4
Aggregates $S_1 = A_2 + A_3 + A_4$
Suppresses four layers $Sd_1 = A_2 + A_3 + A_4 - k_{1,5} - k_{1,6} - k_{1,7} - k_{1,8}$
Computes $V_1 + k_{s,1}$
Adds a layer $A_1 = \sum_{i=1}^{9} V_i + k_{s,2} + k_{s,3} + k_{s,4} + k_{s,1}$

Layer 0

Sink S: Receives A_1
Suppresses all layers $Sd_s = A_1 - k_{s,2} - k_{s,3} - k_{s,4} - k_{s,1}$

6   Related Work

In [3,9], authors propose to use homomorphic encryption schemes to allow secure data aggregation. They implement the Domingo-Ferrer encryption scheme [10] that is based on the computationally expensive discrete exponential technique. The feasibility of this scheme in the context of resource constrained sensor environment is analyzed in [11] and authors gave performance results on the Mica2 motes [12] and show that such measurements were quite reasonable.

In [2], authors propose a secure data aggregation scheme similar to ours that is based on an extension of the one-time pad encryption technique using additive operations modulo n. Even though our scheme seems to be more complex than the solution of [2] due to the use of CTR and multiple encryption layers, our scheme clearly imposes a lower communication overhead than the latter. In [2], each aggregate message is coupled with the list of nodes that failed to contribute to the aggregation because of node or communication failures. As opposed to [2], in our scheme each failure only needs to be reported during m hops from the location of the failure enroute to the sink. Thus, our scheme does not require the reporting of failures beyond the mth parent of the failure point in the tree. Moreover, the security of the additive encryption operation is based on the unique utilization of the encryption key. In order to update keys, [2] proposes to generate a key stream for each node using stream ciphers. This operation implies an additional cost in terms of computation that is higher than the one resulting from our scheme: Indeed, since in [2], sensors share keys only with the sink, each time that a sink receives an aggregated message, it first needs to compute all sensors' keys in order to decrypt the corresponding message where as in our scheme, the sink only needs to update keys that it shares with sensors that are located in the subtree of depth m rooted at the sink.

7   Conclusion

In this paper, we analyze the problem of confidentiality in secure data aggregation mechanisms for wireless sensor networks. We first define two specific confidentiality requirements: the sink should first ensure that sensors not participating to the aggregation mechanism do not access the content of the aggregated data (generic confidentiality); moreover, sensors participating to the aggregation mechanism should not access the already aggregated data without the authorization of the sink (end-to-end confidentiality). We show that the use of homomorphic encryption algorithms is essential for aggregation mechanisms and propose the use of an extension of CTR encryption schemes. In order to protect aggregation mechanisms against node compromise, we first define a key attribution algorithm whereby sensors store several keys with respect to their location in the tree. We then describe a layered secure aggregation mechanism where sensors basically add and suppress some encryption layers with respect to their keying material. We show that this new framework provides both generic and end-to-end confidentiality and is robust against bogus message injections and message losses.

Future work should focus on investigating the problem of key pre-distribution mechanism [13] related to the key attribution algorithm that should be self-organized and efficient. We should also investigate on new solutions that prevent bogus injection rather than minimizing the impact of such attacks.

References

1. Perrig, A., Stankovic, J., Wagner, D.: Security in wireless sensor networks. Communications of the ACM **47** (2004) 53–57
2. Castellucia, C., Mykletun, E., Tsudik, G.: Efficient aggregation of encrypted data in wireless sensor networks. In: Proceedings of the 2nd Annual International Conference on Mobile and Ubiquitous Systems, Mobiquitous, San Diego, CA (2005)
3. Girao, J., Westhoff, D., Schneider, M.: CDA:Concealed Data Aggregation in Wireless Sensor Networks. In: Proceedings of ACM WiSe'04. (2004)
4. Bellare, M., Desai, A., Jokipii, E., Rogaway, P.: A concrete security treatment of symmetric encryption. In: IEEE Symposium on Foundations of Computer Science. (1997) 394–403

5. Pannetrat, A., Molva, R.: Multiple layer encryption for multicast groups. In: The proceedings of CMS'02, Portoroz, Slovenia (2002)
6. of Standards, N.I., Technology: Advanced Encryption Standard (2001)
7. Menezes, A., van Oorschot, P.C., Vanstone, S.A.: Handbook of Applied Cryptography. CRC Press (1996)
8. Bellare, M., Boldyreva, A., Micali, S.: Public-key encryption in a multiuser setting: Security proofs and improvements. In: Eurocrypt 2000. Volume LNCS 1807., Springer Verlag (2000) 259–274.
9. Girao, J., Westhoff, D., Schneider, M.: CDA: Concealed data aggregation for reverse multicast traffic in wireless sensor networks. In: Proceedings of IEEE ICC'05, Korea (2005)
10. Domingo-Ferrer, J.: A provably secure additive and multiplicative privacy homomorphism. In: Proceedings of the Information Security Conference, LNCS2433. (2002)
11. Girao, J., Westhoff, D.: Concealed data aggregation in WSNs (demo). In: EWSN, Switzerland (2006)
12. Crossbow products: (2004)
    http://www.xbow.com/Products/WirelessSensorNetworks.htm.
13. Eschenauer, L., Gligor, V.: A key-management scheme for distributed sensor networks. In: Proceedings of the ACM CCS'02, Washington D.C. (2002)

RIDA: A Robust Information-Driven Data Compression Architecture for Irregular Wireless Sensor Networks

Thanh Dang, Nirupama Bulusu, and Wu-chi Feng

Department of Computer Science,
Portland State University,
PO Box 751, Portland, OR, USA
{dangtx,nbulusu,wuchi}@cs.pdx.edu

Abstract. In this paper, we propose and evaluate RIDA, a novel information-driven architecture for distributed data compression in a sensor network, allowing it to conserve energy and bandwidth and potentially enabling high-rate data sampling. The key idea is to determine the data correlation among a group of sensors based on the value of the data itself to significantly improve compression. Hence, this approach moves beyond traditional data compression schemes which rely only on spatial and temporal data correlation. A logical mapping, which assigns indices to nodes based on the data content, enables simple implementation, on nodes, of data transformation without any other information. The logical mapping approach also adapts particularly well to irregular sensor network topologies. We evaluate our architecture with both Discrete Cosine Transform (DCT) and Discrete Wavelet Transform (DWT) on publicly available real-world data sets. Our experiments on both simulation and real data show that 30% of energy and 80-95% of the bandwidth can be saved for typical multi-hop data networks. Moreover, the original data can be retrieved after decompression with a low error of about 3%. Furthermore, we also propose a mechanism to detect and classify missing or faulty nodes, showing accuracy and recall of 95% when half of the nodes in the network are missing or faulty.

Keywords: Distributed data compression, Error detection, Wavelet analysis, DCT analysis, Sensor networks, Irregular network.

1   Introduction

With the continued development of sensor networking hardware, the ability to deploy large numbers of sensors is becoming possible. Typically, the sensor networks are deployed to gather environmental information over a period of time with the sensors working together to forward data to a central data sink. One of the main challenges with such sensor networking technologies is the need to minimize wireless packet transmissions in order to save power.

There are several basic ways to minimize the amount of traffic generated by the sensor network. Aggregation techniques such as TinyDB [1]and TAG [2] process

K. Langendoen and T. Voigt (Eds.): EWSN 2007, LNCS 4373, pp. 133–149, 2007.

and consume the collected data within the sensor network, forwarding only a small subset of the data to the sink. Query-based techniques such as directed diffusion aim to filter the data within the network to only what the application requires. Low-level networking techniques have been proposed in order to help route data within the sensor network with the hope of minimizing duplicated packets and minimizing the number of hops needed to deliver the data. Finally, data compression techniques are emerging for such sensor networks [3] [4] [5] [6] [7] [8].

Compression can be applied to a single data stream being generated by a single sensor [9]. The advantage of this approach is that the sensor will typically be generating similar data over time. The drawback, however, is that if the data from a single sensor is lost, then a significant amount of data may be lost. An alternative approach is to cluster the sensors together and compress the data across the sensors one snapshot at a time. The main advantage of this approach is that it is more resilient to transmission errors. At the same time, however, all the data needs to be transmitted at least once in order to be collected.

Correlation of data among sensors is determined not only by spatio-temporal proximity, but other factors as well. Building on this observation, we propose a *cluster-based* and *information-driven* architecture for a wide range of compression algorithms for scalar sensor data for a popular class of network of sensors. The key contributions of this paper are as follows.

- The exploration beyond spatial and temporal correlation of data in sensor networks. The key idea here is that correlation of the data is based on the value of the data itself rather than other factors, which we will show later are irrelevant in some cases.
- The information-driven architecture (RIDA) with a logical mapping framework for various compression and analysis algorithms which builds on the above observation. In this approach, data reported by sensors is observed over a short period of time. After that, the pattern of the data can be used to logically assign sensors with indices such that the correlation of data is utilized. Depending on the underlying compression algorithm, an appropriate logical assignment can be used.
- The design, implementation, and evaluation of different compression algorithms (1D and 2D, DCT-based and wavelet-based) on real sensor data.
- A resiliency mechanism in RIDA for missing and faulty nodes in sensor networks. We address a real practical problem in wireless sensor networks where nodes are frequently missing or faulty.

In the next section, we will review related work. Section 3 will point out some key observations about correlation of sensor readings that drive the design of our architecture. Section 4 will describe the proposed information-driven architecture for compression algorithms for sensor networking, including our proposed resiliency mechanism. Section 5 will describe the experiments that we conducted in order to show the efficiency of our approach. We discuss the limitation of our approach and future work, and conclude in section 6.

2   Related Work

In this section, we review related work on data compression with emphasis on data compression in sensor networks.

2.1   Data Compression

There are two main categories of data compression – *lossless* and *lossy* data compression. Lossless compression algorithms usually generate a statistical model of the data and map the data to bit strings based on the generated model. Meanwhile in lossy compression, data is often transformed into a new space using appropriate basis functions. In the new space, the data information or signal energy is usually concentrated in a few coefficients. Hence, compression can be achieved after quantization and entropy coding. For example, discrete fourier transform (DFT), discrete cosine transform (DCT), and discrete wavelet transform (DWT) are used extensively in most image compression applications (e.g. JPEG,JPEG2000). Audio and video compression also use predictive codecs, where previously decoded data is used to predict the current data and only the difference between the predicted and real data is encoded.

For sensor networks, the sensed data of the environment can also be modeled as an image of a temperature, humidity or light map and a standard image compression technique may be subsequently applied. However, sensor networks have some distinct features such as limited computation, distributed processing, degree of correlation and faulty readings, motivating new compression architectures and techniques tailored to meet their requirements. We briefly review recent work in the next section.

2.2   Data Compression in Wireless Sensor Networks

In Distributed Source Coding Using Syndromes (DISCUS), Pradhan *et al* [6] proposed a framework for distributed compression using joint source and channel coding. This approach minimizes the amount of inter-node communication for compression using both a quantized source and correlated side information within each individual node. While it shows an interesting theoretical approach, the choice of the correlated side information is essential to the performance of the algorithm and normally not well known in practice. Unlike this work, we have clearly verified our approach using real data report from sensors at Intel Research Lab at Berkeley.

Based on the recent result of Candes and Tao on near optimal signal recovery from random projections [10], Rabat *et al.* [7][8] propose a distributed matched source-channel communication architecture and reconstruction method from noisy random projections. A similar approach can be found in [8] which uses a gossip communication scheme. Although it is claimed to be universal, there is a trade-off between power-distortion-latency. In addition, they do not consider the correlation of the data itself.

Several methods have been proposed to use wavelets and their variants in analyzing and compressing the sensed data [11] [12][13][14]. Ganesan's DIMEN-SIONS [11] was one of the first systems addressing multi-resolution data access and spatio-temporal pattern mining in a sensor network. In DIMEN-SIONS, nodes are partitioned into different clusters and organized in a multi-level hierarchy. Within each cluster, the cluster head performs a two dimensional wavelet transform and stores the coefficient locally. These coefficients are in turn passed to the next level in the hierarchy for wavelet transform at a coarser resolution. While DIMENSIONS shows interesting results, it makes two main assumptions that we do not: (i) nodes are distributed in a regular grid and (ii) cluster heads can always communicate with their parents. Wagner[13][14] proposed an architecture for distributed wavelet analysis that removes the assumption about the regularity of the grid. In addition, an algorithm for performing the wavelet transform by tracing through the path in the minimum spanning tree and performing the wavelet filter along the path is proposed in [12]. It minimizes inter-node communication by transmitting partial coefficients forward and updating future sensors until the full coefficients are computed. It implicitly assumes that the path will be long enough in order to apply wavelet analysis effectively. Furthermore, it is not clear how to choose an optimal path for compression and the spatial correlation is not fully explored.

Few other works in distributed audio and video compression in wireless sensor networks can be found at [15][16][5]. Other approaches [17][18] try to solve multiple goals such as routing, aggregation, indexing and storage, and energy balancing with compression.

Our approach relies only on the sensing data itself. Therefore it does not make any assumptions about regularity of the network [11] or use any further information such as geographical location [13][14] or routing path [12]. In addition, it guarantees the optimal performance of compression algorithms instead of being universal [10][7][8]. We have also implemented and evaluated our architecture using real sensor data to verify that it works within typical sensor environments. Finally we proposed a resiliency mechanism to ensure a robust compression architecture in sensor networks.

3   Understanding Data Correlation

One of the main challenges of transformed data compression is to explore the correlation of data in time, space, or frequency domains. Most existing approaches try to organize sensors into groups based on spatial relationships in order to obtain some correlation of the readings. However, when we observed the readings over time of 54 sensors deployed at Intel Lab at Berkeley, we found out that (i) Sensors in similar environmental conditions that are not necessarily spatially correlated can report correlated data, (ii) Correlation of data may be independent from external factors such as sensor location and environmental conditions. To illustrate these points, consider the spatial graph of the light sensor readings at night over time as shown in Fig. 1. As you can see, dark areas indicate high light intensity. Hence, sensors nearby opened windows report high readings due to the external light. These readings should be similar to those sensors nearby light sources inside the building. Hence, correlation exists due to the similarity

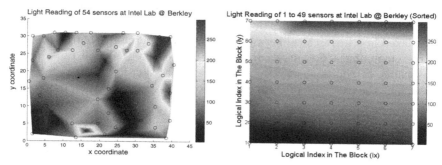

Fig. 1. Nodes nearby open windows and under light bulbs reporting similar reading

of environmental factors as well as the sources. Spatial correlation can be seen as one specific case of this because nearby nodes can have similar condition. The converse, however, is not always true. In addition, Fig. 2 plots voltage readings of sensors. Intuitively, nodes with similar power level should be similar over time regardless of external environmental and spatial factors.

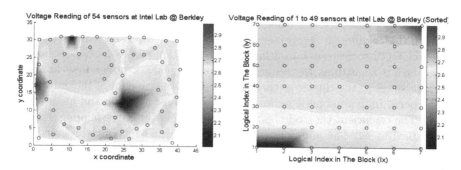

Fig. 2. Correlation of voltage readings is independent of external factors

From these findings, we believe that in order to explore the correlation of data, we should look at the information contained in the data itself rather than considering only attribute meta-data such as location and time. Once the underlying pattern of the data is found, we can assign nodes with appropriate logical indices to ensure the best performance of compression algorithms. The following section describes the information-driven architecture in detail.

4   RIDA: Robust Information-Driven Architecture

4.1   Key Assumptions

We are aware that our approach is only suitable for some types of sensor networks, which are characterized by the following assumptions. The network is fixed and can be partitioned into clusters. We also assume that the communication between any two nodes in a cluster takes one hop. This assumption can be relaxed in a hierarchical network topology. Furthermore, significant changes in the environment do not occur at high frequency eg. several times a day is reasonable. In addition, we only consider compression for scalar data. Finally, we assume the existence of cluster formation and synchronization protocols.

4.2   Overview

The system architecture consists of three main components; *information-driven logical mapping, resiliency mechanism*, and *compression algorithms*. In information-driven logical mapping, nodes within a cluster exchange their readings over a short period of time. During this period, each node learns the pattern of data of the whole cluster. A information-based logical mapping is designed allowing nodes to choose logical indices for themselves. The intuition is that nodes with correlated data should have logical indices near each other. Several mapping schemes will be discussed in more detail later.

The resiliency component involves detecting, isolating, and classifying faulty and missing nodes during the compression and decompression steps. The detail of this mechanism will be discussed in section 4.5. After the mapping is done, the data can be processed using logical indices. The compression algorithms block includes different compression techniques, which can be easily adapted to the architecture. Section 4.4 outlines the integration of two most popular data compression algorithms to the architecture. In general, nodes first broadcast their readings to the cluster so that each node has a snapshot of the data within each epoch. Individual node performs the data transformation and quantization itself. The coefficient the node has is the one having the corresponding index as the logical index. The node only sends its coefficient back to the server if it is non zero. At the sink or back-end server, original data can be reconstructed by decompression from the nonzero coefficients, classification of the missing data, and remapping to physical map of nodes.

4.3   Information-Driven Logical Mapping

The logical mapping gives nodes indices that can be used for data manipulation. This powerful idea keeps the architecture independent from other information such as nodes' locations while still preserving the advantages, such as data correlation, of having that information. The mapping can be formalized as follows.

$$M : (N, N^n) \to L$$
$$M(d(s), D) = l$$

Where: L is the logical index space. N is the natural set representing the value of sensor data. M notates the mapping from a sensor s to a logical index l such as (x, y) in 2D mapping. It uses only the value of the sensor data $d(s)$ and values

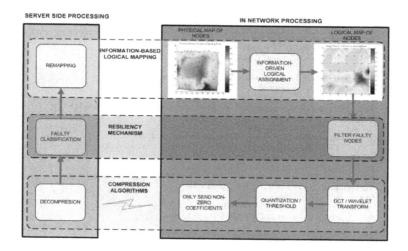

Fig. 3. Detailed System Architecture

of other sensors in the cluster D to determine l. The mapping can be application and algorithm specific. As a first step, we simply sort the data and index the nodes in sequence based on the order of the sorted data.

More specifically, the mapping within a cluster has the following steps. The cluster head broadcasts a *begin_mapping* message. Nodes within the cluster send their sensing data to the cluster head. The cluster head receives data from sensors for a short period of time. It then analyses the pattern of the data values and does the mapping accordingly. For example, in 1D sorted mapping, the cluster head sorts all the data values and sensor ids in ascending order and starts assigning indices sequentially. Once this step is done, the cluster head broadcasts the map and waits for all acknowledgements before sending *end_mapping*, which turns sensors into normal sensing mode.

4.4   Data Transformation

Various algorithms can be easily integrated with the architecture. We have adapted the discrete cosine transform, as well as the first and second generations (lifting scheme) of wavelet transform. Again, depending on the underlying compression algorithm, the logical mapping assigns indices to nodes appropriately. This ensures the flexibility of the architecture for a wide range of applications. In addition, since each node only needs to calculate the coefficient corresponding to its index, it does only the necessary operations. For example, in 2D-DCT, a node only multiplies the corresponding row and column in the block instead of doing a matrix calculation for the whole block. Likewise, in DWT, a node with detail coefficient only needs to run the low pass filter with readings of logically nearby neighbors. Fig. 4 shows an example of distributed DCT.

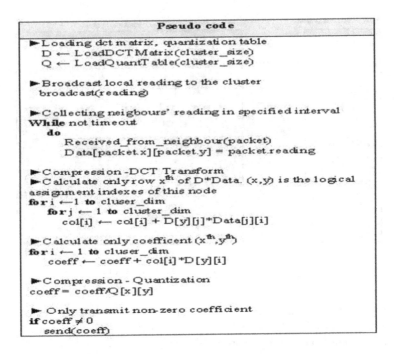

Fig. 4. Pseudo-Code For 2D-DCT

4.5 Error Detection and Classification

Reliability of data is of paramount importance because network nodes fail frequently. Even when nodes have not failed, their operations are typically unstable. Fig. 5 shows the reading history of 54 sensors in a controlled environment. As observed, 53 out of 54 nodes are working. However, the number of nodes reporting data is always around 50% within each epoch. Better design of routing protocols could help increase this rate, but we still have to address the problem of actual faulty and missing nodes. This motivates us to design a simple mechanism to distinguish between missing data and real data at the sink.

All the nonzero data will be projected to an interval (for example [128,255]). The data of different types have different ranges. Although the data value is obtained from the same 10-bit ADC, the ranges of the data are different. Therefore the projection will unify the way we drop coefficients through quantization or thresholding. Missing readings will be set to zero. Hence, we have a set of data from [128,255] for normal data and 0 for missing data of all different scalar types like temperature, humidity, light and voltage. These zero values would result in low values in the reconstructed data. Hence, we can use a threshold to classify them. The threshold we used is 64 which has been shown to classify correctly most of the time. Obviously, there is an inherent trade-off in the ability to detect missing readings and the decompression error.

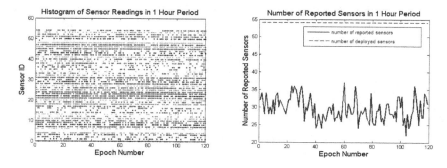

Fig. 5. Reading history over one hour period

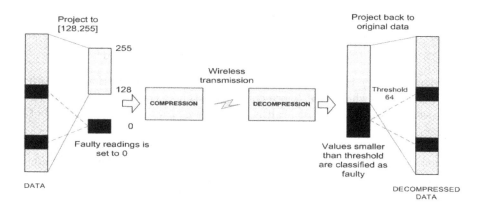

Fig. 6. Resiliency Mechanism

5 Experimental Design and Analysis

This section describes how the experiments are setup to evaluate the architecture and discusses the results.

5.1 Goals and Metrics

The goals of the experiments in this section are four-fold.

- To understand how flexibly the information-driven architecture can adapt to different underlying algorithms, specifically compression algorithms.
- To understand how different compression algorithms perform on real sensor data with different logical mapping schemes.
- To understand how robust the architecture is to missing sensor data and failures using our proposed resiliency mechanism.
- To understand how much energy and bandwidth is saved in a typical multi hop network using our approach.

To evaluate the first goal, we will show that different compression algorithms such as DCT and DWT can be made distributed and integrated with the architecture. The system only needs to change the logical mapping scheme to apply the underlying algorithms.

The second goal is analyzed by observing the tradeoff between compression ratio and normalized mean squared error (MSE) of the compression algorithms using different mapping schemes. We used two main compression algorithms, DCT and DWT, and two simple mapping schemes, one dimensional ordered and two dimensional ordered mappings. Ideally, we aim for a configuration that results in high compression ratios with low normalized MSE.

To evaluate the third goal, we consider the *accuracy* and *recall* of the classification step against the number of faulty nodes. They can be calculated as:

$$accuracy = \frac{TP+TN}{total number of nodes}$$
$$recall = \frac{TP}{total number of healthy nodes}$$

where:

- *TP-True Positive* : Number of correctly classified healthy nodes
- *TN-True Negative* : Number of correctly classified faulty nodes

Therefore *accuracy* indicates how well the system can correctly classify healthy and faulty nodes, while *recall* represents the portion of correctly classified nodes in the set of nodes classified as healthy. Ideally, we wish to see the values of both accuracy and recall as close to 100% as possible.

Finally, we evaluated the energy consumption using PowerTOSSIM. The compression algorithm is implemented for the MicaZ platform and simulated in PowerTOSSIM. The energy consumption can be observed separately by measuring CPU operations and RF transmission. In order to understand how much energy is saved by doing compression in multihop networks, we use the following benchmark.

$$c_b = n(t_x + t_r)h$$
$$c_c = n(t_x + t_r + d) + n'h(t_r + t_x)$$

Where

c_b is the cost to transmit raw data back to the server.

c_c is the cost to transmit data back to the server using compression.

n is the cluster size. In the case of missing sensors, n is the number of healthy nodes.

h is the average hop count.

t_r, t_x are transmitting and receiving power for one package.

d is the cost to compress the data.

n' is the number of non-zero coefficients. n/n' is approximately 20:1 for jpeg.

The energy saving is:

$$r_h = \frac{c_b - c_c}{c_b} = \frac{n(t_x + t_r)h - n(t_x + t_r + d) - n'h(t_r + t_x)}{n(t_x + t_r)h} \qquad (1)$$

In the above equations, we do not consider the cost for mapping. However, as we have assumed previously that the frequency of changes in the environment is low, the mapping cost overall is negligible in comparison to the cost of collecting data. In addition, we only consider energy saving for one cluster because the percentage of energy saving in a fixed diameter network is independent of the number of clusters and determined by the hop count. Finally, we also assume there is no transmission loss for compressed data. However, one can expect that because less data is transmitted in the network, the transmission loss is smaller. Hence, in real world applications, we expect to see slightly higher error when loss in transmitting compressed data occurs.

5.2   Experimental Design

The experiments are designed based on the data collected from 54 sensors between February 28th and April 5th, 2004, which has been made available by Intel Berkeley Research Lab [19]. As discussed in the previous section, the number of sensors reporting data within each epoch is only around 50%. Hence, we decided to design two sets of experiments with two sets of data respectively.

The purpose of the first experiment set is to evaluate how different compression algorithms such as DCT and DWT perform on the real data. It also analyzes different to the mapping schemes such as 1D versus 2D and how robust the system is to the number of missing nodes. The raw data set has its missing values filled in via interpolation to create a complete data set. Thus, it creates an ideal sensor network data set, where every node reports readings within each epoch. In order to evaluate how robust the system is against node failures, we randomly insert faulty readings as zero values and perform the classification during the reconstruction phase.

The second set of experiments is to evaluate our approach on the real raw data without any interpolation. This set of data, as you can see from Fig. 5, has about 50% of its readings missing within each epoch. However, our experiments show that the system still achieves a reasonable compression ratio with low error and high detection rate.

5.3   Results and Analysis

Logical Mapping Schemes. This section discusses several findings on different logical mapping schemes. Basically, there are two logical mapping schemes, 1D content-based and 2D content based mappings, where the data is sorted and indices are assigned based on the order of the data values reported by the sensors. These two mappings are evaluated against two location-based mappings where indices are assigned based on geographical relationships. Nodes which are close together have nearby indices in the block. As we can see in Fig. 7, DCT compression using information-based mappings outperforms those using location-based mappings. With the same compression ratio of 20:1, DCT compression using information-based mappings has a normalized MSE 50% less than location-based mappings. In addition, the 1D transform also gives lower errors in comparison to 2D transform. The normalized MSE is reduced by 30% if we

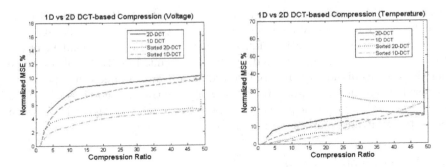

Fig. 7. Location-based mapping versus Content-based mapping and 1D versus 2D Transform

use information-based mappings for voltage. The graph for temperature shows a transition when the compression ratio reaches 25. This is reasonable, because the data set has 49 nodes, so ideally a compression of lower than 25:1 should be considered. Compression ratios of over 25 mean that only one coefficient is left. Therefore, it would be pointless to compare those. This result is even clearer with wavelet transform. One limitation of the 2D transform is that the number of nodes within a cluster must be a square number. Clustering formation is a complex research area and so far no prior work has attempted to constrain the number of nodes in a cluster. In addition, due to the limit on number of nodes within a cluster, we would recommend compression should use 1D mappings.

DCT-based and Wavelet-based Compression. The wavelet-based compression in general shows much lower error that DCT-based compression. While the DCT-based approach shows an error of around 9%, the Wavelet-based approach has an error of only 3%, which is 67% less. However, due to the limit on the length of the data, wavelets with a high number of coefficients can start to diverge much sooner although they have a lower error with the same small compression ratio.

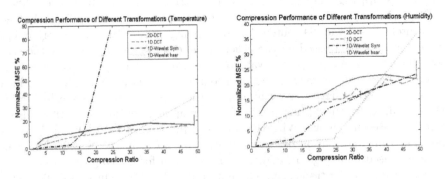

Fig. 8. DCT-based vs Wavelet-based Compression

Error Detection and Classification. By the term faulty node, we mean to describe a node that sends odd data or no data at all. This is similar to a missing node, where the node is missing and does not send any data. Hence, we use the term faulty for both. Faulty data is randomly inserted into the data set before compression. The non-zero data is scaled to the [128,255] interval and we use a threshold of 64 to classify faulty data in both cases. When the number

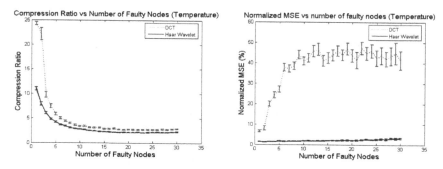

Fig. 9. Compression Performance on Temperature Readings

of faulty nodes increases from 1 to 30, DCT-based compression error increased dramatically from 6% to 45%. But it becomes stable around 45% when the number of faulty nodes reaches above 10. Likewise, the error in wavelet-based approach only slightly increases from 2% to 4%. The compression ratio also decreases gradually from 10:1 to 3:1. This is reasonable because the nature of DCT-based transform is suitable for a smooth signal whereas Wavelet-based transform is more suitable with piecewise constant data. To our surprise, both

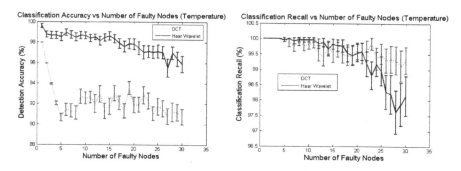

Fig. 10. Classification Accuracy and Recall on Temperature Readings

DCT and Wavelet have very high accuracy and recall rates even when more than half the network is faulty. Haar wavelets can maintain a performance of up to 97% for both accuracy and recall. DCT is slightly lower but, still above 90% for accuracy and 97% for recall. Both of these values decrease gradually as the number of faulty nodes in the network increases. Similar results can be seen for other types of data such as humidity and voltage.

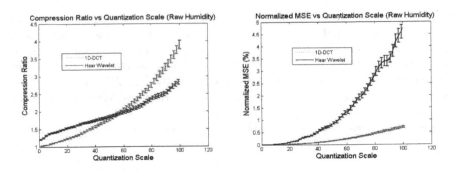

Fig. 11. Compression Performance on Raw Humidity Readings

Performance on Raw Data. The data was collected using TinyDB, which queries data among sensors at the same time. However, collected data has a latency and dropping rate. One way to improve it is to design better routing and data aggregation protocols. However, these are still in development. Hence, we applied our system to this real set of data. Surprisingly, we still get the desired results. A compression ratio of 3:1 can be achieved for both DCT and Wavelet with an error less than 5% as shown in Fig. 11. Moreover, around 90% of nodes are still correctly classified and the recall rate is as high as 98%. In both cases, wavelet performs 3% better than DCT as shown in Fig. 12.

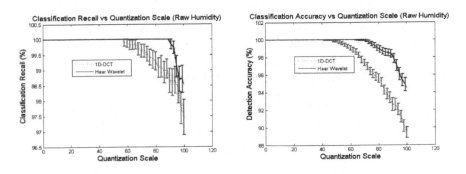

Fig. 12. Classification Accuracy and Recall on Raw Humidity Readings

Energy Consumption. As mentioned at the beginning of the paper, one main purpose of data compression is to conserve energy and bandwidth. We have shown how our system can enable various compression algorithms and save a large amount of bandwidth by logically processing the data and sending only a few non-zero coefficients. We also state that the CPU operations consume much less energy than RF transmission. Indeed, Fig. 13 shows that the total energy consumed by the CPU operations including all normal activities and DCT transform is still only 2.5 times less than that of one RF transmission within each epoch. Hence, for multihop networks where the number of RF retransmissions

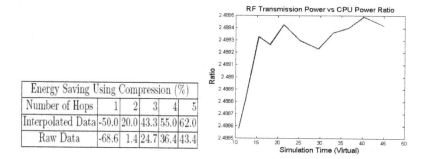

Energy Saving Using Compression (%)				
Number of Hops	1	2	3	4	5
Interpolated Data	-50.0	20.0	43.3	55.0	62.0
Raw Data	-68.6	1.4	24.7	36.4	43.4

Fig. 13. Energy consumption of RF vs CPU

is several times higher, our approach can be expected to save not only a large amount of bandwidth but also a significant amount of energy. Applying Eq. 1, we can know how much energy is saved for multihop networks as shown in Fig. 13. We have seen that different compression algorithms can be easily adapted to our architecture. Moreover, with the introduction of logical mapping, optimal performance can be simply tuned for different applications. In general, due to the limit on the number of nodes within a cluster, 1D mapping and transformation normally gives better performance than 2D mapping and transformation. In addition, Wavelet-based compression gives a lower error bound than DCT-based compression. It is surprising that the wavelet lifting scheme did not perform as well as expected. One of the reasons may once again be the limited length of the signal or the number of nodes within a cluster, correspondingly. Another surprise was that with our resiliency mechanism, the compression system becomes very robust even when half of the cluster is missing. Finally, although DCT transform and wavelet transform require an average amount of work load for Micaz class sensors, we still see that the energy saved by reducing the number of RF transmissions to CPU operations is 2.5. For an average 3-hop network, the energy can be saved by 30%. This ratio will be much higher in multihop networks where the number of RF retransmissions is proportional to the number of hops.

6   Conclusion and Future Work

In conclusion, we have presented RIDA, a novel distributed information-driven architecture for data compression for irregular sensor networks. The key idea is to assign the sensor nodes with logical indices based on the content of the data they report in order to optimally explore the correlation of the sensor data. This approach moves beyond conventional approaches, which have explored how to improve data compression by only exploiting spatial and temporal correlation. We have implemented and evaluated various popular data compression techniques such as DCT-based, Wavelet-based to the architecture. In addition, we also presented a simple method for detecting and classifying faulty nodes. The experimental results on real data show that our architecture can enable high compression ratios, low error and high robustness to faults.

Our current approach is limited to scalar data for environmental monitoring with low changing frequency. We also rely on the clustering structure and assume that the network is fixed. In the future, we would like to investigate further how this approach can be extended to meet the requirements for high rate data compression such as audio and images. Moreover, we would like to consider how it can be adapted to a network of mobile sensors. In addition, we would like to further study several factors that affect compression algorithms such as cluster size, quantization schemes, projection ranges and energy balancing as well as the tradeoff between compression and fault tolerance in sensor networks.

Acknowledgements

The research described in this paper was supported by National Science Foundation grants NSF 05-14818 and 01-21475.

References

1. Madden, S., J.Franklin, M., Hellerstein, J., Hong, W.: Tinydb: An acquisitional query processing system for sensor networks. ACM Trans. Database Syst. **30**(1) (2005) 122–173
2. Madden, S., Franklin, M.J., Hellerstein, J.M., Hong, W.: Tag: A tiny aggregation service for ad-hoc sensor networks. In: OSDI. (2002)
3. Donoho, D.L.: Compressed sensing. In: IEEE Transactions on Information Theory. Volume 52. (2006) 1289–1306
4. Duarte, M.F., Wakin, M.B., Baron, D., Baraniuk, R.G.: Universal distributed sensing via random projections. In: Proceedings of IPSN 2006, Nashville, Tennessee, USA, April 19-21, 2006. (2006) 177–185
5. Gehrig, N., Dragotti, P.L.: Distributed sampling and compression of scenes with finite rate of innovation in camera sensor networks. In: Proceedings of Data Compression Conference, Snowbird, Utah (2006) 83–92
6. Pradhan, S.S., Kusuma, J., Ramchandran, K.: Distributed compression in a dense micro-sensor network. In: IEEE Signal Processing. Volume 19. (2002) 51–60
7. Rabbat, M., Haupt, J., Singh, A., Nowak, R.D.: Decentralized compression and predistribution via randomized gossiping. In: Proceedings of IPSN 2006, Nashville, Tennessee, USA, April 19-21, 2006. (2006) 51–59
8. Bajwa, W.U.Z., Haupt, J., Sayeed, A.M., Nowak, R.D.: Compressive wireless sensing. In: Proceedings of IPSN 2006, Nashville, Tennessee, USA, April 19-21, 2006. (2006) 134–142
9. Sadler, C.M., Martonosi, M.: Data compression algorithms for energy-constrained devices in delay tolerant networks. In: Proccedings of ACM Sensys, Boulder, Colorado (2006)
10. Candes, E., Tao, T.: Near optimal signal recovery from random projections: universal encoding stratergies? In: preprint. (2004)
11. Ganesan, D., Estrin, D., Heidemann, J.: Dimensions: Why do we need a new data handling architecture for sensor networks. (2002)

12. Ciancio, A., Ortega, A.: A distributed wavelet compression algorithm for wireless multihop sensor networks using lifting. In: Proceedings of ICASSP, (Philadelphia, PA)
13. Wagner, R., Choi, H., Baraniuk, R., Delouille, V.: Distributed Wavelet Transform for Irregular Sensor Network Grids. In: IEEE Workshop on Statistical Signal Processing (SSP), Bordeaux, France (2005)
14. Wagner, R.S., Baraniuk, R.G., Du, S., Johnson, D.B., Cohen, A.: An architecture for distributed wavelet analysis and processing in sensor networks. In: Proceedings of IPSN 2006, Nashville, Tennessee, USA, April 19-21, 2006. (2006) 243–250
15. Roy, O., Vetterli, M.: Distributed Compression in Acoustic Sensor Networks Using Oversampled A/D Conversion. In: IEEE International Conference on Acoustic, Speech and Signal Processing (ICASSP). Volume 4. (2006) 165–168
16. Gehrig, N., Dragotti, P.L.: Distributed compression in camera sensor networks. In: Proceeding of MMSP, Siena, Italy (2004)
17. A, S.: Routing and data compression in sensor networks: Stochastic models for sensor data that guarantee scalability. In: Proccedings of ISIT2003, Yokohama, Japan (2003)
18. Petrovic, D., Shah, R.C., Ramchandran, K., Rabaey, J.: Data funneling: routing with aggregation and compression for wireless sensor networks. In: Proceedings of SNPA 2003, Seattle, WA (2003) 156–162
19. Lab, I.B.R.: (http://db.lcs.mit.edu/labdata/labdata.html)

Loss Tomography in Wireless Sensor Network Using Gibbs Sampling

Yongjun Li, Wandong Cai, Guangli Tian, and Wei Wang

School of Computer Science, Northwestern Polytechnical University,
Xi'an 710072, P.R. China
liyongjunxa@hotmail.com

Abstract. The internal link performance inference has become an increasingly important issue in operating and evaluating a sensor network. Since it is usually impractical to directly monitor each node or link in the wireless sensor network, we consider the problem of inferring the internal link loss characteristics from passive end-to-end measurement in this paper. Specifically, the link loss performance inference based on the data aggregation is considered. Under the assumptions that the link losses are mutually independent, we formulate the problem of link loss estimation as a Bayesian inference problem and propose a Markov Chain Monte Carlo algorithm to solve it. Through the simulation, we can safely reach the conclusion that the internal link loss rate can be inferred accurately, comparable to the sampled internal link loss rate, and the simulation also shows that the proposed algorithm scales well according to the sensor network size.

1 Introduction

Recent technological advances have made the development of low cost sensor nodes possible, and this allows the deployment of the large-scale sensor network to be feasible. The accurate network performance plays an important role in the successful design, deployment and management of sensor networks. However, the inherent stringent bandwidth and energy constraints of sensors create challenging problems in the network performance measurement. It is usually impractical to collect sensor network performance statistical data from each sensor node and process it at the sink node.

Motivated by the needs of accurate sensor network performance measurement and the inherent constraint of sensor network, in this paper, we concentrate on the problem of efficiently estimating the internal link loss rate from the passive end-to-end measurement. Particularly, we attempt to estimate the internal link loss rate based on the data aggregation communication paradigm. To determine the loss performance from network edge measurement, a probability model is normally selected to describe the loss characteristic of a link with some or all parameters undetermined. Network tomography is a promising approach proposed in recently years, which investigates the methods and methodologies to identify those parameters from end-to-end measurements.

K. Langendoen and T. Voigt (Eds.): EWSN 2007, LNCS 4373, pp. 150–162, 2007.
© Springer-Verlag Berlin Heidelberg 2007

In this paper, we use the Bayesian inference problem to formulate the sensor network loss inference problem and use the Gibbs Sampling to find out link-level characteristics. The Bayesian network is an active research area by itself that has been producing various methods to overcome the limitation of classical maximum likelihood estimator (MLE), such as sparse data and overfitting. In addition, many stochastic approximation methods, e.g. Markov Chain Monte Carlo (MCMC) and bound and collapse, have been developed for fast convergence, which makes it a competitor to classic MLE. The Gibbs Sampling is a technique for generating Markov Chain whose values converge to the target distribution, without having to calculate the density. Most of applications of the Gibbs Sampling have been in Bayesian models. Recent research makes the Bayesian network an ideal method to systematically discover hidden or missing information. Thus, using the data collected from data aggregation communication paradigm, the Bayesian Network can infer link-level characteristic. [3]

We used the NS2 to simulate a sensor network based on data aggregation communication paradigm. In the process of data aggregation, a subset of nodes in the sensor network attempt to forward the sensor data they have collected to a sink node via a reverse data aggregation tree. Before a node sends its data to the next node in the path to the sink, it waits to receive data from its entire child nodes in the reverse data aggregation tree or until a specified period of time has elapsed. The node then aggregates its own data with the data it has received from its child nodes, and forwards this aggregated data to the sink via the aggregation tree. Information about which nodes' data is present in the aggregated data must also be sent to the sink. By collecting the arrivals of the aggregated data and using the Bayesian network to infer the link loss rate, we found that the inferred results was very close to the true values. This reveals the feasibility and accuracy of our proposed approach.

The rest of this paper is organized as follows. In Section 2, we focus on the related work. The data aggregation tree model and the loss model are described in Section 3. We then introduce the proposed loss inference in section 4 that cover the details of our proposed algorithm. The simulation result inferred by the proposed inference approach is discussed in Section 5. Section 6 concludes the paper.

2   Related Work

There has been much research in the field of network tomography for the wired network. A summary of this research is provided in [1]. Zhu et al [2] proposed an internal link loss inference method for wired network based on Bayesian Network, and use Expectation-Maximization (EM) algorithm to solve it. The simulation shows the feasibility and accuracy of this approach. Dong Guo et al [3][4] also proposed a Bayesian inference of wired network loss. The problems of the link loss inference in a wired network based on end-to-end measurements were formulate as Bayesian inference problems and develop several Markov Chain

Monte Carlo algorithms to solve them. Using this approach can obtain good agreements between the theoretical results and the inferred results.

There has also been much research in the dissemination and propagation of data in wireless sensor networks. The reader is referred to [5] and [6] for discussions of some of the dissemination and propagation techniques proposed. However, there has been little research in the wireless sensor network tomography. G. Hartl et al [7] formulate loss inference as a Maximum-Likelihood Estimation (MLE) problem and infer the loss rate using the Expectation-Maximization (EM) algorithm. Mao et al [8] employ the Factor Graph to solve the internal link loss inference. The proposed algorithm iteratively updates the estimates of link losses upon receiving recently sent packets by the sensors. Jerry Zhao et al [9][10][11] proposed sensor network topography to construct abstracted scans of sensor network health by applying localized algorithms in sensor network for energy-efficient in-network aggregation of local representations of scans. Rather than collect detailed state information from each individual sensor node and then process centrally, this technique builds a composite san by combining local scans piecewise on their way towards the sink node. Meng Xiaoqiao et al [12] proposed an efficient data-collection scheme that can be used for event monitoring or network-wide diagnosis. Their scheme relies on the well-known representation of data-contour maps, which trade off accuracy with the amount of samples. They used three novel algorithms to build contour maps: distributed spatial and temporal data suppression, contour reconstruction at the sink via interpolation and smoothing, and an efficient mechanism to convey routing information over multiple hops. By reducing the number of transmissions, this scheme can improve network lifetime.

3   System Model

In this section, we present the network model and loss model that are used throughout this paper.

3.1   Network Model

Let $T = (V, L)$ denote a reverse aggregation tree with the node set V and link set L. In the T, the root node is the sink node denoted by s. Let a sensor network consist of n internal nodes. The link set, L, contains ordered pairs $(i, j) \in V \times V$ such that node i sends its data, destined for the sink, directly to node j. The link $(i, j) \in L$ is simply denoted by link i. The path from the internal node i to the sink node s is denoted by path i. Let $d(i)$ denote the children set of the node i. That is $d(i) = \{k \in V | (k, i) \in L\}$. Each non-root node i has a unique parent node $f(i)$. Any node on the path i is referred to as an ancestor of i. Let $a(i)$ denote the ancestor set of i.

It is assumed that the topology of the reverse multicast tree is known and remains relatively static. This is a reasonable assumption even if the topology is not known a priori since it is also possible to infer the topology of a network using end-to-end measurements. This process has been presented in many papers. (e.g. [1] and [13])

3.2   Loss Model

We begin this subsection with the similar description of the loss model as presented in [7][8]. Suppose the link losses are mutually independent and the Bernoulli model is adopted in this paper. The flow of data through a reverse aggregation tree is modeled by a stochastic process $Z = \{z_{i,j}, i \in V, j \in a(i)\}$, where each $z_{i,j} \in \{0, 1\}$.

$$z_{i,j} = \begin{cases} 1 & \text{the data sent from node } i \text{ was successfully received by node } j \\ 0 & \text{otherwise} \end{cases}$$

In the data aggregation paradigm, the intermediate node j aggregates its data with that of all its children before sending it to the sink. Information about which nodes' data is present in the aggregated data must also be sent to the sink. From this nature of the data aggregation, we can reach the following conclusion:

- if $z_{i,j} = 0$, we have $z_{k,j} = 0$, $\forall k \in d(i)$.
- if $z_{k,j} = 1, \exists k \in d(i)$, we have $z_{i,j} = 1$.

The probability that the aggregated data is lost on the link i is described as $p[z_{i,f(i)} = 0 | z_{d(i),i} = 1] = \theta_i$. $\Theta = \{\theta_1, \theta_2, ..., \theta_n\}$ is an n-element vector, and each element for one link, which is the parameters to be determined by statistical inference.

Consider the collection of data by the sink to be an experiment. Each round of data collection will be considered a trial within this experiment. Suppose each node tries to send data in each round. The outcome of each trial will be a record of which nodes the sink received data from in that round. We use a Boolean variable $x_k^{(m)}$ to denote the outcome of the node k in mth round, where

$$x_k^{(m)} = \begin{cases} 1 & \text{if } z_{k,s} = 1 \text{ in the } m\text{th round data collection} \\ 0 & \text{otherwise} \end{cases}$$

For N trials, the 0-1 sequences maintained in the sink node for node k are denoted by $X_k = \{x_k^{(m)}, 1 \leq m \leq N\}, k \in V$. Let $X^{(m)} = \{x_k^{(m)}, k \in V\}$. In addition, we denote the unobservable data as $Y = Z \setminus \{X_k\}$, then $y_{i,j} = z_{i,j}$, for each i, j.

4   Loss Inferences

In this section, we firstly formulate the loss rate inference in wireless sensor network. Then the proposed approach is presented in subsection 4.2. Finally, we present the proposed inference algorithm in detail.

4.1   Problem Formulation

After each trial is finished, we will obtain a trial outcome at the sink node. The proposed statistical inference is used here to estimate the loss rate from these outcomes, in particular for those links that cannot be observed directly. Each outcome collected at the sink node corresponds to a set of joint probabilities that lead to the outcome. Take the Fig. 1 for instance, when an outcome $X^{(m)} = \{x_2^{(m)} = 0, x_3^{(m)} = 1\}$ is collected, we have the joint probability $p[X^{(m)}; \Theta] = (1 - \theta_1)\,\theta_2\,(1 - \theta_3)$. If an outcome $X^{(m)} = \{x_2^{(m)} = 0, x_3^{(m)} = 0\}$ is obtained, the joint probability turns to $p[X^{(m)}; \Theta] = \theta_1 + (1 - \theta_1)\,\theta_2\theta_3$.

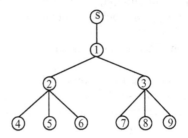

Fig. 1. A simple data aggregation tree

In general, given the loss model and tree structure, we can construct joint probabilities from outcomes as shown in the above example. With a large number of trials, the proposed approach aims to identify the unknown parameters embedded in the joint probabilities. Let the experiment consist of N trials. For each possible outcome $X^{(m)} \in \Omega = \{0, 1\}^{n-1}$, let $n(x)$ denote the number of data collection rounds for which x is the outcome. The probability of observations $X = \{X^{(1)}, X^{(2)}, ..., X^{(N)}\}$ in N trials is given as follows:

$$p\left(X^{(1)}, X^{(2)}, ..., X^{(N)}\right) = \prod_{m=1}^{N} p(X^{(m)}; \Theta) = \prod_{x \in \Phi} p(x; \Theta)^{n(x)}.$$

The proposed loss inference approach aims to make a Bayesian inference to obtain the estimated value $\hat{\Theta} = \{\hat{\theta}_1, \hat{\theta}_2, ..., \hat{\theta}_n\}$ of link loss rate Θ based on the observations X, which amounts to making inference with respect to the posterior density $p(\Theta|X)$.

4.2   Loss Inference Using Gibbs Sampling

In accordance with the correlation among the links introduced by the data aggregation communication paradigm, the statistical inference is used to infer the loss rate of those links from the statistical data. In this paper, our proposed approach is based on the Markov Chain Monte Carlo method and the Gibbs Sampler. In order to implement a Gibbs Sampler for this problem, we assign Beta priors to the link loss rate as described in [3] and [4].

$$\theta_i \sim Beta\,(a_i, b_i) = \frac{\Gamma\,(a_i + b_i)}{\Gamma\,(a_i)\,\Gamma\,(b_i)}\theta_i^{a_i-1}\,(1 - \theta_i)^{b_i-1} \qquad i = 1, 2, ..., n \qquad (1)$$

where the parameters (a_i, b_i) of Beta priors can be obtained by the estimation method of moments according to the measurements.

For the sake of clarity of presentation, we first illustrate our approach by using a simple example network as shown in Fig. 2.

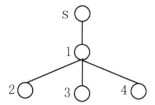

Fig. 2. Simple example network for loss inference

There are 5 nodes connected by 4 links in this network. These links are named 1,2,3 and 4 respectively. Nodes 2, 3 and 4 attempt to forward the sensor data they have collected to node 1. After node 1 has received data from its entire child nodes or until a specified period of time has elapsed. Node 1 then aggregates its own data with data it has received from its child nodes, and forwards the aggregated data to the sink node s. By collecting the arrivals of the aggregated data at the sink node, we can obtain the information about which nodes' data is present in the aggregated data, denoted by X. Suppose the experiment consist of N trials. The loss rate of the four links are $\theta_1, \theta_2, \theta_3$ and θ_4. We are interested in inferring the $\Theta = \{\theta_1, \theta_2, \theta_3, \theta_4\}$ based on the collected data X. According to the relationship between the links, we have

$$
\begin{aligned}
p(\Theta, Y, X) &\propto \prod_{m=1}^{N} p\left(x_2^{(m)}|Y, \Theta\right) p\left(x_3^{(m)}|Y, \Theta\right) p\left(x_4^{(m)}|Y, \Theta\right) p(Y, \Theta) \\
&= \left[\prod_{m=1}^{N} p\left(x_2^{(m)}|y_{2,1}^{(m)}, \theta_1\right) p\left(x_3^{(m)}|y_{3,1}^{(m)}, \theta_1\right) p\left(x_4^{(m)}|y_{4,1}^{(m)}, \theta_1\right)\right] \\
&\quad \left[\prod_{m=1}^{N} p\left(y_{2,1}^{(m)}|\theta_2\right) p\left(y_{3,1}^{(m)}|\theta_3\right) p\left(y_{4,1}^{(m)}|\theta_4\right)\right] \\
&\quad p(\theta_1) p(\theta_2) p(\theta_3) p(\theta_4)
\end{aligned}
\tag{2}
$$

where

$$
\begin{aligned}
p\left(x_k^{(m)}|y_{k,1}^{(m)}, \theta_1\right) &= \theta_1^{1-x_k^{(m)}} \left(1-\theta_1\right)^{x_k^{(m)}} y_{k,1}^{(m)} + \left(1-x_k^{(m)}\right)\left(1-y_{k,1}^{(m)}\right) \\
&= \theta_1^{y_{k,1}^{(m)}\left(1-x_k^{(m)}\right)} \left(1-\theta_1\right)^{x_k^{(m)} y_{k,1}^{(m)}} \qquad k = 2,3,4
\end{aligned}
\tag{3}
$$

and

$$
\begin{aligned}
p\left(y_{k,1}^{(m)}|\theta_k\right) &= \theta_k \left(1-y_{k,1}^{(m)}\right) + (1-\theta_k) y_{k,1}^{(m)} \\
&= \theta_k^{1-y_{k,1}^{(m)}} (1-\theta_k)^{y_{k,1}^{(m)}} \qquad k = 2,3,4.
\end{aligned}
\tag{4}
$$

Substituting (1), (3) and (4) into (2), then we have

$$
p\left(\Theta, Y, X\right) \propto \left[\prod_{m=1}^{N} \theta_1^{y_{2,1}^{(m)}\left(1-x_2^{(m)}\right)} \theta_1^{y_{3,1}^{(m)}\left(1-x_3^{(m)}\right)} \theta_1^{y_{4,1}^{(m)}\left(1-x_4^{(m)}\right)}\right] \tag{5}
$$

$$
\left[\prod_{m=1}^{N} (1-\theta_1)^{x_2^{(m)} y_{2,1}^{(m)}} (1-\theta_1)^{x_3^{(m)} y_{3,1}^{(m)}} (1-\theta_1)^{x_4^{(m)} y_{4,1}^{(m)}}\right]
$$

$$
\left[\prod_{m=1}^{N} \theta_2^{1-y_{2,1}^{(m)}} (1-\theta_2)^{y_{2,1}^{(m)}} \theta_3^{1-y_{3,1}^{(m)}} (1-\theta_3)^{y_{3,1}^{(m)}}\right.
$$

$$
\left.\theta_4^{1-y_{4,1}^{(m)}} (1-\theta_4)^{y_{4,1}^{(m)}}\right] \cdot p\left(\theta_1\right) p\left(\theta_2\right) p\left(\theta_3\right) p\left(\theta_4\right)
$$

$$
= \left[\theta_1^{a_1-1+\sum_{m=1}^{N}\left[y_{2,1}^{(m)}\left(1-x_2^{(m)}\right)+y_{3,1}^{(m)}\left(1-x_3^{(m)}\right)+y_{4,1}^{(m)}\left(1-x_4^{(m)}\right)\right]}\right]
$$

$$
\left[(1-\theta_1)^{b_1-1+\sum_{m=1}^{N}\left(x_2^{(m)} y_{2,1}^{(m)}+x_3^{(m)} y_{3,1}^{(m)}+x_4^{(m)} y_{4,1}^{(m)}\right)}\right]
$$

$$
\left[\theta_2^{a_2-1+\sum_{m=1}^{N}\left(1-y_{2,1}^{(m)}\right)} (1-\theta_2)^{b_2-1+\sum_{m=1}^{N} y_{2,1}^{(m)}}\right]
$$

$$
\left[\theta_3^{a_3-1+\sum_{m=1}^{N}\left(1-y_{3,1}^{(m)}\right)} (1-\theta_3)^{b_3-1+\sum_{m=1}^{N} y_{3,1}^{(m)}}\right]
$$

$$
\left[\theta_4^{a_4-1+\sum_{m=1}^{N}\left(1-y_{4,1}^{(m)}\right)} (1-\theta_4)^{b_4-1+\sum_{m=1}^{N} y_{4,1}^{(m)}}\right]
$$

According to the equation (5), we can easily reach the conclusion that the conditional posterior distributions of link loss rates are still Beta. These conditional posterior distributions are given as following:

$$
p\left(\theta_2 | Y, X, \theta_1, \theta_3, \theta_4\right) \sim Beta(a_2 + \sum_{m=1}^{N}\left(1-y_{2,1}^{(m)}\right), b_2 + \sum_{m=1}^{N} y_{2,1}^{(m)}) \tag{6}
$$

$$p\left(\theta_3|Y, X, \theta_1, \theta_2, \theta_4\right) \sim Beta(a_3 + \sum_{m=1}^{N}\left(1 - y_{3,1}^{(m)}\right), b_3 + \sum_{m=1}^{N} y_{3,1}^{(m)}) \qquad (7)$$

$$p\left(\theta_4|Y, X, \theta_1, \theta_2, \theta_3\right) \sim Beta(a_4 + \sum_{m=1}^{N}\left(1 - y_{4,1}^{(m)}\right), b_4 + \sum_{m=1}^{N} y_{4,1}^{(m)}) \qquad (8)$$

$$p\left(\theta_1|Y, X, \theta_2, \theta_3, \theta_4\right) \sim Beta\left(a_1 + \sum_{m=1}^{N}\left[y_{2,1}^{(m)}\left(1 - x_2^{(m)}\right) + \right.\right. \qquad (9)$$
$$\left. y_{3,1}^{(m)}\left(1 - x_3^{(m)}\right) + y_{4,1}^{(m)}\left(1 - x_4^{(m)}\right)\right],$$
$$\left. b_1 + \sum_{m=1}^{N}\left(x_2^{(m)} y_{2,1}^{(m)} + x_3^{(m)} y_{3,1}^{(m)} + x_4^{(m)} y_{4,1}^{(m)}\right)\right)$$

In addition, the conditional posterior distributions of the unobservable data of the internal nodes are given by

$$p\left(y_{k,1}^{(m)} = 0|x_k^{(m)}, \Theta\right) = p\left(y_{k,1}^{(m)} = 0|x_k^{(m)}, \theta_k, \theta_1\right) \qquad (10)$$
$$\propto p\left(x_k^{(m)}|y_{k,1}^{(m)} = 0, \theta_1\right) p\left(y_{k,1}^{(m)} = 0|\theta_k\right)$$
$$= \left(1 - x_k^{(m)}\right)\theta_k \qquad k = 2, 3, 4$$

$$p\left(y_{k,1}^{(m)} = 1|x_k^{(m)}, \Theta\right) = p\left(y_{k,1}^{(m)} = 1|x_k^{(m)}, \theta_k, \theta_1\right) \qquad (11)$$
$$\propto p\left(x_k^{(m)}|y_{k,1}^{(m)} = 1, \theta_1\right) p\left(y_{k,1}^{(m)} = 1|\theta_k\right)$$
$$= \theta_1^{\left(1 - x_k^{(m)}\right)} (1 - \theta_1)^{x_k^{(m)}} (1 - \theta_k) \qquad k = 2, 3, 4.$$

The Gibbs sampler iteratively draws random samples of $\{\theta_1, \{\theta_k, y_{k,1}, k = 2, 3, 4\}\}$ from the conditional marginal posterior densities (6) $\sim$ (11). When the sample procedure is finished, we can calculate the estimated value of $\hat{\Theta} = \left(\hat{\theta}_1, \hat{\theta}_2, \hat{\theta}_3, \hat{\theta}_4\right)$. For a general sensor network, we can similarly infer link loss rate as in this simple example described above, and expand the sampling strategy as an up-bottom approach where we start from the child node of the sink node, followed by their child nodes, and so on, until we reach the leaf nodes.

4.3   Algorithm Description

By extending the simple example described in subsection 4.2 to a general wireless sensor network, we have the following algorithm for sample from joint posterior density $p\left(\Theta, Y | X\right)$. Suppose the total number of samples is $J = J_0 + J_1$, where J_0 is the number of samples as 'burn-in' period and J_1 is the number of samples used to infer loss rate. Denote $\Theta^{(i)}$ and $Y^{(i)}$ as the ith round sample value.

Initialization: Draw random samples $\Theta^{(0)}$ and $Y^{(0)}$ from their perior.
   Sample: for $j = 1, 2, ..., J$ do
      – Given $Y^{(j-1)}$, for $k \in V \setminus \{s\}$, draw a sample

$$\theta_k^{(j)} \sim p\left(\theta_k | X, \left(Y_{d(k),k}\right)^{(j-1)}\right) \qquad \text{where } d(k) \neq \Phi$$

$$\theta_k^{(j)} \sim p\left(\theta_k | \left(Y_{k,f(k)}\right)^{(j-1)}\right) \qquad \text{where } d(k) \neq \Phi$$

      – Given $\Theta^{(j)}$, for $k \in V \setminus \{s\}$, for $m = 1, 2, ..., N$, draw a sample

$$\left(y_{k,f(k)}^{(m)}\right)^{(j)} \sim p\left(y_{k,f(k)}^{(m)} | \theta_k^{(j)}, \left(y_{f(k),f(f(k))}^{(m)}\right)^{(j)}\right)$$

Inference: Calculate $\hat{\Theta}$ from $\{\Theta^{(J_0+1)}, \Theta^{(J_0+2)}, ..., \Theta^{(J)}\}$
   Output: $\hat{\Theta}$.

5   Simulation Study

We used the ns2 network simulator program to perform the simulation of the sensor network. The ns2 simulator was extended to simulate the data flow through sensor network. For each data collection round, whether a node successfully received data sent to it by its child nodes was determined randomly but with a specified intended loss rate for each link. That is, as the number of data collection rounds increases the actual loss rate of each link should converge to the intended loss rate. The inference algorithm is implemented in MATLAB.

Two networks were used in the simulations. One consisted of 120 nodes while the other contained 10 nodes. Figure 1 shows the topology of the 10-node network. An intended success rate of 0.9 was chosen for all normally links in the simulation network. Each simulation consisted of 1200 data collection trials. Once all of the data was collected, each link loss rate was inferred using the approach presented in Section 4. To estimate the loss rate, we set the number of samples as 'burn-in' period J_0 to be 400, and the number of samples J to be 800.

In the 10-node simulation network, we simulated two possible scenarios that may occur in a real sensor network. These scenarios were: 1) Equal losses throughout the network; 2) Heavy losses at some links. The second scenario was simulated by setting the intended success rates of links 2, 5 and 7 to be 0.7.

Two plots of the inferred and sampled internal link loss rate for all links are shown in Fig.3 and Fig. 4, respectively. We can reach the conclusion that the inferred link loss rate is very close to the sampled link loss rate. In the second scenario the error was significant since some of the losses that should have been attributed to link 2 were instead attributed evenly amongst link 2's child links. However, it is still possible to infer that these lossy links is in fact experiencing the heavy losses.

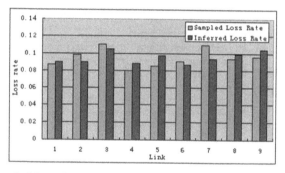

Fig. 3. Sampled Loss Rate vs. Inferred Loss Rate in the equal loss scenarios

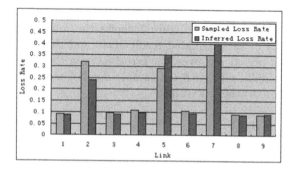

Fig. 4. Sampled Loss Rate vs. Inferred Loss Rate in the heavy loss scenarios

In addition, 100 experiments are used to infer the mean loss rate for each scenario. Two plots of the inferred and sampled internal link mean loss rate for all links are shown in Fig.5 and Fig. 6, respectively. These plots show that the inferred link mean loss rate is much closer to the sampled link loss rate. The same situation occurs in the second scenario as shown in Fig.4, but the difference between the sampled values and the inferred values becomes smaller.

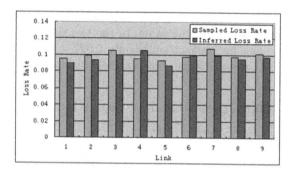

Fig. 5. Sampled Mean Loss Rate vs. Inferred Mean Loss Rate in the equal loss scenarios

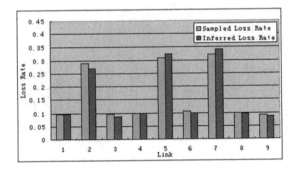

Fig. 6. Sampled Mean Loss Rate vs. Inferred Mean Loss Rate in the heavy loss scenarios

Take the link 2 for instance. Figure 7 shows the relationship between the convergence speeds of the estimated receipt rate and the number of samples. Before the burn-in period was over, the error between the estimated value and the true value is significant. With the sample number increases, the estimated value is approaching to the true value.

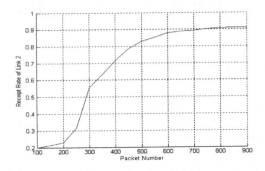

Fig. 7. Inferred Value vs. Sample Number in equal loss scenarios for link 2

Table1 provides the simulation result in 120-node network. It shows that the inferred loss rate is close to its true value. In the two simulation scenarios, the maximum error of link loss estimation is only 0.027 and 0.0312, respectively. These results show that our loss rate inference algorithm scales well.

Table 1. Absolute errors: 120-node network

Equal losses	Mean Error	0.0097
	Max Error	0.0270
Heavy losses on some links	Mean Error	0.0102
	Max Error	0.0312

Finally, we consider the computational cost of the proposed algorithm. We run a simulation program implemented by this algorithm on a PC with 2.8GHz dual processor. The running times of this simulation program are shown in Table 2. From Table 2, we find that the proposed loss inference algorithm using for 120-node sensor network can be done about 4 minutes, which make it good candidate for sensor network monitoring. In addition, the running time increases with the network size.

Table 2. Running Time of the proposed algorithm

Network Size	Number of measurements	Number of iterations	Running time (s)
10-node	1200	800	29.13
120-node	1200	800	249.7

6   Conclusions

In this paper, we apply wired network tomography techniques to the wireless sensor network. An approach to perform inference on sensor network internal link loss characteristics was proposed. We formulate the problem of link loss inference as a Bayesian inference problem and propose a Markov Chain Monte Carlo algorithm using Gibbs Sampling to solve it. Through simulation, we can reach the conclusion that the internal link loss rate can be inferred accurately without any of the internal nodes incurring the additional overhead. Our proposal efficiently solves the problem of link loss characteristics inference. In the future, we will work on finding out better method to decrease the error of inferred link loss rate.

References

[1] M. Coates, A. H. III, R. Nowak, and B. Yu. "Internet Tomography," IEEE Signal Processing Magazine, May 2002, vol.19, no.3, pp.47-65

[2] Zhu,Weiping. "Using Bayesian network on network tomography," Computer Communications, Feb 2003, vol.26, no.2,pp.155-163

[3] Guo Dong, Wang Xiaodong. "Bayesian inference of network loss and delay characteristics with applications to TCP performance prediction," IEEE Transactions on Signal Processing, Aug 2003, vol.51, no.8, pp.2205-2218

[4] Guo, Dong, Wang, Xiaodong. "Bayesian network loss inference," Proceedings of IEEE International Conference on Acoustics, Speech and Signal Processing, Apr 2003, vol.6, pp.33-36

[5] F. Ye, H. Luo, J. Cheng, S. Lu, and L. Zhang. "A Two-tier Data Dissemination Model for Large-Scale Wireless Sensor Networks," Proceedings of ACM Mobicom 2002, Sep 2002 pp.148-159

[6] C. Intanagonwiwat, R. Govindan, D. Estrin, J. Heidemann, and F. Silva. "Directed Diffusion for Wireless Sensor Networking," IEEE Trans. on Networking, Feb 2003, vol.11, no.1, pp.2-16

[7] G. Hartl, Baochun Li, "Loss inference in wireless sensor networks based on data aggregation," Third International Symposium on Information Processing in Sensor Networks, Apr 2004, pp.396-404

[8] Yongyi Mao, Kschischang F.R., Baochun Li, Pasupathy S. "A factor graph approach to link loss monitoring in wireless sensor networks," IEEE Journal on Selected Areas in Communications, Apr 2005, vol.23, no.4, pp.820-829

[9] Jerry Zhao, Govindan Ramesh, Estrin Deborah. "Sensor network tomography: Monitoring wireless sensor networks," Computer Communication Review, Jan 2002, vol.32, no.1, pp.64

[10] J Zhao, R Govindan, D Estrin. "Residual energy scan for monitoring sensor networks," IEEE Wireless Communications and Networking Conference, Mar 2002, vol.1, pp.356-362

[11] Jerry Zhao. "Measurement and Monitoring In Wireless Sensor Networks," Ph.D. Thesis, Department of Computer Science, University of Southern California, Dec 2003

[12] Meng Xiaoqiao, Nandagopal Thyaga, Li Li, Lu Songwu. "Contour maps: Monitoring and diagnosis in sensor networks," Computer Networks, Oct 2006, vol.50, no.15, pp:2820-2838

[13] N. Duffield, J. Horowitz, F. L. Presti, and D. Towsley. "Multicast Topology Inference From Measured End-to-End Loss," IEEE Trans. on Information Theory, Jan 2002, vol 48, no.1, pp. 26-45

Fence Monitoring – Experimental Evaluation of a Use Case for Wireless Sensor Networks

Georg Wittenburg, Kirsten Terfloth, Freddy López Villafuerte,
Tomasz Naumowicz, Hartmut Ritter, and Jochen Schiller

Department of Mathematics and Computer Science
Freie Universität Berlin
Takustr. 9, 14195 Berlin, Germany
{wittenbu,terfloth,lopez,naumowic,hritter,schiller}@inf.fu-berlin.de

Abstract. In-network data processing and event detection on resource-constrained devices are widely regarded as distinctive and novel features of wireless sensor networks. The vision is that through cooperation of many sensor nodes the accuracy of event detection can be greatly improved. On the practical side however, little real-world experience exists in how far these goals can be achieved.

In this paper, we present the results of a small deployment of sensor nodes attached to a fence with the goal of collaboratively detecting and reporting security relevant incidents, such as a person climbing over the fence. Based on experimental data we discuss in detail the process of in-network event detection both from the conceptual side and by evaluating the results obtained. Reusing the same traces in a simulated network, we also look into the impact of multi-hop event reporting.

Keywords: Wireless sensor networks, in-network data processing, event detection, experimental evaluation, use case, fence monitoring.

1 Introduction, Goals and Motivation

The close cooperation of individual sensor nodes in order to achieve a common goal is a key feature of wireless sensor networks (WSNs). While a wealth of distributed algorithms has been proposed and evaluated in the areas of medium access and routing, the situation is different for distributed event detection: Several theoretical approaches have been described [1,2,3], but to the best of our knowledge none of them has been evaluated in a real-world experiment.

On the other hand, several high-profile deployments of WSNs have been undertaken and evaluated by various research groups [4,5,6]. However, they all have in common that they are largely data-agnostic and limit themselves to reporting raw data as collected by the sensor nodes deployed in the field. Only recently we have seen first evaluations of the accuracy of the readings and attempts to perform complex in-network data aggregation and event detection [7,8]. One of the key features of WSNs – in-network data processing and event detection – is thus still widely unexplored in practice.

K. Langendoen and T. Voigt (Eds.): EWSN 2007, LNCS 4373, pp. 163–178, 2007.

Fig. 1. Patio of institute with construction fence

Fig. 2. Sensor node attached to the fence

Fig. 3. Casing of a sensor node

In this paper, we present the results of a real-world experiment on in-network event detection. Our experiment is built around the example of a fence monitoring application whose task it is to detect and report any security related incidents that may occur on a fence, in our case a person climbing over the fence and entering a supposedly restricted area. The focus of this application is thus clearly different from those of other deployments which were mostly concerned with some flavor of environmental monitoring.

Furthermore, fence monitoring is an excellent example for the demand for in-network data processing: Similar to the questions raised in [9], the sheer volume of raw data caused by a single event makes it impractical to transmit the complete data to a base station for processing, especially when keeping energy considerations in mind. Further, the sensor readings caused by a security-related event can be expected to differ sufficiently from those of common every-day events, and thus there should be a reasonable chance for a distributed, in-network event detection algorithm to succeed.

Summing things up, the primary goals of our fence monitoring use case are:

— to establish whether fence monitoring is feasible with current WSN technology by setting up a working system,
— to quantify the accuracy of our event detection algorithm with a special focus on differences between node-local and distributed event detection, thereby putting a number to the value added by networked sensors, and
— to develop and describe a systematic approach to building a robust event detection and reporting algorithm that performs reliably even in a multi-hop scenario.

To these ends, and as shown in Figures 1-3, we deployed a construction fence in the patio of our institute. To each element of the fence we attached a Scatter-Web sensor node equipped with an accelerometer to measure its movement. We then first calibrated the sensors to respond to the typical movements of fence

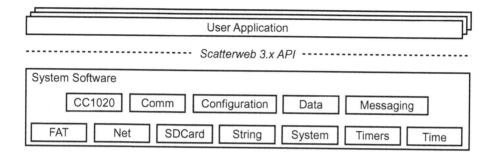

Fig. 4. The ScatterWeb 3.x software architecture

elements, and proceeded afterwards to gather samples of raw data corresponding to different types of events. Based on these, we isolated distinctive features of the raw data corresponding to different types of events, and implemented and evaluated a distributed event detection algorithm.

After a brief introduction into the WSN platform and tools we used in our experiments in Section 2, we present the details of our deployment and the software architecture of our distributed event detection algorithm in Section 3. In Section 4, we thoroughly evaluate this algorithm based on both real-world experiments and simulations. Finally, in Section 5 we review related work and in Section 6 we conclude and point out directions for future research.

2   The ScatterWeb WSN Platform

For setting up our experiment, we used a new version of the ScatterWeb research hardware [10], which has been recently developed with a focus on modularity: The Modular Sensor Board (MSB) as already depicted in Figure 3 consists of a core communication module, add-on sensor modules and an optional interface board. The core communication module consists of the TI MSP430 16-bit microcontroller, the Chipcon CC1020 868MHz radio transceiver, and connectors for analog and digital sensors and actuators. Furthermore, a Freescale Semiconductor MMA7260Q accelerometer is soldered directly onto the board.

An add-on board allows for a broad variety of sensors if needed, ranging from luminosity to motion and from sound to GPS. The core module and the sensors of the add-on board can be powered either by a 3V battery or by the interface board which in addition also provides a flash interface and a USB connection for debugging and power supply.

On the software side, we were able to depend on the broad range of features already available for this platform. These include the ScatterWeb system software, which is responsible for supporting basic tasks such as interrupt handling, packet handling, medium access, management of run levels and debugging options, as well as a rich application programming interface (API) as depicted in Figure 4. Aside from the work on the ScatterWeb core, extensive efforts have been undertaken to supply tool support with the ScatterWeb Software Development Kit (SDK) which is based on Microsoft Visual Studio 2005.

The experiments run on top of the FACTS middleware, a framework especially designed for WSNs and implemented on top of the ScatterWeb platform [11]. Capturing the intrinsic challenges of dealing with low-resource devices and event-centric programming at the language level, the core of FACTS is built around the rule-based Ruleset Definition Language (RDL). Using RDL, a developer is able to specify sets of interacting rules to define node and network behavior. At runtime, these rules are evaluated locally against the fact repository, a central data storage entity on a sensor node, by a sandboxed execution environment.

Currently RDL supports standard operations for fact manipulation, filtering, comparison and different flavors of aggregation. Support for running native code, e.g. to efficiently implement complex mathematical computations or to access hardware directly, is integrated into the language. The design of FACTS aims towards low resource consumption, thus a lot of work has been spent on reducing the memory footprint down to 8KB in terms of the middleware components installed on the sensor nodes.

3   Experimental Setup and Software Architecture

Based on the available hard- and software components introduced in the previous section, we will now present how our construction fence testbed was set up and which types of events we considered in our experiments. We will then continue to describe the architecture of our distributed event detection algorithm.

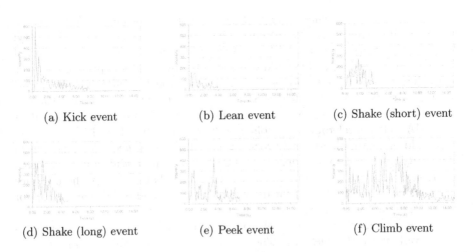

(a) Kick event   (b) Lean event   (c) Shake (short) event

(d) Shake (long) event   (e) Peek event   (f) Climb event

Fig. 5. Raw data of different event types

3.1   Construction Fence Deployment

As already illustrated in Figure 1, we deployed a ten-element construction fence in the patio of our institute. Each fence element is 3.5m wide and 2m high. The exact layout of this deployment is shown in Figure 8. We rigged this installation with one ScatterWeb MSB sensor node per fence element, each node attached to the right hand side of the element at a height of 1.65m (Figure 2). Weather-proof junction boxes with a size of 80mm × 40mm served as casing of the sensor nodes (Figure 3). It is however worth noting that the sensor nodes themselves fit nicely into the hollow metal frame of a fence element, a location at which they would be even more protected from the environment, possibly at the expense of radio transmission quality.

3.2   Types of Events

In our experiments, we considered the following six events as typical scenarios that a fence monitoring system will be exposed to:

Kick: A person kicks against the fence.
Lean: A person gently leans against the fence.
Shake (short): A person shakes the fence for a short period of time.
Shake (long): Same as above, but for a prolonged period of time.
Peek: A person climbs up the fence with the intention to take a look into the restricted area.
Climb: A person climbs over the fence.

Assuming that a person climbing over a fence is the only event with security implications, the important question is how a WSN can be programmed to reliably identify this single type of event that is worth reporting. We did not consider telling the other events apart to keep our use case as realistic as possible, although this would have been possible with additional rules similar to the one shown in Listing 1.1.

We programmed a ScatterWeb MSB sensor node to sample its accelerometer at 10Hz with a sensitivity setting of 1.5g. In Figure 5, we show the raw data in terms of the sum of the differences of elements between the previous three dimensional acceleration vector $\vec{v}_{last}$ and the current vector $\vec{v}_{cur}$. In the following, we will refer to this scalar quantity as the *intensity* I of an event.

$$I = \mid (v_{x\_last} - v_{x\_cur}) \mid + \mid (v_{y\_last} - v_{y\_cur}) \mid + \mid (v_{z\_last} - v_{z\_cur}) \mid$$

Looking at the figures, we note that each event has a more or less unique pattern which may be used for event detection. To prevent problems possibly arising from limited memory resources, we chose not to implement a pattern matching algorithm based on raw data. Instead, we propose a layered architecture to handle this task.

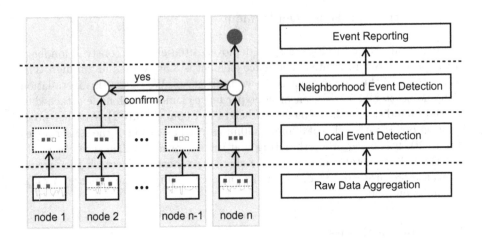

Fig. 6. Layers of the distributed event detection algorithm

3.3   A Layered Software Architecture for Event Detection

The different layers of our architecture implement a distributed, multi-step event detection algorithm. In the lowest layer, raw sensor readings are isolated from background noise and aggregated into a set of characteristic properties. The next layer checks whether known patterns appear in these aggregated values and identifies them as event candidates. In the next layer, the sensor nodes collaboratively decide whether a noteworthy event has in fact occurred within an n-hop neighborhood by exchanging information about recently observed event candidates. Finally, the uppermost layer reports confirmed events to the base station of the deployment. Figure 6 illustrates how these layers interact and the level of abstraction at which they process data.

We first introduce the exact functionality of each layer in this section, while returning to calibration parameters and implementation details in the following section.

Raw Data Aggregation: This layer periodically retrieves the current acceleration vector from the accelerometer and converts it into the intensity as described above. As soon as the intensity surpasses a predetermined threshold value, the sampling rate is increased and new intensity values are aggregated upon retrieval from the sensor. Once the intensity falls below a second threshold value, the sampling rate is decreased for energy efficiency and a tuple of the aggregated data values is reported to the local event detection layer. In the following, we will refer to this tuple of aggregated data values as *basic event*. Typical aggregated data items are the minimum, average, and maximum of all intensity values sampled during the basic event, as well as the total duration of the basic event. Depending on the nature of the event patterns to be recognized, additional aggregated data items may also be considered.

The advantages of this design for the raw data aggregation layer are twofold: Memory usage is kept at a minimum by aggregating sensor readings as they are being sampled, and excessive energy consumption is avoided during intervals in which no events occur. The drawback is that the raw data itself is not available for event detection. However, we regard this as unproblematic given the right selection of data items to aggregate.

Local Event Detection: Based on the basic events reported by the raw data aggregation layer, this layer matches the aggregated data contained in the basic events against previously established patterns. The goal of this procedure is to aggregate one or many basic events into an *event candidate*, i.e. to infer the action that just occurred at the fence from patterns in the aggregated data.

To ensure reliable event detection, patterns in the aggregated data contained in the basic events must be sufficiently distinctive. This of course depends largely on the application and on the types of events that may occur. Hence, the patterns in basic events that lead to event candidates need to be established carefully by the means of either a manual or automatic process before the WSN can be deployed. Once identified, the event candidates are handed up to the neighborhood event detection layer.

Neighborhood Event Detection: In this layer, event candidates are propagated within an n-hop neighborhood of the sensor node that originated the candidate. While theoretically this procedure involves multi-hop communication, given the fact that for the fence monitoring application the radio range of current sensor nodes exceeds the area in which sensors gather data related to an event, we limit ourselves to communication within the one-hop neighborhood.

Upon receiving an event candidate, each sensor node evaluates its own currently available basic events and event candidates and depending on the settings of the distributed aggregation algorithm sends an acknowledgement to the originating node. Similar to the local event detection layer, the parameters of whether to acknowledge an event candidate or not depend on the application and need to be carefully established before an actual deployment. If the sensor node that originally broadcasted the event candidate within its neighborhood receives enough positive replies within a certain period of time, it may safely regard the event candidate as a *confirmed event*, and thus send it to the base station.

Event Reporting: The event reporting layer is not an intrinsic part of in-network event detection and we include it in our model merely for architectural completeness. The task of this layer is to route the confirmed events from the sensor nodes that reported them to the base station. A great variety of routing algorithms for WSNs have been proposed and we omit a thorough evaluation for brevity. In our implementation, we have used a simple spanning tree routing algorithm with the base station being the root of the tree.

At each layer, several parameters need to be configured in order to reliably identify basic events, event candidates, and confirmed events. For different application scenarios, e.g. different types of fence elements, these parameters need to be carefully established, possibly as part of a calibration phase before the system becomes operational. During this calibration phase, one should keep in mind that event detection must be triggered locally on at least one sensor node. Therefore, the calibration should aim at setting the detection threshold rather low for local event detection and only afterwards try to eliminate false positive event candidates in the neighborhood event detection layer.

3.4   Design Alternatives and Robustness Considerations

There are several ways to refine parts of the event detection architecture described in the previous section which we did not implement in our experiments for simplicity. Most of them are related to increasing the robustness of the distributed event detection algorithm with regard to packet loss on the wireless medium.

In our current implementation, there is no mechanism to ensure reliable delivery of event candidates within the neighborhood. As a result, if an event candidate is not delivered due to a packet collision on the wireless medium, no ACKs are sent and a possibly valid event candidate is discarded. The way to solve this issue is by replying to all event candidates with either an ACK as described above or with a NACK in case local data fails to confirm that this event occurred. The originating sensor node can then count the number of ACKs and NACKs received and retransmit the event candidate if this number is below a threshold. This procedure incurs an increase in communication which may well have side effects on energy consumption and packets collisions.

Similar to the problem lined out above, it may also occur that confirmed events are lost on their way to the base station. This may either be solved as part of the routing protocol, or alternatively the sensor node may retransmit the event if no ACK was received from the base station after a certain time interval. Further, it would be desirable to only report exactly one confirmed event to the base station for each real-world event.

4   Deployment and Experimental Results

We conducted over 40 test runs comprising all possible events described in Section 3.2 on the deployed construction fence equipped with our fence monitoring WSN. Each of these runs included one event occurrence per type, thus the fraction of climb events per run is $\frac{1}{6}$. Ten of these runs were used for the calibration of the raw data aggregation layer and 15 runs for the local event detection layer respectively.

4.1   Calibration Values and Implementation Details

From the raw data already presented in Figure 5, we concluded that an intensity threshold of 200 nicely filters out background noise and minor events. As soon as the intensity value surpasses this threshold, the sampling rate is increased from 1Hz to 10Hz, and the values of the accelerometer are aggregated into basic events. Each basic event contains the duration of its sampling period in milliseconds and

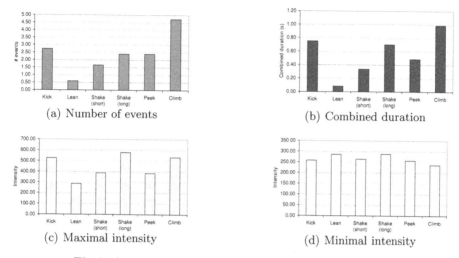

(a) Number of events   (b) Combined duration

(c) Maximal intensity   (d) Minimal intensity

Fig. 7. Aggregated data of different event types on one node

the average intensity during this time. The data did not warrant using a different second threshold value for the hysteresis, hence the sampling rate is reduced to 1Hz again once the intensity falls below the same threshold.

The motivation for chosing the duration and the average intensity as parameters of the basic events is related to the distinctive patterns in different aggregated data values. In Figure 7, we show a selection of these patterns for some of the aggregated data values we considered. For both the number of basic events and their combined duration (Figures 7(a) and 7(b)), we note that the values for climb events differ from all others. On the other hand, no clear pattern can be observed for maximal or minimal intensity (Figures 7(c) and 7(d)). Therefore, on the local event detection layer, the number of basic events produced by the lower layer and their combined duration are suitable values for event detection while maximal and minimal intensity are not. Also note that the average intensity is not used for event detection on this layer, but rather passed to the upper layers for later evaluation.

While there are several options on how to implement our layered event detection architecture, we opted for a rule-based implementation supported by our middleware. Rules such as the one shown in Listing 1.1 suit this particular application because the event-centric semantics of the programming language map nicely to the problem of event detection. For instance, the rule shown will trigger as soon as three conditions evaluate to true: The number of basic events generated has to be greater or equal to three (line 2), the sum of the duration of these events has to be greater or equal to 0.49s (line 3) and smaller or equal to 1.71s (line 4). Once again, we derived these values by studying trace files, thus manually calibrating the local event detection layer. Once all conditions are met and this rule fires, an event candidate is generated which also records the

Listing 1.1. Ruled-based local event detection

```
1  rule aggregateBasicEvents 100
2  <- eval ((count {basicEvent}) >= 3)
3  <- eval ((sum {basicEvent duration}) >= 0.49)
4  <- eval ((sum {basicEvent duration}) <= 1.71)
5  -> define eventCandidate [intensity = (max {basicEvent
     intensity})]
6  -> retract {basicEvent}
```

maximal intensity of the basic events that trigger its creation (line 5) and all basic events are retracted from the system (line 6). The entire event detection ruleset, including for example the rule that purges unused basic events from the system after 30s, consists of 15 rules and has a memory footprint of 1.4KB. A full introduction into the Ruleset Definition Language (RDL) and the exact semantics of the FACTS runtime environment are available in [11].

In the neighborhood event detection layer, we programmed a sensor node to broadcast an event candidate within its one-hop neighborhood since this range covers all nodes that may have been exposed to the possible climb event. Upon reception of an event candidate and given sufficient local information that an event occurred, a node confirms this by sending an ACK to the originating node. If an ACK is received by the originator within a 1s interval, the event is regarded as confirmed and handed to the event reporting layer, which in turn forwards this information to the base station.

In order to properly evaluate the event reporting layer of our WSN use case, we decided to focus on a much larger deployment than the one at our disposal. We therefore resorted to a simulation-based evaluation using the traces of basic events obtained during our experiments and the "ScatterWeb on ns-2" simulation approach which allows to run unmodified algorithms on both ScatterWeb sensor nodes and the ns-2 network simulator [12]. As a typical scenario we chose the construction site of the U.S. embassy located in the center of Berlin.

The layout of the simulated deployment is shown in Figure 10. It consists of 105 sensor nodes placed 3.5m apart from each other along the fence line. Taking into account the expected decrease in signal strength if sensor nodes are placed within the metal frame of a fence element, we set the transmission range to 10m as part of the configuration of the two-ray ground radio propagation model.

4.2   Results and Discussion

We use two statistical metrics for binary classification, sensitivity and specificity, to quantify the accuracy of our event detection algorithm.[1] The goal is to maximize both values, i.e. to correctly classify both events and non-events.

---

[1] Sensitivity is the ratio of correctly identified climb events and all climb events that occurred, i.e. sensitivity = #true positives / (#true positives + #false negatives). Specificity is the ratio of correctly identified other events and all other events, i.e. specificity = #true negatives / (#true negatives + #false positives).

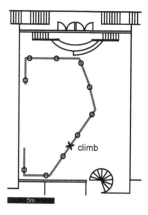

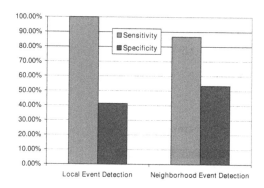

Fig. 8. Construction fence layout in the patio of our institute

Fig. 9. Experimental results of in-network event detection accuracy

In Figures 8 and 9, we illustrate the construction fence deployment in the patio of our institute and the experimental results obtained. At the local event detection layer, a single node of our system performs with a sensitivity of 100% and a specificity of 41.3%. These values indicate that one of our design goals - setting the detection threshold rather low in this layer - has been achieved, since all climb events have been recognized. On the downside, 59.7% of the all other events are also classified as event candidates. We observe that the specificity is increased by 12.0% by the neighborhood event detection layer. This increase comes at the expense of incurring a 13.3% decrease in sensitivity. These values show that our neighborhood event detection layer does well at filtering out false event candidates, but regretably also correct detections. Still, this is consistent with our design principle of a low event detection threshold in the local event detection layer and a higher threshold in the neighborhood event detection layer.

This level of accuracy observed is less than the one we had expected after our initial test runs, especially with regard to the high number of false positives. We attribute this to a variety of factors: On the technical side, we had two node failures during the experiment and of course this resulted in unforeseen inaccuracies during neighborhood event detection. Further, we suspect that gathering trace data at the same time as performing event detection also adversely affected accuracy. More important and consistent with the evaluation found in [7] is however the fact, that the evaluation of the traces suggests that slight variations of the parameters would have significantly improved the results obtained. From this we have to conclude that our manual calibration of the algorithm needs to be improved. On the non-technical side, we note that the event patterns changed over time as our test candidates got more proficient in climbing over the fence.

Before proceeding to simulate a large scale deployment to quantify the impact of multi-hop event reporting, we verified the accuracy of the simulation by rebuilding our original experiment within the simulator and playing back the

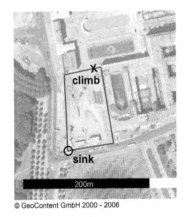

© GeoContent GmbH 2000 - 2006

Fig. 10. Simulated construction fence layout around the U.S. embassy construction site in Berlin

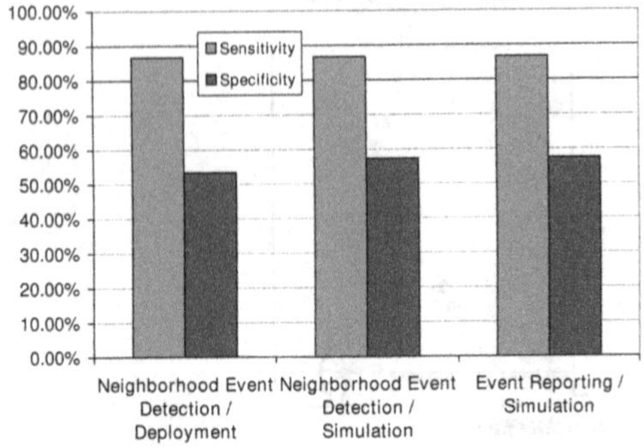

Fig. 11. Experimtental and simulation-based results of in-network event detection and reporting accuracy

original traces. We then ran a series of ten simulations, the average results of which are shown in Figure 11 alongside with the real-world experimental data. As we observed only a minor 4% increase in specificity due to slightly larger packet loss, we concluded that running large scale simulations is appropriate.

The average results of ten simulation runs of the U.S. embassy construction site scenario as illustrated in Figure 10 are included in Figure 11 labeled as "Event Reporting / Simulation". We note that even our very simplistic approach to event reporting, relying on little more than a spanning tree routing, does not have a negative impact on the results, with variations in both sensitivity and specificity below 1%. While our simulation does not include node failures, based on our data and in light of the progress in robust routing protocols for WSN, we still tend to regard event reporting and routing as only a minor problem in the use case of fence monitoring.

Apart from the increase in accuracy, in-network event detection has the additional benefit of reducing the data that needs to be sent to the base station. In Figure 12, we quantify this advantage by looking at the number of packets transmitted during the entire simulation. The figure contains the number of packets sent by our complete layered architecture as well as the same numbers for the two hypothetical cases in which either basic events or event candidates are transmitted to the base station for centralized event detection.

For a transmission range of 10m, our data shows that locally aggregating basic events into event candidates reduces the overall traffic by 79.3%. Aggregating event candidates into confirmed events reduces the overall traffic by another 68.4%. This corresponds to a total reduction of 93.4% of the traffic by our layered event detection architecture.

This reduction of traffic by means of in-network aggregation depends on the topology of the network. For instance, in the trivial case of a network in which all nodes are located within the 1-hop neighborhood of the base station,

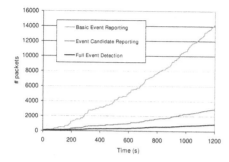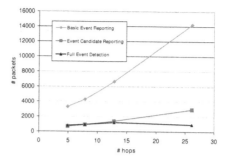

Fig. 12. Number of packets transmitted over time in the simulation with 10m transmission range at different levels of in-network aggregation

Fig. 13. Number of packets transmitted against hops between event source and base station at different levels of in-network aggregation

in-network aggregation will hardly reduce the number of packets transmitted. In fact, the distributed event detection algorithm even incurrs the overhead of data transmissions as part of the neighborhood event detection layer, which is not required if all event candidates are received by the base station.

In order to examine the impact of n-hop event reporting, we ran additional simulations with the transmission range of the simulated sensor nodes set to 10m, 20m, 30m, and 40m. These transmission ranges correspond to an average hop count of 26.14, 12.84, 7.88, and 4.94 between the source of the event and the base station respectively. The number of packets at each level of in-network aggregation for these hop counts is shown in Figure 13. We observe that the reduction of traffic attributed to the neighborhood event detection layer decreases when less hops are required to report the event candidates to the base station. As expected, the diagram also shows the small overhead of in-network aggregation for very well connected topologies. Further, the decrease in confirmed events for a 10m transmission range as opposed to a 20m transmission range, while not directly affecting the accuracy, shows that robustness becomes an issue for reporting events over higher numbers of hops. Possible solutions to this issue have already been discussed in Section 3.4.

Turning our attention to the reduction of traffic due to local aggregation, we note that even at low hop counts the number of packets is still reduced by 75.6%. This underlines that the value added by detecting events locally on the sensor nodes is largely independant of the network topology.

5   Related Work

As already briefly mentioned in the introduction, several theoretical approaches to event detection have been published. On the local and the neighborhood event detection layer, both Petri nets [1] and boolean expressions [2] have been proposed, however no evaluation of these algorithms is presented. In [3], the authors propose to employ Probabilistic Context Free Grammars (PCFGs) in a layered architecture similar to ours and evaluate this approach using a simulation with real traces. Their use case of recognizing motion patterns differs from ours in that it allows to infer semantic meaning of raw data locally on a sensor node, and their evaluation stops short of actually quantifying the accuracy of the system.

On the other hand, a wealth of deployments of WSNs have been described. To mention but a few, deployments have focussed on habitat monitoring [4], fire detection [5], and environmental monitoring [6]. While some of these applications are good candidates for in-network event detection, this functionality neither was an integral part of any of these deployments, nor did the authors report on the level of accuracy of the event detection algorithm used, if any. Instead, reports on deployments mostly limit themselves to describing the raw data collected.

Focussing more on event detection, research undertaken within the NEST project deals with discrimination of people, vehicles and noise using radar-enabled sensor networks [13]. While we opted for classifying the events observed within the network, the authors describe a base-station centerd classification approach and the trade-off between classification accuracy and latency.

The two projects most similar to our work were published by He *et al.* in [7] and by Werner-Allen *et al.* in [14,8]. In [7], He describes the VigilNet project, a system for surveillance missions with applications such as vehicle tracking. It has a broader scope than our work in that it comprises a deployment at a much larger scale and event detection is only one component of their system. The authors did not focus as much on the event detection algorithm as we did, as the only parameter that is mentioned is the degree of aggregation which corresponds to the number of ACKs send at our neighborhood event detection layer. It is also unclear how many different types of events they exposed their system to. Based on our experience, we can however support their claim that slight miscalibrations of the event detection algorithm have an immense impact on its accuracy.

In [14] and later followed-up by [8], Werner-Allen *et al.* evaluate a deployment of sensor nodes on an active volcano with the goal of monitoring volcanic eruptions. The traces obtained during the first deployment were used to both evaluate an offline event detection algorithm and calibrate the event detection algorithm for the second deployment. The architecture of the algorithm deployed differs from ours in that sensor nodes send basic events to the base station and in response to this the base station may decide to collect data from all nodes in the network, while our approach relies entirely on in-network event detection. The results of their second deployment as published in [8] indicate that the accuracy of their event detection architecture faces worse problems than ours under real-world conditions. Sensitivity is very low at 1.2% and specificity is at 100%, which we attribute to a miscalibration of the parameters of the event detection algorithm used during this deployment.

6   Conclusion and Future Work

The goal of this paper was to explore how a security-focussed system relying on the in-network data processing capabilities of WSNs can be constructed. We chose the example of a fence monitoring application due to both its demanding requirements on distributed event detection and realism of the use case. Putting our layered approach to event detection into practice, we have built and evaluated fence monitoring deployments both in real-world and simulated experiments.

Our system showed a sensitivity of of 86.7% and a specificity of 53.3% during these experiments. Distributed event detection contributed to the specificity by eliminating false event candidates, however at the same time decreased the sensitivity by eliminating correct detections. Further, our layered approach to in-network event detection was able to reduce the overall network traffic by up to 93.4% depending on the network topology as compared reporting aggregated sensor data to the base station for centralized processing. Our results are novel in so far as to the best of our knowledge no previous work has quantitatively evaluated the impact of in-network processing based on real-world experiments.

At the same time it must be noted that the level of accuracy we achieved in our experiments is by far not sufficient for a production-level deployment. In the future, we need to focus on refining the calibration phase of the event detection algorithm with the goal of reducing the number of false positive detections. This may include looking at the raw data in a transformed domain to optain a better differentiation of events and examining whether a pattern recognition approach (e.g. k-nearest neighbors) for classification is more suitable. Preferably, calibration should be an automated process instead of the manual calibration we utilized. Fortunately, our comparison between a real deployment and a simulation relying on the same traces indicates that simulation is a viable tool for studying this kind of application. Hence, given enough traces of raw data, it should be feasible to perform the calibration using simulation tools.

Another problem to be tackled is how to avoid that failures of individual nodes and the resulting variation in the average node degree of the WSN adversely affects neighborhood event detection. One possibility we plan to evaluate in this context of self-organization are periodic runs of recalibration phases. Once these adaptations prove successful, we hope to verify our findings in a large scale deployment over a longer period of time as part of which we can also evaluate the long-term energy consumption of our fence monitoring system.

References

1. Jiao, B., Son, S.H., Stankovic, J.A.: GEM: Generic Event Middleware for Wireless Sensor Networks. In: Proceedings of the Second International Workshop on Networked Sensing Systems (INSS'05), San Diego, U.S.A. (2005)
2. Kumar, A.V.U.P., Reddy, A.M., Janakiram, D.: Distributed Collaboration for Event Detection in Wireless Sensor Networks. In: Proceedings of the Third International Workshop on Middleware for Pervasive and Ad-hoc Computing, Grenoble, France (2005) 1–8
3. Lymberopoulos, D., Ogale, A.S., Savvides, A., Aloimonos, Y.: A Sensory Grammar for Inferring Behaviors in Sensor Networks. In: Proceedings of the Fifth International Conference on Information Processing in Sensor Networks (IPSN'06), Nashville, U.S.A. (2006)

4. Szewczyk, R., Polastre, J., Mainwaring, A., Culler, D.: Lessons From a Sensor Network Expedition. In: Proceedings of the First European Workshop on Sensor Networks (EWSN'04), Berlin, Germany (2004)
5. Doolin, D.M., Sitar, N.: Wireless Sensors for Wildfire Monitoring. In: Proceedings of SPIE Symposium on Smart Structures & Materials / NDE'05, San Diego, California, U.S.A. (2005)
6. Martinez, K., Padhy, P., Riddoch, A., Ong, R., Hart, J.: Glacial Environment Monitoring using Sensor Networks. In: Proceedings of the Workshop on Real-World Wireless Sensor Networks (REALWSN'05), Stockholm, Sweden (2005)
7. He, T., Krishnamurthy, S., Stankovic, J.A., Abdelzaher, T., Luo, L., Stoleru, R., Yan, T., Gu, L., Zhou, G., Hui, J., Krogh, B.: VigilNet: An Integrated Sensor Network System for Energy-Efficient Surveillance. ACM Transactions on Sensor Networks (TOSN) 2(1) (2006) 1–38
8. Werner-Allen, G., Lorincz, K., Johnson, J., Lees, J., Welsh, M.: Fidelity and Yield in a Volcano Monitoring Sensor Network. In: Proceedings of the Seventh USENIX Symposium on Operating Systems Design and Implementation (OSDI'06), Seattle, U.S.A (2006)
9. Marrón, P.J., Sauter, R., Saukh, O., Gauger, M., Rothermel, K.: Challenges of Complex Data Processing in Real World Sensor Network Deployments. In: Proceedings of the ACM Workshop on Real-World Wireless Sensor Networks (REALWSN'06), Uppsala, Sweden (2006) 43–48
10. Schiller, J., Liers, A., Ritter, H.: ScatterWeb: A Wireless Sensornet Platform for Research and Teaching. Computer Communications 28 (2005) 1545–1551
11. Terfloth, K., Wittenburg, G., Schiller, J.: FACTS - A Rule-Based Middleware Architecture for Wireless Sensor Networks. In: Proceedings of the First International Conference on COMmunication System softWAre and MiddlewaRE (COMSWARE'06), New Delhi, India (2006)
12. Wittenburg, G., Schiller, J.: Running Real-World Software on Simulated Wireless Sensor Nodes. In: Proceedings of the ACM Workshop on Real-World Wireless Sensor Networks (REALWSN'06), Uppsala, Sweden (2006) 7–11
13. Arora, A., Dutta, P., Bapat, S., Kulathumani, V., Zhang, H., Naik, V., Mittal, V., Cao, H., Demirbas, M., Gouda, M., Choi, Y.R., Herman, T., Kulkarni, S.S., Arumugam, U., Nesterenko, M., Vora, A., Miyashita, M.: A Line in the Sand: A Wireless Sensor Network for Target Detection, Classification, and Tracking. Computer Networks 46(5) (2004) 605–634
14. Werner-Allen, G., Johnson, J., Ruiz, M., Lees, J., Welsh, M.: Monitoring Volcanic Eruptions with a Wireless Sensor Network. In: Proceedings of the Second European Workshop on Wireless Sensor Networks (EWSN'05), Istanbul, Turkey (2005)

Development of a Wireless Sensor Network for Collaborative Agents to Treat Scale Formation in Oil Pipes

Frank Murphy, Dennis Laffey, Brendan O'Flynn, John Buckley, and John Barton

Tyndall Institute, Lee Maltings, Prospect Row, Cork, Ireland
fmurphy@tyndall.ie

Abstract. A wireless network system (WSN) has been developed for a team of underwater Collaborative Autonomous Agents (CAAs) that are capable of repairing and locating scale formations in tanks and pipes within inaccessible environments. The design of the hardware is miniaturised and it consists of a stackable 25mm form-factor that includes the appropriate functionality and ISM wireless communications for the application. Sourcing of relevant sensors for the application was based on having the necessary sensing range; being miniature in size and having low power consumption. Once agent functionality was achieved, antennas were placed within the infrastructure of the pipe and CAAs to realise direct and indirect communication for the WSN.

Keywords: FPGA, WSN, robotic development, underwater sensors, Zigbee communication protocol.

1 Introduction

This paper describes the exploitative and investigative methods for the engineering of emergent collective behaviour in societies of miniature agents. These multi-agents can be utilised to expand the action-horizon of humans in inaccessible fluidic environments such as those found in critical components of material/industrial systems. Such agents have been given the acronym CAAs (Collaborative Autonomous Agents) and can be viewed as having identical simple structures capable of perceiving and exploring their environment, selectively focusing their attention, communicating with peers, initiating and completing corrective tasks as appropriate.

The application chosen to show these properties concentrates on the development of CAAs that can be deployed for the repair of bypass pipes used in the oil-industry. Pipelines can deteriorate due to scale formation and this can be detected in the vicinity of the fault as a variation in pH value due to the formation of scale due to CaCoO3 deposits when the pipes are flushed with water. Each of the CAAs have four pH sensors integrated on its shell to locate these faults and have the ability to navigate, explore and avoid collisions with the wall of the pipe and each other using proximity sensors integrated on the outside surface of the CAA. The geometry of the test-pipe is cylindrical and has dimensions of 0.5m in diameter and 2m in length.

As CAAs are part of an underwater system and care needs to be taken in the sourcing of sensors [1] particularly as small form factor sensors are required within

K. Langendoen and T. Voigt (Eds.): EWSN 2007, LNCS 4373, pp. 179–194, 2007.

the agent. This was a point of significance as sensors were to be integrated on the CAAs surface and needed to be in contact with the water medium. The Ingress Protection (IP67) property used for the packaging of submerged sensors also needed to be considered for sensors used in such an aqueous application and the power consumption it required.

Once the sensors were integrated, Finite State Machines (FSMs) were designed to test the CAAs hydrodynamics and to develop the appropriate algorithms for the sensor/actuator feedback loop for pH following behaviour, within the pipe. These results then formed the basis for the development of the simulation environment (emulator), which had an embedded physics engine that was capable of modelling the test pipe environment and CAAs. For synchronised updates of the sensors within the water medium wireless transceivers were embedded in the pipe and passed data to the simulation environment. This was enabled using direct RF communication, which also provided RSSI (Received Signal Strength Indictor) data allowing the tracking of agents within the pipe by applying a triangulation algorithm. Indirect communication was also built into the system and this enabled the swarm-like social collaborative behaviour.

A 25mm form-factor platform, Fig. 1, was developed that can host algorithms for autonomy for instance a FSM and potentially an SNN [2][3]. This platform consists of a 3-D programmable modular system that can embed such algorithms on the FPGA [4][5] module; the platform also houses the sensory and communication modules that are vital for the agent to interact autonomously with their environment.

Fig. 1. WSN 25mm form factor

Other research institutes have developed similar underwater robotic systems [6] using alternative mote technologies, which have measured depth and temperature, however, an ad-hoc wireless communication test-bed has not been described. One of the main challenges of using Wireless Sensor Networks in miniaturized robotic agents in underwater applications, is the natural occurrence of RF attenuation through water (382 dB/m at 3 GHz) this results in a loss of transmitter signal strength and reduced range of RF systems underwater [7]. The antennas described in this paper use miniaturised versions that are spatially arranged on the CAA for RF coverage around its shell.

2 Hardware Development

The hardware has been designed to be versatile since its wireless core system can utilise custom interfaces and so can be used in a host of ad-hoc networks and applications/scenarios. The design of the WSN hardware supports autonomous formats and uses wireless units that are designed to collect data and transmit to a central host (or distributed hosts). The unit is made up of a modular system (Fig 2) of hardware components that include resources for computation, communications and sensor implementation for its system. Thus the module is adaptable to various configurations due to its flexible and generic design capabilities.

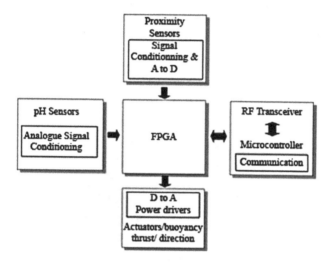

Fig. 2. A modular description of the CAA

2.1 Description of Hardware Used on the WSN

2.1.1 FPGA
A Spartan2E FPGA module was used to host the algorithms that is needed for the autonomy of the agent. In addition the FPGA provides a re-configurable processing solution where algorithms can be tested and updated, when required. This provides flexibility to the system in regards to the development and optimisation of algorithms.

2.1.2 Communications Module
A communications module was designed and built to the 25mm stackable architecture specifications. This module supports the direct communications of the CAA to simulation environment as well as the CAA-to-CAA indirect communication mechanisms. The module is based upon the CC2420 transceiver from Chipcon, which implements a Zigbee compatible IEEE802, 15.4 standard. The transceiver is supported by an ATMEL ATMega128L micro-controller that allows the communication mechanisms to be programmed. The features of the CC2420 that make it attractive are low power consumption for extended battery life and support for RSSI so that the strength of the RF gradient fields can be measured for the indirect communication and the location can be estimated for the direct communication.

Additional hardware was also designed for the implementation of direct and indirect communication. This led to the development of two extra modules that are part of the 25mm hardware platform. These namely are the 4-way and 6-way antenna switch modules, which provide the essential building blocks for the communications mechanism. The 4-way board is integrated within the agent for RF transmission by the CAA and the 6-way module is placed along the demonstration pipe to receive the data from the CAAs. This RF system when combined enables RF coverage through out the pipe.

2.1.2.1 25mm 4-Way Communications Mechanism. This board is designed to allow the antennas to be consecutively activated under the control of the 25mm transceiver board. The switching of the antennas is generated at least 10 times per second. Obviously the RF field is constantly changing due to the switching effect but when the RF pattern generated by each antenna is integrated the field can be viewed as spherical. In addition since the CAA moves at a rate of 9cm/min, it was possible to receive multiple readings from all the antennas in less than a second, in which time the CAA would have moved very little indeed.

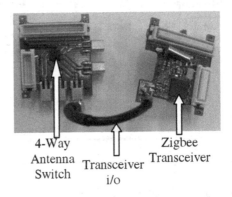

Fig. 3. Four-Way Switch and Transceiver

The chip visible on the board is a MASWSS0018 part from M/A COM (Tyco Electronics). The board uses MMCX connectors to connect the antennas to the board.

2.1.2.2 25mm 6-Way Communications Mechanism. This board also works on the principle of connecting the antennas in a consecutive manner to the transceiver. It

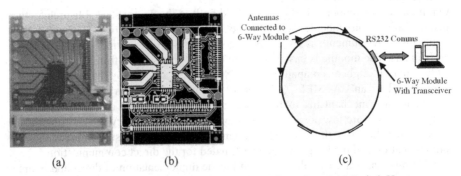

Fig. 4. (a) Six-Way Switch (b) Switch Layout Schematic and (c) Switch Usage

uses an SW90-0004A (MASWCC0008) RF switch, again from M/A COM (Tyco Electronics). This allowed sufficient antennas to be attached to the pipe so that the resultant RF field covered all the interior space.

RF coverage is generated in the pipe by a series of three six-way (hexagonal) rings that are placed every 25cm. One of these rings ("C") is connected serially to a PC and is considered a master module and handles all the communication between other modules and the simulation environment.

Once a message is received the module forwards the information about the received message along with the location of the antennae (there are a number of challenges involved with the localisation of the antennas and will be discussed in later on the evaluation and design of suitable antennas) to the "C" antenna ring.

The data acquired by the simulation environment is broken into six bytes. The first two bytes consist of the ring address and its antennae position. The third byte provides the RSSI strength. If the message is initially detected by ring "A" the information is routed to ring "B" and "C" before finally being sent to the simulation environment.

Byte 1	Byte 2	Byte 3	Byte 4	Byte 5	Byte 6
Acquires ring address	Acquires antennae number	Acquires RSSI	Original message first byte	Original message second byte	Original messages third byte

Fig. 5. Byte information

2.2 Integration of the 25mm Hardware Platform Interfaced to the CAA

The agent used is spherical; 10cm in diameter see Fig. 6. The CAA has four inbuilt behaviours these are (a) pH following, (b) collision avoidance, (c) vertical motion and (d) repair actuation once point defects are found.

Fig. 6. CAA with fitted sensors, integrated on the 25mm module

3 Sensors Integration on the Agent

An appropriate sensor set was decided upon for the application. The main criteria used for the sourcing of the sensors were (a) the size of the sensors, (b) the power consumed by the sensor and (c) the sensors ability to perform in an underwater environment.

3.1 pH

CAAs are capable of biologically inspired, indirect communication that can be observed by other agents. This is accomplished by sending a "quorum signal" which is a simple RF signal that can be detected by other wandering agents (indirect communication). When these wandering agents detect this "quorum signal" they cooperate collaboratively to form a swarm capable of pH following utilising pH sensors integrated on the agents. The "swarm" can thus detect and neutralize the build up of Calcium Carbonate formations in the monitored pipe. To establish this pH gradient following behaviour, appropriate pH sensors (ISFET) were used. These sensors are fitted to the agent to detect point defects occurring on the wall of the pipe. Once the point has been located by a single agent a "quorum signal" is emitted in its vicinity and the repair actuator releases the anti-corrosion chemical to neutralize the build up of CaCO3 in the pipe.

A circuit described by Casans et al [8] was prototyped to condition the ISFET signal appropriately. This circuit uses precision REF200 current sources to accurately ensure a 100uA bias current, and TL084 high input impedance operational amplifiers. Having developed a suitable circuit for the design, the pH module was built on the 25mm stackable platform.

3.2 Proximity Detection

To enable CAAs to avoid collisions they must be able to sense the boundaries of their vicinity and other agents in space see Fig. 7. This prevents collisions with the walls of the pipes and other robots, to protect their electronics and external sensors. A number of proximity sensor options were investigated. However in sourcing these sensors there are numerous physical constraints that needed to be factored-in i.e. the available room needed for the sensors inside the shell, the power consumption of the sensors and a suitable sensing range underwater. Since the sensors were used on the outside of the shell they required waterproof specifications that meant they required more power from the battery to operate and were large in size and sometimes in weight. However after an exhaustive search LED/Photodiode pairs were deemed the most suitable solution.

Fig. 7. Proximity sensors operating on the principle of reflections from wall and other CAAs

To facilitate collision avoidance behaviour the sensor properties for the Proximity System consisted of LEDs and photodiodes that had the following physical properties.

- Low power consumption system – The photodiodes consume minimum (just forA2D to convert their readings to a digital output) power, while the operating power of the LEDs is around 120 mW.

- Extremely small area of both units – Offers minimal resistance to the motion of the agent.
- Reasonable sensing range with low cost.
- Capability of fitting design to the units' need – Power saving scheme, implementation etc.

3.3 Pressure Sensor and Syringe Feedback Loop

To facilitate each CAA with vertical movement capability, a Buoyancy System was required and therefore the CAA was fitted with a LEGO^{TM} - like designed syringe, and a pressure sensor. The syringe when filled with water supplied sufficient extra mass to submerge the CAA and when empty, allows the unit to float. This theory forms the foundation in achieving neutral buoyancy. A pressure sensor was installed to provide feedback on the "current depth", and hence the FPGA could determine whether the CAA is either sinking or floating.

3.4 Repair Actuator

The repair actuator is a device that can treat the calcium carbonate site with a repair fluid/chemical, once it has being detected and located by the agent. The repair actuator is made up of a number of subcomponents that are:

- A sealed reservoir to store the repair fluid/chemical inside the agent.
- A pump to draw the fluid from the reservoir through plastic tubing.
- A valve to prevent a flow of water from the outside into the agent.
- Nozzle to spray the liquid pumped from the reservoir over the affected area.

The reservoir is a watertight container and was designed to prevent leakage of the repair fluid into the agent. In addition, an outlet tube to connect to the pump needed to be attached. An air inlet also has to be attached to prevent the container from collapsing under the pressure of the pump.

A miniaturised pump was sourced, as room within the agent was limited. A miniature diaphragm pump with dimensions 25x16x35mm produced by Schwarzer Precision was implemented. The pump operates on a 5V supply.

4 Field Studies of the Agents Underwater and Sensor Characterisation

A FSM was used to monitor sensor and actuator feedback from CAAs submerged underwater. The use of a FSM is a prior step to the development of a simulation environment, which can be used for creating algorithmic routines for example SNNs. The FSM were a requirement since an understanding of the robots hydrodynamics and sensor feedback loops are an advantage when the Simulation Environment was under design and in addition it explored the autonomy of the CAAs functionality. This understanding provided a description of how the pH following behaviours within the pipe operated for the CAAs and it also provided the framework for which the learning curve of the SNN controllers needed to aspire to [9].

The SNN controllers needed for the application described in this paper are the first of its kind and are extremely difficult to evolve under the normal paradigm of "training without a teacher". This is due to the harsh environment the CAAs need to navigate through, the complexity of the robotic agent (operates in a 3-D water environment) and the resources available on the FPGA for porting of the SNN controllers on the CAA. However, to compliment the learning curve for the training of the SNNs, FSMs were used to describe the operation of the CAAs within the pipe. This has established the initial definitions and requirements for the SNN topologies, to build on.

4.1 Algorithms Generated by the FSM

The development of the FSM were initially based on the characterisation results for the sensors, but for the completion of the FSM a trial and error method was devised for the deployment of the CAAs in the pipe. The following section examines the FSM for the various behaviours innate to the CAA , for pH following.

4.1.1 Buoyancy

Functional buoyancy control was delivered by recording the various depths and altering the direction of the syringe motion (i.e. either expelling or absorbing water); this was controlled using the FPGA. The algorithm designed for its control continuously compares, current readings from the pressure sensor against desired depths the agent required for the treating of scale formations. The following shows the pseudo-code to describe such a setup.

```
If((CurrentDepth < DesiredDepth ))
  THEN
    The CAA sinks towards the desired depth.
  Elseif((CurrentDepth - PreviousReading ) = "smallest
  discrete voltage step for the controller")
THEN
If the difference between the current reading and the
desired reading do not vary between 0.01 Volt
Syringe = 1; (the syringe will take in water).
    Elseif((CurrentDepth - PreviousReading ) > " smallest
  discrete voltage step for the controller ")
    Then;
```

The syringe is turned off. This ensures the syringe is activated slowly i.e. until the currentdepth is found. The CAA is then left to sink very slowly and is compared with the currentdepth until this too is reached. The currentdepth and the previousdepth are also assigned to each other based on a timer.

```
    End if;
```

4.1.2 Proximity

Each of the Photodiodes is identified in the algorithm and a specific Voltage threshold point is used for deciding collision avoidance based on the reflections from the walled surface or the LED light generated from the other agents. The design code operates in a true/false state manner:

1. The different readings from all diodes are received and compared to a set threshold value, which signifies whether or not the direction currently taken should be altered.
2. The direction chosen is decided by a sequence of AND/OR statements, which are formulated in a manner that collision is prevented if required. This procedure is applied to the five photodiodes located at the centre of the CAA.
3. If the photodiode located at the top identifies an object, the desired depth is altered. This method forces the Buoyancy System to establish the CAA at a new depth. The pseudo-code description is the following.

```
If [(PDIODE1 > threshold) OR (PDIODE4 > threshold) OR
(PDIODE5 > threshold)) AND
        (PDIODE2 < threshold) AND (PDIODE3 < threshold)]
THEN
Activate the west position jet exhaust
Elseif[(PDIODE4 < threshold) and (PDIODE5 < threshold)
and ((PDIODE1 < threshold) and ((PDIODE2 > threshold)
or (PDIODE3 > threshold)))]
THEN
Activate the East position exhaust
Elseif [(((PDIODE4 > threshold) or (PDIODE5 >
threshold)) and ((PDIODE2 > threshold) or (PDIODE3 >
threshold)))]
THEN
Activate the North position exhaust
Elseif ((PDIODE6 > threshold))
THEN
Change the depth of the CAA.
End if;
```

4.1.3 pH

The algorithm code caries the identity and the sensor data. The four triangular planes compare each other and the plane with the strongest signal indicates the direction of motion. The code block for this system works in the following manner

1. The recordings from each sensor are compared to one another, through a series of true or false statements. This establishes which plane detects the strongest pH gradient.
2. Note that the Collision Avoidance System overwrites the course of direction if required

Like the other processes this procedure is also continuously ongoing for the period the CAA is operating. Note in the following pseudo-code for the FSM the term collision_depth refers to obstacle hasn't been located.

```
If (collision_direct ='0' AND ((ph_sensor1 >
ph_sensor0) AND (ph_sensor2 > ph_sensor0) AND
(ph_sensor3 > ph_sensor0))
THEN
Activate the south position exhaust tube
Elsif (collision_direct ='0' AND ((ph_sensor0 >
ph_sensor2) AND (ph_sensor1 > ph_sensor2) AND
(ph_sensor3 > ph_sensor2))
THEN
Activate the east exhaust tube
Elsif (collision_direct ='0' and((ph_sensor0 >
ph_sensor1) and (ph_sensor2 > ph_sensor1) and
(ph_sensor3 > ph_sensor1))
THEN
Activate the west exhaust tube
End if;
```

4.1.4 Repair

The CAAs are continuously scanning the vicinity for calcium carbonate. Once a point of defect has been detected and located, the repair actuator treats the area with its chemicals. Each Collaborative Autonomous Agent has been equipped with a reservoir to contain the chemicals, and a pump to expel the fluid over the affected area.

```
If (collision_direct ='1' AND ((ph_sensor0 >
ph_sensor2) AND (ph_sensor1 > ph_sensor2) AND
(ph_sensor3 > ph_sensor2))
THEN
Turn on pump
Else
Keep pump off
End if.
```

4.2 Results Generated by the FSM for Field-Tests

4.2.1 pH Sensor Results

Four ISFET pH sensors were arranged on the CAA so that they could detect a gradient in all 6-degrees of freedom. Calculations for optimal positioning of sensors were carried out and it was shown 120° separations for the four integrated sensors on the unit was the most efficient arrangement. This arrangement is shown in Fig. 8, the four sensors generate four equal triangular planes and have the ability to distinguish between a pH gradient in all spatial planes within the pipe. These planes are used in the agent's controllers to manoeuvre the CAA to the centre of the gradient where the CAA activates "quorum sense" and the other CAAs collaborate together to repair the defected area.

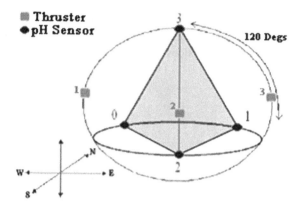

Fig. 8. Position of pH sensors

Fig. 9 shows results for the CAA immersed in a homogeneous solution of pH 7 within the pipe. For demonstration purposes a solution of pH 4 was then added to this solution. The results show that when the pH 4 is initially included the pH sensor closest to the inserted solution has the greatest change. Then it settles while the solution diffuses, but remains strongest relative to the other pH sensors.

Normalised Chart

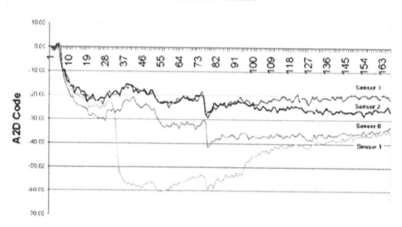

Fig. 9. Results acquired for pH sensors

4.2.2 Proximity Sensor Results

The proximity sensing unit was also calibrated underwater and it was shown to provide suitable detection for both reflections from CAA to CAA and CAA to wall. Fig. 10 shows the detection of light versus distance. From the graph a common voltage threshold was used to activate the exhaust tube on the agent to steer away from an obstacle. The distances found for CAA to CAA and CAA to wall detection was found at

25 and 5cm respectively. The detection distance found for the CAA-CAA was greater since there was a direct propagation of light between the LED and Photodiode (integrated on CAAs) whereas reflections from the wall of the pipe were less intense.

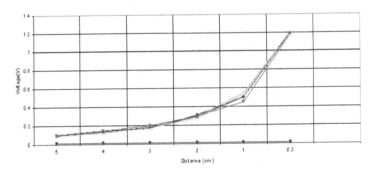

Fig. 10. Proximity Sensors calibration and sensor readings

4.2.3 Pressure Sensor and Syringe Feedback Loop

The Honeywell 26PC series psi pressure sensor is a water applicable sensor, which varies consistently within a depth range of 0 to approx 65 centimetres. The feedback from the sensor requires op-amp conditioning circuit, which was connected to its output. This configuration merely obtains the difference reading and amplifies the milli-volt output signal to a range within 0-3.3 volt. The feedback from the pressure sensor provided a linear relationship between depth and Voltage.

5 Testing of the SRM0 - SNN on the FPGA

This section outlines the steps required for the implementation of SNN model known as a Spike Response Model (SRM0) and is used for purposes of verification on the amount of resources are used up on the FPGA and it is also provides a means of optimising the requirements of the fixed point arithmetic required for the VHDL coding in respect to the data that will be acquired by the sensors. Although the SRM0 is an initial SNN for evaluation on how VHDL coding can be designed it also provides an insight to how this coding can be developed in a generic manner for a range of more sophisticated SNN nets, such as the controllers required for the CAA. Moreover the SRM0 model also provides the most important characteristics of SNN functionality that is; it provides appropriate kernel functions for membrane potential calculations, kernel functions for relative refractory period calculations and a spiking history of the neurons.

A simple 3x3x3 neuron (sensory inputs, intermediate layer, and actuator output) SNN (SRM0) network architecture was tested and this showed that the maximum frequency for the network is 22MHz. This is well within the requirements of the sampling frequency of the SNN, which is only 1 KHz.

6 RF System Design and Characterisation for Use Underwater

6.1 Antenna Design

When designing an antenna there are a number of desirable antenna characteristics that are striven for. These include:

1. A low S_{11} at the resonant frequency of 2.45GHz. S_{11} is ratio of power reflected against power absorbed (return loss).
2. High Gain and bandwidth (BW).
3. Large groundplane for higher efficiency.

However due to the particular nature of the CAA these normally imperative design features come under a great deal of pressure from other considerations. The main conflicting design point was the size of the antennas and the groundplanes. These had to be kept small to allow them to fit inside the CAA, but at the same time they had to be large enough to ensure that the antennas could perform to a good standard. The antennas shown in Fig. 11 are used inside the CAA. It has an S_{11} of roughly –13dB to –15dB in air at 2.45GHz. It has an MMCX connector, a 50Ω transmission line, and the groundplane is 25mm*25mm. The total size of the board is 25mm*32.5mm. The antenna component is a Lynx ANT-2.45-CHP commercial chip antenna.

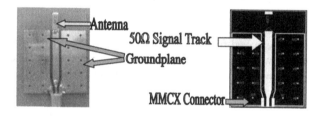

Fig. 11. The antenna design used inside the CAA

6.2 Tuning the Antennae for Optimal Transmission

The proximity of the water to the antennas has a "detuning" effect. This means that the resonant frequency is shifted from the designed 2.45GHz to something other than that and/or the return loss is increased at the resonant frequency. In order to minimise

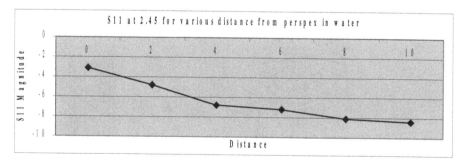

Fig. 12. The S_{11} characteristic of the antenna versus distance from Perspex in water at 2.45GHz

the effects of this, a number of experiments were done to find an optimal distance for the antennas to be placed from the Perspex shell of the CAA. It was found that the further away from the Perspex the antennas were placed the better, but given that there is a limited amount of free space in the CAA it was necessary to select a distance that achieved a good balance of space vs. performance. The distance chosen was 8mm performance and beyond this distance a limited improvement was observed, see Fig. 12.

6.3 Underwater Tests

In order to be able to characterise the system fully it was not an option to simply test the RSSI in an open - environment. It was a requirement that the antenna system and the fields generated by it be in full underwater testing. This would take into account a number of issues that would be overlooked in an air test; the rate of attenuation due to the medium and also the interference due to the reflection of the signal back into the CAA at the water interface. In order to perform the tests under-water it was required that a special setup was developed to hold the CAA at a specific depth and angle while underwater. This "gantry" consisted of two parts, a frame to hold the CAA to allow it to be rotated in order to measure all three of the principle axes, and a rotation gantry that held the frame and allowed it to be rotated by hand to any angle on the axis. The gantry was designed to be totally devoid of metallic parts so as to have as little effect as possible on the parts. Every test run involved taking approximately 50 readings of the RSSI for each antenna every 10 to 20 degrees until the entire axis was described. The frame was then removed from the gantry and was rotated to a different principle axis, then the gantry was returned and the readings were repeated. The advantage of using the 2.4 GHz band was for the miniaturisation aspects of the CAA in regards to the space allowed for the placement of antennas within the shell. However a scaling technique was devised for achieving greater transmission coverage.

The results found represent the shape of the RF field in each plane, and although they are not omni-directional they can be made to appear so by applying a scaling factor Fig. 13b.

The scaling factor does not alter the actual shape of the field but can be used in control software to make the field "appear" more omni-directional to a positioning algorithm. The scaling factor however decreases the resolution of the positioning

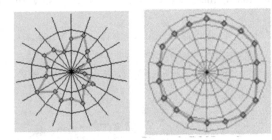

Fig. 13a, 13b. An example of the RF field shapes about an axis in a water 3cm from the shell for scaling factor 1 and 2.5 respectively

algorithm by a proportion equal to the scaling factor. The results showed a near omni-directional pattern about the main axes. The field generated about the CAA is usable not only for communication, but also it is usable for the function of tracking the CAA.

7 Future Work

The next phase of work will concentrate on developing evolved SNN controllers on the FPGA. Currently the SNN controllers have been shown to function in the virtual environment as "a proof of concept". But more experimentation will be required to move from a virtual environment to a real hardware setup as effects due to the amount of resources available on the FPGA (3k system gates) mean that topologies need to be managed succinctly. Thus the topology requires three different entities that are defined and written in VHDL for implementation to the FPGA. These namely are (a) Sensory Neurons that receive an "analog" i.e. non-spiking based neuron, (b) intermediate layer/command neurons and (c) control neurons. The common goal in all entities as stated is to minimise resource allocation so that computation of the total induced membrane potential is calculated in fixed-point precision in each entity in the network. So far SNNs have been ported onto the FPGA and were successfully implemented but functionality of the SNNs on a real agent will still need to be explored.

The wireless communications setup can also be improved by making sure that antennas are placed in the optimal positions. This work would be extremely time-consuming however, involving many minute movements of each antenna, exact recording of placement and orientation as well as the chore of having to re-run each and every axis reading for each movement.

8 Conclusions

The specification and adaptation of the sensors used in the CAA was a key factor in monitoring what could be implemented in the design of the CAA in terms of sensors for the pH following application. Properties such as size, power consumption, and sensing capability i.e. range and scope all needed to be factored into the delivered agent.

Multiple hardware modules were also needed and all these were implemented onto the generic 25mm hardware platform. The unit as a whole was interlinked so that software protocols were easily transferable to the hardware. In addition these modules have a plug and play feature for reprogramming of the software if needed in the early stages for the training of SNNs.

ISM wireless communications were delivered and are capable of underwater communication this is a progressive result as it demonstrates RF communication can be used for the proliferation of mobile agents capable to perceive RF signals within a water medium.

Acknowledgment

We are pleased to acknowledge the funding support from the EU Future and Emerging Technology programme for the project entitled "Self-Organised Societies of Connectionist Intelligent Agents Capable of Learning", No IST-2001-38911. We are also pleased to acknowledge our project partners: the University of Patras, Greece, CTI, Greece and University of Essex, UK.

References

[1] J. Engel, Z. Fan, L. Zhao, J. Chen and C. Liu, "Smart Brick – A low cost, modular Wireless Sensor For Civil Structure Monitoring ", International Conference on Computing, Communications and Control Technologies (CCCT 2004), August 2004.

[2] W. Mass, "Networks of spiking neuron networks: The third generation of Neural Network Models", Neural Networks, Vol. 10(9), 1997, pp 1659-1671

[3] H Hagras, A Pounds-Cornish, Martin Colley, V. Callaghan and G. Clarke, "Evolving Spiking Neural Network Controllers for Autonomous Robots", Proceedings of the 2004 IEEE International Conference on Robotics & Automation, New Orleans April 2004.

[4] Ponca M and G. Scarbata, "Implementation of Artificial Neurons Using Programmable Hardware", Synopsys User Group Conference – SNUG Europe 2001, 12-13 March, Munich, Germany, 2001.

[5] D. Roggen, S. Hofmann, Y. Thoma, D. Floreano, "Hardware spiking neural network with run-time reconfigurable connectivity", 2003 NASA/DoD Conference on Evolvable Hardware, 2003, pp. 189-198.

[6] Vitaly Bokser, Carl Oberg, Gaurav S. Sukhatme, and Aristides A. Requicha, "A Small Submarine Robot for Experiments in Underwater Sensor Networks," In IFAC - International Federation of Automatic Control Symposium on Intelligent Autonomous Vehicles, 2004

[7] J. H. Jacobi and L. E. Larsen, "Water immersed microwave antennas and their applications to Microwave Interrogation of Biological Targets,", Microwave Theory and Techniques, IEEE Transactions on, vol.27, no.1pp. 70-78, Jan 1979

[8] Casans, S, AE Navarro, and D Ramirez, "Circuit forms novel floating current source," EDN, May 1, 2003, pp 92-94.

[9] J.J. Hopfield and Carlos D. Brody, "Learning rules and network repair in spike-timing-based computation networks", Proceedings of the National Academy of Sciences of the USA, Jan 2004; 101: 337-342

Deployment Support Network
A Toolkit for the Development of WSNs

Matthias Dyer[1], Jan Beutel[1], Thomas Kalt[1], Patrice Oehen[1], Lothar Thiele[1],
Kevin Martin[2], and Philipp Blum[2]

[1] Computer Engineering and Networks Laboratory, ETH Zurich, Switzerland
[2] Siemens Building Technologies Group, Switzerland

Abstract. In this paper, we present the Deployment Support Network (DSN), a new methodology for developing and testing wireless sensor networks (WSN) in a realistic environment. With an additional wireless backbone network a deployed WSN can be observed, controlled, and re-programmed completely over the air. The DSN provides visibility and control in a similar way as existing emulation testbeds, but overcomes the limitations of wired infrastructures. As a result, development and experiments can be conducted with realistic in- and outdoor deployments. The paper describes the new concept and methodology. Additionally, an architecture-independent implementation of the toolkit is presented, which has been used in an industrial case-study.

1 Introduction

The validation and testing of wireless sensor network (WSN) algorithms and software components is an indispensable part of the design-flow. However, this is not a trivial task because of the limited resources of the nodes. Considering further the distributed nature of the algorithms, the large number of nodes, and the interaction of the nodes with the environment, leads to the fact that the nodes are not only hard to debug, but also hard to access.

Access to the state of the nodes, often referred to as visibility, is fundamental for testing and debugging. More visibility means faster development. But not only the amount of state information, but also their quality is important. Simulators for sensor networks for example, provide almost unlimited visibility. But on the other hand they use simplistic models for the abstraction of the environment. They fail to capture the complex physical phenomena that appear in real deployments. Therefore, the visibility of simulations is of low quality.

For this reason, researchers have built emulation testbeds with real devices. Existing testbeds consist of a collection of sensor nodes that are connected to a fixed infrastructure, such as serial cables or ethernet boxes. Testbeds are more realistic than simulators because they use the real devices and communication channels. The problem that remains is that the conditions in the field where the WSN should be deployed in the end can be significantly different from the testbed in a laboratory. In particular, with a cable-based infrastructure it is impossible to test the application with a large number of nodes out in the field.

K. Langendoen and T. Voigt (Eds.): EWSN 2007, LNCS 4373, pp. 195–211, 2007.

In evaluations of real deployment experiments like the ones presented in [1,2,3], a gap between simulation-emulation-results and the measured results of the real deployment has been reported. Measured packet yields of 50%, reduced transmission ranges, dirty sensors and short life-times of nodes did not match the expectations and the results obtained through simulation and emulation. The unforseen nuances of a deployment in a physical environment forced the developers to redesign and test their hardware- and software components in several iterations. It has also been shown that sacrificing visibility, such as switching off the debugging LEDs on the nodes in favor of energy-efficiency is problematic during the first deployment experiments [4].

In this paper, we present the *Deployment Support Network*, a toolkit for developing, testing and monitoring sensor-network applications in a realistic environment. The presented methodology is a new approach, since it is wireless and separates the debugging and testing services from the WSN application. Thus it is not dependent on a single architecture or operating system. In contrast to existing approaches, our method *combines* the visibility of emulation testbeds with the high quality of information that can only be achieved in real deployments. The DSN has been implemented and applied in an industrial case-study.

The remaining of the paper is organized as follows: section 2 presents related work, sections 3 and 4 describe our approach and its realization. In section 5 an industrial case-study is presented and finally, in section 6, we discuss the advantages and limitations of our method and conclude the paper.

2   Related Work

To support the development and test of sensor-network applications various approaches have been proposed. On the one hand, simulation and emulation testbeds allow for observation of behaviour and performance. On the other hand, services for reprogramming and remote control facilitate the work with real-world deployments.

Simulation. Network simulators such as *ns-2* [5] and Glomosim [6] are tools for simulation of TCP, routing, and multicast protocols over wired and wireless networks. They provide a set of protocols and models for different layers including mobility, radio propagation and routing. TOSSIM [7] is a discrete event simulator that simulates a TinyOS mote on bit-level. TOSSIM compiles directly from TinyOS code allowing experimentation with low-level protocols in addition to top-level application systems.

Emulation Testbeds and Hybrid Techniques. Indoor testbeds use the real sensor node hardware which provides much greater sensing-, computation-, and communication realism than simulations. In some testbeds the nodes are arranged in a fix grid, e.g. on a large table or in the ceiling. They are connected via a serial cable to a central control PC. In the MoteLab testbed [8], each node is attached to a small embedded PC-box that acts as a serial-forwarder. The control PC can then access the nodes via the serial-forwarders via ethernet or 802.11.

The *EmStar* framework [9] with its *Ceiling–Array* is also an indoor testbed. It additionally provides the ability to shift the border between simulation and emulation. For instance, the application can run on the simulator whereas for the communication the radio hardware of the testbed is used. This hybrid solution combines the good visibility of simulators and the communication realism of real radio hardware. Another feature of *Emstar* is its hardware abstraction layer. It allows the developers to use the same application-code for simulation and for emulation without modification, which enables a fast transition between different simulation- and emulation modes. The operation mode that provides the best sensing-, computation-, and communication realism within *Emstar* is called *Portable–Array*. It is still a wired testbed but with its long serial cables it can be used also for outdoor experiments.

SeNeTs [10] is in many aspects similar to *Emstar*. Both run the same code on simulation and on the real node hardware and both incorporate an environment model. The main difference is that in *SeNeTs* the simulation part runs on distributed PCs, which improves scalability.

Services for real-world deployments. Deluge [11] is a data-dissemination protocol used for sending new code images over the air to deployed TinyOS sensor nodes. It uses the local memory on the nodes for caching the received images. A disseminated buggy code image could render a network unusable. This problem can be addressed with a *golden image* in combination with a watchdog-timer [3]. The golden image is a know-working program that resides on every node, preferably on a write-protected memory section. Once a unrecoverable state is reached the watchdog-timer fires and the bootloader loads the golden image, which reestablishes the operability of the network.

Marionette [12] is an embedded RPC service for TinyOS programs. With some simple annotations, the compiler adds hooks into the code which allow a developer at run-time to remotely call functions and read or write variables. The main cost of using Marionette is that each interaction with a node requires network communication. Sharing the wireless channel with the application could adversely affect the behavior of the network algorithm that is being developed or debugged.

3   Deployment Support Networks

The Deployment Support Network (DSN) is a tool for the development, debugging and monitoring of distributed wireless embedded systems in a realistic environment. The basic idea is to use a second wireless network consisting of so-called DSN-nodes that are directly attached to the target nodes.

The DSN provides a separate reliable wireless backbone network for the transport of debug and control information from and to the target-nodes. However, it is not only a replacement for the cables in wired testbeds but it also implements interactive debugging services such as remote reprogramming, RPC and data/event-logging.

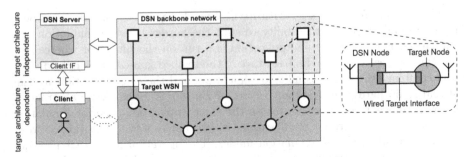

Fig. 1. Conceptual view of a DSN-system with five DSN-node/target-node pairs

3.1   DSN–Architecture

Overview. Figure 1 shows an overview of the different parts in a DSN-system. On the right hand side is the *DSN-node/target-node pair* that is connected via a short cable, referred to as the *wired target interface*. DSN-nodes are battery-operated wireless nodes with a microcontroller and a radio-module, similar to the target-nodes.

In the center of the figure, there is a conceptual view of the DSN with the two separate wireless networks: the one of the DSN-nodes and the one of the target-nodes. The network of the DSN-nodes is a automatically formed and maintained multi-hop backbone network, that is optimized for connectivity, reliability and robustness.

The *DSN-server* is connected with the DSN-backbone-network and provides the client interface, over which the client can communicate and use the implemented DSN-services. The *client* is a target-specific application or script. The information flow goes from the client over the DSN-server to the DSN-nodes and finally to the target nodes and vice versa. The DSN-server decouples the client from the target WSN both in time and space. In particular, data from the target nodes are stored in a database and can be requested anytime, and commands can be scheduled on the DSN-nodes. Separation in space is given through the client interface that allows for an IP-based remote access.

Target-Architecture-Independent Services. A key feature of the DSN-system is the clear separation of the target-system and the DSN-services. As a result, the DSN can be used for the development and testing of different target-architectures. The DSN-services are target-architecture-independent. Only the *wired target interface* and a small part of the software on the DSN-nodes to control it must be adapted. However, this adaptation is typically a matter of I/O configuration which is completed fast.

Client Interface. The DSN-server provides a flexible RPC user interface for the DSN-services. A developer can write his own client scripts and test applications. The client virtually communicates over the DSN with the WSN application on the target-nodes.

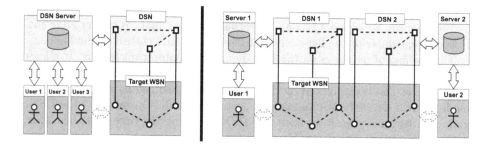

Fig. 2. DSN multi-user and multi-network

The DSN supports multiple users. Figure 2 shows two examples. Multiple users can connect to one DSN-server. Different access privileges can be assigned to users. For example this allows for read-only access or for power-users that are permitted to reprogram the target nodes or to reconfigure the DSN. The second example shows two separate DSN-networks, each with its own server. By this means, two developers can work independently in the same location without interfering each other. Additionally this setup balances the load onto two networks, i.e. yielding a better performance. The separation is achieved by a unique DSN-network-ID that is checked on the DSN connection setup.

3.2   DSN–Services

In this section we describe the debugging services that are provided by the DSN. Each service has a part which is implemented on the DSN-server and a part that is implemented on the DSN-nodes.

Data- and Event-Logging. Probably the most important service of the DSN is the data- and event-logging. It gives the developers insight into the state of the target nodes. The basic concept is as follows: The target-nodes write logging-strings to the wired target-interface (by using e.g. printf-like statements for writing to a debug-UART). The DSN-node receives the log-string, annotates it with a time-stamp and stores it in a local logfile. On the other side, the DSN-server has a logging database, where it collects the log-messages from all the DSN-nodes. For that purpose there are two mechanisms: In *pull-mode*, the DSN-server requests the log-messages, where in *push-mode*, the DSN-nodes sends the log-messages proactively to the server. Finally, the user can query the database to access the log-messages from all target-nodes.

String-based messages are very convenient for debugging and monitoring sensor network applications. They can be transmitted via a serial two-wire cable to the DSN-node with only little overhead on the target-nodes. The majority of the work is done on the DSN-nodes: They run a time-synchronization protocol for accurate time-stamping and they are responsible for transmitting the messages to the server. However, for certain experiments, even the overhead of writing short log-messages to a serial interface is not acceptable. Therefore, there is a second mechanism which uses I/O and external interrupt-lines to trigger an event. Events are, similar to the log-strings, time-stamped and cached in the logfile.

The caching of messages on the DSN-nodes is an important feature. It allows for a delayed transmission to the server, which is necessary for reducing the interference. The transmission can for example be scheduled by the server (pull-mode) or it is delayed until an experiment has finished. It even allows the DSN-nodes to disconnect entirely from the DSN for a certain time and then after reconnection to send all cached log-messages.

For the sake of platform-independence, the content of the log-messages is generally neither parsed by the DSN-nodes nor the DSN-server. This is the responsibility of the user application written by the developer who knows how to interpret the format. However, the DSN-nodes can optionally classify the messages into classes such as *Errors, Warnings* and *Debug*. This can be useful if one wishes to directly receive critical error-messages using the push-mode, while the bulky rest of the debugging messages can be pulled after the experiment.

Commands. The counterparts of the log-messages are the commands. With this service, string-based messages can be sent from the client to the target-nodes. There are two types of commands: *instant commands* that are executed immediately and *timed commands* that are schedulable. A destination-identifier that is given as a parameter, lets the client select either a single node or all nodes. Once the command is delivered to the DSN-server, it is transmitted immediately to the selected DSN-nodes. Then, in the case of an instant command, the message-string is sent over the wired target interface to the target-nodes. For the timed commands, a timer on the DSN-node is started which delays the delivery of the message. Again, the content of the message-string is not specified. It can be binary data or command-strings that are interpreted on the target-nodes.

Together with the data-logging, this service can be applied for the emulation of interactive terminal sessions with the target-nodes. This service sends commands to the nodes while the replies are sent back as log-messages to the user. In other words, this is a remote procedure call (RPC) that goes over the backbone network of the DSN. The wireless multi-hop network introduces a considerably larger delay than direct wired connections. However, even with a few seconds it is still acceptable for human interaction.

Timed commands are necessary if messages should be delivered at the same time to multiple target-nodes. The accuracy of time-synchronization of the DSN-nodes is orders of magnitude higher than the time-of-arrival of broadcasted messages. In addition this service can be used to upload a script with a set commands that will get executed on the specified time.

In addition to the described commands, there is an additional command for the wired target interface which lets the developer control the target-architecture specific functions such as switching on/off the target power, reading the target voltage, and controlling custom I/O lines.

Remote Reprogramming. The DSN has a convenient remote-reprogramming service. The developer uploads a code image for the target-nodes to the server, which forwards it to the first DSN-node. The DSN-nodes have an extra memory section that is large enough to store a complete code image. They run a data-dissemination protocol to distribute the code image to all nodes over the backbone network. The nodes periodically send status-information to the direct neighbors including a version number and the type of the image. By doing so, also newly joined nodes with an old version get updated.

At any time, the developer can monitor the progress of the data dissemination. Once all DSN-nodes have received the code image, he can, with an additional command, select a set of DSN-nodes for the reprogramming of the target-nodes. The DSN-node is connected to the programming-port of the target-node through the wired target interface. This programming connection and its software driver on the DSN-nodes is one of the few parts of the DSN-system that is architecture-dependent. It must be adapted if target-nodes with a new processor type are used.

DSN configuration and DSN status. The DSN is configurable. The user can set different operation-modes and parameters both at setup-time and at run-time. One such mode is the *low-power/low-interference mode*. When this mode is set, the DSN-nodes switch off their radio for a given time-interval. This might be important if the radio of the DSN and the one of the target-system interfere with each other. If this is the case, the DSN radio should be switched off during the experiment. As this mode is also very energy-efficient, it could be set whenever the DSN remains unused for a known time, e.g. during the night. This will significantly increase the life-time because only a timer on the microcontroller of the DSN-nodes needs to be powered.

The DSN further provides the developer with the possibility to gain information about the state of the DSN. In particular, the following information is provided:

- a *list of connected DSN-nodes* with a *last-seen* timestamp,
- a *location-identifier*,
- the *connectivity information* of the DSN-nodes,
- the *versions and types* of the stored code images, and
- the battery voltages of the DSN-nodes

The location-identifier is a string that is stored on every DSN-node containing e.g. the coordinates for positioning. It can be set via the user-interface when the DSN is deployed.

The gathering of the DSN-status requires bandwith on the DSN backbone network. To minimize this overhead, the DSN-server only fetches the information from the DSN-nodes when it is explicitly requested by the client. Otherwise it provides a cached version of the DSN-status.

3.3   Test Automation

It is often not enough to have an interactive terminal session to the nodes. There is a need for automation and scripting support for the following reasons:

(a) Experiments have to be repeated many times, either for statistically validity or to explore different parameter settings. (b) The execution of an experiment has to be delayed, e.g. since interference caused by human activity is minimized during nighttime. (c) Experiments last longer than an operator can assist.

One possibility to automate tests is to send once a set of timed commands to the DSN-nodes (see section 3.2). However, a more sophisticated method for test automation is to use scripts that interact with the DSN-server. This has the advantage that a script can evaluate the state of the targets during test execution and adapt its further actions. For example, only when a particular message from node A is received, a command to node B is sent.

The above described DSN-services are accessible as RPC functions and can therefore be called easily from scripts. Table 1 shows some functions for the different parts.

Table 1. Pseudo-syntax of the RPC functions

```
test-setup:
    loadImage(type, version, code image)
    targetFlash(selected-nodes)
    dsnConfig([selected-nodes], property, value)
    setLogMode(selected-nodes, class, push|pull)
test-execution:
    instantCommand(selected-nodes, command)
    timedCommand(selected-nodes, command, time)
result gathering:
    getDSNStatus()
    getLog(filter)
```

4   Realization

In the previous section, we described the general concept and methodology of the DSN. In this section we present our implementation. Figure 3 shows an overview of the technologies used in our implementation. See also [13] for details.

For the DSN-nodes we use the BTnodes rev3 [14]. This platform has proven to be a good choice since it has a relatively large memory and a robust radio.

4.1   Bluetooth Scatternets

Bluetooth is not often seen on sensor-networks, due to its high energy-consumption (BTnode: 100 mW). However, it has a number of properties that the traditional sensor-network radios do not have and which are very important for the DSN backbone network. Bluetooth was initially designed as a cable-replacement. It provides very robust connections. Using a spread-spectrum frequency-hopping scheme, it is resilient against interference and has a high spatial capacity. Robustness and spatial capacity are mission-critical for the DSN.

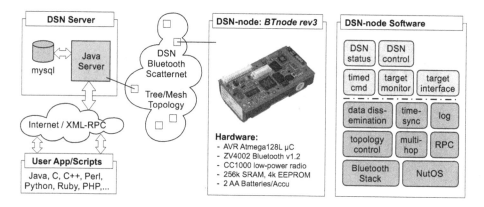

Fig. 3. Technology overview of the DSN implementation on the BTnodes rev3

Using Bluetooth for the DSN has further the benefit that it is potentially accessible from PDAs and mobile phones. Although this not utilized in our current implementation, it opens interesting new usage scenarios for the future.

We use the BTnut system software on the BTnodes which comes with an embedded Bluetooth stack. For the automatic formation and maintenance of a connected Bluetooth scatternet, we have implemented two topology control and routing algorithms: a simple, fast tree-builder and a more sophisticated mesh algorithm. They are both adaptive algorithms, i.e. taking network changes due to link-losses and leaving or joining nodes into account. For more details on these topology control implementations see [15] and [16].

4.2 Wired Target Interface

The only part of the DSN-node software that must be adapted for new target architectures is the *target interface*. Common to most platforms is that data transport is possible through a serial RS232-like connection. The BTnode provides a hardware UART for this purpose. Porting this interface to similar platforms consist of adapting the bitrate and configuring flow control.

More problematic is the programming connection, since different platforms have quite different solutions. Some target-architectures provide direct access to the programming port (ISP). For this case the target-interface must execute the ISP protocol of the appropriate microcontroller type. We have this currently implemented for the AVR and the MSP430 microcontroller family. Some other target-architectures use the same serial port both for data transport and programming. The appropriate control signals for the multiplexing must then be issued by a custom function of the target interface on the DSN-node.

A third programming method is applied on the *Tmote Sky* target: We had to programm the targets with a custom bootloader that is able to receive the code image over the external pins (instead of the USB-connector). Figure 4 shows four different DSN-node - target-node pairs for which our implementation supports the general DSN-services. For the BTnode- and the A80 target we

Fig. 4. Realized target interfaces: 4 different DSN-node–target-node pairs are shown (from left to right): BTnode rev3, Moteiv Tmote Sky, Shockfish TinyNode 584, and Siemens SBT A80

added additional target-monitoring functions such as target-power sensing and control to the wired target interface.

4.3   Client Interface

All DSN-services are accessible as RPC functions. We use XML-RPC, since it is platform independent and there exist API-libraries for a large number of programming- and scripting languages. The application or script which uses the DSN-services is target-architecture dependent and must therefore be written by the user. The script in Figure 5 demonstrates how simple automation and experimental setups can be written. In this example, a code image is uploaded to the server, the data dissemination is started, and then the targets are programmed. The DSN does not perform a version check of the targets since this is dependent on the target-application. This must therefore be a part of the client script. In the example it is assumed that the targets write out a boot-message, such as "Version:X375". The script uses both a time-string and a text-filter-string to query the server for the corresponding log-messages.

4.4   Performance Evaluation

The performance of our implementation on the BTnodes is mostly limited by the packet processing soft- and hardware. In fact, the microcontroller is too slow for the packet processing at full Bluetooth-speed. Incoming packets are stored in a receive buffer. If the arrival rate of packets is higher than the processing rate for a certain time, packets are dropped due to the limited capacity of the receive buffer. This affects the performance of the DSN in several ways: (a) pushed log-messages might get lost, (b) pulled log-messages might get lost, (c) commands might get lost, and (d) data-dissemination packets might get lost. The probability of these cases increases with the amount of traffic on the DSN backbone network. For many scenarios the user can control what and when data is sent on the DSN. He

```
_____ user script example (Perl) _____

require RPC::XML::Client;

# creates an xml-rpc connection to the dsn-server
$serverURL='http://tec-pc-btnode.ethz.ch:8888';
$client = RPC::XML::Client->new($serverURL);

# sends the code image to the dsn-server with xml-rpc
$filename = 'experiment2.hex';
$handle = fopen($filename, 'r');
$req = RPC::XML::request->new('dsnService.uploadFile',
                              $filename,
                              RPC::XML::base64->new($handle));
$resp = $client->send_request($req);

# initiates the data-dissemination on the dsn-nodes
$type = 1; # code image is for target nodes
$resp = $client->send_request('dsnService.loadFile', $filename, $type);

# wrapped function that uses 'dsnService.getDSNstatus' to wait until
# all targets have received the code image
waitDataDisseminationComplete($filename);

# programm the targets
$flashtime = $client->send_request('dsnService.getServerTime');
$resp = $client->send_request('dsnService.targetFlash', 'all');
sleep(5);

# collects the target-versions sent as boot-message by targets
$resp = $client->send_request('dsnLog.getLog',
                              'all', 31, 18, 'Version: X', $flashtime, '');
@versions = ();
for $entry (@{$resp}){
  $entry{'LogText'} =~ m/^Version: X(\d+)/;
  push(@versions, {'node' => $entry('DSNID'), 'version' => $1});
}
```

Fig. 5. User script example in Perl

can e.g. wait for the completion of the data-dissemination bevor he starts pulling messages. In general, cases (b)-(d) are not critical, as they can be resolved with retransmission. However, in a scenario, where all nodes periodically generate log-messages that are pushed simultaneously to the server, the log-messages can not be retransmitted. So for case (a), the user wants to know the transport-capacity of the DSN, such that he can adjust the parameters of the setup.

In Figure 6, we show the measured yield of correctly received log-messages at the server. We varied the message-generation rate from 0.5 to 4 packets per node per second and the DSN size from 10 to 25 nodes. Each message carries 86 bytes payload. We left this value constant, because sending the double amount of data would result in sending two packets, which is the same as doubling the message rate. The measurements are performed on random topologies that were generated by the integrated tree topology algorithm. We observed slightly different results for different topologies, but all with the same characteristic: Starting with slow message rates, all packets are received correctly. However, there is a certain rate, from which on the yield decreases very quickly. This cut-off point is between 0.5 and 1 messages per second for 25 and 20 nodes, between

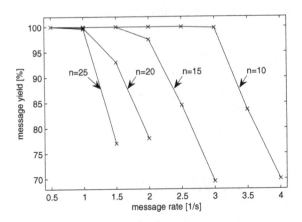

Fig. 6. Yield of correctly received log-messages that are pushed periodically to the server for different message-rates and different sizes of the DSN. For the measurement each node sent 100 log-messages with 86 bytes payload.

1.5 and 2 for 15 nodes, and between 2.5 and 3 for 10 nodes. Thus, if for this streaming scenario a developer needs all pushed log-messages, he must set the message-rate or the DSN size below this cut-off point.

5   Case-Study: Link Characterization in Buildings

Some wireless applications in buildings require highly reliable communication. A thorough understanding of radio propagation characteristics in buildings is necessary for a system design that can provide this reliability. Engineers of Siemens Building Technologies use a BTnode-based DSN system to measure and evaluate link characteristics. To this purpose, the DSN system remotely controls the target nodes and collects measurement data. In the following, the measurement setup is described and the *type* of results that can be obtained is presented. The purpose of the case study is to proof the concept of the DSN system, therefore the obtained data is not discussed in detail.

Experiments. The measurement setup consists of up to 30 target nodes, each connected to a DSN node (see Figure 7). Nodes are placed at exactly the locations required by the actual application (see Figure 8). We measure signal strength (RSSI) and frame error rates for every link between any two target nodes. Additionally, noise levels and bit error rates are evaluated. One target node is sending a fixed number of test frames while all the others are listening and recording errors by comparing the received frame to a reference-frame. Two messages are generated per second. During and after the reception of every frame, the RSSI is recorded in order to provide information about the signal and noise levels.

Fig. 7. Siemens "Blue Box" with BTn-ode, A80 target node and batteries. The Adapter Board acts as a connecting cable.

Fig. 8. Blue Box placed at location defined by the application

In the *detailed mode*, receiving target nodes create a message after every frame reception. Figure 9 shows the data collected by one target node in detailed mode. In *summary mode*, receiving target nodes only create a message after a complete sequence of frames has been received. Figure 10 shows the data collected by 14 nodes in summary mode. In summary mode, the amount of data is significantly reduced compared to detailed mode. This allowed us to concurrently evaluate all 30 target nodes in the test setup. On the other hand, only detailed mode (with maximally 10 nodes, see also Figure 6) allowed us to analyze the temporal properties of collected data. E.g. Figure 9 shows that frames with low signal strength do not occur at random times, but are concentrated towards the end of the experiment. Thus channel properties seem to vary over time.

The procedure described above provides data for the links between one sending target and all other targets. Test automation is used to repeat this procedure with different senders such that finally the links between any two nodes in the

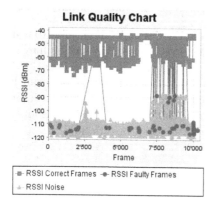

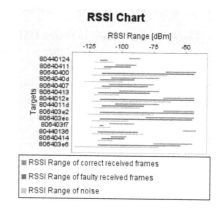

Fig. 9. Detailed mode

Fig. 10. Summary mode

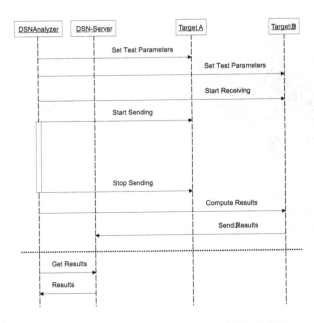

Fig. 11. The automated execution of a simple test from the *DSNAnalyzer* which is a client of the DSN

target system are evaluated. Test automation is also used to repeat tests with different WSN-system parameters like e.g. transmit power. Finally tests are executed during day- and nighttime to observe the influence of human interference. In this case a Java application acts as the user of the DSN-system (see Figure 1). The interaction of this application with the DSN system is illustrated in Figure 11.

Discussion. The BTnode based DSN system has proved to be very useful for SBT's development teams. The following advantages are most relevant to us:

- The simple interface between DSN and target nodes makes it possible to work with existing target platforms. Alternative systems require specific hard or software on the target side.
- The DSN-node/target-node pairs are completely wireless and thus can be deployed quickly and even in inaccessible locations. This is important in our use-case since we are collecting data from a wide range of buildings, some of them in use by our customers, which excludes wired installations.

6   Conclusion

We have presented the Deployment Support Network. It is a new methodology to design and test sensor-network applications in a realistic environment. Existing solutions fail at providing at the same time both visibility and the high quality information from real deployments.

The DSN is wireless, which is the key difference to existing emulation testbeds. The deployment of DSN-node/target-node pairs is much easier than handling hundreds of meters of cables. This means that the positions of the nodes and thus the density of the network can be chosen and adjusted quickly according to the application requirements and is no longer dictated by the testbed setup.

However, using wireless ad-hoc communication instead of cabled infrastructure introduces also new limitations. One is the limited range of the DSN radio. If the range of the targets radio is larger than the one of the DSN-nodes and if a sparse deployment with maximal distances between the nodes is to be tested, additional DSN-nodes have to be inserted that act as repeaters. Another limitation is obviously the lower throughput for debugging and control information. The researcher must be aware of this and choose the rate of generated pushed messages accordingly or change to pull mode if possible. In our implementation Bluetooth provides the necessary robustness and reliability needed for the DSN. With its high spatial capacity it allows not only for large deployments, but also for very dense ones.

Compared to existing services for real-world deployments such as Deluge and Marionette, the DSN is different in the sense that the services run on a separate hardware and not on the target-nodes itself. This solution causes less interference since debugging services and the sensor-network application are clearly separated and do not share the same computing and radio resources. The resources demand of the DSN-services is different from the resources demand of the target-application which asks for different architectures. If in an application scenario the nodes only have to transmit a few bits once every 10 minutes with best effort, the developer would choose an appropriate low-power/low-bandwidth technology. Running the DSN-services over such a network is not feasible. Another approach is over-engineering. One could use more powerful nodes for the sake of better visibility and flexibility during development. Running a data-dissemination service on the target-nodes would require additional memory that is large enough for a whole code image. Expensive extra memory that is only used for development is no feasible option for industrial products.

During development and test, the DSN-nodes execute the services on dedicated optimized hardware. After that, they can be detached from the target-nodes. Since the services are implemented on the DSN they can be used for different target architectures and independently of their operating system.

Both hard- and software of our BTnode-based implementation of the DSN are publicly available at [13].

Acknowledgement

The work presented in this paper was partially supported by Siemens Building Technologies Group Switzerland and by the National Competence Center in

Research on Mobile Information and Communication Systems (NCCR-MICS), a center supported by the Swiss National Science Foundation under grant number 5005-67322.

References

1. Szewczyk, R., Polastre, J., Mainwaring, A., Culler, D.: Lessons from a sensor network expedition. In: Proceedings of the First European Workshop on Sensor Networks (EWSN). (2004)
2. Tolle, G., Polastre, J., Szewczyk, R., Culler, D., Turner, N., Tu, K., Burgess, S., Dawson, T., Buonadonna, P., Gay, D., Hong, W.: A macroscope in the redwoods. In: Proc. 3rd International Conference on Embedded Networked Sensor Systems (SenSys), New York, NY, USA, ACM Press (2005) 51–63
3. Dutta, P., Hui, J., Jeong, J., Kim, S., Sharp, C., Taneja, J., Tolle, G., Whitehouse, K., Culler, D.: Trio: enabling sustainable and scalable outdoor wireless sensor network deployments. In: Proc. of the fifth international conference on Information processing in sensor networks (IPSN), ACM Press, New York (2006) 407–415
4. Langendoen, K., Baggio, A., Visser, O.: Murphy loves potatoes: experiences from a pilot sensor network deployment in precision agriculture. In: Parallel and Distributed Processing Symposium20th International. (2006) 8 pp.
5. ns-2: (The network simulator - ns-2) Available via http://www.isi.edu/nsnam/ns/ (accessed July 2006).
6. Zeng, X., Bagrodia, R., Gerla, M.: Glomosim: a library for parallel simulation of large-scale wireless networks. In: Proc. Twelfth Workshop on Parallel and Distributed Simulation (PADS). (1998) 154–61
7. Levis, P., Lee, N., Welsh, M., Culler, D.: TOSSIM: Accurate and scalable simulation of entire TinyOS applications. In: Proc. of the 1st int'l conference on Embedded networked sensor systems (SenSys), ACM Press, New York (2003) 126–137
8. Werner-Allen, G., Swieskowski, P., , Welsh, M.: Motelab: A wireless sensor network testbed. In: Proceedings of the Fourth International Conference on Information Processing in Sensor Networks (IPSN'05), Special Track on Platform Tools and Design Methods for Network Embedded Sensors (SPOTS), IEEE, Piscataway, NJ (2005)
9. Elson, J., Girod, L., Estrin, D.: Emstar: development with high system visibility. Wireless Communications, IEEE [see also IEEE Personal Communications] 11 (2004) 70–77
10. Blumenthal, J., Reichenbach, F., Golatowski, F., Timmermann, D.: Controlling wireless sensor networks using senets and envisense. In: Proc. 3rd IEEE International Conference on Industrial Informatics (INDIN). (2005) 262 – 267
11. Hui, J.W., Culler, D.: The dynamic behavior of a data dissemination protocol for network programming at scale. In: SenSys '04: Proceedings of the 2nd international conference on Embedded networked sensor systems, New York, NY, USA, ACM Press (2004) 81–94
12. Whitehouse, K., Tolle, G., Taneja, J., Sharp, C., Kim, S., Jeong, J., Hui, J., Dutta, P., Culler, D.: Marionette: using rpc for interactive development and debugging of wireless embedded networks. In: IPSN '06: Proceedings of the fifth international conference on Information processing in sensor networks, New York, NY, USA, ACM Press (2006) 416–423

13. BTnodes: (A distributed environment for prototyping ad hoc networks) http://www.btnode.ethz.ch.
14. Beutel, J., Dyer, M., Hinz, M., Meier, L., Ringwald, M.: Next-generation prototyping of sensor networks. In: Proc. 2nd ACM Conf. Embedded Networked Sensor Systems (SenSys 2004), ACM Press, New York (2004) 291–292
15. Beutel, J., Dyer, M., Meier, L., Thiele, L.:   Scalable topology control for deployment-support networks. In: Proc. 4th Int'l Conf. Information Processing in Sensor Networks (IPSN '05), IEEE, Piscataway, NJ (2005) 359–363
16. Dyer, M.: S-XTC: A signal-strength based topology control algorithm. Technical Report TIK Report Nr. 235, ETH Zurich, Switzerland (2005)

Energy Consumption of Minimum Energy Coding in CDMA Wireless Sensor Networks*

Benigno Zurita Ares, Carlo Fischione, and Karl Henrik Johansson

Royal Institute of Technology, Automatic Control Lab
Osquldas väg 10, 10044 Stockholm, Sweden
benigno@kth.se, {carlofi,kallej}@ee.kth.se
http://www.ee.kth.se/control

Abstract. A theoretical framework is proposed for accurate performance analysis of minimum energy coding schemes in Coded Division Multiple Access (CDMA) wireless sensor networks. Bit error rate and average energy consumption is analyzed for two coding schemes proposed in the literature: Minimum Energy coding (ME), and Modified Minimum Energy coding (MME). Since CDMA wireless systems are strongly limited by multi access interference, the system model includes all the relevant characteristics of the wireless propagation. Furthermore, a detailed model of the energy consumption is described as function of the coding schemes, the radio transmit powers, the characteristics of the transceivers, and the dynamics of the wireless channel. A distributed radio power minimization algorithm is also addressed. Numerical results show that ME and MME coding schemes exhibit similar bit error probabilities, whereas MME outperforms ME only in the case of low data rate and large coding codewords.

Keywords: Wireless Sensor Network (WSNs), Minimum Energy Coding, CDMA, OOK, Power Control, Outages.

1 Introduction

Despite the advancements in hardware and software technologies, one of the most relevant constraints to embody in the design of wireless sensor networks is the energy efficiency. The nodes are supposed to be deployed with reduced energy resources and without battery replacement. Motivating examples are found in areas such as industrial automation, environmental monitoring, and surveillance. Hence, the implementation of this technology has pushed the development

* Work done in the framework of the HYCON Network of Excellence, contract number FP6-IST-511368, and RUNES Integrated Project, contract number FP6-IST-004536. The work by C. Fischione and K. H. Johansson was partially funded also by the Swedish Foundation for Strategic Research through an Individual Grant for the Advancement of Research Leaders and by the Swedish Research Council. Corresponding author: C. Fischione.

K. Langendoen and T. Voigt (Eds.): EWSN 2007, LNCS 4373, pp. 212–227, 2007.
© Springer-Verlag Berlin Heidelberg 2007

of techniques, protocols, and algorithms able to cope with the scarcity of communication and computation resources of the nodes.

Several techniques have been proposed to reduce the energy consumption of WSNs, while ensuring adequate performance. Often, cross-layer approaches are necessary in order to take into account several interacting techniques and protocols, as for example, distributed source coding [1] and sleep discipline [2]. In this paper, we restrict our attention to minimum energy coding schemes. Indeed, these schemes are easily implementable in real wireless sensor networks, and offer potentially several benefits.

Minimum Energy (ME) coding [3] is a technique to reduce the power consumption in digital transmitters when it is employed with On-Off Keying (OOK) modulation. The salient characteristic of ME coding and OOK is the reduction of information actually transmitted, with obvious energy savings. The advantages of ME coding have been investigated also in [4], where the authors proposed optimal ME coding along with channel coding. In [5], a closed-form expression of the bit error probability of ME coding and OOK modulation has been analyzed. In [6], ME coding has been applied to CDMA wireless systems. The authors have shown that, when ME coding technique is used with CDMA, multi access interference (MAI) is reduced. Therefore, ME enables better performance not only at the transmitter side, but also at the receiver, without the need of sophisticated correlation filters that increase the complexity and cost of the receiver node. In [7], the Modified Minimum Energy (MME) coding strategy has been proposed. MME is a variant of the ME coding strategy in that it aims at further reducing the energy consumption with sleep policies at the receiver.

In this paper we propose a detailed analysis of ME coding and MME coding in terms of energy consumption in CDMA WSNs. Since CDMA wireless systems are strongly limited in interference, we adopt a detailed model of the wireless channel, including path loss and shadowing. In the analysis, we accurately study the energy spent for coding, transmitting and receiving. The application of a decentralized radio power allocation strategy, which ensures transmit power consumption minimization, is addressed. Furthermore, by resorting to the extended Wilkinson moment matching method, we are able to characterize the bit error probability, which is a relevant factor of the total energy consumption of ME coding and MME coding.

With respect to existing relevant contributions [3], [4], [6] and [7], our approach is original because we provide a complete theoretical framework for characterization of the total energy consumption with respect to all the parameters of the system scenario, namely: ME, MME, CDMA, wireless channel, and actual energy consumption of the transceiver. For example, MME coding requires frequent startup of the radio, which cause severe influence on the average energy consumption for that scheme. We are able to accurately predict the performance of both ME coding and MME coding on realistic models of wireless sensor networks.

The remainder of the paper is organized as follows. In Section 2 the system model is described, and the main parameters and energy consumption of ME and MME are reported along with a description of the wireless scenario. The various components of the average energy consumption expressions are then investigated in the following sections. In Section 3, an algorithm for the minimization of the radio power consumption is discussed. A performance analysis of ME and MME in terms of radio power, bit error rate and total energy consumption is carried out in Sections 4 and 5. Numerical results are presented and discussed in Section 6. Finally, conclusions are given in Section 7.

2   System Description

Let us consider a scenario where there are K transmitter-receiver pairs of nodes (see Fig. 1). Data sensed by a node are firstly coded according to a Minimum Energy coding scheme. The corresponding bits are then handled by a OOK modulator: only the bits having value 1 are transmitted over the wireless interface after a DS-CDMA spreading operation. The power level per bit is denoted with P_i. The transmitted signal, after being attenuated by a flat fading wireless channel, is received corrupted by an additive Gaussian noise, having power spectral density $N_0/2$, and multi access interference caused by other transmitting nodes. At the receiver, the signal is de-spread, demodulated, and decoded in order to get the source data.

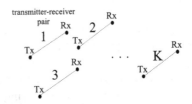

Fig. 1. System scenario: K pairs of nodes are simultaneously transmitting

2.1   ME Coding

With ME coding [3], each codeword of the source code-book is mapped into a new codeword having larger length but less number of 1 (or high) bits. Let us denote with L_0 the length of the source codeword, and with L_{ME} the length of the ME codeword. Thus, $L_0 < L_{ME}$, and the extra bits added are called redundant bits (see Fig. 2). The mapping is done such that source codewords having large probability of occurrence are associated to ME codewords with less high bits. Since only high bits are transmitted through the wireless interface, the transmission of ME codewords enable consistent energy savings. We denote with α_{ME} the probability of having high bits in a ME codeword. Note that, since there are several alternatives to associate source codewords to ME codewords, α_{ME} may assume different values.

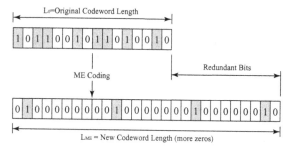

Fig. 2. Mapping of the source codewords into the codewords of the Minimum Energy Coding

Consider the link i between a transmitter and a receiver node. The energy consumption per ME codeword spent over the link can be expressed as follows:

$$
\begin{aligned}
E_i^{(ME)} &= E_i^{(tx)} + E_i^{(rx)} \\
&= P^{(tx,ckt)}\left(T^{(on,tx,ME)} + T_s\right) + \alpha_{ME}P_iT^{(on,tx,ME)} + \\
&\quad + P^{(rx,ckt)}\left(T^{(on,rx,ME)} + T_s\right),
\end{aligned}
\tag{1}
$$

where $E_i^{(tx)}$ and $E_i^{(rx)}$ are the average energy consumption of a node while transmitting and receiving, respectively; the power consumption of the electronic circuits, while transmitting and processing a codeword, is denoted with $P^{(tx,ckt)}$, and while receiving is denoted with $P^{(rx,ckt)}$; note that $P^{(tx,ckt)}$ and $P^{(rx,ckt)}$ do not include the radio power, which is P_i; $T^{(on,tx,ME)}$ is the transmitter activity time per ME codeword, and $T^{(on,rx,ME)}$ is the receiver activity time per codeword; finally, T_s is the start up time of the transceiver. In the above expressions, we have also modelled the major characteristic brought about by the ME and OOK modulation: the effective transmit time is only the fraction α_{ME} of the transmitter ontime.

With respect to the original codeword, the ME coding increases the value of two system parameters: the codeword length, L_{ME}, and the transmitter/receiver active time, $T^{(on,tx,ME)}$ and $T^{(on,rx,ME)}$. The increase of the transmitter active time is negligible with respect to the radio power consumption P_i ($P_i \gg P^{(tx,ckt,ME)}$). Increasing the receiver active time, however, may be harmful at the receiver itself, since the power spent to receive is approximately the same as that used to transmit. Furthermore, the larger codeword length of ME may increase the codeword error probability. These drawbacks of ME are compensated by the reduction of the multiple access interference caused by the decreased number of high bits.

2.2 MME Coding

The MME coding [7] exploits a structure of the codeword that allows the receiver to go in a sleep state, where the radio electronic circuitry is switched off[2]. In the MME coding technique, the ME codewords are partitioned into N_s sub-frames of length L_s, where each sub-frame starts with an indicator bit. When the indicator bit, which we denote with b_{ind}, is a high bit, it indicates that there are not high bits in that sub-frame, so there is no need for decoding, and the receiver can go to the sleep state. Conversely, if b_{ind} is a low bit, it indicates that there are high bits in the sub-frame, so the decoding operation must be performed, and the receiver cannot go to sleep. In Fig. 3, the MME codeword structure is reported. Note that the length of a MME codeword, L_{MME} is the same as L_{ME}. It should be noted that the MME coding may increase the length of the codeword of N_s bits with respect to ME coding, due to presence of the indicator bit. This drawback is, however, compensated by the potential energy savings that MME offers at the receiver.

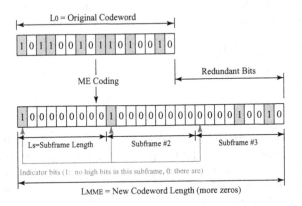

Fig. 3. MME codeword. The original codeword is mapped into a MME codeword partitioned in sub-frames. Each sub-frame starts with an indicator bit.

By adopting the same parameter definition employed in (1), the energy consumption per MME codeword can be modelled as follows:

$$
\begin{aligned}
E_i^{(MME)} &= E_i^{(tx)} + E_i^{(rx)} \\
&= P^{(tx,ckt)} \left[T^{(on,tx,MME)} + T_s \right] + \alpha_{MME} P_i T^{(on,tx,MME)} + \\
&\quad + P^{(rx,ckt)} \left[T^{(on,rx,MME)} + (N_i + 1) T_s \right] .
\end{aligned}
\tag{2}
$$

In (2) we have introduced the average number of times, denoted with N_i, that the receiver has to awake from the sleep state. This term plays a fundamental role when evaluating the energy consumption: each time a radio receiver component is turned on, it spends an amount of energy given by $P^{(rx,ckt)} T_s$. Since $P^{(rx,ckt)}$ is the largest term among the powers at the receiver, and T_s is not negligible: when it is amplified by N_i, the resulting energy may be very large. The consequences are that MME may not offer an adequate performance improvement with respect to ME. Note that the term N_i has not been included in the energy model proposed in [7].

2.3 Wireless Channel

We consider an asynchronous DS-CDMA wireless access scheme, where the same fixed bandwidth W, and hence the same chip interval T_c, is allocated to each transmitter-receiver pair. The processing gain is denoted with $G = \frac{W}{R_b} = \frac{T_b}{T_c}$, where the bit interval is T_b.

Following an approach similar to that found in [9] and references therein, we can express the output of the correlation receiver of the link i as

$$Z_i(t) = D_i(t) + I_i(t) + N_g(t) , \qquad (3)$$

where $D_i(t)$ is the desired signal for the pair i, $I_i(t)$ is the interference term due to the presence of multiple transmitting nodes (causing MAI) and $N_g(t)$ is a Gaussian random variable with zero mean and variance $\frac{N_0 T_b}{4}$. Specifically, it can be proved that

$$D_i(t) = \sqrt{\frac{P_i \Omega_{i,i}(t)}{2}} T_b b_i(t) . \qquad (4)$$

and that the variance (correlation) of the MAI term is:

$$E\{I_i^2(t)\} = \sum_{\substack{j=1 \\ j \neq i}}^{K} \nu(t) P_j \Omega_{j,i}(t) \frac{T_b^2}{6G} . \qquad (5)$$

In the expression (4) and (5), P_i, for $i = 1, \ldots, K$, denotes the radio power of the transmitter node in link i. We introduce the vector $\mathbf{P}$ for notational convenience:

$$\mathbf{P} = [P_1, \ldots, P_i, \ldots, P_K]^T . \qquad (6)$$

The term $\nu(t)$ is a binary random variable that describes the transmission of a high bit ($\nu(t) = 1$) or low bits ($\nu(t) = 0$), with probability $\Pr(\nu(t) = 1) = \alpha$ and $\Pr(\nu(t) = 0) = 1 - \alpha$, respectively. In particular, $\alpha = \alpha_{ME}$ for ME coding, whereas $\alpha = \alpha_{MME}$ for MME coding. The wireless channel coefficient associated to the path from the transmitter of the link j to the receiver of the link i is denoted with $\Omega_{j,i}(t)$, and it is defined as

$$\Omega_{j,i}(t) = \mathrm{PL}_{j,i} e^{\xi_{j,i}(t)} . \qquad (7)$$

where $\mathrm{PL}_{j,i}$ is the path loss, and $e^{\xi_{j,i}(t)}$ is the shadow fading component over the same path, with $\xi_{j,i}(t)$ being a Gaussian random variable having zero average and standard deviation $\sigma_{\xi_{j,i}}$. The path loss can be further written (in dBs) as follows

$$\mathrm{PL}_{j,i}|_{dB} = -P_l(d_r)|_{dB} - 10n \log_{10}\left(\frac{d_{j,i}}{d_r}\right) . \qquad (8)$$

where d_r is the reference distance and $d_{j,i}$ is the distance between the transmitter in link j and the receiver of the link i, the term $P_l(d_r)|_{dB}$ denotes the path loss attenuation at the reference distance, and n is the path-loss decay constant. For notational convenience, we introduce the following vector to denote the wireless channel coefficients seen by the receiver of the pair i:

$$\mathbf{\Omega}_i(t) = [\Omega_{1,i}(t), \ldots, \Omega_{i,i}(t), \ldots \Omega_{K,i}(t)]^T . \tag{9}$$

When a high bit is transmitted, i.e. $b_i(t) = 1$, the quality of the received signal is measured by the Signal to Interference plus Noise Ratio. For the generic transmitter-receiver pair i, the SINR is defined as follows

$$SINR_i(t) = \frac{\sqrt{\frac{P_i \Omega_{i,i}(t)}{2}} T_b b_i(t)}{\sqrt{\frac{N_0 T_b}{4} + \sum_{\substack{j=1 \\ j \neq i}}^{K} \nu(t) P_j \Omega_{j,i}(t) \frac{T_b^2}{6G}}} . \tag{10}$$

Note that the SINR is a stochastic process, since it is dependent on the wireless channel coefficients $\mathbf{\Omega}_i(t)$, as well as on the binary on/off source activity $\nu(t)$. Moreover, it can be directly influenced by the transmit powers $\mathbf{P}$. When $b_i(t) = 0$, the SINR is obviously zero.

3   Optimal Transmission Power

In this section, we study the optimal value of the radio power P_i that appears in (1) and (2). In order to minimize the transmission power of the overall system, we adopt an optimization problem whose objective function is the sum of the powers of all the transmit nodes, while the constraints are expressed in terms of link outage probability [2], namely

$$\min_{\mathbf{P}} \sum_{i=1}^{K} P_i$$
$$s.t. \ P[SINR_i(t) \leq \gamma] \leq \bar{P}_{out} \ , \forall \, i = 1...K \tag{11}$$
$$P_i > 0 \quad \forall \, i = 1, \ldots, K .$$

In the optimization problem, note that γ is defined as the SINR threshold for the computation of the outage probability. In particular, the solution of the optimization problem ensures that the outage probability remains below the maximum value $\bar{P}_{out}$. Furthermore, note that the computation of the outage probability is performed with respect to the statistics of the wireless channel, and the distribution of high bits.

To solve the optimization problem (11), we have to model the constraints related to the outages of the links. Since the statistics of the SINR are in general unknown, we resort to the well know extended Wilkinson moment-matching method [9]. We approximate the SINR with an overall Log-normal distribution, thus obtaining that

$$SINR_i(t) = L_i(t)^{-\frac{1}{2}} \approx e^{-\frac{1}{2}X_i(t)} , \qquad (12)$$

where $X_i(t)$ is a Gaussian process having average and standard deviation, respectively, given by μ_{X_i} and σ_{X_i}, i.e., $X_i \sim \mathcal{N}(\mu_{X_i}, \sigma_{X_i})$. The expression of the parameters of the Gaussian distribution are provided in the Appendix. The approximation is useful because allows for computing the outage probability while taking into account all the relevant aspects of the wireless propagation, the transmission power, and the distribution of high bit. It trivially results that

$$P\left[SINR_i(t) \le \gamma\right] \approx P\left[e^{-\frac{X_i(t)}{2}} \le \gamma\right] = Q\left(\frac{-2\ln\gamma - \mu_{X_i}}{\sigma_{X_i}}\right) . \qquad (13)$$

The constraint on the outage probability can be easily rewritten in order to evidence the dependence on the transmission power coefficients. After some algebra, a relaxation of the program (11) can be rewritten as follows:

$$\min_{\mathbf{P}} \sum_{i=1}^{K} P_i$$

$$s.t. \ P_i \ge 2T_b^{-2}\mathrm{PL}_{i,i}^{-1}\left\{\beta_i^{(1)}[\mathbf{P}_{-i}]\right\}^{2(1-q_i)}\left\{\beta_i^{(2)}[\mathbf{P}_{-i}]\right\}^{-\frac{1}{2}+q_i}\gamma^2, \ i = 1\ldots K$$

$$(14)$$

$$P_i > 0 \quad \forall\, i = 1,\ldots,K ,$$

where $q_i = Q^{-1}(\bar{P}_{out})$, and $Q(x) = 1/\sqrt{2\pi}\int_x^\infty e^{-t^2/2}dt$ is the complementary standard Gaussian distribution. The expressions for $\beta_i^{(1)}[\mathbf{P}_{-i}]$ and $\beta_i^{(2)}[\mathbf{P}_{-i}]$ are provided in the Appendix. The problem (14) is a relaxation since σ_{X_i} has been replaced with its square. This is equivalent to say that the outage constraints are tighter. It is possible to see that the relaxation reduces the computational burden, and that the solution is an upper bound of the solution of the original problem. The program (14) is a centralized problem, in the sense that, to compute the solution, a central node should be able to collect all information related to radio link coefficients, it should be able to solve the program, and finally it should broadcast the optimized powers to all other nodes. A centralized implementation exhibits clear disadvantages in terms of communication resources. Nevertheless, by following the same method proposed in [11], it can be proved that (14) can be solved with a fully distributed strategy. Each receiver node can find iteratively the optimal power as follows

$$P_i(n) = 2T_b^{-2}\mathrm{PL}_{i,i}^{-1}\left\{\beta_i^{(1)}[\mathbf{P}_{-i}(n-1)]\right\}^{2(1-q_i)}\left\{\beta_i^{(2)}[\mathbf{P}_{-i}(n-1)]\right\}^{-\frac{1}{2}+q_i}\gamma^2 ,$$

$$(15)$$

where $\mathbf{P}_{-i}(n-1)$ are the powers that the node i sees at the iteration n. The power updating can be done asynchronously by each node, and it can be proved that for

$n \longrightarrow \infty$ the power converges to the optimal value of (14). The algorithm (15) is fully distributed, since the computation of the path loss parameter, as well as the other coefficients, is done locally by the nodes. In particular, note that the node i has just to compute the expectations $\beta_i^{(1)}[\mathbf{P}_{-i}(n-1)]$ and $\beta_i^{(2)}[\mathbf{P}_{-i}(n-1)]$, through (44) and (45).

4   Performance Analysis: Error Probability

In this section we characterize the average bit error probability for the ME coding, as well as for the MME coding. The characterization is useful to express the total energy consumption (2). With this goal in mind, we first derive the error probability for the decision variable (3). In particular, two cases are possible: the decision variable is decoded as a low bit, when a high bit was transmitted; or the decision variable is decoded as a high bit when a low bit was actually transmitted. We denote such probabilities with $p_{i|0}$ and $p_{i|1}$, respectively, where:

$$p_{i|0} = \Pr\left[Z_i(t) > \delta_i(t)|b_i(t) = 0, \mathbf{\Omega}_i(t), \nu(t)\right] , \qquad (16)$$

$$p_{i|1} = \Pr\left[Z_i(t) < \delta_i(t)|b_i(t) = 1, \mathbf{\Omega}_i(t), \nu(t)\right] , \qquad (17)$$

where $\delta_i(t)$ is the decision threshold for the variable $Z_i(t)$. The probabilities in (16) and (17) are computed adopting the usual standard Gaussian approximation [14], where $Z_i(t)$ is modelled as a Gaussian random variable conditioned to the distribution of the channel coefficients and coding. Specifically, it is assumed that:

$$Z_i(t) \sim \mathcal{N}\left(\mu_{Z_i(t)}, \sigma_{Z_i(t)}\right) , \qquad (18)$$

where

$$\mu_{Z_i(t)} = \begin{cases} \mu_{Z_i(t)|0} = 0 & \text{if } b_i(t) = 0 \\ \mu_{Z_i(t)|1} = \sqrt{\dfrac{P_i \Omega_{i,i}(t)}{2}} T_b^2 & \text{if } b_i(t) = 1 \end{cases} , \qquad (19)$$

and

$$\sigma_{Z_i(t)} = \sqrt{\frac{N_0 T_b}{4} + \sum_{\substack{j=1 \\ j \neq i}}^{K} \nu(t) P_j \Omega_{j,i}(t) \frac{T_b^2}{6G}} . \qquad (20)$$

Hence, it is easy to compute the probabilities (16) and (17), which are given by

$$p_{i|0} = Q\left(\frac{\delta_i(t)}{\sigma_{Z_i(t)}}\right) ,$$

$$p_{i|1} = Q\left(\frac{\mu_{Z_i(t)|1} - \delta_i(t)}{\sigma_{Z_i(t)}}\right) .$$

The bit error probability, conditioned to the channel coefficients and coding, can be expressed as:

$$\begin{aligned} \Phi_i[e|\mathbf{\Omega}_i(t), \nu(t)] &= \Pr\left[b_i(t) = 0\right] p_{i|0} + \Pr\left[b_i(t) = 1\right] p_{i|1} \\ &= (1-\alpha) p_{i|0} + \alpha \cdot p_{i|1} . \end{aligned} \qquad (21)$$

Finally, averaging with respect to the distribution of the channel coefficients and the distribution of the high bits,

$$\Phi_i = E_{\Omega_i(t),\nu(t)} \left[(1-\alpha) Q \left(\frac{\delta_i(t)}{\sigma_{Z_i(t)}} \right) + \alpha \cdot Q \left(\frac{\mu_{Z_i(t)|1} - \delta_i(t)}{\sigma_{Z_i(t)}} \right) \right] . \quad (22)$$

The expression (22) should be minimized with respect to $\delta_i(t)$. However, it has to be remarked that it is hard to compute the expectation in (22), since the argument is non linear. Hence, no closed-form is available for Φ_i, and, as a consequence, it is difficult to find the optimal $\delta_i(t)$. Therefore, we resort to the heuristic

$$\delta_i^{opt}(t) = \frac{\mu_{Z_i(t)|1}}{2} . \quad (23)$$

Using (23), the probability of error turns out to be

$$\Phi_i = E_{\Omega_i(t),\nu(t)} \left[Q \left(\frac{\mu_{Z_i(t)|1}}{2\sigma_{Z_i(t)}} \right) \right] = E_{\Omega_i(t),\nu(t)} \left[Q \left(\frac{1}{2} e^{-\frac{1}{2} X_i(t)} \right) \right] . \quad (24)$$

Let us define $\zeta_i = \frac{1}{2} e^{-\frac{1}{2} X_i(t)}$. Then, using the Stirling approximation [14] for the computation of the expectation in (24), we obtain that

$$E_{\Omega_i(t),\nu(t)} [Q(\zeta_i)] \approx \frac{2}{3} Q(\mu_{\zeta_i}) + \frac{1}{6} Q \left(\mu_{\zeta_i} + \sqrt{3}\sigma_{\zeta_i} \right) + \frac{1}{6} Q \left(\mu_{\zeta_i} - \sqrt{3}\sigma_{\zeta_i} \right) , \quad (25)$$

where, recalling the computation of the average and standard deviation of log-normal random variables (see also the Appendix), we have that

$$\begin{aligned} \mu_{\zeta_i} &= \frac{1}{2} e^{-\frac{1}{2}\mu_{X_i} + \frac{1}{8}\sigma_{X_i}^2} , \\ r_{\zeta_i} &= \frac{1}{4} e^{-\frac{1}{2}\mu_{X_i} + \frac{1}{8}\sigma_{X_i}^2} , \\ \sigma_{\zeta_i}^2 &= r_{\zeta i} - \mu_{\zeta_i}^2 . \end{aligned} \quad (26)$$

4.1 Error Probability in ME Coding

The probability of bit error in the ME case, denoted with $\Phi_i^{(ME)}$, can be easily computed by using Eq. (25), along with (26), (42) and (43), where α takes the value α_{ME}.

4.2 Error Probability in MME Coding

An analysis on the MME performance regarding its probability of error demands a careful study which takes into account the special nature of the MME codeword. As done in [7], we compute the average equivalent bit error probability as the ratio between the average number of erroneous bits per MME codeword and the codeword length, namely

$$\Phi_i^{(MME)} = \frac{\overline{n}_{i,sf} N_s}{L_{MME}} , \quad (27)$$

where N_s is the number of sub-frames per codeword and $\overline{n}_{i,sf}$ is the average number of erroneous bits in a subframe transmitted over the link i:

$$\overline{n}_{i,sf} = \sum_{n=1}^{L_s-1} n p_i^{(n)} , \tag{28}$$

where $p_i^{(n)}$ stands for the probability of having n errors in the sub-frame, and, recalling that each sub-frame starts with an indicator bit, it can be computed as follows

$$p_i^{(n)} = \Pr\left[b_{ind} = 1\right] \Phi_i \Pr(\mathcal{A}_i) + \Pr\left[b_{ind} = 0\right] \left[(1 - \Phi_i) \Pr(\mathcal{A}_i) + \Phi_i \Pr(\mathcal{B}_i)\right] , \tag{29}$$

where the event $\mathcal{A}_i$ happens when there are n decoding errors in a sub-frame, and $\mathcal{B}_i$ happens when there are n high bits in the codeword. Note that in (29) we have actually considered that an error in decoding of an indicator bit has catastrophic consequences in the entire following sub-frame.

It is not difficult to see that [7]:

$$\Pr(\mathcal{A}_i) = \binom{L_s - 1}{n} \Phi_i^n \left(1 - \Phi_i\right)^{L_s-1-n} , \tag{30}$$

$$\Pr(\mathcal{B}_i) = \binom{L_s - 1}{n} \alpha_{MME}^n \left(1 - \alpha_{MME}\right)^{L_s-1-n} , \tag{31}$$

while

$$\Pr\left[b_{ind} = 0\right] = 1 - \left(1 - \alpha_{MME}\right)^{L_s-1} , \tag{32}$$

and

$$\Pr\left[b_{ind} = 1\right] = \left(1 - \alpha_{MME}\right)^{L_s-1} . \tag{33}$$

5 Performance Analysis: Energy Consumption

5.1 ME Coding

The energy consumption of the ME coding scheme is defined as the average of the energy consumption of all the sensor nodes, namely

$$E^{(ME)} = \frac{1}{K} \sum_{i=1}^{K} E_i^{(ME)} , \tag{34}$$

where the term $E_i^{(ME)}$ is defined as in (2), and it takes into account the radio power minimization discussed in section 3.

Looking at the energy model for a system using ME coding (1) it is easy to see that setting $\alpha_{ME} = 1$, one obtains the energy consumption of the BPSK case. The energy gain of the ME coding with respect to BPSK can be defined as the ratio of the energy used in a BPSK system and the energy used in a ME coding system:

$$\rho_{dB} = \left(\frac{E_{radio}^{BPSK}}{E_{radio}^{ME}}\right)_{dB} . \tag{35}$$

5.2 MME Coding

In order to investigate the energy of MME coding, it is necessary to characterize the values of $T^{(on,rx,MME)}$ and N_i in (2).

The value of $T^{(on,rx,MME)}$ is given by the average number of high bits in a MME codeword times the bit time, namely

$$T^{(on,rx,MME)} = \frac{\overline{n}_i}{R_b} . \tag{36}$$

In particular, having in mind the sub-frame structure, the average number of received high bits is given by

$$\overline{n}_i = N_s \left\{ 1 + \Pr\left[b_{ind} = 0\right](1 - \Phi_i)(L_s - 1) + \Pr\left[b_{ind} = 1\right]\Phi_i(L_s - 1) \right\} . \tag{37}$$

In order to compute the average number of times that the radio module has to be active, first we have to consider that it has to be on for each indicator bit. Moreover, the radio is turned active for every sub-frame, with the exception of the case in which the previous sub-frame has been decoded (the radio is already on). This can be expressed as follows:

$$N_i = N_s \left[1 - \Pr(b_{ind} = 0)(1 - \Phi_i) - \Pr(b_{ind} = 1)\Phi_i \right] . \tag{38}$$

Eq. (36) and Eq. (38) can be plugged into (2) to obtain the energy consumption for the generic link i. Thus, averaging over all the links, the energy consumption for the MME case is:

$$E^{(MME)} = \frac{1}{K} \sum_{i=1}^{K} E_i^{(MME)} . \tag{39}$$

Finally, the receive energy gain is defined as:

$$\rho_{dB} = \left(\frac{E_{radio}^{ME}}{E_{radio}^{MME}} \right)_{dB} . \tag{40}$$

6 Numerical Results

In this section we provide numerical evaluation of the bit error probability, and the total energy consumption of ME and MME coding.

In the numerical results, we consider a system scenario with $K = 10$ pairs of nodes. Each pair is randomly placed, and the minimum distance among nodes is 3 m, while the maximum distance is 15 m. We have considered a homogeneous environment, where the path loss at the reference distance is set to $P_l(d_r)|_{dB} = 55$ dB, $d_r = 1$m, $n = 4$, and $\sigma_{\xi_{j,i}} = 5$dB, for $i, j = 1 \ldots K$. The source data rate is assumed to be $R_b = 1$Kbps. A spreading gain $G = 64$ has been used. We set the value of the power spectral density of the noise to $N_0/2|_{dB} = -174$dBm, and the threshold for the SINR $\gamma = 3.1$ dB. Finally, we have taken as reference the

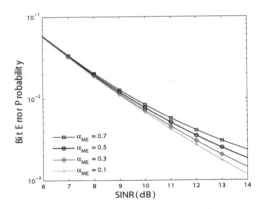

Fig. 4. Bit error probability for both the ME and MME cases. Note that they overlap.

CC2420 radio transceiver module by Chipcon [10], as is the one incorporated in the Telos motes, to set the values of the energy parameters. Namely: $P^{(tx,ckt)} = 36 \cdot 10^{-3}$ mW, $T_s = 0.58 \cdot 10^{-3}$ ms, $P^{(rx,ctk)} = 33.84$ mW.

In Fig. 4, the bit error probability is reported for both the case of ME and MME coding. Each curve is associated to a different value of $\alpha = \alpha_{ME} = \alpha_{MME}$. The probabilities are reported as function of the average received SINR, and are computed using $\Phi^{(ME)}$ and $\Phi^{(MME)}$ after the power minimization algorithm (15) provided the optimal powers. Details on the numerical results of the power minimization algorithm can be found in [16]. It is interesting to observe that there is not noticeable difference among the ME and MME cases. This can be explained by considering that the outage probability is the dominant term in the computation of the bit error probability, and the optimal powers ensure that the constraint of the outage probability is fulfilled in the same way for ME case and MME cases. A decreasing of the bit error probability can be evidenced when α decreases. This is obviously due to the fact that lower values of α decrease the multi access interference.

In Fig. 5, the energy gain is reported for MME case as computed with (40) for different values of the α coefficient and as function of the sub-frame length. As it can be observed, an optimum value can be found for the energy gain as function of L_s, for each value of α. The energy gain decreases as L_s increases since this causes the receive time to be longer. Low values of α determine good performance of MME. It is interesting to remark, however, that as α increases, there is a sharp decrease of the energy gain. When α increases more then 0.3, there is no advantage in using the MME coding with respect to the ME. This can be explained by observing that large probabilities of having high bits lead to large average number of wake-ups of the radio receiver.

Numerical values have been derived also with higher source data rate. Due to lack of space, we cannot report them in this paper. However, it could be possible to observe that as the source data rate increases, the MME receive energy gain quickly decreases.

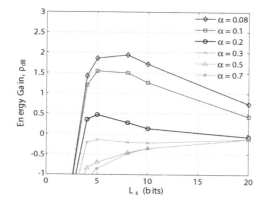

Fig. 5. MME Energy Gain as function of the sub-frame length for different values of α

7 Conclusions

In this paper, a general framework for accurate analysis of the performance of ME coding and MME coding in CDMA WSNs has been proposed. The analysis has been carried out in terms of radio power consumption, and energy consumption of the electronic circuit transceivers. Specifically, an accurate wireless propagation scenario has been taken into account, including path loss and shadowing. A distributed power minimization strategy has been described and implemented.

Numerical results show that, in the scenario considered, ME and MME codings do not have significant differences in terms of bit error probability. MME outperforms ME only for low bit rate data transmission and low probability of high bits. Therefore, MME is a good candidate for low rate applications. However, as technology evolves and smaller startup times might be reached, MME could be useful with higher data rates as well.

Future studies include extension of the analysis to optimizing the decision threshold, and investigating performance for a large set of channel conditions. Furthermore, experimental validation of the performance we have analytically predicted will be carried out.

References

1. Chou, J., Petrovic, D., Ramchandran, K.: A Distributed and Adaptive Signal Processing Approach to Reducing Energy Consumption in Sensor Networks. In proc of IEEE INFOCOM, (2003)
2. Fischione, C., Bonivento, A., Johansson, K.H., Sangiovanni-Vincentelli, A.: Cooperative Diversity with Disconnection Constraints and Sleep Discipline for Power Control in Wireless Sensor Networks. In: Proc. of the 63rd IEEE Vehicular Technology Conference, Vol. 2 (2006) 578–582
3. Erin, C., Asada, H.H.: Energy Optimal Codes fo Wireless Communications. In: Proc. of the 38th IEEE Conference of Decision and Control, Vol. 5 (1999) 4446–4453

4. Prakash, Y., Gupta, S.K.: Energy Efficient Source Coding and Modulation for Wireless Applications. In: Proc. of the IEEE Wireless Communications and Networking Conference, Vol. 1 (1999) 212–217

5. Tang, Q., Gupta, S., Schwiebert, L.: BER Performance Analysis of an On-off Keying based Minimum Energy Coding for Energy Constrained Wireless Sensor Application. In IEEE ICC (2005)

6. Liu, C.H., Asada, H.H.: A Source Coding and Modulation Method for Power Saving and Interference Reduction in DS-CDMA Sensor Networks Systems. In: Proc. of American Control Conference, Vol. 4 (2002) 3003–3008

7. Kim, J., Andrews, J.G.: An Energy Efficient Source Coding and Modulation Scheme for Wireless Sensor Networks. In: 6th IEEE Workshop on Signal Processing Advances in Wireless Communications (2005) 710–714

8. Yao, S., Geraniotis, E.: Optimal Power Control Law for Multimedia Multirate CDMA Systems. In: IEEE 46th Vehicular Technology Conference: 'Mobile Technology for the Human Race', Vol. 1 (1996) 392–396

9. Santucci, F., Durastante, G., Graziosi, F., Fischione, C.: Power Allocation and Control in Multimedia CDMA Wireless Systems. In: Telecommunication Systems, Vol. 23. Springer Netherlands (2003) 69-94

10. 2.4 GHz IEEE 802.15.4 / ZigBee-ready RF Transceiver. Chipcon Products by Texas Instruments (2006)

11. Fischione, C., Butussi, M.: Power and Rate Control Outage Based in CDMA Wireless Networks under MAI and Heterogeneous Traffic Sources. Technical report IR-EE-RT_2006:033, Royal institute of Technology, Stockholm, Sweden, (Sept. 2006)

12. Bertsekas, D.P., Tsitsiklis, J.N.: Parallel and Distribuited Computation: Numerical Methods, Athen Scientific, (1997)

13. Proakis, J.G.: Digital Communications. 3rd edn. McGraw Hill International Editions (1995)

14. Stüber, G.L.: Principles of Mobile Communication. Kluwer Academic Publishers (1996)

15. Rå de, L., Westergren, B.: Mathematics Handbook for Science and Engineering. Studentlitteratur (2006)

16. Zurita Ares, B.: Adaptive Source and Channel Coding Algorithms for Energy saving in Wireless Sensor Networks. Master Thesis, Royal Institute of Technology, (Sept. 2006)

Appendix

By definition, we have that

$$L_i(t) = \frac{2}{P_i T_b^2 \mathrm{PL}_{ii}} \left(\sum_{\substack{j=1 \\ j \neq i}}^{K} \alpha_{ME} P_j \mathrm{PL}_{j,i} e^{\xi_{j,i} - \xi_{ii}} \frac{T_b^2}{6G} + \frac{N_0 T_b}{4} e^{-\xi_{ii}} \right) . \tag{41}$$

The extended Wilkinson moment matching method [9], allows for the computation of the average and standard deviation of X_i by matching the average and autocorrelation of $L_i(t)$ with those of $e^{X_i(t)}$, thus obtaining

$$\mu_{X_i} = 2 \ln M_i^{(1)} - \frac{1}{2} \ln M_i^{(2)} , \tag{42}$$

$$\sigma_{X_i}^2 = \ln M_i^{(2)} - 2\ln M_i^{(1)} \, , \tag{43}$$

with

$$M_i^{(1)} \triangleq E_{\Omega_i(t),\nu(t)}\{L_i\} \, , \tag{44}$$

$$M_i^{(2)} \triangleq E_{\Omega_i(t),\nu(t)}\{L_i^2\} \, , \tag{45}$$

where the statistical expectation is taken with respect to the distributions of the channel coefficients and the high bit. Therefore, by recalling that $\Omega_i(t)$ and $\nu(t)$ are statistically independent, and the definition of moments of log normal random variables [15], it is easy to show that

$$M_i^{(1)} = \frac{2}{P_i T_b^2 \mathrm{PL}_{i,i}} \beta_i^{(1)}[\mathbf{P}_{-i}] \, , \tag{46}$$

$$M_i^{(2)} = \frac{4}{P_i^2 T_b^4 \mathrm{PL}_{i,i}^2} \beta_i^{(2)}[\mathbf{P}_{-i}] \, , \tag{47}$$

where

$$\beta_1^i[\mathbf{P}_{-i}] = \sum_{\substack{j=1 \\ j\neq i}}^{K} \alpha P_j \mathrm{PL}_{j,i} e^{\frac{1}{2}\left(\sigma_{\xi_{j,i}}^2 + \sigma_{\xi_{i,i}}^2\right)} \frac{T_b^2}{6G} + \frac{N_0 T_b}{4} e^{\frac{1}{2}\sigma_{\xi_{i,i}}^2} \, , \tag{48}$$

$$\beta_2^i[\mathbf{P}_{-i}] = \sum_{\substack{j=1 \\ j\neq i}}^{K} \alpha^2 P_j^2 \mathrm{PL}_{j,i}^2 e^{2\left(\sigma_{\xi_{j,i}}^2 + \sigma_{\xi_{i,i}}^2\right)} \frac{T_b^4}{36G^2} + \frac{N_0^2 T_b^2}{16} e^{2\sigma_{\xi_{i,i}}^2}$$

$$+ \sum_{\substack{j=1 \\ j\neq i}}^{K} \sum_{\substack{k=1 \\ k\neq i \\ k\neq j}}^{K} \alpha^2 P_j P_k \mathrm{PL}_{j,i} \mathrm{PL}_{k,i} e^{\frac{1}{2}\left(\sigma_{\xi_{j,i}}^2 + \sigma_{\xi_{k,i}}^2 + 4\sigma_{\xi_{i,i}}^2\right)} \frac{T_b^4}{36G^2}$$

$$+ \frac{N_0 T_b}{2} \sum_{\substack{j=1 \\ j\neq i}}^{K} \alpha P_j \mathrm{PL}_{j,i} e^{\frac{1}{2}\left(\sigma_{\xi_{j,i}}^2 + 4\sigma_{\xi_{i,i}}^2\right)} \frac{T_b^2}{6G} \, . \tag{49}$$

In previous expressions, we have defined

$$\mathbf{P}_{-i} = [P_1, P_2, \ldots, P_{(i-1)}, P_{(i+1)}, \ldots, P_K]^T \, , \tag{50}$$

with the purpose to evidence that nor in $\beta_i^{(1)}[\mathbf{P}_{-i}]$, nor in $\beta_i^{(2)}[\mathbf{P}_{-i}]$ there is dependence with the transmission power of the link i.

Crankshaft: An Energy-Efficient MAC-Protocol for Dense Wireless Sensor Networks

G.P. Halkes and K.G. Langendoen

Faculty of Electrical Engineering, Mathematics and Computer Science
Delft University of Technology, The Netherlands
{g.p.halkes, k.g.langendoen}@tudelft.nl

Abstract. This paper introduces Crankshaft, a MAC protocol specifically targeted at dense wireless sensor networks. Crankshaft employs node synchronisation and offset wake-up schedules to combat the main cause of inefficiency in dense networks: overhearing by neighbouring nodes. Further energy savings are gained by using efficient channel polling and contention resolution techniques.

Simulations show that Crankshaft achieves high delivery ratios at low power consumption under the common convergecast traffic pattern in dense networks. This performance is achieved by trading broadcast bandwidth for energy efficiency. Finally, tests with a TinyOS implementation demonstrate the real-world feasibility of the protocol.

Keywords: Wireless Sensor Networks, MAC Protocol, Dense Networks.

1 Introduction

In Wireless Sensor Networks (WSNs) energy efficiency is a major consideration. Sensor nodes are expected to operate for long periods of time, running of batteries or ambient energy sources. Because the biggest consumer of energy is the radio, many researchers have focused on creating energy efficient MAC protocols [1,2,3,4,5,6,7].

Recent experiences with real-world deployments [8] have shown that the number of neighbours in WSNs can be higher than 15, which exceeds the 5–10 that MAC protocol designers have typically assumed. The "smart-dust" vision of WSNs also incorporates these dense deployments. Dense deployments have their own specific challenges, due to the high connectivity. Below we list the most important problems in current MAC protocols arising from dense networks:

Overhearing. Overhearing of messages destined for other nodes is a source of energy waste in any deployment. However, in dense deployments there are more neighbours that will overhear a message which exacerbates the problem. Furthermore, having more neighbours also means there may be more messages to overhear.

Communication grouping. Several protocols, like S-MAC [1] and T-MAC [2], group communication into active parts of frames. This is done to allow the

K. Langendoen and T. Voigt (Eds.): EWSN 2007, LNCS 4373, pp. 228–244, 2007.

network to go to sleep during the inactive parts of frames. The approach has a significant drawback: the grouping increases contention and collisions. Collisions cause retries, which in turn increases the traffic load. Furthermore, for adaptive protocols like T-MAC the increased traffic will keep nodes awake longer without increasing useful energy consumption.

Over-provisioning. TDMA protocols like LMAC [6] schedule send-slots for participating nodes. However, if a node has nothing to send, the slot goes unused. In a dense deployment, a frame has to be split into many slots to allow all nodes to participate in the network. Most of these slots go unused, but as a node has to wait for its send slot before it is allowed to send, latency increases and throughput decreases. Also, all the non-sender nodes will have to listen for at least a short amount of time to check if the scheduled sender is actually using the slot, and to check if they are being addressed by the sender.

Neighbour state. Protocols that save neighbour state as for example PMAC [7] and WiseMAC [9] do, also run into problems in dense deployments. Because in a dense deployment each node has many neighbours, the MAC protocol will have to either maintain a lot of state or discard some of the neighbours. Maintaining state for over 20 neighbours is undesirable as it uses precious RAM. However, discarding neighbour information means that communication with certain nodes is not possible or at least severely hindered. Furthermore, the routing protocol also maintains a neighbour list. If the neighbour list of the routing layer contains different nodes than the neighbour list of the MAC protocol, considerable problems arise.

This paper introduces the Crankshaft MAC protocol, which is specifically designed to perform well in dense deployments. It reduces overhearing and communication grouping by letting nodes power-down their radios alternately, rather than simultaneously. It does not keep per-neighbour state and receive-slot scheduling ensures that over-provisioning is bounded. The trade-off is that the maximum throughput is reduced, especially for broadcast traffic. For many applications however, this trade-off is acceptable.

The rest of this paper is organised as follows: First we will present related work. Then, in Section 3 we discuss the design of the Crankshaft protocol. In Section 4 we discuss the setup of our simulations, followed by the simulation results in Section 5. In Section 6 we present our results with our TinyOS implementation. Finally in Sections 7 and 8 we provide more discussion of the results and finish with our conclusions and future work.

2   Related Work

Many MAC protocols have been designed for WSNs. Below we present a selection of protocols that have relevance to our new Crankshaft protocol.

One of the earliest proposals is Low Power Listening [3] (LPL). LPL uses a simple Data/Ack scheme to ensure reliability. This is combined with efficient channel polling to reduce the energy spent on listening for incoming messages.

Instead of simply turning the radio on, LPL periodically checks the channel. To ensure that messages are properly received the preamble of each message is stretched to include an additional poll period. The B-MAC [4] protocol is an evolution of LPL, whereby the application can tweak the poll period depending on its bandwidth usage.

The channel polling mechanism of LPL has been further refined in the SCP-MAC [5] protocol. It uses channel polling, but it synchronises all nodes to poll at the same time, essentially implementing a slotting mechanism. This allows potential senders to do contention resolution before the intended receiver wakes up. Furthermore, the message preambles do not have to be stretched for a complete poll period because the poll moment is known. Crankshaft employs a mechanism of channel polling very similar to the SCP-MAC protocol.

Several TDMA protocols have also been developed. A good example is the LMAC [6] protocol. Contrary to many other TDMA protocols, the LMAC protocol uses a completely distributed slot assignment mechanism. Each slot owner sends at least a packet header in the slot the node owns. Neighbouring nodes listen to the start of each slot, and detect which slots are free. However, for a TDMA protocol it is required that a slot is not reused within a two-hop neighbourhood. The LMAC protocol therefore includes a bitmap with all the slots assigned to a node's neighbours in the header. By combining the bitmaps of all neighbours, a node can determine which slots are free within a two-hop neighbourhood. Crankshaft also uses frames and slots, but schedules receivers rather than senders. However, the mechanisms employed by LMAC to achieve synchronisation, framing and slotting are used in Crankshaft.

Pattern MAC [7], or PMAC, also divides time into frames. Each frame consists of two parts: the Pattern Repeat part and the Pattern Exchange part. Both parts are divided into slots. During the Pattern Repeat part, nodes follow the sleep/wake pattern they have advertised. Nodes also wake up when a neighbour for which they have a packet to send has advertised it will be awake during a particular slot. Nodes advertise their chosen patterns during the Pattern Exchange part. Each slot in the Pattern Exchange part is long enough to send a node's pattern information and nodes have to contend for these slots. To enable all nodes to send their pattern information, the Pattern Exchange part has as many slots as the maximum number of neighbours a node is expected to have. The sleep/wake patterns are adapted to the traffic going through a node, to achieve maximal energy savings. The PMAC protocol is similar to the Crankshaft protocol in that it also schedules nodes to be awake for reception on a slot basis. However, the PMAC protocol requires nodes to exchange and store schedules.

Although unrelated to the Crankshaft protocol, we also briefly introduce the S-MAC and T-MAC protocols, as they have become a standard benchmark for WSN MAC protocols. The S-MAC [1] protocol attacks the idle listening problem by introducing a coarse duty-cycling mechanism. It divides time into frames with an active part and a sleeping part. All communication between nodes is performed in the active part. In a later paper [10] the S-MAC protocol was extended with "adaptive listening". This incarnation of the S-MAC protocol uses the same idea as the T-MAC [2] protocol: group all communication at the start of the active period, and go to sleep if no more activity is sensed. This adapts the length of the active period to the available traffic.

When employed in dense networks all the above protocols suffer from one or more of the problems signalled in the introduction. This results in suboptimal energy use.

3   Crankshaft

Having signalled the problems MAC protocols face in dense wireless-networks, we designed the Crankshaft protocol. The basic principle of the protocol is that nodes are only awake to receive messages at fixed offsets from the start of a frame. This is analogous to an internal combustion engine where the moment a piston fires is a fixed offset from the start of the rotation of the crankshaft. Allowing different nodes to wake up for reception at different offsets from the start of the frame means that there are fewer nodes overhearing messages and spreads out the communication between unrelated receivers. Below we detail the working of the Crankshaft protocol.

The Crankshaft protocol divides time into frames, and each frame is divided into slots. There are two types of slots in the Crankshaft protocol: broadcast slots and unicast slots. During a broadcast slot all nodes wake up to listen for an incoming message. Any node that has a broadcast message to send contends with all other nodes to send that message. A frame starts with all the unicast slots, followed by the broadcast slots.

Each node also listens for one unicast slot every frame. During that slot a neighbouring node can send a message to that node, provided it wins the contention. The slot a node listens to is determined by the node's MAC address. Therefore, a node wanting to send a message knows precisely in which slot the destination wakes up. Crankshaft uses a Data/Ack sequence for unicast messages, and the slot length is such that it is long enough for the contention period, maximum-length data message and acknowledgement message. If the sender does not receive an acknowledgement, the protocol is set to retry each message three times in subsequent frames. However, to reduce contention when retrying the transmission the node will only retry in the next frame with a probability of 70%. Otherwise it will wait for another frame.

Special provisions are made for base-station or sink nodes. Sink nodes will listen to all unicast slots. The rationale for this is that the sink is the destination for most traffic in the network and therefore requires more receive bandwidth. Furthermore, the sink is typically connected to either a much larger battery or mains power, which will allow it to spend more energy. To allow other nodes to determine whether a neighbour is a sink node, sink nodes use specially reserved addresses. For example, in TinyOS node 0 is always considered a sink node.

Although many complicated methods of slot assignment are possible (e.g. Time Division Hashing [11]), we have chosen to use a simple mechanism to limit the amount of processing power required. Each frame has n unicast slots, and the slot assignment is performed by calculating *MAC address* modulo n. Using a static slot assignment like this may result in two neighbours being assigned the same slot. To allow such neighbours to communicate, nodes are allowed to act as senders in their own receive slot. A node that acts as a sender in its own receive slot will revert to receive mode if it loses contention.

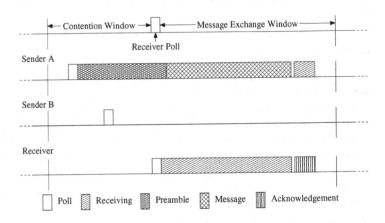

Fig. 1. Contention and message exchange in the Crankshaft protocol

Clearly, using frames requires that nodes are synchronised. Synchronisation can be achieved both through a reference node (i.e., the base-station or sink node), or through a distributed algorithm like GSA [12]. This synchronisation can also be used to achieve increased energy savings. Nodes need not wake up for an entire slot, but only for a small amount of time at a fixed offset to the start of the slot (see Figure 1). The period between the start of the slot and the moment the listening node turns on its radio is used to resolve contention. A node that wants to send a message in a particular slot chooses a moment in the contention window. The sending node listens for a short amount of time just prior to its chosen moment to detect other nodes contending for the same slot. If no other nodes are sending, the sending node starts sending a preamble to notify other nodes of its intention to send. Shortly after the receiving node is known to wake up, the sending node transmits the start symbol and the actual message. This is similar to the channel polling mechanism in the SCP-MAC protocol [5]. Note that during the contention window only the contending senders are awake, and only the winner of the contention is awake for more than a short poll. This results in very energy efficient contention resolution.

To improve contention resolution, the Crankshaft protocol also employs the Sift distribution [13] for choosing the moment to start sending. The Sift distribution is essentially a truncated geometric distribution, which results in fewer collisions than using a uniform distribution. Using Sift also reduces the average amount of time between the start of sending and the wake up moment of the receiver, saving even more energy.

The header for Crankshaft packets consists of a one byte length field, two byte *to* and *from* addresses, a one byte message type field, three bytes of clock synchronisation information, and two CRC bytes. For broadcast messages, the type field is set to broadcast and the *to* address is omitted. In our simulations, the synchronisation information contains the number of hops to the reference node, and the current (estimated) clock at the reference node.

Although not implemented in our simulations or real-world implementation, the Crankshaft protocol can use address filtering to reduce overhearing. A node would then simply turn of its radio after receiving the *to* address if the message is for another node.

4   Simulation Setup

To evaluate the Crankshaft protocol we created an implementation in our OM-NeT++ [14] based simulator called MiXiM. The simulator contains a model of the EYES wireless sensor node, which includes an RFM TR1001 radio. The radio model is an SNR-based model, on top of a simple path-loss propagation model. For timing the nodes use a 32 KHz crystal, and the nodes are powered by two 1.5 V AA batteries supplying 3 V.

For our experiments we use the layout of a real-world potato-field experiment [8]. This setup includes 96 nodes on a field of approximately 90×50 meters. The simulated nodes have a radio range of 25 meters, which is similar to the radio range in the real-world experiment. The base station is situated near a corner. Average connectivity in the network is approximately 17.3.

In our simulations we have included five protocols: Low Power Listening (LPL), T-MAC, LMAC, SCP-MAC*, and of course Crankshaft. The SCP-MAC* protocol is our variation of the SCP-MAC protocol. Instead of using two contention periods, one of which the receiver overhears, it uses the Sift distribution for a single contention period before the receiver wakes up. This way the SCP-MAC protocol can easily be implemented as a variation of the Crankshaft protocol, where each slot is a receive and broadcast slot at the same time, and acknowledgements are disabled.

We have focused our simulations on traffic patterns we consider most important for wireless sensor networks: convergecast and broadcast flood. The convergecast pattern is the pattern used in most monitoring applications. All nodes periodically send data to a sink node, which then processes the data or stores the data for further processing. Broadcast floods are typically found in routing protocols and in distributing queries over the network.

Table 1 lists the simulation parameters. Each simulation lasts 200 seconds of simulated time and the results are the average of 20 runs with different random seeds. Routing is done using a static routing table. Therefore there is no routing traffic exchanged during the simulation.

Table 1. Simulation parameters

General			LMAC		
Message payload	25 bytes		Maximum data length	64 bytes	
			Slots per frame	80	
Radio			Packet header	20 bytes	
Effective data rate	61 kbps				
Preamble + start byte	433 μs		SCP-MAC* and Crankshaft		
Transmit	12 mA		Contention window	9.15 ms	
Receive	3.8 mA		Poll length	300 μs	
Sleep	0.7 μA		Maximum data length	64 bytes	
			Sift nodes parameter	512	
LPL			Packet header (max.)	11 bytes	
Sample period	300 μs				
			Crankshaft specific		
T-MAC			Unicast slots	8	
Frame length	610 ms		Broadcast slots	2	
Contention window	9.15 ms				
Packet header	8 bytes				
Maximum data length	250 bytes				
Activity timeout	15 ms				

5   Simulation Results

Below we present our simulation results. In Section 5.1 we present the results for the convergecast pattern followed by the results for the broadcast flood pattern in Section 5.2. In Section 5.3 we revisit the convergecast pattern results and show how the latency of the Crankshaft protocol can be improved.

5.1   Convergecast

Figure 2 shows the results of our convergecast experiments. It is clear that the LPL protocol has the highest delivery ratio (top graph) except for high message rates, but at the expense of consuming a lot of energy (middle graph). The high energy consumption is due to the the high connectivity which causes many nodes to overhear each transmission. As nodes using LPL can send their message any time, i.e. they do not have to wait for a slot or frame to start, the latency remains low until the network is saturated (bottom graph).

The delivery ratio of the SCP-MAC* protocol is clearly adversely affected by the lack of acknowledgement messages for low message rates. Even for low message rates SCP-MAC* does not achieve perfect delivery. However, the lack of acknowledgements also means that there are fewer messages to send. For high messages rates the lack of acknowledgements is beneficial. For protocols using acknowledgements the increasing collisions at high message rates will induce more retransmissions, which in turn increase the network load. This effect can be seen in that the SCP-MAC* curve does not drop like the LPL and Crankshaft curves do. SCP-MAC*'s energy consumption is much better than LPL, but for high message rates increases quickly as well.

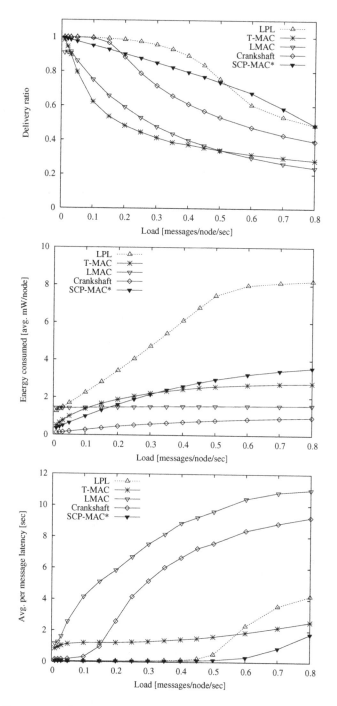

Fig. 2. Performance under convergecast traffic: delivery ratio (top), energy consumption (middle) and latency (bottom)

Compared to the LPL protocol, Crankshaft's delivery ratio starts to drop at lower message rates. This is caused by limiting the per-node receive bandwidth through selecting only one receive slot per frame. For low message rates Crankshaft does manage perfect delivery. The bandwidth limitation does mean that for medium and high message rates the Crankshaft protocol cannot achieve the high delivery ratios of LPL and SCP-MAC*.

The Crankshaft protocol is very energy efficient. It consumes a factor of 3.5 less energy than SCP-MAC*. There are two factors which contribute to the energy efficiency: firstly, because only a subset of the nodes is awake in each slot overhearing is reduced. Secondly, contention is reduced. When using SCP-MAC* and node A wants to send to node B and node C wants to send to node D, and A and C are within communications range, nodes A and C contend for the right to send. However, when using Crankshaft nodes B and D generally wake up in different slots, automatically resolving the contention between nodes A and C.

LMAC suffers from the need to assign a contention-free slot to all nodes in the network. To allow such an assignment to exist 80 slots are required. Even at low message rates the LMAC protocol does not achieve a perfect delivery ratio. Network congestion caused by low per-node bandwidth prevents this. The energy consumption remains nearly constant, because the LMAC protocol already saturates at low message rates. The small increase in energy consumption is due to more messages that are sent one hop, only to be discarded because of full message queues at the receiver. The large number of slots also induces a high message latency for the LMAC protocol.

Finally, T-MAC is unable to cope with the flood of messages directed towards the sink node. The aggressive sleep policy is causing nodes to go to sleep too often, which hinders throughput. Although latency seems low for high message rates, this is caused by only the nodes near the sink being able to reach the sink. The aggressive sleep policy does provide low energy consumption, even though the T-MAC protocol suffers from communication grouping and overhearing.

Of all the protocols compared, SCP-MAC* has the lowest latency. Again this is caused by the lack of acknowledgements and retries. Messages are not kept in queues waiting for retransmissions of other messages, which means latency is kept down. Crankshaft's latency rises quickly as the delivery ratio drops. This is partly caused by messages having to wait in queues due to congestion, and partly caused by messages having to wait a full frame (150 ms) when contention is lost. However, Crankshaft's latency can be improved, as we will show in Section 5.3.

5.2   Broadcast Flood

With our second experiment we investigate the performance under broadcast flood traffic. In this experiment the sink node initiates the floods. The delivery ratio is calculated as the total of unique flood messages received by all nodes, divided by the total of unique messages that should have been received by all nodes. To allow nodes to determine the uniqueness of a message, each message contains a serial number. Nodes compare the serial number in the message with the highest serial number received so far. If the serial number in the message is lower or equal, the message is discarded. Note that this may result in messages not previously received being discarded, if a message with a higher serial number has already been delivered. For this to happen, collisions or link errors must have resulted in the failed reception of a lower numbered message first.

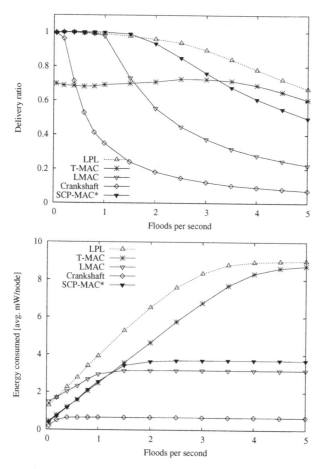

Fig. 3. Performance under broadcast-flood traffic: delivery ratio (top), energy consumption (bottom)

Figure 3 shows the delivery ratio (top) and energy consumption (bottom) for all protocols under the broadcast flood traffic pattern. LPL outperforms all other protocols in terms of delivery ratio for high message rates, but at the expense of high energy consumption. Again, because it does not use any slotting or framing it can quickly move messages through the network. Although it uses much energy, the energy is mostly put to good use.

The T-MAC curve shows a remarkable artifact. As the amount of traffic in the network increases, so does the delivery ratio. The cause is again T-MAC's aggressive sleep policy. In low traffic conditions, most of the network is asleep after the sink initiated the broadcast flood. Although all nodes that heard the sink's broadcast repeat the message, the sleeping part of the network does not receive most of these. Depending on the collisions and back-off, parts of the network may not receive any of these messages at all. Increasing the traffic load will keep more nodes awake for more time, increasing the number of nodes receiving re-sends. However, it also increases the chance of messages arriving out of order, thereby causing nodes to disregard previously unseen messages arriving later.

LMAC's performance is not hampered by the 80 slots in this scenario, because all nodes need to send the same number of messages. Therefore, there is little over-provisioning. Protocols like LPL and SCP-MAC* can support more simultaneous transmissions than LMAC, because they do not require all nodes in a two-hop neighbourhood to remain quiet. Of course this leads to collisions, but because every message is sent multiple times, although by different nodes, this is not a problem. If a node does not receive the first transmission, it probably receives a second or third. Hence, the LPL and SCP-MAC* protocols outperform LMAC.

The Crankshaft protocol shares the SCP-MAC* characteristics in the broadcast case. However, because only two out of every 10 slots are broadcast slots Crankshaft can cope with roughly one sixth of the traffic that SCP-MAC* can. It only uses approximately one sixth of the energy as well. Crankshaft's broadcast flood performance can be tuned to the amount of broadcast flood traffic is expected, by increasing the number of broadcast slots. Of course the broadcast performance is then traded for unicast performance, as unicast traffic will receive a smaller share of the available time.

5.3   Crankshaft Latency

The average message latency for the Crankshaft protocol under convergecast traffic increases quickly as the number of messages per node per second exceeds 0.15. However, the design of the Crankshaft protocol leaves an option to improve the latency. Recall that the cause of the quickly increasing latency is that a node that loses contention or does not receive an acknowledgement has to wait for an entire frame to retry. Given that a dense network provides many alternate paths to the sink, a node that loses contention or does not receive an acknowledgement could also try to send its message to another next hop.

Of course the routing layer has to cooperate with the Crankshaft protocol to make this work. To this end the interface between the routing layer and the MAC protocol is augmented. First of all, the routing layer can query Crankshaft about which of a list of neighbours wakes up first. Secondly, Crankshaft will return a message that it could not deliver in the first try to the routing layer. That is, it will not block and try at some later moment as most MAC layers do. The routing layer will then decide if and to whom to retry sending the message.

Figure 4 shows the latency (bottom) for the Crankshaft protocol with the low-latency option, marked *Crankshaft LL*. For reference the results for the regular Crankshaft protocol and the SCP-MAC* protocol are repeated.

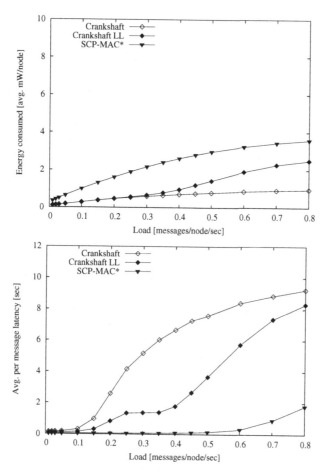

Fig. 4. Crankshaft energy consumption (top) and latency (bottom) with low-latency option

Even for Crankshaft's low-latency version, average latency starts to increase noticeably at approximately 0.15 messages per node per second. The latency is however reduced to approximately 37% of the regular Crankshaft protocol's latency. The increase at 0.15 is almost entirely due to a small group of 15 nodes that are in the corner opposite the sink. These nodes do not have many next hop neighbours. As the network load increases these nodes are having increasingly more difficulty in sending their messages to the next hop. Average latency for the messages for these nodes increases to some eight seconds and more. From 0.25 through 0.35 messages per node per second the increase in latency stops. On this interval the number of messages that arrive at the sink from the 15 distant nodes decreases in such a way that it compensates for the increased latency. Most of the other 80 nodes still have average per message latencies in the range of 0–0.7 seconds. Using the regular Crankshaft protocol, approximately half of the nodes already have average per message latencies (much) larger than one second. For message rates larger than 0.35 the other 80 nodes are also seriously affected by the increasing network load. This is reflected by the increasing latency.

As can be seen from the top graph in Figure 4, Crankshaft's energy consumption does not change for message rates below 0.35 messages per node per second. At higher rates the energy consumption does increase significantly, to 2.7 times the energy consumption without the low-latency option at a rate of 0.8 messages per node per second. The congestion in the network is causing increasing numbers of retransmissions, which consume much energy. The delivery ratio is affected very little by the low-latency option. For message rates between 0.15 and 0.5, at most 7 percentage points are gained, while at 0.8 approximately 10 percentage points are lost.

6 TinyOS Implementation

To demonstrate the real world feasibility of the Crankshaft protocol, we have created an implementation of Crankshaft for the TinyOS operating system. We have tested our implementation by running a convergecast scenario on our 26 node testbed consisting of mica2 clones named TNOdes. The nodes in our testbed can all hear one another, but not all pairs of nodes have good links. We have created a static routing table in which 12 of the 26 nodes use other nodes to forward messages to the sink. All nodes, with the exception of the sink, repeatedly send messages to the sink at fixed intervals. For comparison, we have included our implementations of T-MAC and LMAC, and the default MAC protocol for mica2 nodes, i.e. BMAC.

Table 2 shows the parameters for the experiment and the protocols. We have strived to make the parameters match those of our simulations as closely as possible, but the hardware used does dictate many of the protocol timings. Also, the physical layers in our TinyOS framework include extra header fields, and the time synchronisation fields take five bytes instead of three. Therefore the packet headers are longer than in simulation. Furthermore, the BMAC protocol as implemented in TinyOS does not provide for retries, where the simulated LPL protocol does. The Crankshaft protocol is implemented without the use of the Sift distribution. A standard uniform distribution is used instead for ease of implementation.

The experiments only show the results of a single run, due to time constraints. Therefore it is not possible to draw firm conclusions from these results. However, the results do provide an indication of the performance.

Figure 5 shows our results. The first thing to note is that even for low message rates, none of the protocols achieves perfect delivery. This is due to the use of

Table 2. Real-world experiment parameters

Experiment		LMAC	
Time per message rate	5 min	Slots per frame	32
Message payload	10 bytes	Packet header	24 bytes
Maximum data length	29 bytes		
(all protocols)		Crankshaft	
		Contention window	5.8 ms
Radio		Poll length	4 ms
Effective data rate	19 kbps	Packet header	18 bytes
Preamble + start byte	2.1 ms	Unicast slots	8
		Broadcast slots	2
T-MAC			
Frame length	610 ms	BMAC	
Contention window	5.8 ms	Sample period	20 ms
Packet header	18 bytes		
Activity timeout	18 ms		

non-perfect radio links. The LMAC protocol copes best, because only one node will try to send in each slot, ensuring the best possible link quality.

The LMAC protocol also shows the same sudden drop in delivery ratio as our simulation results. Again this is due to the bandwidth limitations imposed by the TDMA structure of the protocol. The T-MAC protocol shows erratic behaviour for low message rates. This is probably due to the aggressive sleep strategy used in the T-MAC protocol. As in the simulations, the T-MAC protocol shows it does not deal well with high load situations.

The Crankshaft protocol and the BMAC protocol show similar performance. For low message rates, the use of retries in the Crankshaft protocol means its delivery ratio is higher than BMAC's. For high message rates the difference between Crankshaft and BMAC is too small to draw any conclusions.

7   Discussion

The simulations results show that the Crankshaft protocol can provide good convergecast performance at low energy consumption in dense networks. Latency can be a problem in the unoptimised protocol. However, by spending a little more energy latency can be kept down if the routing layer is modified as well. Furthermore, message rates of more than 0.5 messages per node per second are infrequent in monitoring applications.

The trade-off is that broadcast bandwidth is significantly reduced. This means that to use the Crankshaft protocol effectively, broadcast flooding must be minimised. Flooding is used mostly for two purposes in WSNs: collecting routing information and pushing queries into the network. For the former purpose broadcast flooding is required to operate correctly. The latter can be achieved by more bandwidth efficient broadcasting schemes, especially in dense networks. This would eliminate the need for high broadcast throughput. Also, sustained flood rates of more than one flood per second are probably excessive.

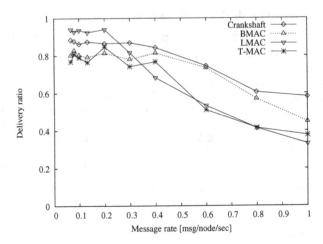

Fig. 5. Delivery ratio for convergecast with TinyOS implementation

A point to consider with respect to the implementation of the Crankshaft protocol is the recent trend towards packet-based radios. To implement Crankshaft variable preamble lengths are required. Packet radios in general do not provide sufficient flexibility to implement this directly. However, the creators of the WiseMAC protocol [9] already provide a solution: repeatedly sending the packet for the required duration. Although this may seem wasteful, one has to consider that sending is the infrequent operation. Letting the sender spend more energy to allow multiple (overhearing) receivers to save energy is usually more energy efficient on balance.

The Crankshaft protocol can also be tuned to the specific application and network density. By increasing the number of unicast slots the consumed energy can be brought down further, although maximum bandwidth will be decreased and latency will go up. By decreasing the number of unicast slots, the maximum per node bandwidth can be increased and the latency decreased, at the expense of more energy consumption and more collisions. Similar considerations hold for the number of broadcast slots.

7.1   Variations

The Crankshaft protocol design allows for some variations in the slot assignment mechanism. For example, we have tested using meta frames consisting of four frames. Each of the four frames would use a different assignment calculation, in our case different parts of the MAC address.

As nodes are usually numbered sequentially, simply using the higher bits of the MAC addresses would not give enough variation. Therefore the calculations were more complex than simple modulo calculation. We also disallowed sending in a node's receive slot, because there always is at least one of the four frames in which the slot assignment for two neighbours differs.

Although this assignment scheme resulted in a small performance increase, we felt the difference did not compensate for the added code complexity and processing requirements.

Other options we tested are Time Division Hashing [11], and using broadcast slots for unicast if two neighbours share a slot assignment. None of these options gave a significant performance benefit, so they are not included in the results.

8 Conclusions and Future Work

In this paper we have presented Crankshaft, a MAC protocol for dense wireless sensor networks. It employs receive slot scheduling to reduce overhearing and bases the schedule on MAC addresses to obviate the need to keep neighbour state. We have shown through simulation and real-world experiments that Crankshaft can provide good delivery ratios in convergecast scenarios with respect to Low Power Listening, T-MAC, LMAC and SCP-MAC*. Simulations also show that Crankshaft manages to do so while consuming very little energy.

Further simulations show that the Crankshaft protocol cannot provide good broadcast flood delivery. However, Crankshaft's energy consumption does not suffer from broadcast flooding either. Most applications only require sporadic flooding, for which Crankshaft provides adequate performance.

We conclude that the Crankshaft protocol is suitable for long-lived monitoring applications, where energy efficiency is key. The Crankshaft protocol can provide the required delivery ratios for convergecast traffic at extremely low energy consumption.

The Crankshaft protocol as proposed has a very rigid structure. This limits the applicability of the protocol. For future work we intend to look at adaptive scheduling of extra receive slots to facilitate more application types and mitigate bottlenecks that can occur near sink nodes and elsewhere in the network. Another research item is improving the broadcast capabilities of the Crankshaft protocol.

A final research direction for the Crankshaft protocol is leveraging multi-channel radios. In principle this is as simple as assigning nodes a channel as well as a time within a frame.

Acknowledgements

We would like to thank the anonymous reviewers for their comments. Furthermore we would like to thank Otto Visser and Ivaylo Haratcherev for their work on the testbed and Tom Parker for his work on his TinyOS MAC-framework which made developing the TinyOS implementation so much easier.

References

1. Ye, W., Heidemann, J., Estrin, D.: An energy-efficient MAC protocol for wireless sensor networks. In: Proc. of the 21st Conf. of the IEEE Computer and Communications Societies (INFOCOM). Volume 3. (2002) 1567–1576

2. van Dam, T., Langendoen, K.: An adaptive energy-efficient MAC protocol for wireless sensor networks. In: Proc. of the 1st ACM Conf. on Embedded Networked Sensor Systems (SenSys 2003), Los Angeles, CA (2003) 171–180

3. Hill, J., Culler, D.: Mica: a wireless platform for deeply embedded networks. IEEE Micro **22** (2002) 12–24

4. Polastre, J., Hill, J., Culler, D.: Versatile low power media access for wireless sensor networks. In: Proc. of the 2nd ACM Conf. on Embedded Networked Sensor Systems (SenSys 2004), Baltimore, MD (2004) 95–107

5. Ye, W., Heidemann, J.: Ultra-low duty cycle MAC with scheduled channel polling. Technical Report ISI-TR-604, USC Information Sciences Institute (2005)

6. van Hoesel, L., Havinga, P.: A lightweight medium access protocol (LMAC) for wireless sensor networks. In: Proc. of the 1st Int. Workshop on Networked Sensing Systems (INSS 2004), Tokyo, Japan (2004)

7. Zheng, T., Radhakrishnan, S., Sarangan, V.: PMAC: an adaptive energy-efficient MAC protocol for wireless sensor networks. In: Proc. of the 19th IEEE Int. Parallel and Distributed Processing Symp. (IPDPS'05). (2005) 65–72

8. Langendoen, K., Baggio, A., Visser, O.: Murphy loves potatoes: Experiences from a pilot sensor network deployment in precision agriculture. In: Proc. of the 14th Int. Workshop on Parallel and Distributed Real-Time Systems (WPDRTS), Rhodes, Greece (2006)

9. El-Hoiydi, A., Decotignie, J.D.: WiseMAC: An ultra low power MAC protocol for the downlink of infrastructure wireless sensor networks. In: Proc. of the Ninth Int. Symp. on Computers and Communications, 2004 (ISCC 2004). Volume 1. (2004) 244–251

10. Ye, W., Heidemann, J., Estrin, D.: Medium access control with coordinated, adaptive sleeping for wireless sensor networks. IEEE/ACM Trans. on Networking **12** (2004) 493–506

11. Cheng, W., Lee, I.T.A., Singh, N.: Time division hashing (TDH): A new scheduling scheme for wireless ad-hoc networks. In: Proc. of the Int. Symp. on Advanced Radio Technologies (ISART). (2005) 91–100

12. Li, Y., Ye, W., Heidemann, J.: Energy and latency control in low duty cycle MAC protocols. In: Proc. of the IEEE Wireless Communications and Networking Conf., New Orleans, LA, USA (2005)

13. Jamieson, K., Balakrishnan, H., Tay, Y.C.: Sift: a MAC protocol for event-driven wireless sensor networks. In: Proc. of the 3rd European Workshop on Wireless Sensor Networks (EWSN). (2006) 260–275

14. Varga, A.: The OMNeT++ discrete event simulation system. In: Proc. of the European Simulation Multiconference (ESM'2001), Prague, Czech Republic (2001)

Decentralized Scattering of Wake-Up Times in Wireless Sensor Networks

Alessandro Giusti[1], Amy L. Murphy[2,3], and Gian Pietro Picco[1,4]

[1] Politecnico di Milano, Italy
giusti@elet.polimi.it
[2] University of Lugano, Switzerland
[3] ITC-IRST, Povo, Italy
murphy@itc.it
[4] University of Trento, Italy
picco@dit.unitn.it

Abstract. Duty-cycling in wireless sensor networks (WSNs) has both beneficial effects on network lifetime and negative effects on application performance due to the inability of a sensor to perform while it is sleeping. In a typical scenario, the active periods of nodes are randomly initialized, leading to unpredictable and often sub-optimal performance. In this paper, we propose a fully decentralized *wake-up scattering* algorithm that uniformly spreads wake-up times of nearby sensors. Interestingly, our approach is complementary and dual to existing approaches that aim at synchronizing (instead of scattering) times, and to those that focus on spatial (instead of temporal) coverage. Wake-up scattering is beneficial in several application scenarios, three of which are considered here: responsiveness to one-hop queries from a mobile base station, sensing coverage for event detection, and latency in multi-hop communication. Our evaluation shows that, w.r.t. a random assignment of wake-up times, wake-up scattering brings improvements in all these measures, along with a positive impact on the network lifetime.

1 Introduction

One of the primary challenges for wireless sensor network (WSN) applications is energy management. A common solution that dramatically increases sensor lifetime is duty-cycling, i.e., periodically switching on and off communication and/or sensing capabilities. The major factors that affect lifetime are the length of the period (the *epoch period*) and the duration of the on-time (the *awake interval*). However, another variable critically affects the *performance* of the network, namely *when* in each period each node activates. We refer to this as the *wake-up time* of the sensor node. Typically, the wake-up time is randomly established, relating only to when the sensor is initially activated.

We first encountered the potential negative performance impact of wake-up times during our work on TinyLIME [1], a middleware that allows applications running on mobile bases stations to access the data (e.g., temperature) of nearby (one-hop) sensors through a tuple space interface. The system is designed to account for sensors that duty-cycle their communication components, therefore each time a base station needs to contact a sensor, it repeats its request until a sensor wakes up, receives the request,

K. Langendoen and T. Voigt (Eds.): EWSN 2007, LNCS 4373, pp. 245–260, 2007.

and replies. In the best case, one of the sensors is awake when the first request is sent and responds immediately. However, in the worst case, all sensors in range have just cycled off and will not reactivate communication until the next epoch. Therefore, the base station repeatedly sends the request until the sensors wake up and one replies. In a system with an epoch of minutes, such delays in response time can be significant.

Our solution is to introduce a calibration phase to deliberately select the time within the epoch in which each sensor wakes up. To improve performance, the wake-up times should be scattered evenly throughout the epoch, minimizing the time that a base station must wait before a sensor becomes active. Scattering is performed such that response to a base station at any location in the system is minimized, thus avoiding the need to track and adjust to a possibly rapidly moving base station.

We achieve this goal with a fully decentralized algorithm that incrementally improves the scattering of wake-up times among neighboring nodes. Essentially, each node periodically determines the wake-up times closest to its own among its one-hop neighbors, then moves its own wake-up time so as to minimally overlap with others. Because decisions are made entirely locally and independently, a single run of this algorithm may result in poor scattering. However, the system quickly stabilizes to a scattered network in very few repetitions.

Interestingly, this *wake-up scattering* approach can be naturally applied in many other situations. For example, in contrast to the aforementioned scenario which duty-cycles *communication*, consider a system that duty-cycles *sensing* activities. Scattering the wake-up time for sensing allows the area to be more effectively covered at all times, as opposed to activating all sensors in a given area at the same time. More importantly, the guarantee of a better scattering in time enables one to design a network with shorter awake intervals, therefore achieving a longer overall network lifetime. Another use is in a system that exploits a tree for communication from sensors to a fixed, centralized sink. To speed up communication from the edge of the network to the base station, parent nodes should be active *after* their children. In this case, proper scattering of wake-up times can decrease the average latency for data traveling on the network towards the root, thus increasing network performance.

Finally, it is worth noting how the problem of *wake-up scattering* is complementary and dual to other problems in WSNs. For instance, the idea of controlling wake-up times to enable communication has been studied in the context of MAC protocols, but with the goal of *synchronizing*, instead of scattering, the wake-up times. Similarly, the problem of covering an area to detect an event has been studied only for what concerns *spatial* coverage of an area and not, to our knowledge, in terms of coverage in time.

Summarizing, in this paper we put forth the following main contributions:

- we introduce for the first time the notion of wake-up scattering;
- we present a fully decentralized algorithm solving this problem;
- we evaluate this algorithm in three application scenarios common in WSNs.

These contributions are presented in Section 2, 3, and 4, respectively. The paper concludes by reporting related work in Section 5, followed by a brief summary.

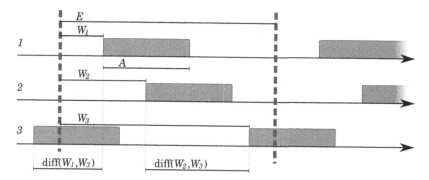

Fig. 1. Key definitions illustrated with three nodes. Time increases left to right. E is the epoch period, A the awake interval, W_i the wake-up time for node i, and $\text{diff}(W_i, W_j)$ the length of time between the wake-up times of nodes i and j.

2 Model and Motivation

Before presenting the details of our protocol, we briefly formulate the wake-up scattering problem and outline three reference scenarios that benefit from our approach.

2.1 Model

For the purposes of this work, we assume a straightforward network model in which non-mobile sensor nodes with circular communication and sensing radii are deployed in an unobstructed field. We further assume that all nodes have the same communication range. While these assumptions significantly simplify our analysis, they can be altered without affecting the algorithm's fundamental validity. Finally, we assume that the topology is not known and nodes are only aware of the neighboring nodes they can directly communicate with.

The primary premise of our work is that sensors operate in a duty-cycling manner, turning on and off certain capabilities at regular intervals. The length of the interval is the *epoch period E*, while the time during which a node is on is the *awake interval A*. Although it is possible to allow both E and A to vary for each node, in this work we assume they are system-wide, deployment-time parameters, equal for all nodes. These parameters are illustrated in Figure 1. Although this figure shows that the epochs at all three nodes are synchronized, this is not a requirement for our approach.

The figure also represents the *wake-up time W_i*, for each node i, and the interval between wake-up times measured with $\text{diff}(W_i, W_j)$. This operator accounts for the fact that the wake-up patterns repeat across epochs, therefore it measures the difference in the start of the awake intervals between any two nodes, even those waking up at the beginning or end of an epoch.

2.2 Wake-Up Scattering: Objectives and Usage Scenarios

This work illustrates an approach to modify, in a decentralized fashion, the wake-up time W_i of the nodes in a WSN such that they are scattered as much as possible. We

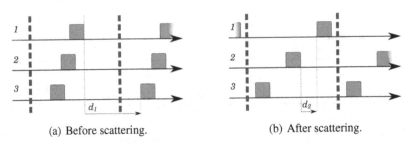

(a) Before scattering.   (b) After scattering.

Fig. 2. Three connected nodes before and after scattering. d_i shows the maximum delay for a base station to wait for a response in each setting.

maintain that such *wake-up scattering* improves application performance in many situations. Here, we focus on three representative scenarios with different characteristics, for which we detail the application functionality and goal as well as the improvement expected from wake-up scattering. In Section 4 we use these same scenarios to evaluate the effectiveness of our approach.

Responsiveness to Local Queries. As mentioned in the introduction, our first scenario is motivated by our work on the TinyLIME middleware [1]. In TinyLIME applications, sensor nodes are distributed through a region and a mobile base station queries for sensor data close to it. The goals in this environment are two-fold. First, we wish to minimize the time that a base station needs to wait to receive data. In other words, the goal is to always have at least one node near the base station awake, or about to wake up, in order to respond to queries. Second, we wish to minimize the maximum number of nodes that are awake at the same time, therefore reducing the possibility of collisions among query responses issued simultaneously by awake nodes.

Rather than trying to adapt to the possibly rapidly moving base station, our approach yields a wake-up scattering solution that suffices for any location of the base station. We accomplish this by considering the wake-up times among *nearby* nodes, motivated by the fact that such nodes are likely to be in contact with the base station at the same time, while those farther away will not. In this case the problem can be defined as the search for a global configuration of wake-up times that maximizes the minimum difference in wake-up times for any pair of nearby nodes. Put another way, our goal is that any pair of nearby motes should have their wake-up times as far away from each other as possible.

Figure 2 intuitively demonstrates the benefits of wake-up scattering with three nodes in a fully connected network (i.e., each pair can communicate) both before and after scattering. It can clearly be seen that after scattering, fewer nodes are awake at any given time, therefore reducing the possibility of communication interference. The figure also shows the maximum time, d_i that an unlucky base station needs to wait before receiving a response to a query, with the maximum delay d_1 much larger than d_2. On average, a base station initiating a query at any point during the epoch will have less delay to receive a response after scattering.

Event Coverage. Another popular use for sensor networks is detection of an event occurring somewhere in the field covered by the sensors. In this scenario, the critical parameters are the sensing range of the devices and the amount of time that the sensors are active. To detect an event, it must occur both *spatially* inside the sensing range of a node and *temporally* during the awake time of the node.

Our goal in this scenario is to maximize the percentage of events detected. By treating sensing analogous to communication, we can reuse the previous wake-up scattering technique to manage the wake-up times of *sensing* devices, thus guaranteeing that the intervals of data acquisition are spread as evenly as possible throughout the epoch thus improving event detection. Figure 2 can be used to visualize the concept, by defining the awake interval as the active time of the sensor devices. Although after scattering there are still gaps in the sensed time, these gaps are smaller than before scattering. To completely eliminate these breaks in sensing coverage, the awake interval of the sensors should be modified dynamically. However, in this paper we do not consider this additional optimization and limit ourselves to the management of wake-up times.

Data Latency in Tree-Based Networks. The third scenario we consider is the construction of a tree to funnel data from the edges of the network to a centralized base station, a common approach for applications such as TinyDB [2]. When considering nodes that duty-cycle their communication capabilities, we want to guarantee that when a child has data to send, either its parent in the tree is immediately active or it will be soon, thus minimizing the latency of a data packet on the path to the sink.

If we ignore propagation delays, the trivial solution is to force all nodes to turn on their communication at the same time. Not only does this solution exhibit a high collision probability, if sensors are active only at the same time as communication, sensing will also be synchronized and the potential benefits of scattering for event detection will not be achieved. Therefore, our goal is to maintain good event coverage while simultaneously reducing data latency.

To achieve this, we require that all nodes keep track of which of their neighbors can serve as parents towards the sink. We assume this is accomplished by broadcasting a message from the sink, that allows nodes to know their distance from it, and to infer that *all* neighbors with distances less than their own are *potential* parents.

When a node has a message to propagate to the sink (i.e., data collected from one of its own sensors or a message from one of its children), it must forward this to one of its (potential) parents, determined as above. We assume that the node tracks the wake-up time of its parents, and thus knows which parent will be awake next. If one is currently awake, the packet can be immediately sent; if not, the node must wait until a parent is awake, then forward the message. If the parent's wake-up time is much after the end of the awake interval of the child, rather than stay awake waiting, energy-savings may be achieved by putting the child to sleep and waking it up later when the parent is awake.

Intuitively, this gap between the readiness of the data at the child and the readiness of the parent to receive the data is minimized if the parent node is the next node to wake up in the sequence of wake-up times. If, instead, the next node is a sibling or child, data cannot make quick progress. Therefore, our goal is to introduce *into the scattering algorithm* the constraint that the next node should be a parent. Clearly this cannot be a strict requirement, because a node that must serve as a parent for multiple children can only have one previous to it in the wake-up order. However, we enforce the constraint that every node has either a parent or a sibling next in the wake-up order.

3   A Decentralized Wake-Up Scattering Algorithm

With the previous application targets in mind, we now present the details of our wake-up scattering approach. The algorithm is designed to generate low communication overhead and is easily implementable in a real WSN system. Our presentation first addresses the general scattering necessary for the first two application scenarios, then introduces extensions for multi-hop tree-based communication.

3.1   Overview

To simplify the explanation of the algorithm, we assume that the epoch starting times are synchronized at all nodes and that all start the scattering algorithm at the same time. Section 3.4 outlines the minimal changes required to remove these constraints.

Our wake-up scattering algorithm is inherently distributed among the sensor nodes, with each node making decisions with information only about nodes it can directly communicate with. Wake-up scattering iteratively refines the wake-up times of nodes in a series of calibration rounds. Each calibration round lasts one epoch, after which each node selects its new wake-up time. Our experiments, presented in the next section, demonstrate that after few rounds (on the order of 3-5) the network stabilizes to a well-scattered configuration.

It is worth noting that calibration rounds need not occur in successive epochs, but can be spread out over time, further limiting the already minimal impact of wake-up scattering on the normal operation of the WSN. Furthermore, after calibration stabilizes, it is meaningful to periodically repeat a calibration round to account for the insertion or removal of sensors.

The processing on a node inside a calibration phase is as follows:

1. Each node must learn the wake-up times of *some of* its neighbors. In a synchronized system, the nodes exchange their W_i values at the beginning of the calibration epoch. Each node is only interested in the wake-up times of the neighbor that wakes up immediately before it, prev, and immediately after it, next.

   The computation of W_{prev} and W_{next} must take into account the fact that the scheduling of wake-up times is repeated across epochs. Therefore, if a mote is the first to wake up in its neighborhood, $W_{prev} = W_{last} - E$, i.e., the wake-up time of the last node that wakes up in the epoch, minus the duration of the epoch E. Similarly, if the node is the last to wake up in the epoch, $W_{next} = W_{first} + E$.

2. Based on the collected information, each node selects a new wake-up time *near* the center of the time interval between W_{prev} and W_{next}. The motivations for not moving to the precise center are discussed later. Also, the target is calculated modulo E, forcing the wake-up time to fall inside the epoch.

Figure 3 shows a single calibration round for node 1 and the four nodes in communication with it. In this example, only nodes 1, 2, and 3 change their wake-up times, as indicated by the shift from the light to dark wake-up intervals, while nodes 4 and 5 are already well scattered w.r.t. all their neighbors and therefore do not adjust their wake-up times. The figure shows the key control information for node 1, namely the wake-up time of its prev (node 3) and next (node 2). W_{target} is the midpoint between these values, although node 1 does not move exactly to this time.

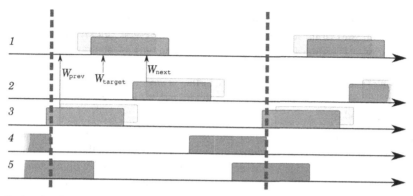

Fig. 3. A scenario with five nodes in the same 1-hop neighborhood, scattering their wake-up times. Light shading indicates the old awake interval, and dark shading the new one. Arrows indicate the W_{prev}, W_{next}, and the computed target wake-up time for node 1, W_{target}.

Indeed, the actual new wake-up time is calculated as a weighted average of W_{target} and the current wake-up time W_1. This weight, $0 < \alpha \leq 1$, is a parameter to the algorithm whose primary effect is to regulate the speed at which the algorithm stabilizes, i.e., the number of required calibration rounds. Small values reduce the convergence speed, while larger values generally converge faster. However, if the value is too large, the evolution to new configuration is not stable. Moreover, if we consider unreliable communication in which packets containing information about W_{next} and W_{prev} are lost, a smaller α value improves robustness.

Finally, it is worth noting that each calibration phase requires only a single, one-hop broadcast message from each node. Therefore, a calibration epoch can overlap with an epoch in which data is also exchanged.

3.2   Extensions for Tree-Based Communication

As noted in Section 2.2, a good wake-up configuration for multi-hop tree-based communication is one in which every node has either a sibling or a parent as its next in the wake-up sequence. Further, latency can be reduced by moving the wake-up time of the child close to the wake-up time of the parent. In this section we introduce two extensions to achieve these goals, namely *jumping* and *waving*.

"Jumping" Wake-up Times to Allow a Parent to Follow a Child. While ideally a parent should wake up after a child to forward data upstream as quickly as possible, the previously presented scattering algorithm never changes the sequence that nodes wake up inside an epoch. In other words, if a parent wakes up before its child, our scattering algorithm will never swap this order. Therefore, to reach a *better* configuration for tree-based communication, we introduce a new behavior in the scattering algorithm, namely the ability to *jump* over a neighbor w.r.t. wake-up time.

Specifically, if a node detects that its next node is one of its children, it sets its new wake-up time in the middle of the wake-up times of W_{next} and $W_{\text{afternext}}$, where $W_{\text{afternext}}$ is the node to wake up immediately following next. To avoid unstable behaviors such as nodes continuously jumping back and forth, jumping is applied only with a given probability β, a parameter of our algorithm. In experiments with $\beta = 0.6$, shown in Section 4, all topologies converged quickly to "tree-friendly" configurations. The time to convergence depends mainly on the depth of the tree. In fact, a faster convergence could be achieved by using a high value of β for nodes close to the sink, and decreasing it for nodes farther away. In this way, the nodes closer to the root stabilize their configuration quickly, allowing incremental stabilization of downstream nodes.

"Waving" Wake-up Times to Reduce Latency. While jumping generally retains both short intervals between wake-up times and good event detection, the latency for a message to move from the edge of the network to the sink is not fully optimized. In fact, the optimal wake-up configuration is achieved when the time between a node and its parent's wake-up time is fixed to the message passing time. Enforcing such a wake-up schedule is relatively trivial and results in a wake-up pattern in which nodes one hop from the sink wake up together, those two hops away wake up immediately before, and so on to the edge of the network. The result is a "wave" of wake-up times originating with nodes at the edges and ending at the sink. Any scattering away from this wave pattern negatively affects the optimal latency for a packet traveling to the sink.

To counteract this, we introduce controlled *waving*, i.e., setting wake-up times to reduce the interval between a node's wake-up time and $W_{\texttt{next}}$. However, our goal is not simply to form a tree, but also to retain the benefits of wake-up scattering, namely a short time to communication and a good event coverage. Such a compromise is reached by enforcing a maximum wake-up distance between a sensor and its $\texttt{next}$. This distance, γ, is another parameter of our protocol allowing the application to tune the tradeoff between a good scattering and the latency to reach the sink.

3.3   Pseudocode

Figure 4 shows the full pseudocode for a *single* calibration round of our scattering algorithm, including the extensions for managing a tree. For convenience, we use the notation W_i^j to indicate the wake-up time of node i in calibration round j. Initially, $j = 0$ and the wake-up time for each node, W_i^0, is assumed to be random. The key parameters already mentioned are α, affecting the convergence speed, β, establishing the jumping probability, and γ determining the waving behavior. When $\beta = 0$, no jumping optimization is performed. The γ parameter has meaning only if jumping is on, i.e., $\beta \neq 0$. $\gamma = 0$ represents perfect synchronization of wake-up times; meaning all nodes wake up at the same time.

Notably, the first steps of the algorithm establish the values of $W_{\texttt{next}}$ and $W_{\texttt{prev}}$ by assuming that all nodes receive the full configuration R of wake-up times before the round starts. Next we consider an alternate approach that does not require synchronization among the nodes.

3.4   Removing Synchronization Requirements

In some cases, it may not be reasonable to assume that nodes share a clock and therefore that epochs are synchronized among the nodes. This makes a direct comparison among the wake-up times impossible, and demands an alternate mechanism to learn $W_{\texttt{prev}}$, $W_{\texttt{next}}$ and, if necessary, $W_{\texttt{afternext}}$.

```
// Exchange wake-up times with neighbors
Broadcast W_i^j
Receive R = {W_n^j : n is a neighbor of i}
if R is empty then exit                              // i is alone

// Initialization of W_next and W_prev
W_first ⇐ min(R)
W_last ⇐ max(R)
if W_i^j > W_last then W_next ⇐ W_first + E          // i is the last
else W_next ⇐ min(W_n^j ∈ R : W_n^j > W_i^j)
if W_i^j < W_first then W_prev ⇐ W_last − E          // i is the first
else W_prev ⇐ max(W_n^j ∈ R : W_n^j < W_i^j)

// Scattering for next round
target ⇐ (W_prev + W_next)/2
W_i^{j+1} ⇐ (W_i^j · (1 − α) + target · α) mod E

// Extensions for the tree scenario
if i belongs to a tree and is not the root then
   // Waving
   if W_i^{j+1} < W_next − γ then W_i^{j+1} ⇐ W_next − γ
   // Jumping
   if next is a child then
      with probability (1 − β) exit                  // abort jumping
      if i is the last or second to last then
         W_afternext ⇐ min(W_n^j ∈ R : W_n^j + E > W_next) + E
      else W_afternext ⇐ min(W_n^j ∈ R : W_n^j > W_next)
      W_i^{j+1} ⇐ ((W_next + W_afternext)/2) mod E    // jump
```

Fig. 4. A single calibration round j of the wake-up scattering for node i

A simple solution is to gather these wake-up times *relative* to a nodes own epoch. This can be achieved by requiring each node to broadcast a message upon waking up, and having all nodes listen for two epochs. The latter constraint ensures that a node receives the wake-up time of nodes that were already awake when its epoch started. The algorithm in Figure 4 remains fundamentally unchanged after the wake-up times are collected. One additional advantage of this mechanism is that it reduces the probability of collisions among calibration messages, as they are sent at the wake-up times of the nodes and are naturally scattered.

Another practical concern is the initiation of the calibration round. While we have so far considered that all nodes are aware of the calibration at the same moment, it is trivial to extend the algorithm to allow a node to start a calibration round when it receives a calibration message from one of its neighbors. In this manner, knowledge of calibration will propagate to the whole system regardless of the node where it originates.

4   Evaluation

Our wake-up scattering algorithm potentially supports many applications. Our evaluation shows the achievable benefits for three, distinct scenarios as we vary the key parameters. Table 1 shows the most important parameters along with the default values used during simulation.

Table 1. Key simulation parameters and their default values. Those in italics remain constant throughout the evaluation.

Parameter	Value	Parameter	Value	Parameter	Value
Number of Nodes	200	Awake interval	0.25	α, *scattering weight*	0.5
Size of area	1000 x 660	Radio range	70	β, jumping probability	0
Epoch period	1	Sensing range	70	γ, maximum waving distance	–

The evaluation was performed with a custom Java simulator.[1] As previously mentioned, the simulator assumes a straightforward communication model where nodes have configurable, circular communication and sensing ranges. The results presented here assume messages are never lost, although we also performed experiments (not presented here for space reasons) showing that even with up to 10% loss, the system is still able to quickly converge to a good wake-up configuration.

Most of the reported results are calculated as averages over 10 different random topologies, each with 5 different initial wake-up configurations. Our baseline for comparison are the initial, random configurations.

Responsiveness to Local Queries. In our scenario with a mobile base station and many scattered sensors, the primary goal to minimize the time that the base station waits for a query response. This corresponds to the average response delay between when a base station first requests data, until a sensor in range is awake and sends the data. To measure this quantitatively, we use a Monte-Carlo sampling technique that randomly selects and point (x, y) and time t such that (x, y) is within communication range of at least one sensor and t is inside the epoch. The response delay is 0 if at least one sensor in radio range is awake at t, otherwise it is calculated as the difference between t and the closest wake-up time of an in-range sensor. Thousands of samples are taken and averaged to compute the overall average response delay.

One of the major factors affecting radio responsiveness is the duration of the awake interval for each of the nodes. The longer the nodes are active, the greater the chance that a node will be available to respond immediately. In our default setting with 200 nodes and radio range of 70, a node has on average 4.2 neighbors. Therefore, with a wake-up time near to 1/4 of the epoch, we expect very short response delays, as it is likely that at least one node is awake when a query is made. However, as the awake interval shrinks, the probability of finding a gap between the query and the first wake-up time increases. Figure 5 shows the average response delay in both absolute (left) and relative (right) terms. The absolute response delay is in terms of the fraction of an epoch while the relative is in percentage improvement over the initial wake-up configuration. From the left side of the figure, it is important to notice that in all cases, our scattering approach converges in few configuration rounds, with most improvements taking place in the first three rounds.

Figure 5 also evidences that our wake-up scattering approach can be used to dramatically improve the lifetime of the network. Consider that a randomly initialized network

---

[1] An online demo is available to test and visualize the effect of wake-up scattering on custom configurations: http://www.elet.polimi.it/upload/giusti/scattering/

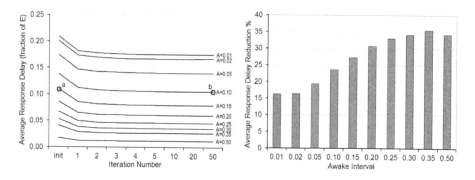

Fig. 5. Response delay with various awake intervals

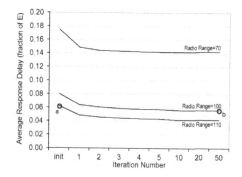

Fig. 6. Response delay with various communication ranges. The three lines correspond to networks with on average 4.3, 8.4 and 10.1 neighbors.

with an awake interval of 0.15 has an initial average response delay of 0.110, labeled a in the figure. A similar response delay of 0.106, b in the figure, can be achieved after wake-up scattering with a shorter awake interval of 0.10. This means that by applying wake-up scattering, the awake interval can be decreased by 33% while the application performance is preserved at what can, on average, be achieved with a random initial configuration. Similar significant results can be observed by comparing the initial response delay with a given awake interval compared to similar response delays achieved after scattering, but with shorter awake intervals.

We also analyzed our approach for different network densities, observing from Figure 6 that with less dense networks, the percentage improvement after scattering tends to be larger. Also, a similar lifetime argument can be made by observing that with a radio range of 100, after scattering, b in the figure, the response delay achieved is that of randomly initialized network with a range of 110, a in the figure. Because higher transmission ranges require more energy, again, wake-up scattering can be exploited to improve network lifetime.

Event Coverage. When applying wake-up scattering to sensor activation, as opposed to communication activation, we consider the probability that an event occurring in the

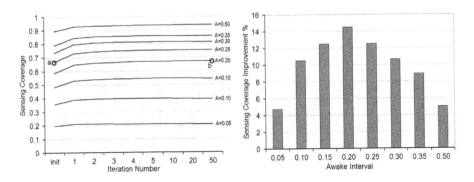

Fig. 7. Sensing coverage for various awake intervals

sensed region is detected. To measure this, we use a sampling technique similar to that used for response delay, selecting a point (x, y) that is covered by at least one sensor, and a time in the epoch t. If a sensor covering this point is active at time t, then the event is detected, otherwise it is not. As before, several thousand samples are taken and the results averaged. It should be noted that perfect event detection is unlikely to be attained, except with contrived topologies. Consider a simple setting with two sensors, each awake half of the epoch, and located just within communication range. Even with perfect scattering, only the events located in the overlapping area will be reliably detected. Instead, those in regions covered only by one sensor will be detected half the time, leading to an average event coverage much less than 1.

In contrast to the scattering for response delay discussed previously, event coverage scenarios are heavily dependent on the length of the awake intervals. With response delay, if a node is inactive when a query is made, the base station simply waits. Instead, if an event occurs and no sensor is active, the event is not detected. Therefore, in Figure 7 we show the effect of awake intervals on the sensing coverage. Although the percentage improvement in the probability of detecting an event is small, less than 15%, we can make similar network lifetime arguments as before by comparing the achieved coverage of a network with an awake interval of 0.20 (0.671, b in the figure) in comparison to the initial coverage of a network with 20% more awake time (0.667, a in the figure). In other words, the lifetime of the network can be increased by 20% while achieving the same coverage as a random initialization with a longer awake interval.

Another important consideration is the relationship between the communication radius and the sensing range. Our wake-up scattering is based only on the ability of two nodes to communicate with one another, ignoring any difference between sensing and communication ranges, however such differences are possible with real sensing devices. Figure 8 shows that if the communication radius remains fixed while the sensing range varies, wake-up scattering still achieves gains.

Data Latency in Tree-Based Networks. When considering a tree, the primary factor to improve is the time it takes a message to reach the collection point, the root. Therefore, we consider the time-to-root averaged over all sensors, assuming the message is sent just

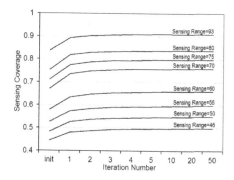

Fig. 8. Effect of sensing range on wake-up scattering

before the end of the sender's awake interval. If the parent is not immediately awake, the sending node wakes up outside of its normal awake interval to forward the message.

The top of Figure 9 gives a first impression of the effect of wake-up scattering on time-to-root, and the tradeoffs introduced with jumping and waving. The chart shows how time-to-root changes from the initial random configuration (labeled init), after the basic wake-up scattering stabilizes (scattering), after the application and stabilization of jumping (jumping), and after applying waving with various γ parameters. It should be noted that this plot represents the *independent* effects of the scattering, jumping, and waving techniques, not a progression of time-to-root values over time.

The first observation is that time-to-root is only marginally worse after scattering. This is because, except with long awake times, scattering removes any overlap of awake intervals between parents and children that occurred in the random initialization. Second, the addition of jumping significantly improves time-to-root, reducing the latency by approximately one third of the total time. Finally, as expected, waving further reduces time-to-root with smaller values of the waving factor, γ, leading to greater improvements because of the reduction of the required gap between the wake-up times of the child and parent.

While the previous plot shows that both jumping and waving have significant, positive impacts on time-to-root, it is reasonable to consider combining the tree scenario with event coverage, for example to send notifications of detected events to a centralized sink. Therefore, the bottom of Figure 9 shows the effect of jumping and waving on the coverage achieved with scattering alone. Most importantly this plot shows that jumping does not significantly affect sensing coverage, however waving does. This is to be expected because jumping maintains the scattering properties while simply changing the order of awake intervals, instead waving causes the wake-up intervals to overlap. Such overlapping intervals lead to an increase in missed events because the nodes tend to be active for event detection at the same times when γ is small. Put another way, when a sensor node is used for event detection where the results are sent to a centralized root, wake-up scattering and jumping provide a solution that has good coverage and time-to-root values. To our knowledge, our work is the first to consider such a combination.

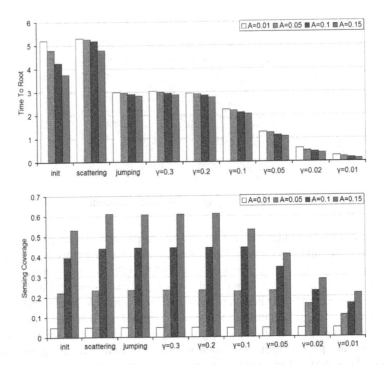

Fig. 9. Average time-to-root and sensing coverage for various awake intervals after enabling the various scattering, jumping, and waving phases of the algorithm. The results are averaged over 50 random topologies, each tested with a single initialization of wake-up times.

We ran similar experiments to evaluate the effects of jumping and waving on response delays in the first scenario. The results are similar to those for coverage, showing that jumping has minimal effect, while waving has negative effects.

5   Related Work

To the best of our knowledge, our approach to scatter the wake-up times of nearby sensors is novel. Nevertheless, it is related to several other directions in the literature, investigated here from the bottom (MAC) up (applications).

Many MAC layer protocols explicitly introduce their own duty cycling as a means to save energy, thus on the surface the two approaches are similar. However, it is important to note that the duration of duty cycles at the MAC-layer and those we consider are orders of magnitude different.

As our approach focuses on assigning wake-up times to nodes, it is interesting to compare the wake-up scattering assignments to those of MAC protocols. For example, SMAC [3] and TMAC [4] attempt to synchronize all nodes to a single awake interval, allowing communication during a short interval, then putting the whole network to sleep for an extended time. While this has the same lifetime extension potential as our approach, it cannot achieve the benefits for average response delay or sensor coverage. In contrast to the whole-network synchronization of SMAC and TMAC, LMAC [5] and

ZMAC [6] are TDMA-like approaches that divide and assign a set of communication slots among all nodes, eliminating overlap as much as possible. While this is related to wake-up scattering as the assigned slots are spread over time, these systems work with an assumption of a fixed number of time slots, eliminating all possible overlapping. Wake-up scattering, on the other hand, scatters as much as possible without discrete, fixed time intervals, allowing overlap if the awake interval is long, but still spreading out over the full epoch even if awake intervals are short.

Finally, DMAC [7] is designed to allow efficient communication along a tree, termed convergecast communication. It performs synchronization similar to SMAC/TMAC, then staggers the wake-up such that messages are forwarded without delay. This spreading of wake-up intervals is analogous to our waving approach that moves wake-up intervals closer together, similarly reducing latency. However, as observed in Section 4, placing wake-up times close together negatively affects all benefits to coverage that can be achieved with scattering.

Above the MAC layer, extensive work exists on managing sensor coverage by intentionally setting the physical sensor locations, as opposed to our approach which deals with temporal coverage. In fact, this field has been studied since the early 1990's in the context of the cellular network. More recent work approaches the same issues in WSNs [8] with a variety of techniques such as Integer Programming [9], greedy heuristics [10,11,12] and Virtual Force Methods [13]. Interestingly, [14] studies sensor placement in combination with varying the ratio of sensing and communication range, supporting our desire to present the evaluation of the same ratio when studying sensing coverage. These spatial techniques can be applied in parallel to our approach, however, it is worth noting that our study measured only the coverage that could be achieved with random placement, ignoring any areas of the field not covered by the sensors.

6   Conclusions

In this paper we presented and evaluated a fully decentralized wake-up scattering algorithm whose goal is to spread uniformly the wake-up times of the nodes in a WSN. We illustrated common application scenarios where this functionality is beneficial, and verified through simulation that indeed our algorithm provides improvements in the WSN performance and lifetime over a random assignment of wake-up times. The algorithm is very simple, and therefore not only is easily implementable on resource-scarce WSN devices, but it also introduces a negligible communication and computational overhead.

Acknowledgments. This work is partially supported by the European Union under the IST-004536 RUNES project and by the National Competence Center in Research on Mobile Information and Communication Systems (NCCR-MICS), a center supported by the Swiss National Science Foundation under grant number 5005-67322.

References

1. Curino, C., Giani, M., Giorgetta, M., Giusti, A., Murphy, A.L., Picco, G.P.: Mobile data collection in sensor networks: The TinyLIME Middleware. Elsevier Pervasive and Mobile Computing Journal **4**(1) (2005) 446–469

2. Madden, S., M.J. Franklin, J.M. Hellerstein, Hong, W.: TinyDB: An acquisitional query processing system for sensor networks. ACM Trans. Database Syst. **30**(1) (2005) 122–173

3. Ye, W., Heidemann, J., Estrin, D.: An energy-efficient MAC protocol for wireless sensor networks. In: Proceedings of the 21st IEEE INFOCOM. (2002) 1567–1576

4. van Dam, T., Langendoen, K.: An adaptive energy-efficient MAC protocol for wireless sensor networks. In: Proc. of the 1st ACM Conf. on Embedded Networked Sensor Systems (SenSys), Los Angeles, CA, USA (2003) 171–180

5. van Hoesel, L., Havinga, P.: A lightweight medium access protocol (LMAC) for wireless sensor networks. In: Proc. of 1st Int. Wkshp. on Networked Sensing Systems, Tokyo, Japan (2004)

6. Rhee, I., Warrier, A., Aia, M., Min, J.: Z-MAC: A hybrid MAC for wireless sensor networks. In: Proc. of the 3rd ACM Conf. on Embedded Networked Sensor Systems (SenSys), San Diego, CA, USA (2005) 90–101

7. Lu, G., Krishnamachari, B., Raghavendra, C.S.: An adaptive energy-efficient and low-latency MAC for data gathering in sensor networks. In: Proc. of the Int. Wkshp. on Algorithms for Wireless, Mobile, Ad Hoc and Sensor Networks (WMAN), Santa Fe, NM, USA (2004)

8. Meguerdichian, S., Koushanfar, F., Potkonjak, M., Srivastava, M.: Coverage problems in wireless ad-hoc sensor networks. In: Proc. of 20th IEEE INFOCOM, Anchorage, Alaska, USA (2001) 1380–1387

9. Chakrabarty, K., Iyengar, S.S., Qi, H., Cho, E.: Grid coverage for surveillance and target location in distributed sensor networks. IEEE Trans. on Computers **51**(12) (2002) 1448–1453

10. Bulusu, N., Estrin, D., Heidemann, J.: Adaptive beacon placement. In: Proc. of the 21st Int. Conf. on Distributed Computing Systems (ICDCS), Phoenix, AZ, USA (2001) 489–498

11. Howard, A., Mataric, M.J., Sukhatme, G.S.: An incremental self-deployment algorithm for mobile sensor networks. Auton. Robots **13**(2) (2002) 113–126

12. Howard, A., Mataric, M.J., Sukhatme, G.S.: Mobile sensor network deployment using potential fields: A distributed, scalable solution to the area coverage problem. In: Proc. of the 7th Int. Symp. on Distributed Autonomous Robotic Systems (DARS). (2002)

13. Zou, Y., Chakrabarty, K.: Sensor deployment and target localization in distributed sensor networks. Trans. on Embedded Computing Sys. **3**(1) (2004) 61–91

14. Jourdan, D.B., de Weck, O.L.: Layout optimization for a wireless sensor network using a multi-objective genetic algorithm. In: Proc. of the Vehicular Technology Conf., Los Angeles, CA, USA (2004) 2466–2470

Improving the Energy Efficiency of the MANTIS Kernel

Cormac Duffy[1], Utz Roedig[2], John Herbert[1], and Cormac J. Sreenan[1]

[1] Computer Science Dept., University College Cork, Cork
[2] InfoLab21, Lancaster University, Lancaster

Abstract. Event-driven operating systems such as TinyOS are the pre-ferred choice for wireless sensor networks. Alternative designs following a classical multi-threaded approach are also available. A popular im-plementation of such a multi-threaded sensor network operating system is MANTIS. The event-based TinyOS is more energy efficient than the multi-threaded MANTIS system. However, MANTIS is more capable than TinyOS of supporting time critical tasks as task preemption is sup-ported. Thus, timeliness can be traded for energy efficiency by choosing the appropriate operating system. In this paper we present a MANTIS kernel modification that enables MANTIS to be as power-efficient as TinyOS. Results from an experimental analysis demonstrate that the modified MANTIS can be used to fit *both* sensor network design goals of energy efficiency and timeliness.

1 Introduction

Sensor nodes must be designed to be energy efficient in order to allow long peri-ods of unattended network operation. However, energy efficiency is not the only design goal in a sensor network. For example, timely processing and reporting of sensing information is often required as well. This might be needed to guar-antee a maximum delivery time of sensing information from a sensor, through a multi-hop network, to a base-station. To be able to give such assurances, net-work components with a deterministic behavior will be required. The operating system running on sensor nodes is one such component.

Event-based operating systems are considered to be the best choice for build-ing energy efficient sensor networks as they require little memory and processing resources. Hence, the event-based TinyOS [1] is currently the preferred operating system for sensor networks. Event-based operating systems are not very useful in situations where tasks have strict processing deadlines. Tasks are processed sequentially, a prioritization of important tasks to meet processing deadlines is not possible. Multi-threaded operating systems are more suitable if such re-quirements must be fulfilled. Thread preemption and context switching enables such systems to prioritize tasks and meet deadlines. The MANTIS [2] operating system is the first multi-threaded operating system designed specifically for wire-less sensor networks. Unfortunately, MANTIS has a relatively high processing

K. Langendoen and T. Voigt (Eds.): EWSN 2007, LNCS 4373, pp. 261–276, 2007.
© Springer-Verlag Berlin Heidelberg 2007

overhead for thread management. This processing overhead is directly related to reduced energy efficiency because of the relative increase in CPU activity.

This creates the dilemma that both design goals - energy efficiency and timeliness - can only currently be optimized independently. One is forced to choose which goal is of higher importance in the considered application scenario. Therefore, it would be good if the dilemma could be resolved by either making TinyOS more responsive or MANTIS more energy efficient. In this paper the later problem is solved: We present a MANTIS kernel modification to increase power efficiency. As the results show, MANTIS can be modified to be as power-efficient as TinyOS without impacting vital kernel functionality. Thus, the modified MANTIS can be used to solve both important sensor network design goals.

The next Section of the paper presents related work. Section 3 presets preliminary research comparing TinyOS and MANTIS regarding event processing capabilities and energy consumption. This comparison motivates the modifications of the MANTIS kernel for better energy efficiency. Section 4 explains in detail the MANTIS kernel. Section 5 presents and explains the MANTIS kernel modifications. Section 6 shows an evaluation of the modified kernel. Section 7 concludes the paper.

2   Related Work

Problems arise when a sensor network applications require to be energy efficient and have to provide timely processing capabilities at the same time.

One example of an operating system that tries to bridge the gap is Contiki [3]. Contiki is an event-based sensor network operating system that includes a threaded library that can be optionally compiled to facilitate multi-threaded applications. Thus multi-threaded capabilities can be selectively designated to specific processes, without the processing and memory overhead in all parts of the system.

A similar approach can be seen in [4,5]. In both works the TinyOS operating system is encapsulated in a multi-threaded kernel. The operating system is then scheduled as a thread such that it can be preempted by complex threads if required. Thus TinyOS still achieves preemption without sacrificing the lightweight scheduling characteristics. In summary, the research focus of [3,4,5] is to minimize the processing overhead of a multi-threaded system, by isolating only the processes that require multi-threaded capabilities. However no effort is made to reduce the overhead of the multi-threaded processes.

In [6] a programming concept called "proto-threads" is described which allows the programmer to develop a program using a multi-threaded programming syntax. It is argued that an event-based system is more power-efficient but that programming concurrent (sensor network) applications with threads, as opposed to event handlers, is easier for the programmer. Proto-threads are, however, merely a thread abstraction. They do not provide thread preemption, thus complex processes cannot easily be multiplexed with high priority tasks without introducing blocking.

The research listed above tries to compromise between power-efficient event-based schedulers and multi-threaded schedulers. The work presented in this paper focus on the reduction of processing overheads in multi threaded sensor network operating systems.

3 Preliminary Research

The preliminary research investigates the differences of the multi-threaded MANTIS [2] and the event-based TinyOS [1] operating systems. More details on the preliminary research can be found in [7]. The experimental methodology is re-used for the evaluation of the optimized MANTIS presented in Section 6.

3.1 Evaluation Goals

It is generally assumed that an event-driven operating system is very suitable for sensor networks because few resources are needed, resulting in an energy-efficient system. However, the exact figures are unknown and therefore quantified in this preliminary research. On the other hand it is claimed that a multi-threaded operating system has good event processing capabilities in terms of meeting processing deadlines. Again, an in-depth analysis is currently missing and is therefore conducted. For comparison purposes, the event-based system *TinyOS* and the multi-threaded system *MANTIS* executing the same sensor network applications on the [8] are investigated.

The following parameters - while the sensor node is executing a generic application - are evaluated:

1. *Event Processing*: The average task execution time E_t of a particular re-occurring sensor task is measured. Average task execution time and its variance are a measure for the event handling capabilities of the system.
2. *Energy Consumption*: The percentage of experiment time I_t spent with an idle CPU is measured. CPU idle time can be used to suspend the CPU and thus relates directly to the energy efficiency of a system.

An application scenario for the evaluation has to be defined, as the parameters of interest are influenced significantly by the scenario. It was decided to use a scenario of a generic nature so that the results are applicable to a range of real-world applications.

3.2 Evaluation Setup

In many cases, a sensor network is used to collect periodically obtained measurement data at a central point (sink or base-station) for further analysis. The sensor nodes in such a network execute two major tasks. Sensor nodes perform the sensing task and they are used to forward the gathered data to the sink. If the sink is not in direct radio range of a node, other nodes closer to the sink are used to forward data. The execution time of the sensing task will depend on the nature of the physical phenomenon monitored and the complexity of the algorithm used to analyze it. Therefore, the position of the node in such a network and the complexity of the sensing task define the operating system load of the sensor node. The complexity of the sensing task is varied in the experiments and hence the application scenario is considered abstract, as it can be compared with many different real-world deployment scenarios.

The complexity of the sensing operation depends on the phenomenon monitored, the sensor device used and the data pre-processing required. As a result, the operating system can be stressed very differently. If, for example, an ATMEGA128 CPU with a processing speed of $4Mhz$ is considered (a currently popular choice for sensor nodes), a simple temperature sensing task processed through the Analogue to Digital Converter can be performed in less than $1ms$ [9]. In this case only a $16bit$ value has to be transferred from the sensing device to the CPU. If the same device is used in conjunction with a camera, image processing might take some time before a decision is made. Depending on camera resolution and image processing performed, a sensing task can easily take more than $100ms$ [10]. Other application examples documented in the literature are situated in between these values. Note that a long sensing task can be split-up into several sub-tasks but in practice this is not always possible. The experimental evaluation spans the task sizes described ($1ms...100ms$).

The following paragraphs give an exact specification of the abstract application scenario used, which is defined by its topology, traffic pattern and sensing pattern. The application scenario is then implemented using TinyOS and MANTIS on the DSYS25[8] sensor platform for evaluation.

Topology. The sensor network is used to forward sensor data towards a single base-station in the network. It is assumed that a binary tree topology is formed in the network (see Fig. 1). Depending on the position n in the tree, a sensor node might process varying amounts of packets. Nodes closer to the root are more involved in packet forwarding as these nodes have to multiplex packet forwarding operations with their sensing operations. In the experiments, the behaviour of a single node at all possible positions n is emulated and measured by applying the sensing pattern and network traffic as described next.

Fig. 1. Binary Tree

Sensing Pattern. A homogeneous activity in the sensor field is assumed for the abstract application scenario. Each sensor gathers data with a fixed frequency f_s. Thus, every $t_s = 1/f_s$ a sensing task of the duration l_s has to be processed. As mentioned, the duration l_s is variable between $l_s = 4000$ and $l_s = 400000$ clock cycles depending on the type of sensing task under consideration (Which corresponds to $1ms/100ms$ on a $4MHz$ CPU).

Traffic Pattern. Depending on the position n of a node in the tree, varying amounts of forwarding tasks have to be performed. It is assumed that no time synchronization among the sensors in the network exists. Thus, even if each sensor produces data with a fixed frequency, data forwarding tasks are not created at fixed points in time. The arrival rate λ_n of packets at a node at tree-level n is modeled as a Poisson process. As the packet forwarding activity is related to the sensing activity in the field, λ_n is given by:

$$\lambda_n = (2^n - 1) \cdot f_s \tag{1}$$

This equation is a simplification; queuing effects and losses are neglected, but nevertheless provides a good method to scale the processing performance requirements of a sensor network application. It is assumed that the duration (complexity) l_p of the packet-processing task, is $l_p = 4000$ clock cycles. This is the effort necessary to read a packet from the transceiver, perform routing and re-send the packet over the transceiver. This is a common processing time and was obtained analyzing the DSYS25 sensor nodes using the Nordic radio [11].

3.3   Event Processing

It is assumed that the packet-processing task within the nodes has priority so that deadlines regarding packet forwarding can be met. Thus, in the MANTIS implementation, the packet-processing task has a higher priority than the sensing task. In the TinyOS implementation, no prioritization is implemented as this feature is not provided by the operating system.

Task Execution Time. To characterize processing performance of the operating system, the average task execution time E_t of the packet forwarding task, is measured. During the experiment, J packet-processing times e_j are recorded. To do so, the task start time e_{start} and the task completion time e_{stop} are measured and the packet-processing time is recorded as $e = e_{stop} - e_{start}$. The average task execution time E_t is calculated at the end of the experiment as: $E_t = \sum e_j / J$. For each tree position n, the experiment is run until $J = 25000$ packet-processing events are recorded.

Results. In the experiment, the average task execution time E_t is determined for TinyOS and MANTIS supporting the abstract application scenario (see Fig. 2).

Where MANTIS is used, it can be observed that the average packet-processing time is independent of the sensing task execution time. Furthermore, E_t is also independent from the position n of the node in the tree. The average processing time increases slightly, under a heavy load. This is due to the fact that under heavy load packet forwarding tasks have to be queued (see Fig. 2 a)).

Where TinyOS is used, the average processing time for the packet forwarding task E_t depends on the length of the sensing l_s of the sensing task. In addition, under heavy load the queuing effects of the packet forwarding tasks also contribute somewhat to the average processing time (see Fig. 2 b)).

The variance in the packet-processing time E_t is also recorded but is not shown due to space restrictions. However, it has to be noted that this variance

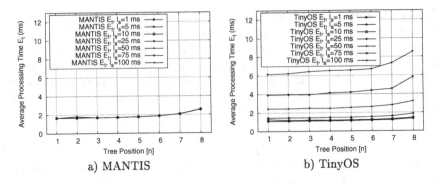

Fig. 2. Average packet-processing time E_t

is significantly smaller in MANTIS than in TinyOS (see [7] for details). Thus, MANTIS is better able to support scenarios which require predictable processing behaviour.

The thread prioritization capability of MANTIS is clearly visible in the experimental results. Packet processing times are independent of the concurrently executed and lower priority sensing task. In TinyOS, sensing and packet forwarding task delays are coupled, and the influence of the sensing activity on the packet forwarding activity is clearly visible.

3.4   Energy Consumption

To evaluate power-efficiency, This study investigates the available idle time in which low-power operations can be scheduled. Thus the comparative effectiveness of specific power management policies can be guaged on the amount of potential low-power (idle) time available.

Idle time. In the experiment, the abstract application scenario is executed by the sensor node running TinyOS or MANTIS. The duration of the experiment T and the duration i_k of K idle time periods during the experiment is recorded. i is defined as $i = i_{stop} - i_{start}$. All idle periods i_k are summarized and the percentage idle time, I_t, the percent of experiment time, in which the processor is idle, which is calculated as follows: $I_t = (\sum i_k/T) \cdot 100$. Again, for each tree position n, the experiment is run until $J = 25000$ packet-processing events are recorded.

Results. In the first experiment, the percentage idle time I_t is determined for TinyOS and MANTIS supporting the abstract application scenario. (see Fig. 3).

The time spent in idle mode drops for both operating systems exponentially with the increasing node position in the tree described by the parameter n. This behavior is expected as the number of packet tasks increases accordingly. Less obvious is the fact that the available idle time drops faster in MANTIS than in TinyOS. The fast drop in idle time is caused by the context switches in the MANTIS operating system. The more packet forwarding tasks are created, the

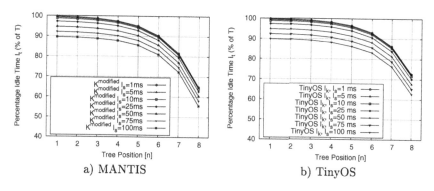

Fig. 3. Percentage idle time I_t for both operating systems

more likely it is that a sensing task is currently running when a packet interrupt occurs. Subsequently, a context switch to the higher prioritized forwarding task is needed.

3.5 Findings

The experimental results show that MANTIS has a much more predictive behavior executing the packet-processing task than TinyOS. More precise, the execution time in MANTIS has a low variation and is independent of other activity such as the sensing task. Thus, MANTIS would be preferable in situations that need deterministic and timely processing. However, the MANTIS system is not as power-efficient as TinyOS. Thus, TinyOS would seem preferable if energy consumption is deemed to be of primary importance. If the system is not loaded (leaf node with $n = 1$ and a sensing task with the size of $l_s = 1ms$) a difference of only 0.1% in idle time is measured. However, if the system is under a heavy load (leaf node with $n = 8$ and a sensing task with the size of $l_s = 100ms$) a 6.9% difference in the idle time is encountered. The biggest difference is measured for $n = 8$ with a task size of $l_s = 1ms$ which results in a difference of 7.6%.

4 The MANTIS Kernel Architecture

The threaded MANTIS architecture implements thread-preemption, allowing the operating system to interrupt any active thread to immediately begin processing a thread of higher priority. As a result, the operating system can respond faster to critical events. In general, the system architecture follows the design principles of classical multi-threaded operating systems. However, to facilitate the necessary power management requirements, energy saving mechanisms are integrated in the thread scheduling. The processing states (e.g. sleeping, waiting) of all threads are monitored and used to decide which power saving modes of the CPU should be activated. Power saving is activated through a so-called *idle task* which is special purpose thread with the lowest possible thread priority, that is scheduled when all other threads are inactive.

Algorithm 1. Thread structure

```
1: mos_thread_new(thread_A,128, PRIORITY_HIGH)

2: thread_A
3:   while(running)
4:     ...
5:     mos_semaphore_wait(A1)
6:     ....

7: int_A
8:   ...
9:   mos_semaphore_post(A1)
10:  ...
```

```
1:dispatch_thread()
2:   PUSH_THREAD_STACK()
3:   CURRENT_THREAD = readyQ.getThread()
4:   CURRENT_THREAD.state=RUNNING
5:   POP_THREAD_STACK()
```

part A   part B

4.1   Overview

Each task the operating system must support can be implemented as a separate MANTIS thread. A simplified view of this thread structure is shown in Alg. 1, part A. A new thread is initialized via the function *mos_thread_new* (line 1). Subsequently the thread processing, often implemented as an infinite loop, is started (line 3). Processing might be halted using the function *mos_semaphore_wait* when a thread has to wait for a resource to become available (line 5). An interrupt handler (line 7) using the function *mos_semaphore_post* (line 9) is used to signal the waiting thread that the resource is now available and thread processing is resumed. While a thread is waiting on a resource to become available, other threads might be activated or if no other processing is required, a power saving mode is entered.

As an example, a thread might be used to process incoming packets from a transceiver chip. In this case, the *mos_semaphore_wait* is used to suspend the thread until a new packet arrives at the transceiver. If the transceiver receives a packet, an interrupt is executed and the thread is resumed to read the currently available packet and process it.

4.2   Scheduling

Thread scheduling is performed within the kernel function *dispatch_thread* shown in Alg. 1, part B. This function searches a data structure called *readyQ* for the highest prioritized thread and activates it. The *readyQ* is an array of linked lists containing pointers to the currently active threads. Each index of the array corresponds to a thread priority level.

When the *dispatch_thread* function is called, the current active thread is suspended calling *PUSH_THREAD_STACK* (line 2). Thus, the current CPU register information is saved to the heap memory allocated to the current thread. The highest priority thread is then selected from the *readyQ* (line 3) and its register values are restored by the *POP_THREAD_STACK* function (line 5). The thread can then resume processing at the exact point it was previously suspended.

Algorithm 2. Semaphore

```
1: mos_semaphore_wait(Semaphore s)
2:   s.val--
3:   if (s.val<0)
4:     s.addThread(CURRENT_THREAD)
5:     CURRENT_THREAD.state=BLOCKED
6:     update_sleep_counters()
7:     dispatch_thread()
```

part A

```
1: mos_semaphore_post(Semaphore s)
2:   s.val++
3:   if (s.getThread()!=NULL)
4:     s.getThread().state=RUNNING
5:     readyQ.addThread(s.getThread())
6:     update_sleep_counters()
7:     dispatch_thread()
```

part B

Algorithm 3. Timer Interrupt

```
1: t_slice_int()
2:   readyQ.addThread(CURRENT_THREAD)
3:   update_sleep_counters()
4:   dispatch_thread()
```

Before the *dispatch_thread* function is called, the *readyQ* structure is updated. Threads that are currently sleeping or that are waiting on a semaphore are excluded from the *readyQ*. The scheduling through the *dispatch_thread* function can be initiated by two different means: initiation within a semaphore operation or initiation through a time slice timer event.

Semaphore. A thread uses the function *mos_semaphore_wait* to coordinate access to a shared resource. If the resource is not ready, processing is suspended until the resource associated with the semaphore becomes available (Alg. 2, part A). If the resource is not immediately available (, line 3), the current thread is suspended and a context switch using the previously explained function *dispatch_thread* is performed (line 7). Before the context switch is performed, the function *update_sleep_counters* is executed (line 6). This function is used to check if currently sleeping threads have to wake up and join the *readyQ* structure. In the MANTIS operating system, the user has the ability to make a thread sleep for a period of time. Thus, suspended threads either wait on a semaphore or they sleep. Pointers to the sleeping threads are stored in a sorted list, the *sleepQ*. Sleeping threads are sorted according to their wakeup time, such that the earliest thread to wake-up will be at the head of the queue. The function *update_sleep_counters* updates the wakeup times and if threads in the *sleepQ* are due, they are moved to the *readyQ*. Within an interrupt routine, *mos_semaphore_post* is called to inform a waiting thread that a resource is now available for processing (Alg. 2, part B). If a thread is waiting for the resource (line 3), the thread is activated and added to the *readyQ* structure. Thereafter, the *update_sleep_counters* function is called to check if sleeping threads have to be activated as well. Finally, the thread waiting for the semaphore (or a higher prioritized thread that was moved from the *sleepQ*) is activated using *dispatch_thread*.

Time Slice Timer. A timer is set to create an interrupt every $20ms$ (Alg. 3). This interrupt serves two purposes. First, the interrupt acts as a time slice for

Algorithm 4. Modified semaphore functions

```
1: mos_semaphore_wait(Semaphore s)
2:   s.val--
3:   if (s.val<0)
4:     if(readyQ.getThread!=NULL)
5:       if(CURRENT_THREAD.state==BLOCKED_RUNNING)
6:         CURRENT_THREAD.state==BLOCKED
7:       s.addThread(CURRENT_THREAD)
8:       #ifdef MANTIS_SLEEP
9:         update_sleep_counters()
10:      dispatch_thread()
11:    else
12:      CURRENT_THREAD.state=BLOCKED_RUNNING
13:      do_power_management()
```

```
1: mos_semaphore_post(Semaphore s)
2:   s.val++
3:   if (s.thread.state==BLOCKED)
4:     s.getThread().state=RUNNING
5:     readyQ.addThread(s.getThread())
6:     #ifdef MANTIS_SLEEP
7:       update_sleep_counters()
8:     dispatch_thread()
9:   else
10:    s.getThread().state=RUNNING
```

part A   part B

the Round Robin scheduler, in which lengthly tasks are interrupted to give other equal priority threads a processing time-slice, thus preventing process starvation. Second, the periodic interrupts are used to check if threads in the *sleepQ* have to wake-up. The *update_ sleep_ counters* function is called from the timer interrupt to reactivate and reschedule sleeping threads. Obviously, threads sent to sleep using this mechanism do not expect to sleep with a period less than the periodic interrupt, $20ms$. Finally, *dispatch_ thread* is called to perform the context switch to the new thread. In many application cases, the new thread will be the same as the old thread.

4.3   Power Management

In MANTIS, thread state information is used to determine the level of power management to be initiated. Sensor network processors have a number of different low-power modes, providing a range of energy conserving states, varying in power-conserving performance and wake-up responsiveness.

Thread state information is used in MANTIS to determine if a thread requires a responsive wake-up, or if more relaxed wake-up times can be accepted. If the thread is *BLOCKED* (Alg. 2, part A:line 3), it is assumed that fast wake-up times are required and an idle power mode with fast wake-up response time is chosen. If all threads reside in a SLEEPING state, then the thread sleep counters are used to determine the next wakeup period. A timer is set to wakeup the processor in time for the next thread event. Thus the processor can be put into a deep sleep power mode and wakeup early enough to compensate for the slow processor wake-up period.

Power management in the MANTIS kernel is implemented as a separate thread, the idle thread. The idle thread is assigned the lowest priority and is always in a ready state. Thus, if no threads are ready to be processed the idle thread by default will be the next thread to be activated and the processor will be transitioned into a low power state determined as previously explained.

5   MANTIS Kernel Modifications

As shown in the preliminary research, MANTIS has the capability of task pre-emption and thus critical high priority tasks can be executed deterministically. However, the power consumption of a node running MANTIS is considerably higher than the power consumption of a node running TinyOS. The high energy consumption of the MANTIS operating system is caused by the processing over-head for thread management. This relatively high overhead is mainly caused by the (i) idle thread, the (ii) time slicing and the inefficient use of the (iii) kernel queuing structures.

5.1   Idle Thread

As previously explained, power management is implemented in MANTIS within the idle thread. If no other thread is currently active, the idle thread is dispatched which subsequently initiates the appropriate power-saving state. This method of power management is elegant as all power management code is contained in a thread but it is also highly inefficient.

When all threads are inactive (*SLEEPING* or *BLOCKED*), a context switch to the idle-thread is performed. Thereafter, as soon as one thread resumes activity, another context switch is required. The new active thread might even be the same thread that was active before the idle thread was called. Thus, for each sleep activity two context switches have to be performed which are in most cases not necessary on a typical sensor node running a single application.

To reduce the problem, the idle thread concept can be abandoned and threads initiate a sleep state directly. Thus, the kernel thread handling overhead can be greatly reduced, especially in scenarios where the same thread has to be activated after a sleep phase, avoiding context switching.

In the modified MANTIS kernel, the power-management procedure that was implemented as a thread is now implemented as a separate function that is invoked directly by the kernel when no more threads are available to process. The optimization requires a modification of the idle loop function. In the original MANTIS kernel the idle loop is initially invoked by the *kernel_init* function to execute for the duration of operating system operation as a separate thread. In the modified MANTIS kernel, the idle loop is no longer encapsulated as a thread, but instead directly invoked from the kernel blocking procedures, i.e. *mos_semaphore_sleep* and *mos_semaphore_wait* (see Alg. 4). A new thread state is added to the kernel, the *BLOCKED_RUNNING* state is used to signify if a thread can be reactivated after power management without a thread switch. A thread is first transitioned to this state when waiting for a semaphore while no other thread is active (Alg. 4, part A:line 12). Thereafter, the power management function is involved (line 13). If the processor is later reactivated and a resource is then ready, the *mos_semaphore_post* function will be called and the condition at Alg. 4 part B:line 3 will be used to determine if the blocked thread was already running before the power-management was invoked. If this is the case, all thread registers values still reside in the processor registers and a context switch is not necessary. Instead, the thread state is changed to *RUNNING*, and the thread resumes processing.

5.2   Time Slice Timer

As mentioned, MANTIS creates a time slice interrupt every $20ms$ to alternately process threads of equal priority and addtionally update the *sleepQ*.

The periodic execution of the interrupt routine, and especially the necessary updates to determine which threads from the *sleepQ* have to be woken, represents a significant thread management overhead. Additionally, the *sleepQ* is also checked with each semaphore operation.

Round robin execution of equal priority threads is not really required in a sensor node. Either, one thread can wait for the other to finish execution or, if starvation is a concern, another priority level can be assigned to the thread. The sleep function using the *sleepQ* can be implemented alternatively using a timer interrupt combined with a semaphore. Therefore, the time slice timer can be removed from the MANTIS kernel without losing vital kernel functionality.

In the modified MANTIS kernel, the time slicing functionality and the associated sleep function using the *sleepQ* are removed. More specificly, this functionality is moved to a separate library that can be included in the kernel if needed. Applications can decide not to include the time slice timer and the associated sleep functionality in favor of more efficient processing. Such applications can therefor *not* invoke the *mos_thread_sleep* function to block a thread and must instead call a semaphore and a timer to block a thread for a predefined period of time. Equally prioritized threads in such applications execute sequentially until completion instead of being processed in a round-robin fashion.

To include the default MANTIS time slice timer, the user need only specify *#define MANTIS_SLEEP* in the application code. The *MANTIS_SLEEP* environment variable is used at part A:lines 8 and part B:6 in Alg. 4 to determine if the thread sleep functionality is required and the thread sleep counters must be updated with the *update_sleep_counters* function. Additionally, the time slice timer is set active.

5.3   The Kenel Queues

The MANTIS kernel maintains 3 types of link-list quing structures. The readyQ, sleepQ and semaphore queue are used to store threads in a READY, SLEEPING or BLOCKED state respectivly. A thread cannot reside in more than one queue at a time, and will therefore frequently switch between the queues as it changes state. As MANTIS normally handles a small number of threads (12 is the default number of threads supported [12]) simple data structures and ways of using them can be implemented. For example, all thread pointers can be kept in a simple array of pointers ordered by thread priority. Thread priority's and the number of threads normally do not change while an application is running and thus, the structure can be kept fairly static. Refrencing threads with static arrays requires far less processing that using a link-list.

In the modified MANTIS kernel all linked list structures are removed from kernel methods. The *readyQ* is changed from being an array of linked lists to a simple array of thread pointers. The thread pointers are kept permanently in the array while the threads exist. The thread pointers stored in this array are sorted regarding thread priority. Thus, addition and deletion of threads is costly but should not be common during a node's operation as threads are normally created at system startup. This change simplifies operations on the *readyQ* structure when semaphore functions are called. Threads need not switch between queues, a simple change of the thread state variable is all that is needed for a thread to switch state. The function *readyQ.getThread* (Alg. 4, part A:line 4) returns the first thread pointer in the *readyQ* array where the thread is in state *READY*.

If a thread is suspended and waits for a semaphore, the thread pointer is added to the semaphore structure. However, a copy of the thread pointer remains in the *readyQ*. The semaphore structure is also modified to point directly to a single thread rather than a link-list of multiple threads. Thus, the function *s.addThread* (Alg. 4, part B:line 5) is reduced to a simple pointer copy operation. The flexibility of using a semaphore to block multiple threads is obviously traded for efficiency.

6 Experimental Evaluation

The MANTIS kernel modifications are evaluated using exactly the same setup that was used in the preliminary research. Again, the average task execution time E_t and the percentage of experiment time I_t spent with an idle CPU are measured. According to the goals of the kernel modifications, the event processing capabilities of MANTIS should not be shortened and the energy consumption should be improved due to a reduction of processing overhead.

6.1 Event Processing

Fig. 4 shows the measured average packet-processing time E_t of the original and the modified MANTIS kernel for sensing tasks of two different sizes.

The results show that the average processing time of the packet forwarding task is reduced significantly. This decrease is due to the reduced processing overhead of the modified MANTIS kernel. The processing time is measured from the point the packet arrives to the time the packet is processed which includes possible context switching time (see Section 3.3). The pure packet-processing within the packet-processing thread accounts for $1ms$. Thus, the operating system can not execute the packet forwarding faster than $1ms$.

The trend in the packet-processing time is due to the fact that the packet-processing might sometimes preempt an active sensing task. Additionally, packet queuing effects become more dominant with increasing network load (an increasing n).

It can be deduced from the measurements that no significant difference in the variance of packet-processing timesbetween the orignial and modified MANTIS

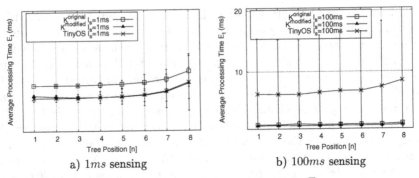

a) $1ms$ sensing   b) $100ms$ sensing

Fig. 4. Average packet-processing time E_t

kernel(same magnitude of variation in the execution times). Additionally the processing speed is increased as the number of kernel overheads are reduced.

6.2 Energy Consumption

The percentage idle time is compared with the theoretical maximal possible percentage idle time, I_k^{max}. I_k^{max} is calculated by taking only the application processing of the abstract application scenario into account (see.Section 3.2). Thus, I_k^{max} represents the percentage running time that the processor would be idle using an ideal operating system which would have no operating system processing overhead. I_k^{max} depends on the task durations l_s and l_p of sensing and packet forwarding task respectively, the frequency of the sensing task f_s, the CPU speed s_{cpu} and the position n of the node in the abstract application scenario. I_k^{max} is calculated using Equation (1):

$$I_k^{max} = \left(1 - \frac{f_s}{s_{cpu}} \cdot (l_s + l_p \cdot (2^n - 1))\right) \cdot 100 \qquad (2)$$

Fig. 5 shows the measured average idle time I_t of the original and the modified MANTIS kernel for sensing tasks of two different sizes. Additionally, the maximum possible idle time I_k^{max} is shown in the graph.

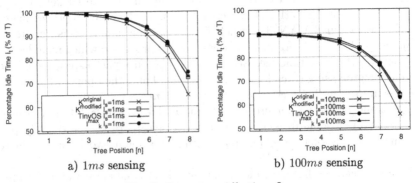

a) $1ms$ sensing   b) $100ms$ sensing

Fig. 5. Percentage idle time I_t

The results show that the available idle time is now very close to the theoretical maximum. The difference is especially visible under high network load (high n). The modified MANTIS kernel reduces overheads in context switches which is valuable in cases of a high system load.

Compared with the original MANTIS, the kernel modifications improve the idle time (by 8% for $n = 8$ with $l_s = 100ms$). Compared with the TinyOS operating system, the optimized MANTIS is now even outperforming TinyOS in some cases. For example for $l_s = 100ms$, $n = 8$, the modified MANTIS is 1% better than TinyOS. If $l_s = 1ms$, $n = 8$, the modified MANTIS is 0.3% worse than TinyOS under a heavy load.

7   Conclusion

As it is shown in the paper, it is possible to make a multi-threaded sensor network operating system as power-efficient as an event-based system. Thus, the commonly accepted fact that multi threaded systems are not useful for sensor networks due to their heigh energy consumption is invalid. Especially in scenarios that require timely event processing, multi threaded systems can be considered a useful option.

The MANTIS kernel modifications reduce the processing overhead needed for thread management dramatically. This overhead is reduced to such an extent that in usual sensor network application scenarios MANTIS has a similar overall performance to TinyOS. As kernel overhead is directly related to energy efficiency, the energy consumption of a MANTIS node is now similar to that of a TinyOS node. After the kernel modifications, MANTIS is 1% more energy efficient than TinyOS (in case of heavy load with $n = 8$, $l_s = 100ms$). With the original MANTIS kernel, TinyOS is 6.9% better than MANTIS (in case of heavy load with $n = 8$, $l_s = 100ms$).

We conclude that multi threaded systems can be used in sensor networks if designed carefully.

References

1. J. Hill, R. Szewczyk, A. Woo, S. Hollar, D. Culler, and K. Pister, "System architecture directions for networked sensors," in *ACM SIGOPS Operating Systems Review*, vol. 34, pp. 93–104, December 2000.
2. H. Abrach, S. Bhatti, J. Carlson, H. Dai, J. Rose, A. Sheth, B. Shucker, and R. Han, "MANTIS: System support for multimodal networks of in-situ sensors," in *2nd ACM International Workshop on Wireless Sensor Networks and Applications*, pp. 50–59, September 2003.
3. A. Dunkels, B. Gronvall, and T. Voigt, "Contiki - a lightweight and flexible operating system for tiny networked sensors," in *29th Annual IEEE International Conference on Local Computer Networks*, pp. 455–462, November 2004.
4. E. Trumpler and R. Han., "A systematic framework for evolving TinyOS," in *IEEE Workshop on Embedded Networked Sensors*, pp. 61–65, May 2006.

5. J. Regehr, A. Reid, K. Webb, M. Parker, and J. Lepreau, "Evolving real-time systems using hierarchical scheduling and concurrency analysis," in 24th *IEEE Internation Real-Time Systems Symposium*, pp. 25–36, December 2003.

6. A. Dunkels, O. Schmidt, and T. Voigt, "Using protothreads for sensor node programming," in *Workshop on Real-World Wireless Sensor Networks*, June 2005.

7. C. Duffy, U. Roedig, J. Herbert, and C. J. Sreenan, "A performance analysis of TinyOS and MANTIS," tech. rep., University College Cork, November 2006.

8. A. Barroso, J. Benson, T. Murphy, U. Roedig, C. Sreenan, J. Barton, S. Bellis, B. O'Flynn, and K. Delaney, "Demo abstract: The DSYS25 sensor platform," in 2nd *international conference on Embedded networked sensor systems*, pp. 314–314, November 2004.

9. Atmel Corporation, *Atmega128 Datasheet*, rev n ed., March 2006.

10. M. Rahimi, R. Baer, O. I. Iroezi, J. C. Garcia, J. Warrior, D. Estrin, and M. Srivastava., "Cyclops: In situ image sensing and interpretation in wireless sensor networks," in *In proc. 3rd international conference on Embedded Networked Sensor Systems,*, pp. 192–204, November 2005.

11. Nordic Semiconductor, *Datasheet NRF2401*, rev 1.1 ed., June 2004.

12. S. Bhatti, J. Carlson, H. Dai, J. Deng, J. Rose, A. Sheth, B. Shucker, C. Gruenwald, A. Torgenson, and R. Han., "MANTIS OS: An embedded multithreaded operating system for wireless micro sensor platforms," *ACM kluwer Mobile Networks & Applications Journal, special Issue on Wireless Sensor Networks*, August 2005.

Model-Based Design Exploration of Wireless Sensor Node Lifetimes

Deokwoo Jung, Thiago Teixeira, Andrew Barton-Sweeney,
and Andreas Savvides

Embedded Networks and Applications Lab, ENALAB
Yale Univerisity, New Haven, CT 06520, USA
firstname.lastname@yale.edu

Abstract. This paper presents two lifetime models that describe two of the most common modes of operation of sensor nodes today, trigger-driven and duty-cycle driven. The models use a set of hardware parameters such as power consumption per task, state transition overheads, and communication cost to compute a node's average lifetime for a given event arrival rate. Through comparison of the two models and a case study from a real camera sensor node design we show how the models can be applied to drive architectural decisions, compute energy budgets and duty-cycles, and to preform side-by-side comparison of different platforms.

1 Introduction

The rapid progress of sensor networks in many applications is constantly fueling the quest for extending the lifetime of battery-operated wireless sensor nodes. In fact, many innovative platforms [9,3,8,11,13] have recently demonstrated several important new techniques for increasing node lifetime. Despite these efforts however, there are numerous situations where design decisions are rather opportunistic and tend to be influenced on the availability of low-power components and techniques without considering the longer term trends in platform design.

To complement these effort, we draw from our experiences in building and using sensor nodes to develop detailed models that characterize two widely used operation patterns for sensor nodes today: trigger-driven and schedule-driven. The models are constructed using Semi-Markov models by considering the power consumption in different operational modes and the energy overheads incurred during transitions. While similar predictions about lifetime could be obtained using simulations, we argue that detailed models are also needed to provide additional insight into how individual platform and application parameters affect lifetime. For instance, one can use the lifetime models presented here to evaluate potential gains from the design of hardware triggering mechanisms, software driven scheduling and duty-cycle modes and power budgets. The models presented here can also be used to perform side-by-side comparison between existing platforms under different application requirements, event arrival rates and detection probabilities. With this, our models can be used as a deployment analysis tool to determine which design is more appropriate for a certain application.

K. Langendoen and T. Voigt (Eds.): EWSN 2007, LNCS 4373, pp. 277–292, 2007.

Our presentation is divided into two main parts. The first part states our assumptions and derives our models. The second part demonstrates the usefulness of our models in a case study drawn from our own experiences during the design of a camera sensor node. The case study shows how the models developed here can be applied to analyze the lifetime properties of a sensor node architecture based on application characteristics, hardware properties and changing trends in microprocessor and radio technologies.

2   Related Work

Node lifetime is a frequently discussed topic in platform design and analysis. In the last couple of years new platforms such as LEAP[9], XYZ[8], iMote2[3] and the Hitachi watch in [15] have demonstrated several new techniques for reducing power leakage during sleep time. The LEAP [9] platform adopted a dual processor/radio architecture to exploit the tradeoffs between power efficient and high-power components. An Energy Management and Accounting Preprocessor (EMAP) module based on a low-power MSP 430 processor has been designed to manage different power domains on the LEAP board, enabling the high-end sensors and processors only when needed. Intel's iMote2 [3] uses dynamic frequency and voltage scaling and a power management IC (PMIC) to control different voltage domains on the node. The XYZ [8] node and the Hitachi watch [15] have used an external real-time clock circuit to wake up the node processor from ultra-low power deep-sleep modes. A number of proposals [10],[13],[4] described energy dissipation at the node level. Nath et al.[10] used Markov chains to analyze energy dissipation behavior per node. Each node is assumed to have six distinct power modes and transitions over different modes with given probabilities. Despite the detailed power mode consideration, this work is mostly simulation-based (in ns-2) and does not consider the energy dissipation models pertaining to the power modes. Snyder et al. [13] demonstrated the validity and effectiveness of their power consumption simulation tool, PowerTOSSIM, by predicting energy consumption per node. Hardware components are characterized at a very detailed level to simulate power consumption of a node as close as possible. Another approach presented in [4] uses hybrid automata models for analyzing power consumption of a node at the operating system level (TinyOS).

Our work differs from the above in that it tries to derive longer-term models by considering a node's hardware characteristics and operation patterns. Instead of considering software optimizations, the emphasis of our analysis is in exposing how a chosen combination of hardware components and operation patterns can influence lifetime.

3   Model Overview and Assumptions

The analysis described below models two main sensing schemes commonly employed in sensor nodes today: trigger-driven and schedule-driven. In trigger-driven operation, the sensors are managed by a low-power pre-processing unit

Table 1. List of variables

Symbol	Description	Symbol	Description
E_{Total}	Total amount of energy per node	Z	Transmission time per packet
S_i	Power state of mode i	σ	Job inter arrival time per event
P_M	Power consumption at power mode M, where $M \in S_i, i = 1...5$	λ	Average event inter arrival rate
		$n_{ij}(t)$	# of $i \rightarrow j$ transitions during t
P_S	Power consumption at asleep period of schedule driven node	P_W	Power consumption at awake period of schedule driven node
p_j	Steady state probability of mode j	N_σ	The number of jobs per event
p_{ij}	Transition probability from mode i to j	C_{ij}	Transition energy cost from mode i to j
C_P	CPU wake-up energy cost	N_P	Number of packets per event
C_R	Radio wake-up energy cost	T_W	CPU awake duration
L	Channel-listening time of radio	T_S	CPU asleep duration
Y	Processing time per event	T_c	Duty period, $T_c = T_1 + T_2$
u	Detection probability	d	Duty cycle, $d = T_1/(T_1 + T_2)$

that continuously samples the sensors. This preprocessor performs a first-order filtering of the data and wakes up a more powerful main processing unit if certain criteria are met. The LEAP node [9] and image sensors described in [14] follow this model. In schedule-driven operation, the node's sensors are connected directly to the node's main processor. To conserve energy, the processor follows a schedule that alternates between a low-power mode (e.g sleep, deep-sleep or shutdown) and a short, full-power mode in which the processor (or its ADC) samples the sensors for interesting activity. If the desired event types are sensed, it proceeds to make the necessary computations and transmits the outcome with the radio if needed. The sentry nodes used in the Vigilnet project [5] follow this type of model. In this case the sentry are asleep most of the time, and periodically wake up to sample for activity.

3.1   Assumptions

The models described in this paper make the following assumptions:

1. The first-order statistical characteristic (mean value) of all random quantities (events, processing time, etc) is known by observation and experiment from the Ergodic property.
2. Event arrivals follow a Poisson distribution.
3. Processing and radio-transmission times are independent and identically distributed (i.i.d.) with arbitrary distribution.
4. When an event is detected, the node processes it and sends the information to a base station (or another node) with probability α.
5. During the processing period, the CPU visits a limited number of low-power states (e.g. idle state).

Table 2. Power state description

Mode	Trigger-Driven Node			Schedule-Driven Node		
	Preprocessor	CPU	Radio	Sensor	CPU	Radio
S_0	–	–	–	Off	Off	Off
S_1	On	Off	Off	–	–	–
S_2	On	On	Off	On	On	Off
S_3	On	On	TX	On	On	TX
S_4	On	Idle	Off	On	Idle	Off
S_5	On	On	RX	On	On	RX

6. During the communication period, the radio visits a limited number of listen (idle) states.
7. All power consumptions are constant during an operation and a fixed amount of energy is required to turn on or off the CPU and radio.

The first three assumptions imply that the power state transitions may be modeled as a semi-Markov chain [12] that can be used to compute a node's average power consumption and lifetime. While assumption 2 may not always hold true in all deployments a Poisson arrival rate is a representative model for many applications. For example, the number of people entering a building is a well known example of Poisson arrival [6]. For the purposes of our analysis we argue that the Poisson assumption is a reasonable choice because our main interest is to exercise the node hardware parameters that influence lifetime. Furthermore, by fixing the distribution of arrival events in our models we provide a common baseline for the comparison of many platforms by exercising their features under the same underlying distribution. In order to include communication overhead in the lifetime analysis, the same communication paradigm is adopted for both the trigger-driven and schedule-driven models as stated in assumption 4. The next two assumptions, 5 and 6, related to the idle state of the CPU and listening state of the radio, are necessary to more accurately describe the power consumption of those components. When an event is sensed by the node, the CPU will usually go to a full-power, active mode to perform some processing or additional sensing, but may alternate it with a temporary lower-power state to conserve energy. This is accounted for in assumption 5. Meanwhile, it is common for MAC protocols to listen to the radio channel before any transmission, to avoid packet collisions [2]. For this we have introduced assumption 6. We also emphasize that our models focus on node-level behaviors by examining the parameters of the node hardware under different event arrival rates. Software and network level optimizations are therefore not considered in this analysis.

3.2   Node Power Modes and Variables

Our analysis considers a simplified version of the power modes available on sensor nodes, eliminating some of the impractical modes. The modes considered are described in Table 2. To develop our models we also introduce a set of variables.

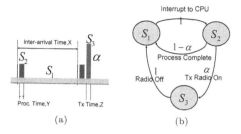

Fig. 1. (a) Power profile of simplified trigger-driven node model, (b) Semi-Markov chain of simplified trigger-driven node model

These are described Table 1. Our notation also uses a bar to denote expected value (i.e the expected value of the variable A is $\bar{A}$).

4   Lifetime Models

In this section, we will show that each sensor node can be modeled by an embedded semi-Markov Chain. Let $X(t)$ denote the power state at time t. Then change of state $X(t)$, $t \geq 0$ does not solely depend on the present state, but also the length of time that has been spent in that state. This characterizes a semi-Markov chain, as states change in accordance with a Markov chain but there is a random length of time between the changes. Let H_i denote the distribution of time that the semi-Markov process spends in state i before making a transition, and let the mean be $\mu_i = \int_0^\infty x dH_i(x)$. With X_n denoting the nth state visit, $X_n, n \geq 0$ becomes a Markov chain with transition probabilities p_{ij}. It is also called the embedded Markov chain of the semi-Markov process [12]. Let T_{ii} denote the time between successive transitions into state i and let $\mu_{ii} = E[T_{ii}]$. If the semi-Markov process is irreducible and if T_{ii} has nonlattice distribution with finite mean, then

$$p_i \equiv \lim_{t \to \infty} P[X(t) = i | X(0) = j] = \lim_{t \to \infty} \frac{T_t}{t}, \tag{1}$$

where T_t is the amount of time in i during $[0, t]$, exists and is independent of the initial state, j. In other words, p_i equals the long-run proportion of time in state i (the time spent in i over the combined time spent in all states). Suppose further that the embedded-Markov chain X_n, $n \geq 0$ is positive recurrent. Then a stationary probability exists, which is the frequency of visiting each state for infinite time duration . Let its stationary probability be π_j, $j \geq 0$. Then π_j is the unique solution of

$$\pi_j = \sum_i \pi_i p_{ij}, \sum_j \pi_j = 1 \tag{2}$$

and π_j can be interpreted as the proportion of transitions into state j (over the sum of all state transitions). Then the following theorem holds

$$p_i = \frac{\mu_i}{\mu_{ii}} = \frac{\pi_i \mu_i}{\sum_j \pi_j \mu_j} \tag{3}$$

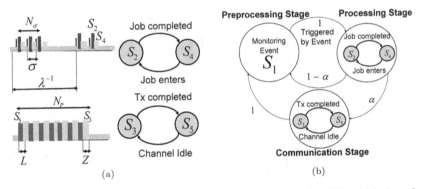

Fig. 2. (a) Power profile of complete trigger-driven node model, (b) Semi-Markov chain of complete trigger-triven node model

Using equations (2) and (3), one can compute the long-run proportion of time in state i.

4.1   Trigger-Driven Lifetime Model

Figure 1a shows the simplest power model. In this model, the sensor node has only three states, which can be represented by the semi-Markov chain in Figure 1b. This model does not account for any Idle or Listening modes on the CPU or radio, respectively. However, in reality the CPU and radio often enter Idle mode during the processing and communication stages. For example, when an event is detected, the CPU has a choice of either processing the data, or deciding to drop it (or quickly store it for later). In these situations, the CPU may go back into an idle state to wait for the next job. Meanwhile, radios tend to spend considerable energy listening to the channel before any actual transmission due to impositions of the underlying MAC protocol. In IEEE 802.15.4, for instance, less than 50 percent of energy is spent for actual transmission, and listening activity accounts for more than 40 percent of energy consumption [2]. To take these factors into account, Figure 2a deals with the addition of the idle and listening states of the CPU and radio. The updated semi-Markov chain in Figure 2b shows that each processing and communication stage contains a two-state embedded chain.

Given a long enough time period, T, the total time spent at state i can be approximated as $\lim_{T \to \infty} T_i = T p_i$. Therefore, the total energy spent at state i is $E_{S_i} = T p_i \times P_{S_i}$, for $i \in \{1, 2, 3\}$, and the transition energy cost from state i to j during T can be obtained as $E_{S_{ij}} = C_{ij} \bar{n}_{ij}(T)$. However, only the CPU and radio wake-up costs (C_P and C_R, or, in $E_{S_{ij}}$ notation, $E_{S_{12}}$ and $E_{S_{23}}$) need to be taken into consideration since the sleep cost ($E_{S_{31}}$) is negligible in comparison. Since the total amount of energy spent at each state, E_{S_i}, and the transition energy, $E_{S_{ij}}$, cannot exceed the energy resource, E_{total}, the following inequality holds:

$$\sum_{1 \le k \le 3} E_{S_k} + E_{S_{12}} + E_{S_{23}} \le E_{total} \tag{4}$$

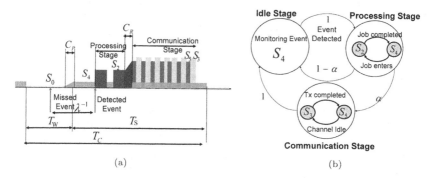

Fig. 3. (a) Schedule-driven node power profile, (b) Power state transition during wake-period

By applying (2) and (3) to Figure 1b, we can obtain the asymptotic node lifetime as follows. A more detailed derivation can be found in [7].

$$T_L(\lambda) \leq \frac{[1 + \lambda K_T] E_{Total}}{P_{S_1} + \lambda K_E} \tag{5}$$

In (5), K_T and K_E represent the average time and energy spent for a sensed event respectively. Typically, $K_E \gg P_{S_1}$ and $\lambda \ll 1sec^{-1}$. As shown in the denominator of (5), the power component can be roughly broken down into two parts: λK_E, the average power spent for computation and communication per sensed event; and P_{S_1}, the power spent to monitor the events. It can be easily found that a sensor node spends more power monitoring an event than processing it at $\lambda \leq \frac{P_{S_1}}{K_E}$. The average steady-state power consumption of the trigger-driven sensor node is simply given as:

$$\overline{P}_{ST,td}(\lambda) = \frac{P_{S_1} + \lambda K_E}{[1 + \lambda K_T]} \tag{6}$$

For the simplest power model, Figure 1a, K_T and K_E are given as:

$$K_T = \overline{Y} + \alpha \overline{Z}, \quad K_E = \overline{Y} P_{S_2} + \alpha \overline{Z} P_{S_3} + \frac{C_P + \alpha C_R}{1 + \alpha} \tag{7}$$

By taking into consideration the average power consumption and sojourn time in these two-state chains as shown Figure 2b, K_T and K_E are given as:

$$K_T = (\overline{\sigma} + \overline{Y})\overline{N}_\sigma + \alpha(\overline{L} + \overline{Z})\tilde{N}_P$$

$$K_E = (\overline{\sigma} P_{S_4} + \overline{Y} P_{S_2})\overline{N}_\sigma + \alpha(\overline{L} P_{S_5} + \overline{Z} P_{S_3})\tilde{N}_P + \frac{C_P + \alpha C_R}{1 + \alpha} \tag{8}$$

4.2   Schedule-Driven Lifetime Model

Let k be the total number of duty cycles during the node's entire lifetime, and each ϵ_i the residual processing time after the ith awake state of the node.

Additionally, let T_W be the length of time when the node is awake. Then the average node lifetime is obtained as following:

$$\sum_{0 \leq i \leq k} ((T_W + \epsilon_i)\bar{P}_{W,i} + (T_S - \epsilon_i)\bar{P}_{S,i} + C_P) \leq E_{Total} \tag{9}$$

where $\bar{P}_{W,i}$ and $\bar{P}_{S,i}$ denote average power consumption of awake and asleep periods during cycle i respectively. Note that each $\bar{P}_{W,i}$ incorporates the power expenditure of four power states: S_2, S_3, S_4 and S_5. As for the power computation, the schedule-driven node performs the same function as the trigger-driven node when an event occurs during the awake period (Figure 3). Therefore, given a long enough timespan, the average power consumption of the node during the active period ($\bar{P}_{W,i}$) can be approximated by replacing in (6) the preprocessing power with idle power, and setting $C_P = 0$. The result is shown below:

$$\lim_{i \longrightarrow \infty} \bar{P}_{W,i} = \overline{P}_W(\lambda) = \frac{P_{S_2} + \lambda K'_E}{1 + \lambda K'_T} \tag{10}$$

In (10), K'_T and K'_E represent the average time and energy spent for a sensed event respectively during awake period. Typically, $K'_E > P_{S_2}$ and $\lambda \ll 1sec^{-1}$. As before, the nominator of (10) shows the power component during the awake period can be roughly broken down into two factors, namely $\lambda K'_E$, the average power spent for computation and communication per sensed event, and P_{S_2}, the static power spent during the awake period. It can be easily found that a sensor node spends more power for the idle state than processing events at $\lambda \leq \frac{P_{S_2}}{K'_E}$.

For the awake period of the schedule-driven power model, (Figure 1b) K'_T and K'_E are given as using (8):

$$K'_E = (\overline{\sigma}P_{S_4} + \overline{Y}P_{S_2})\overline{N}_\sigma + \alpha(\overline{L}P_{S_5} + \overline{Z}P_{S_3})\tilde{N}_P + \frac{\alpha C_R}{1 + \alpha} \tag{11}$$

$$K'_T = (\overline{\sigma} + \overline{Y})\overline{N}_\sigma + \alpha(\overline{L} + \overline{Z})\tilde{N}_P$$

Using the fact that $\bar{P}_{S,i}(t)$ is constant ($\bar{P}_{S,i} \equiv P_{S_0}$), the average node lifetime can be obtained by applying (10) to equation (9):

$$\overline{T_L} \approx (T_W + T_S)k \leq \frac{E_{Total}(T_W + T_S)}{[T_W \overline{P}_W(\lambda) + T_S P_{S_0} + (\overline{P}_W(\lambda) - P_{S_0})\overline{\epsilon} + C_P]} \tag{12}$$

Since it is typically the case that $T_W \gg \epsilon$, the term $(\bar{P}_W(\lambda) - P_{S_0})\bar{\epsilon}$ can often be ignored as $T_W \bar{P}_W(\lambda) \gg \bar{\epsilon}\bar{P}_W(\lambda) \geq \bar{\epsilon}(\bar{P}_W(\lambda) - P_{S_0})$.

The model derivation is now complete. Before applying these models, we have verified their numerical correctness through simulation. The simulation iterates through each state visited for a certain time period summing up all the power overheads during the lifetime of the node. Due to space limitations, these results are omitted from this paper.

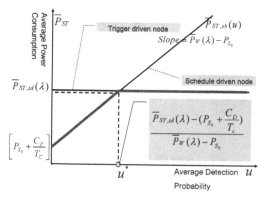

Fig. 4. Trade-Off Diagram: Power versus Average Detection Probability

4.3   Trigger-Driven and Schedule-Driven Comparison

To meaningfully compare the two models, the event detection probability also needs to be considered. For the trigger-driven case, the sensor and preprocessor are always on, so we can assume that event detection happens with probability one. This comes at a price, of course, of added power cost for the preprocessor. The schedule-driven scheme, however, takes no such toll on power, but does so at the expense of event detection probability. All events that do not coincide with the node's duty-cycle remain undetected. To compare, let us define two random variables U and V to describe the number of Poisson sensor events during T_W and T_c respectively. Then the average detection probability, $E\left[\frac{U}{V}\right]$, can be computed as:

$$E\left[\frac{U}{V}\right] = \sum_{0 \leq v \leq \infty} E\left[\frac{U}{v}\middle| V = v\right] P_V(v) = \sum_{0 \leq v \leq \infty} \frac{1}{v}\left[v\frac{T_W}{T_c}\right] P_V(v) = \frac{T_W}{T_c} = d$$

(13)

The second equality of Equation (13) comes from the fact that $P(U = u|V = v)$ has a binomial distribution, $B(v, d)$, where $d = \frac{T_W}{T_c}$. As shown in Equation (13), the detection probability is simply the duty cycle of the schedule-driven node. Therefore, we can express the trade-off diagram between the trigger-driven and schedule-driven schemes as a function of the detection probability u (shown in Figure 4), where the node lifetime of the schedule-driven node follows the equation:

$$\bar{T}_L(u) \leq \frac{E_{Total}}{(\bar{P}_W(\lambda) - P_{S_0})u + (P_{S_0} + \frac{C_P}{T_c})}$$

(14)

From (14), the average steady-state power consumption of the schedule-driven node can be found:

$$\bar{P}_{ST,sb}(u) = (\bar{P}_W(\lambda) - P_{S_0})u + \left(P_{S_0} + \frac{C_P}{T_c}\right)$$

(15)

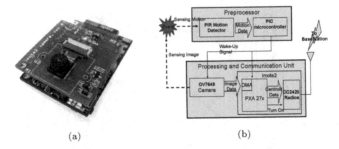

Fig. 5. (a) *iMote2* node with a COTS camera board, (b) Trigger-driven sensor node with *iMote2* fitted with a PIC microcontroller and PIR motion sensor

By superimposing the two average power consumption formulas (Equations (15) and (6)), we can obtain a trade-off diagram as Figure 4. The thick line denotes the lowest-power choice for a given detection probability. The two curves meet at $u^* = \frac{\bar{P}_{ST,td}(\lambda) - (P_{S_0} + \frac{C_P}{T_c})}{P_W(\lambda) - P_{S_0}}$. The figure shows that for an application that allows the use of sensors with detection probability smaller than u^*, the schedule-driven scheme is a sound choice. For events with larger arrival rates, u^* gets shifted to the right, further favoring the schedule-driven scheme for frequent, non-critical detections. Otherwise, if the application demands high-accuracy, the trigger-driven scheme is a better alternative. Of course, multiple nodes with complementary schedules may reduce the number of events that are globally missed, but such a network-wide power analysis is out of the scope of this paper.

5   Case Study: Using the Models to Characterize and Make Decisions About a Camera Sensor Node

To demonstrate the usefulness of the models derived in the previous sections, we now demonstrate their application in the decision-making process of an experimental camera sensor node designed for the BehaviorScope project at Yale. Our goal is to decide whether it makes sense to develop an improved version of the camera node shown in Figure 5a. This camera node is an Intel *iMote2* [3] coupled with a custom camera board we have designed with a commercial, off-the-shelf (COTS) image sensor, the Omnivision's OV7649. The node is powered by three AAA batteries (1150mAh capacity). The alternative design we are considering is a new camera board that supports a wakeup preprocessor mechanism comprised of a passive infrared (PIR) sensor for detecting motion and a small 8-bit PIC 10F200 microcontroller to act as a preprocessor. This configuration (described in Figure 5b) would allow the node to follow a trigger-driven mode of operation. Instead of periodically sampling the camera to detect activity, with this improvement the PXA 271 processor onboard the *iMote2* will wait in a low-power state until triggered by the PIC-based preprocessor that is always kept on for a small energy overhead (Mode S_1 in Table 5). In this state, the preprocessor will

Table 3. Reference scenario, measured ($*$)

Parameter	Value	Parameter	Value
λ	0.1/min	Y	$2sec^*$
$\bar{Z}$	$3.8msec$	$\bar{L}$	0 msec
$\bar{\sigma}$	0 min	$\bar{N}_\sigma$	1
α	1	T_c	10 min
$\bar{N}_P$	1	Total Energy	18.63 kJ

apply a thresholding algorithm to the samples it collects from the PIR sensor. If the observed motion exceeds a predefined value, the preprocessor will power up the $iMote2$ and camera board to acquire and process the images. If the image processing reveals something of interest, the node the transmits the information to a basestation. These transmissions take place with probability α. To provide more concrete numbers in our case study, we set up the camera node to act as a simple single target localization device. An event is defined as the complete trajectory of human centroid in the range of camera sensor. In this setting, the camera sensor node performs the following functions in order.

1. When a person enters the camera's field-of-view, the preprocessor wakes up the iMote2 and camera (only for the trigger-driven node).
2. When awake, the iMote2 continually computes the location of the person at a frequency of 8Hz (8fps) until the person exits the coverage area of the camera.
3. Once the person is out of the sensing range, the node transitions back into the low power mode after sending a stream of locations to the base station.

According to our experiment, event duration is roughly 2 seconds. From our event definition, *processing time* is actually the same as *event duration*, and any incomplete trajectory (set of centroids) of a person is considered a *missed event* (hard-decision). For example, if a person is entering into camera view, and 1 sec later a node wakes up and observes only half of the trajectory, then the event is considered *missed*. For real-time computation, the node may transmit the centroids as soon as they are acquired. Notice, however, that whether the centroids are sent immediatelly or left for transmitting later is not of relevance to our models, as long as the energy consumption of both cases is still the same. From a lifetime perspective, the summation of the energy spent at each stage will be same regardless of the processing order. The time between capturing a frame to extracting a centroid is 123msec/centroid. Therefore, a node generates a total of roughly 16 centroids per event and the total amount of information per event is 96 Bytes. With a packet size of 119 Bytes (including 23 Byte of packet header) transmitted at the rate of 250 kbps, the packet transmission takes $3.8msec$. As a reference scenario, we set the system parameter values as specified in Table 3.

The PXA271 processor provides six power modes: Normal, Idle, Deep Idle, Standby, Sleep and Deep Sleep. Each of the six modes have different levels of power consumption and different transition times to the Normal mode. The Normal mode is the state where all internal power domains and clocks are enabled

Table 4. Typical power-consumption specifications of schedule-driven camera sensor node ($iMote2$) at 104 MHz CPU Core frequency, 4MHz PIC and 0dBm TX Power

Mode	CPU PXA271	Camera OV7649	Radio CC2420	Total
S_0	Deep Sleep	Standby	Shutdown	
	$1.8mW$	$8mW$	$144nW$	$9.8mW$
C_P	$48.63mJ$	-	$691pJ$	$48.63\ mJ$
	$252msec$	-	$970\mu sec$	$253msec$
S_2	Normal	Active	Idle	
	$193mW$	$44mW$	$712\mu W$	$237.7mW$
S_4	Deep Idle	Active	Idle	
	$88mW$	$44mW$	$712\mu W$	$132.7mW$
C_R	-	-	$6.63\mu J$	$6.63\mu J$
	-	-	$194\mu sec$	$194\mu sec$
S_3	Normal	Active	TX	
	$193mW$	$44mW$	$78mW$	$315mW$
S_5	Normal	Active	RX	
	$193mW$	$44mW$	$78mW$	$315mW$

and running. At Idle and Deep Idle modes, the CPU core stops being clocked, but for the latter the PXA is first switched into 13 MHz frequency. Standby mode puts all internal power domains into their lowest power mode except for the real-time clock and the PLL for the core. At Sleep and Deep Sleep modes, the PXA271 core power is turned off. Furthermore, in Deep Sleep mode all clock sources are also disabled. Therefore, Standby mode is the lowest power mode that does not require the node to reboot. To reason with the different design possibilities, we measured the power consumption and transient time of the $iMote2$ at different operational modes that correspond to the schedule-driven and trigger-driven modes we have previously defined in our models. The measurements for these modes are shown in Tables 4 and 5[1]. More detailed information can be found in [1]. Both tables follow the power mode definitions introduced in Table 2. Since the $iMote2$ does not provide any special interface for measuring the power of the PXA CPU, we measured the total power drawn when the radio is shutdown.

Question 1: *What is the expected lifetime for the existing (schedule-driven, Figure 5a) and proposed (Figure 5b) configuration?* Using our measurements in Table 4, the schedule-driven node will last for only 1.61 days if it is always on, continuously sampling, since $\bar{T}_L(1) = \frac{E_{Total}}{P_W(0.1/min)}$ by plugging $u = 1$ and $T_c = \infty$ in Equation (14). The lifetime of the alternative, trigger-driven configuration depends on the event arrival rate and can be computed using the model in

---

[1] In our tables Normal and Active modes have similar meanings. We opted on using two different terms to be consistent with the naming conventions of the datasheet for each device.

Table 5. Typical power-consumption specifications of trigger-driven camera sensor node($iMote2$) at 104 MHz CPU Core frequency, 4MHz PIC and 0dBm Tx Power on a CC2420 radio

| | Preprocessor | | CPU | Camera | Radio | |
Mode	Motion Sensor	PIC10F200	PXA271	OV7649	CC2420	Total
S_1	On	On	Standby	Standby	Shutdown	
	$3.6\mu W$	$340\mu W$	$17mW$	$8mW$	$144nW$	$25.34mW$
C_P	-	-	2.2mJ	-	114nJ	2.2mJ
	-	-	11.432msec	-	$970\mu sec$	12.4msec
S_2	On	On	Normal	Active	Idle	
	$3.6\mu W$	$340\mu W$	$193mW$	$44mW$	$712\mu W$	$238.05mW$
S_4	On	On	Deep Idle	Active	Idle	
	$3.6\mu W$	$340\mu W$	$88mW$	$44mW$	$712\mu W$	$133.05mW$
C_R	-	-	-	-	$6.63\mu J$	$6.63\mu J$
	-	-	-	-	$194\mu sec$	$194\mu sec$
S_3	On	On	Normal	Active	TX	
	$3.6\mu W$	$340\mu W$	$193mW$	$44mW$	$78mW$	$315.34mW$
S_5	On	On	Normal	Active	RX	
	$3.6\mu W$	$340\mu W$	$193mW$	$44mW$	$78mW$	$315.34mW$

Equation (8). The trend for different arrival rates is shown in Figure 6b. At our default configuration (PXA and Camera in Standby Mode), the trigger-driven iMote2 would only last 8.45 days at most (1.03 days at least). Figure 6b shows that less than 4 days of lifetime gain would be achieved by completely turning off the camera sensor board. It reveals the important design guide that in order to obtain a significant lifetime gain (more than 10 times), the trigger-driven node ultimately has to stay at Deep-Sleep mode during preprocessing stage, which is the lowest power state that can be achieved by the node with software control.
Question 2: *Given a specific arrival rate for a certain application, and a lifetime requirement, what is the maximum power a pre-processor(and sensor) can consume?* To obtain the power budget for the pre-processor we need to solve for P_{S_1} of the trigger-driven model in (5). The lifetime trend at different event arrival times as a function of preprocessor power is shown in Figure 6c.
Question 3: *If we don't build the proposed board and use a duty-cycle instead, what is the expected lifetime for a certain detection probability?* We can answer this question by plugging in the detection probability u in the lifetime model for the schedule-driven node described by Equation (14). The expected lifetimes for different detection probabilities are shown in Figure 6a.
Question 4: *Suppose we had an ideal sensor preprocessor (power cost=0) what would be the lifetime of the node at a certain arrival rate?* This trend is shown in Figure 6d. If we use Standby mode as the lowest power mode, in a trigger-driven configuration, the node will last for only 8.62 days! Also, if we entirely disable the preprocessor, the node will operate as in the schedule-driven model with duty-cyle=0, missing all events. Even so, the node lifetime is only 8.62

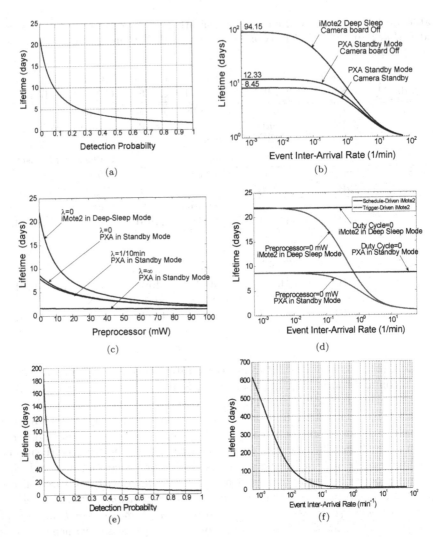

Fig. 6. a) Lifetime trend versus detection probability for question 1, b) Lifetime trend versus arrival rate for question 1, c) Lifetime trend for question 2, d) Lifetime trend for question 3, e) Lifetime trend versus detection probability for the sentry node described in VigilNet[5], f) Predicted hypothetical lifetime trend versus arrival rate for the sentry node described in VigilNet[5]

days, indicating that we should try to operate at power levels lower than the Standby mode. Comparing Figure 6c and Figure 6d, we notice that just lowering power consumption of preprocessor does not impact the lifetime trend of the trigger-driven node since P_{S_1} is heavily dominated by the power consumption of the camera board and PXA at Standby mode. Indeed, our computation shows that for rare events the lifetime increases to 94 days, with the camera board off and the iMote2 in Deep Sleep mode (Figure 6b). Much to our surprise, our models have shown that the addition of a preprocessor and trigger-driven operation will not provide substantial lifetime gains. This is mainly due to the high power consumption in the Standby mode of the PXA and camera. The trends also indicate that it is unlikely to significantly improve lifetime by manipulating the processor power modes alone. A better strategy would be to consider mechanisms that disconnect the entire node from the power supply as suggested in [8]. According to our models, the use of such a mechanism would increase the lifetime of the schedule-driven node to 552 days, a large improvement over the currently predicted 8.45 days for a non-ideal preprocessor (see Figure 6d).

As a sanity check, we also used our model to predict the lifetime of the Micaz nodes used in the Vigilnet project [5]. Using our model, we computed the expected lifetime of a sentry node to be about 442 hours (18.5) days as shown in Figure 6d. According to [5], a sentry node will last 90 days with a role rotation of 4-5 nodes and 25% of sentry duty cycle. Multiplying our prediction by 5 to account for role rotation, our model will anticipate a lifetime of 92.5 days, an estimate that is very close to the lifetime of the real deployment reported by the authors of [5]. Furthermore, Figure 6f shows that the lifetime of the sentry node will significantly increase if we convert it into a trigger-driven node using the same preprocessor as before.[2] Such a high lifetime gain comes from the fact that the power consumption of sentry node at Sleep state is extremely low (42 μW).

6   Conclusion

In this paper, we presented parametric lifetime model for trigger-driven node and schedule-driven node that also takes the associated transition overheads into consideration. The application of the models in making decisions about a camera node platform has helped us to isolate the dominant factors that limit lifetime in our design and provided valuable insight on how to proceed with the architecture. In the near future we are working on extending our models to cover more complex cases involving multiple processors and radios. Additional updates about this work can be found on our website at http://www.eng.yale.edu/enalab.

Acknowledgements

This work is funded in part by the NSF under contracts 0615226 and 0448082. The authors are also thankful to their collaborators Mani Srivastava (UCLA), Deepak Ganessan (UMASS Amherst), Mark Corner (UMASS Amherst), Prashant Shenoy (UMASS Amherst) and Lama Nachman (Intel) for the fruitful discussions around this work.

---

[2] This is a hypothetical lifetime since [5] does not consider a trigger-driven sentry node.

References

1. A. Barton-Sweeney, D. Jung, and A. Savvides. imote2 node and ENALAB camera module power measurements. In *ENALAB Technical Report: 090601*, Sep 2006.
2. B. Bougard, F. Catthoor, D. C. Daly, A. Chandrakasan, and W. Dehaene. Energy efficiency of the IEEE 802.15.4 standard in dense wireless microsensor networks: Modeling and improvement perspectives. In *Design, Automation, and Test in Europe (DATE), pp.196-201*, March 2005.
3. L. Nachman. Intel Corporation Research Santa Clara. CA. New tinyos platforms panel:iMote2. In *The Second International TinyOS Technology Exchange*, Feb 2005.
4. S. Coleri, M. Ergen, and T. Koo. Lifetime analysis of a sensor network with hybrid automata modeling. In *1st ACM International Workshop on Wireless Sensor Networks and Applications (WSNA)*, September 2002.
5. T. He, P. Vicaire, T. Yan, Q. Cao, G. Zhou, L. Gu, L. Luo, R. Stoleru, J. A. Stankovic, and T. Abdelzaher. Achieving long-termsurveillance in vigilnet. In *Infocom 2006*, April 2006.
6. A. Ihler, J. Hutchins, and P. Smyth. Adaptive event detection with time-varying poisson processes. In *KDD '06: Proceedings of the 12th ACM SIGKDD international conference on Knowledge discovery and data mining*, 2006.
7. D. Jung, A. Barton-Sweeney, T. Teixeira, and A. Savvides. Model-based design exploration of wireless sensor node lifetimes. In *ENALAB Technical Report: 090602*, Sep 2006.
8. D. Lymberopoulos and A. Savvides. XYZ: A motion-enabled, power aware sensor node platform for distributed sensor network applications. In *Information Processing in Sensor Networks (IPSN), SPOTS track*, April 2005.
9. D. McIntire, K. Ho, B. Yip, A. Singh, W. Wu, and W. J. Kaiser. The low power energy aware processing (LEAP) embedded networked sensor system. In *Proceedings of Information Processing in Sensor Networks, IPSN/SPOTS*, April 2005.
10. R. A. F. Mini, M. V. Machado, A. A. F. Loureiro, and Badri Nath. Prediction-based energy map for wireless sensor networks. In *Elsevier Ad-hoc Networks Journal (special issue on Ad Hoc Networking for Pervasive Systems)*, March 2005.
11. J. Polastre, R. Szewczyk, and D. Culler. Telos: Enabling ultra-low power wireless research. In *The Fourth International Conference on IPSN/SPOTS*, April 2005.
12. S. M. Ross. Stochastic processes, second edition, pp213-218. In *Jonn Wiley and Sons,Inc.*, April 1996.
13. V. Shnayder, M. Hempstead, B. Chen, G. Werner-Allen, and M. Welsh. Simulating the power consumption of large-scale sensor network applications. In *SenSys'04*, November 2004.
14. T. Teixeira, E. Culurciello, D. Lymberopoulos J. Park, A. Barton-Sweeney, and A. Savvides. Address-event imagers for sensor networks: Evaluation and programming. In *Proceedings of Information Processing in Sensor Networks (IPSN)*, April 2006.
15. S. Yamashita, S. Takanori, K. Aiki, K. Ara, Y. Ogata, I. Simokawa, T. Tanaka, K. Shimada, and Ltd.) H. Kuriyama (Hitachi. A 15x15mm, 1ua, reliable sensor-net module: Enabling application-specific nodes. In *IPSN SPOTS 2006*, April 2006.

Multithreading Optimization Techniques for Sensor Network Operating Systems

Hyoseung Kim and Hojung Cha

Department of Computer Science, Yonsei University
Seodaemun-gu, Shinchon-dong 134, Seoul 120-749, Korea
{hskim, hjcha}@cs.yonsei.ac.kr

Abstract. While a multithreading approach provides a convenient sensor application developing environment with automatic control flow and stack managment, it is considered to have a larger data memory requirement and energy consumption than an event-driven model. Current threaded sensor operating systems unfortunately do not provide appropriate solutions. This paper presents multithreading optimization techniques for sensor network operating systems. Our work focuses on the three major problems of implementing threads on resource-constraint sensor nodes—memory resources, energy consumption, and scheduling policy. Single kernel stack and the thread stack-size analysis techniques reduce the RAM requirement of thread model. The variable timer saves energy consumption and the event-boosting thread scheduling reflects the characteristics of sensor applications and provides fast response time to threads. The experimental results on a common sensor node show that the multithreaded system could be effectively implemented with reasonable overhead.

Keywords: sensor network operating system, multithreading optimization technique.

1 Introduction

Wireless sensor networks have been well-studied in terms of the increasing variety of hardware and the development of diverse applications which now require sophisticated system software. Sensor nodes are normally battery-operated, memory-limited and have low computational power. Sensor network operating systems, therefore, should support high concurrency with minimal memory usage and low energy consumption. Unlike general purpose operating systems, popular sensor operating systems such as TinyOS [1] and SOS [2] adopt an event-driven model to meet these tight constraints. They execute applications with reactive event handlers and cooperatively-operated run-to-completion tasks. Li *et al.* [3] reported that the event-driven TinyOS achieves about a 30-fold improvement in data memory requirement and a 12-fold reduction in power consumption over general purpose multithreaded embedded operating systems.

Although the event-driven sensor operating systems are implemented efficiently in a resource-constraint environment, they do not provide all the functions of general

K. Langendoen and T. Voigt (Eds.): EWSN 2007, LNCS 4373, pp. 293–308, 2007.
© Springer-Verlag Berlin Heidelberg 2007

purpose operating systems. Developers typically suffer from the manual configuration when programming applications. With TinyOS and SOS, for example, developers have to split a long-running task, which can unnecessarily delay other tasks, into several phases. Programmers also take responsibility for managing event handlers' states. As tasks are inter-dependent in the execution context, the repeated analysis of system concurrency and system restructuring is inevitable in order to meet the changes in application requirements [4].

In contrast to the event-driven approach, multithreading inherently provides high concurrency with preemption and automatic state management. It also allows programmers to specify control flow. Sensor applications frequently request sensing and radio communication. With an event-driven model, the programmers may split one conceptual function into multiple functions for I/O operations, but multithread systems easily handle it by blocking the I/O interface. Synchronization and deadlock problems experienced with thread [5] can be managed by compiler support and development tools [6]. As most existing development tools are based on threads, multithread systems could provide a general and more efficient development environment. However, threads tend to incur more time and space overhead than events. Stack reservation for each stack is indispensable for multithreading systems. Context switching overhead is caused by preemption and blocking. Kernel services, such as a scheduler and system timer management, are also required. Data memory and energy requirement of multithreading is an obvious obstacle to the resource-constraint sensor nodes. In addition, a scheduling policy optimized for sensor applications should be developed. Although the multithreading approach is attractive in sensor application developments, current thread-based sensor operating systems [7, 8] do not provide appropriate solutions for overhead problems or a scheduling issue. This has motivated us to develop multithreading techniques specifically designed for sensor nodes.

This paper presents optimized techniques for the implementation of multithreaded sensor network operating systems. The thread model for sensor nodes should consider memory resource, energy consumption, and scheduling policy. The proposed techniques contribute to each issue by providing multithreading functions while consuming reasonable overhead compared to existing event-driven sensor operating systems. Our techniques are implemented in the RETOS operating system [9, 10, 11], although they are applicable to other thread-based sensor operating systems. The effectiveness of the proposed techniques is validated by experiments conducted on a commercial mote running the RETOS operating system.

The rest of this paper is organized as follows: Section 2 describes the proposed multithreading optimization techniques; Section 3 validates the effectiveness of the mechanism through real experiments; Section 4 discusses related work; and Section 5 concludes the paper.

2   Thread Optimization for Sensor Applications

This section explains optimization techniques for implementing threads on sensor nodes. Considering the resource constraints of conventional sensor hardware, we propose various techniques in our work: *Single kernel stack* reduces the size of thread stack requirement, and *Stack-size analysis* automatically assigns an appropriate stack size to each thread. *Variable timer* reduces the overhead of system timer, hence reducing energy consumption. *Event-boosting thread scheduler* satisfies the response time requirement for sensor applications.

2.1 Single Kernel Stack

Multithread systems require stack reservation for each thread. The amount of the required stack of a thread is the sum of the resource required by thread functions, system calls, interrupt handlers and hardware context saving. In general, sensor applications are implemented with system API such as radio packet transmission, and system calls and interrupt handlers use a large portion of the thread stack. Considering these characteristics, we propose single kernel stack management for data memory efficiency. Single kernel stack management separates the thread stack into kernel and user stacks, and maintains a unitary kernel stack for system calls and interrupt handlers to reduce the thread stack bound. Equation 1 explains the total stack size for the multiple kernel stack system. The size for the single kernel stack system is obtained by Equation 2. The sum is computed for the number of application threads. Without any threads, multiple kernel stack systems and single kernel stack systems have the same data memory usage for stack. However, the effect of the single kernel stack becomes more significant when the number of threads increases.

$$\sum \{ \max(system\,call) + \max(ISR) + h\,/\,w\,context \} \tag{1}$$

$$\max(system\,call) + \max(ISR) + \sum (h\,/\,w\,context) \tag{2}$$

In the single kernel stack system, the kernel stack is shared among every thread. A controlled access to the kernel stack is implemented in such a way that the system does not arbitrarily interleave execution flow, including thread preemption, while in the kernel mode. Thread switching could be performed immediately prior to returning to user mode and executing an idle function, such as at the time when all work pushed on the kernel stack is completed. With thread preemption, hardware contexts are saved in each thread's thread control block (TCB) due to kernel stack sharing.

Although the single kernel stack is unable to preempt threads in the kernel mode, it does not inhibit real-time operation of the kernel. With this technique, the execution context and the development environment of the kernel and the user are isolated. Because the kernel is interrupt-driven, the kernel developer, based on underlying system analysis, gives high concurrency to system components such as device drivers or the network stack.

2.2 Stack-Size Analysis

With MMU-less hardware, application developers must estimate accurate thread stack size to optimize the memory usage. A given stack size that is less than the size required by the thread causes stack overflow and easily crashes a system. Assigning a large stack would cause data memory overhead. The proposed stack-size analysis provides minimal and system-safe stack requirements for each thread, so the kernel automatically allocates an appropriate stack size for threads.

Table 1. MSP430 instructions concerned with stack usage

Instruction	Stack usages	Description
push var	$+2$	Push a value
pop var	-2	Pop a value
call #label	$+2$	Push return address
sub SP, N	$+N$	Directly adjust stack pointer (function prologue)
add SP, N	$-N$	Directly adjust stack pointer (function epilogue)

The proposed stack analysis produces a control flow graph of an application. Function label, start address and internal stack usage are used as nodes in the graph, and branch instructions are used as edges. The technique then calculates the maximum possible thread stack size with a straightforward depth-first search. The operations are conducted with a binary image, which results from linking the application programmer's code with libraries and compiler-generated codes. Table 1 shows the TI MSP430 instructions, which are related to detecting a function's stack usage. Unlike previous stack bounding techniques [12, 13], which focus on the behavior of the interrupt handler, the proposed technique is based on a system where interrupts are handled by the kernel stack. Thus, this technique determines exact stack usages of functions using the instructions listed in Table 1 only.

The set of start nodes for traversing the flow graph consists of every thread function in an application. Finding out the start nodes depends on the programming language and thread library. On the RETOS operating system, where a user programs a sensor application with standard C and pthread library, we can detect the start node for the main thread with the label "main" and each child thread with the parameter of pthread_create(). The thread start address and stack requirement are stored in the header field of application files, and the kernel looks up the information to create a new thread with optimal stack size.

The proposed technique, however, cannot analyze stack size if the application uses recursive calls or indirectly addressed function calls. Recursive calls create cycles in the flow graph and indirect calls cause a disconnect in the flow graph. In these cases, there is no proper way to know the accurate thread stack size. We have implemented the proposed technique as a tool that notifies users if the analysis fails. In addition, we allow users to determine the default thread size on the RETOS operating system, which is equipped with the application safety mechanism [9]. The mechanism inserts dynamic checking code for stack safety to the application, when the stack-size analysis fails. With the safety mechanism, users do not need to be aware of any restrictions such as explicit prohibition of recursive calls, and the system is safe.

2.3 Variable Timer

The multithreading model of computation generally incurs energy overhead due to context switching, scheduler execution, and system timer management. Context switching and scheduling are known to be the source of major overhead in threaded systems. However, the frequency of scheduling in the threaded system is much lower than that of passing messages between handlers in the event-driven system [6], and the context saving and restoring overhead is only a moderate issue in common sensor nodes [8]. In our work, we propose a variable timer technique to minimize energy consumption of the multithreading system.

The system timer manages timer requests from threads and updates the remaining time quantum of currently running threads. In general-purpose threaded systems, the timer management relies on a periodic timer interrupt. This continuously triggers the interrupt handler whether timer handling requests are present or not, and so increases energy consumption of the sensor node, which stays idle most of the time. Moreover, the periodic timer interrupt restricts the time accuracy within the timer interval. If the interrupt interval is reduced, a significant amount of system power is wasted in order to handle the interrupt. Instead of the periodic timer, the system may use a variable-time tick rate by way of reprogramming the tick rate with an upcoming timeout request. The variable timer can solve these problems. General purpose systems do not use the variable timer because the cost of reprogramming timer requests from hundreds of threads is much higher than for the periodic timer interrupt. Alternately, sensor network applications are typically programmed with a relatively small number of threads and timer requests. Thus, it is reasonable to adopt the variable timer tick rate for threaded sensor systems.

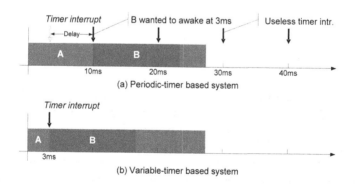

Fig. 1. Variable- and periodic-timer based systems

The variable timer reprograms the timer interrupt interval to the earliest upcoming timeout among the time quantum of currently running thread and the timer requests, such as the sleep() system-call. Figure 1 compares the periodic timer and variable timer systems. General-purpose systems handle the time quantum expiration through the periodic timer interrupt. In Figure 1(a), thread B wants to wake up after 3ms, but with the 10ms interval it is difficult to meet this request in the system. Unnecessary timer interrupts are generated per 10ms. Figure 1(b) shows the case of the variable timer system; thread B can preempt other threads at 3ms, which is the time when thread B is originally requested, and no more timer interrupts are invoked. The effect of the variable timer system depends on the cost and frequency of timer reprogramming. Section 3 evaluates the correlation of the cost for reprogramming a timer and the frequency on a real sensor node device.

2.4 Event-Boosting Thread Scheduling

The RETOS operating system supports the POSIX 1003.1b real-time scheduling interface [19] to enable both programmers' explicit priority assignment and kernel's dynamic priority management. Threads are scheduled by three policies, SCHED_RR, SCHED_FIFO, and SCHED_OTHER, and the system-calls are provided for programmers to adjust their policy and priority. SCHED_OTHER is the default policy and always has less priority than SCHED_RR or SCHED_FIFO.

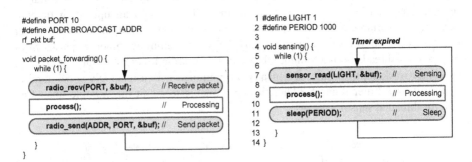

Fig. 2. Typical sensor applications on the multithreading system

We now describe the SCHED_OTHER policy proposed in our work. Although users do not manually give priority assignment to application threads, the operating system should satisfy threads with fast response time. Figure 2 shows typical sensor application codes. The key objectives of common sensor applications are packet forwarding and sensing. Threads usually receive a packet, process data, and forward the result. Threads also collect sensor data, process it, and sleep for a regular period. General operating systems typically classify threads into I/O bound and CPU bound, and they prefer I/O bound threads for high interactivity. From the aspect of sensor node operation, almost every sensor thread is treated as I/O bound, or else the thread property is infinitely switched between I/O bound and CPU bound due to the iteration of I/O and computation in the sensor thread. Therefore, a scheduling policy which specifically concerns sensor network applications should be developed to provide fast response time.

Table 2. Priority adjustment for event-boosting

	Dynamic priority	Description
Init.	4	Thread created
sleep()	+3	Timer request
radio_recv()	+2	Radio event request
sensor_read()	+1	Sensor event request
Consuming CPU time	- 1 per 8ms	Decrease dynamic priority

In our work, we propose an event-boosting thread scheduler to increase the event response time of threads. The scheduler directly boosts the priority of the thread requesting to handle a specific event. Events in the sensor network applications are defined as the expiration of the timer request, the reception of a packet, and the completion of sensing. A thread issues a blocking system-call to handle one of these events, and the kernel enhances the thread's priority according to the type of system-call. When an event occurs, the priority-boosted thread will be able to rapidly preempt other threads. The priority of the thread reduces with the CPU-consumed time. Hence, other threads have chances to be re-scheduled. Table 2 shows the priority adjustment for event-boosting scheduling policy. Threads are created with the initial priority, and obtain higher priority if they call sleep(), radio_recv(), and sensor_read() system-calls. Thread priority is decreased by 1 per 8ms of consumed CPU time. Concerning the priority adjustment, we have not conducted any formal evaluation on the value of adjustment, but rather used a subjective user study on the RETOS operating system. We considered that the explicit timer request is the most critical job and the radio event is more important than the sensor event.

In the real implementation, it is also important to avoid starvation and to provide fairness. Therefore, we compare the remaining thread time quantum if there are equally prioritized SCHED_OTHER threads. When all threads in the run-queue have exhausted their time quanta, the scheduler re-computes the time quantum duration of all threads in the system. The idea for assigning a new quantum is adopted from Linux, which gives half the previously remaining quantum plus a default time quantum to threads.

3 Evaluation

This section presents the experimental results of the proposed multithreading techniques. The experiment evaluates the efficiency of single kernel stack and stack-size analysis, the timer handling overhead of variable timer management, and the concurrency supports of an event-boosting scheduler. Furthermore, the overall effect of optimization techniques are validated by running a real sensor application both on RETOS and TinyOS, the former being a dual mode based multithreaded system and the latter being a single mode and event-driven operating system. RETOS have been implemented for the TI MSP430 F1611 (8Mhz, 10Kb RAM, 48Kb Flash) and CC2420 (IEEE 802.15.4) based Tmote Sky hardware platform [14]. The execution results are based on the average results over 10 sets of 30 runs.

3.1   Effect of Stack Optimization

The single kernel stack and stack-size analyses are to optimize stack usage of the multithreaded system. To adequately evaluate the efficiency of these techniques, we considered entire stack usage on the system. Seven sensor network applications were used for the test. *MPT_mobile* and *MPT_backbone* are decentralized multiple-object tracking programs [15]. When the *MPT_mobile* node moves around, it sends both an ultrasound signal and beacon messages every 300ms to nearby *MPT_backbone* nodes. *MPT_backbone* nodes then report their distance to the mobile node, and *MPT_mobile* computes its location using trilateration. *R_send* and *R_recv* are programs to send and receive radio packets with reliability. *Sensing* samples the data and forwards it to the neighbor node. *Pingpong* makes two nodes blink in turns by means of a counter-exchange. *Surge* is a multihop data collecting application which manages a neighbor table and routes the packet.

Table 3. Kernel stack and thread context block requirements

	Kernel stack size (byte)	Increase of TCB+ H/W context (byte)
Single kernel stack system	76	18
Multiple kernel stack system	76	16

Table 4. Efficiency of a single kernel stack based system

Applications	Num. of Threads	User stack (byte)	Data section (byte)	Kernel stack (byte)	
				Multiple	Single
MPT_backbone	1	68	131	152	76
MPT_mobile	2	78	416	228	76
R_send	3	78	217	304	76
R_recv	3	50	214	304	76
Sensing	2	18	157	228	76
Pingpong	1	8	106	152	76
Surge	4	98	336	380	76

In order to evaluate the single kernel stack, we have implemented two versions of RETOS to measure the effectiveness of stack usage reduction. For the easy stack size comparison, the multiple kernel stack system also stores the hardware context in the TCB. Table 3 shows the size of the required kernel stack and the increase of TCB plus the hardware context for each kernel. The kernel stack requirement is detected by executing all system-calls and interrupt handlers in each system. As the two systems have the same kernel control flow except the kernel stack management scheme, the kernel stack size on the single kernel stack system is identical with the size on the multiple kernel stack system. The increase of TCB plus the amount of saving the hardware context on the single kernel stack system, however, differs from the multiple kernel stack system, since the single kernel stack system requires two more bytes to store the thread return address.

Table 4 shows the results of running sensor applications on two systems. With the multiple kernel stack system, the kernel stack is required for the idle thread and each application thread. Meanwhile, the single kernel stack system uses only 76 bytes of RAM for the kernel stack independent of the number of application threads. The more threads that are created, the more significant the expected stack efficiency on the this system. Our results also show that the stack reservation overhead on the threaded system is trivial. Most of sensor application threads require a little stack size. *Sensing* and *Pingpong* applications, for instance, can be implemented with 18 and 8 bytes of user stack, respectively.

As described in Section 2.2, we have developed a stack-size analysis technique. For the seven sensor applications, the estimated maximum stack size was compared with the worst stack depth via simulation. The sensor application does not use an indirectly addressed function call, so the technique successfully analyzes each program's stack size. The results of the proposed technique were equal to 1 or 2 words more than the results of simulation, and the technique gave the same call graph with the program's control flow, which was determined manually. We also tested this technique on a program which uses indirect function calls. For this program, the technique could not produce a call graph. However, the stack overflow of an application with an immediate stack size was detected in run-time, indicating that the system safety was maintained.

3.2 Effect of Variable Timer

We have implemented two versions of the system using the variable and periodic timer techniques. Since the major difference in the energy consumption between the two systems is the amount of CPU usage, we measured the active CPU time to estimate the energy consumption. Figure 3(a) shows the performance efficiency of the variable timer compared to the periodic timer. One tick in the variable timer is 1ms, and 10ms on the periodic timer. The experimental results include the execution time of a timer interrupt handler and a timer reprogramming routine. The effectiveness of variable timer differs from the execution cycle of applications. *MPT_mobile, R_send, Sensing, Pingpong,* and *Surge* are periodic programs and are executed every 300ms, 100ms, 1000ms, 1500ms, and 2048ms, respectively. *R_send* is the most energy consuming program among the seven benchmark applications. Because *R_send* transmits a radio packet every 100ms and performs ACK and the timeout-based packet retransmission, it creates more frequent timer requests than other applications. *MPT_backbone* and *R_recv* are reactive applications, which are only executed with radio packet reception. *Pingpong* and *Surge* have a relatively slow execution period. Therefore, these applications get significant energy reduction on the variable timer based system.

In order to clearly compare the performance of variable timer and the periodic timer by the timer request interval, we measured the overhead of the timer management routine. The blink application was used for the evaluation by adjusting the period from 20ms to 1000ms. Figure 3(b) shows the results of this evaluation. When the timer request interval is long, variable timer system spends definitively less overhead than the periodic timer system. However, as the timer interval increases, the overhead on the variable timer becomes larger. At the 20ms of interval, two systems

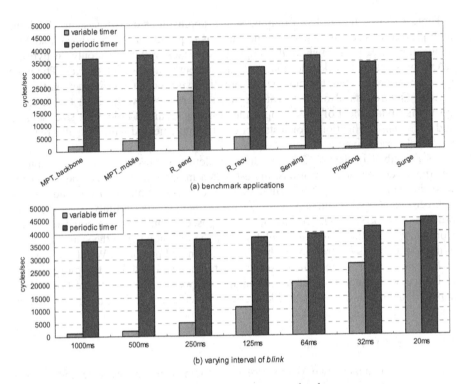

(a) benchmark applications

(b) varying interval of *blink*

Fig. 3. Timer management overhead

have almost the same overhead because the variable timer takes a longer time per each timer request than the periodic timer, due to the time required to determine the next upcoming timeout event and reprogram the system timer. In this experiment, the periodic timer system has a 10ms tick. If the periodic timer system is implemented to use a 1ms tick as with the variable timer, more overhead would be required to handle timer interrupts.

3.3 Effect of Event-Boosting Scheduling Policy

This section shows that the event-boosting scheduler can effectively satisfy sensor applications' event requests. The test application is a packet round-trip program which continuously sends and receives a packet between two nodes. The first node sends a packet out while the second node receives and returns it to the first node. The first node waits for a reply from the second node and then repeats this process. The round-trip application runs with only two nodes, so that the influence of radio channel and back-off time of the MAC is minimized. The response time for the thread to handle a packet depends on the number of other threads in the system and the scheduling policy. Hence, we can evaluate the functionality of a thread scheduler with radio throughput of the application. The other threads in our experiment are designed to add loads to the scheduler, and perform 10ms of computation each at 100ms intervals.

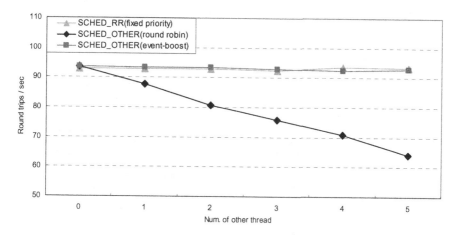

Fig. 4. Scheduling policy comparison

Figure 4 represents the number of round-trips per minute according to the scheduling policy. If users are not concerned with adjusting scheduling policy, SCHED_OTHER is the default policy for threads. In the case of implementing SCHED_OTHER as a simple round-robin, the number of round-trips decreases according to the increment of the other threads. Because preemption is not performed when other threads do not finish their execution or exhaust their time quantum, the radio packet handling is delayed. In the case of explicitly configuration of the round-trip thread as SCHED_RR, the application, which has always higher priority than others, maintains a fixed round-trip performance independent of the number of other threads. The performance of the system, which uses the proposed event-boosting technique for SCHED_OTHER threads, is nearly the same as the case of SCHED_RR. Although users do not manually configure the priority of threads, the dynamic priority adjustment of the event-boosting scheduler minimizes the event handling delay of sensor application threads.

3.4   RETOS vs. TinyOS

This section compares the multithreaded operating system RETOS with the event-driven TinyOS by developing a sensor application. TinyOS is a component-based operating system, and has no distinction between the kernel and the application. Components are programmed with event-driven model and compiled to a single binary image. RETOS provides a rich development environment with preemptive threads. The proposed thread optimization reduces the overhead of traditional multithreading and increases thread response time. We used RETOS v0.96 and TinyOS v1.1.13 for this experiment, and the applications used in the experiment are MPT and a simple packet transmission. MPT is a mobile object tracking program [15] based on ultrasound localization technique. MPT consists of mobile node and backbone node, and the mobile node computes its location using trilateration every 300ms. The trilateration takes approximately 16ms to determine the location. We have considered inserting a simple code which periodically sends and receives a radio

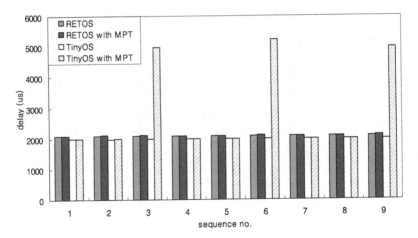

Fig. 5. Packet handling delay

packet to the above application. The sink node transfers a packet every 100ms, and the mobile node receives and counts it. We measured the time from the FIFOP interrupt handling at the CC2420 radio driver to the packet at the thread.

Figure 5 shows the packet-handling latency on RETOS and TinyOS. The purpose of this experiment was to understand the dependency of MPT execution time and packet handling. The results were measured after the two applications' start time was synchronized. With the RETOS system, the packet-handling latency was almost the same whether or not MPT was run, because application threads are preemptive and a packet was received by the radio device driver located in the kernel. In the case of the TinyOS system, the packet-handling latency without MPT was slightly shorter than RETOS. With MPT, the latency was considerably longer than in the other three cases. The extended latency was caused by long computation time of trilateration in the MPT application, which can delay the packet-handler task's execution on the TinyOS.

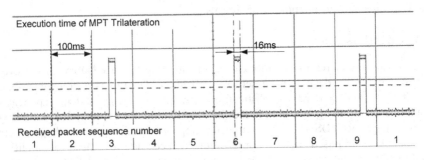

Fig. 6. Execution time of MPT Trilateration observed by oscilloscope

Figure 6 shows the execution pattern of trilateration as observed by oscilloscope. Trilateration was performed every 300ms and took approximately 16ms. We tried to reduce the delay by splitting the trilateration into several phases, but this made the

Table 5. Code size for MPT application

	TinyOS (bytes)		RETOS Kernel (bytes)		RETOS Lib. + App. (bytes)		RETOS Total (bytes)	
	ROM	RAM	ROM	RAM	ROM	RAM	ROM	RAM
MPT Backbone	12614	467	18314	748	492	143	18806	891
MPT Mobile	17222	701	18314	748	6848	434	25162	1182

program control flow complex and rendered it difficult to manage the increased number of states. Moreover, measurement of the execution time of each code fragment was necessary to determine whether the split provided reasonable performance.

As RETOS is a multithreaded operating system, it is considered to have more time and space overhead than the event-driven TinyOS. Table 5 shows the code size of MPT on RETOS and TinyOS. The RETOS system uses less than 30Kbytes of flash memory and 2Kbytes of RAM. Although the code size of RETOS is bigger than that of TinyOS, RETOS supports functionality such as application safety mechanism [9], dynamic loadable module [10] and the network stack [11], which are barely supported by the native TinyOS system.

Figure 7(a) compares the computational overhead of MPT with RETOS and TinyOS. *MPT_mobile* spends 2% more overhead with RETOS; it performs thread preemption and scheduling, and also dynamic code checking for system safety. Figure 7(b) shows

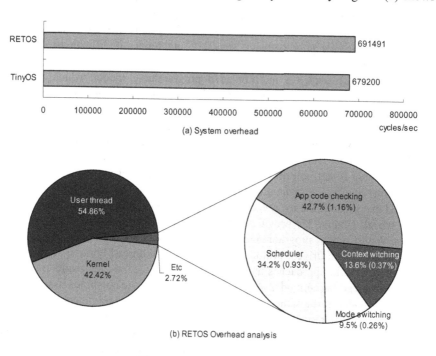

(a) System overhead

(b) RETOS Overhead analysis

Fig. 7. Computational overhead

the CPU usage distribution of the RETOS system. The user thread occupies 55% of total processing time. The kernel portion is approximately 42% due to the frequent use of radio communication. On the other hand, the amount of calculation time caused by mode switching, scheduler execution and context switching is trivial, compared with the entire processing time. The portion of context switching, mode switching and scheduler execution overhead may be bigger when an application requires little radio communication or computations. Nevertheless, the experiment results show that multithreading could be implemented with reasonable overhead on current sensor node hardware.

4 Related Work

TinyOS [1], the industry defacto sensor network operating system, is based on an event-driven model and provides nesC [16] programming language. TinyOS is considered to provide high concurrency without thread stack reservation, which is essential to multithreading. SOS [2] provides dynamically loadable modules and adopts an event-driven model to avoid context switching overhead for multithreading. However, event-driven models can be inconvenient when developing applications. As event handlers are run to completion, programmers must split long-lived tasks into several phases of codes for concurrency. The tasks of the event-model cannot be blocked, hence a single conceptual function with an I/O operation should be divided into two separate sub functions, one for before and the other for after the I/O operation. The stack frame in the split function is manually maintained by programmers, and it increases the use of global variables. These issues of event-driven model induce poor software structure and render it difficult to debug and develop applications [6, 17].

MANTIS [8] provides a multithreaded programming model, which implement traditional multithreading in sensor nodes. The system shows that programming long-running tasks is much easier than in an event-driven model. With the MANTIS system, programmers heuristically assign a stack size to each thread. If the stack size is too big, the system will suffer from memory insufficiency. If the stack is too small, stack may overflow and system will fail. In MANTIS, fixed priority scheduling based on round-robin is not able to fully utilize the advantage of preemption without the programmer making a manual priority adjustment. As the MANTIS scheduler is executed every 10ms, the overhead for context switching and timer interrupt handling is not trivial. Contiki [7] provides a thread library that works on the event-driven system. With Contiki, programmers empirically choose an appropriate programming model among event-driven, protothread [18], and multithread libraries to develop an application. Hybrid approaches have been studied to integrate the merits of an event model and thread-based model. Adya et al. [17] suggest the combined usage of event and thread model in the same program, but this requires programmers to thoroughly understand the differences between the two models and to appropriately choose the alternatives. Protothread [18] does not require stack reservation; however it cannot maintain local variables and can block only in an explicitly declared area.

5 Conclusion

In this paper, we described multithreading optimization techniques for sensor applications development. Our techniques contribute to possible solutions toward three major problems involved in the implementation of threaded operating systems on resource-constraint sensor nodes—memory resource, energy consumption, and scheduling policy. Single kernel stack and stack-size analysis techniques reduce the memory requirement of a thread model. Variable timer achieves power reduction by improving the timer management scheme. Event-boosting scheduling policy reflects the characteristics of sensor applications and provides fast response time of threads without explicit priority configuration. With the proposed techniques, the overhead of multithreading is reported to be approximately 2% of the total execution time on the TI MSP430 processor, and the system guarantees minimal response delay to sensor applications.

Application libraries or system calls are being implemented, and extensive testing is also conducted on the RETOS sensor operating system. We are presently improving the performance and the energy efficiency of the network stack for radio communication on RETOS, as well as implementing device drivers for diverse sensors and porting them to other processors.

Acknowledgements

This work was supported by the National Research Laboratory (NRL) program of the Korea Science and Engineering Foundation (2005-01352), and the MIC(Ministry of Information and Communication), Korea, under the ITRC(Information Technology Research Center) support program supervised by the IITA(Institute of Information Technology Advancement) (IITA-2006-C1090-0603-0015).

References

1. Hill, J., Szewczyk, R., Woo, A, Hollar, S., Culler, D., and Pister, K.: System architecture directions for network sensors. In Proceedings of the 9th International Conference on Architectural Support for Programming Languages and Operating Systems (ASPLOS), Cambridge, MA, 2000.
2. Han, C. C., Rengaswamy, R. K., Shea, R., Kohler, E., and Srivastava, M.: SOS: A dynamic operating system for sensor networks. In Proceedings of the 3rd International Conference on Mobile Systems, Applications, and Services (Mobisys), Seattle, WA, 2005.
3. Li, S.-F., Sutton, R., and Rabaey, J.: Low Power Operating System for Heterogeneous Wireless Communication Systems. In Proceedings of the Workshop on Compilers and Operating Systems for Low Power, Barcelona, Spain, 2001.
4. Regehr, J., Reid, A., Webb, K., Parker, M., and Lepreau, J.: Evolving real-time systems using hierarchical scheduling and concurrency analysis. In Proceedings of the 24th IEEE Real-Time Systems Symposium (RTSS), Cancun, Mexico, 2003.
5. Ousterhout, J. K.: Why threads are a bad idea (for most purposes). Invited Talk at the 1996 USENIX Technical Conference, 1996.

6. Behren, R., Condit, J., and Brewer, E.: Why events are a bad idea (for high-concurrency servers). In Proceedings of the 9th Workshop on Hot Topics in Operating Systems (HotOS), Lihue, Hawaii, 2003.
7. Dunkels, A., Grönvall, B., and Voigt, T.: Contiki - a Lightweight and Flexible Operating System for Tiny Networked Sensors. In Proceedings of the 1st IEEE Workshop on Embedded Networked Sensors (EmNetS), Tampa, Florida, 2004.
8. Bhatti, S., Carlson, J., Dai, H., Deng, J., Rose, J., Sheth, A., Shucker, B., Gruenwald, C., Torgerson, A., and Han, R.: MANTIS OS: An Embedded Multithreaded Operating System for Wireless Micro Sensor Platforms. ACM/Kluwer Mobile Networks & Applications, Special Issue on Wireless Sensor Networks, vol.10, no.4, 2005.
9. Kim, H., and Cha, H.: Towards a Resilient Operating System for Wireless Sensor Networks. In Proceedings of the 2006 USENIX Annual Technical Conference, Boston, MA, 2006.
10. Shin, H., and Cha, H.: Supporting Application-Oriented Kernel Functionality for Resource Constrained Wireless Sensor Nodes. In Proceedings of the 2nd International Conference on Mobile Ad-hoc and Sensor Networks, Hong Kong, China, 2006.
11. Choi, S., and Cha, H.: Application-Centric Networking Framework for Wireless Sensor Nodes. In Proceedings of the 3rd Annual International Conference on Mobile and Ubiquitous Systems: Networks and Services, San Jose, CA, 2006.
12. Regehr, J., Reid, A., and Webb, K.: Eliminating stack overflow by abstract interpretation. In Proceedings of the 3rd International Conference on Embedded Software, Philadelphia, PA, 2003.
13. Brylow, D., Damgaard, N., and Palsberg, J.: Static checking of interrupt-driven software. In Proceedings of the 23rd International Conference on Software Engineering, Toronto, Canada, 2001.
14. Tmote Sky. http://www.moteiv.com.
15. Yi, S., and Cha, H.: Active Tracking System using IEEE 802.15.4-based Ultrasonic Sensor Devices. In Proceedings of the 2nd International Workshop on RFID and Ubiquitous Sensor Networks, Seoul, Korea, 2006.
16. Gay, D., Levis, P., Behren, R., Welsh, M., Brewer, E., and Culler, D.: The nesC Language: A Holistic Approach to Network Embedded Systems. In Proceedings of the ACM SIGPLAN 2003 Conference on Programming Language Design and Implementation (PLDI), San Diego, CA, 2003.
17. Adya, A., Howell, J., Theimer, M., Bolosky, W. J., and Douceur, J. R.: Cooperative Task Management Without Manual Stack Management. In Proceedings of the 2002 USENIX Annual Technical Conference, Monterey, CA, 2002.
18. Dunkels, A., Schmidt, O., and Voigt, T.: Protothreads: Simplifying Event-Driven Programming of Memory-Constrained Embedded Systems. In Proceedings of the 4th ACM Conference on Embedded Networked Sensor Systems (Sensys), Boulder, Colorado, 2006.
19. POSIX 1003.1B. http://www.unix.org/version3

An Empirical Study of Antenna Characteristics Toward RF-Based Localization for IEEE 802.15.4 Sensor Nodes

Sungwon Yang and Hojung Cha

Department of Computer Science, Yonsei University,
Seodaemun-gu, Sinchon-dong 134, Seoul 120-749, Korea
{swyang, hjcha}@cs.yonsei.ac.kr

Abstract. Localization using the characteristics of the Radio Frequency (RF) in wireless sensor networks is attractive because the method does not require additional measuring devices, and hence satisfies low cost and low power consumption needs. The range information derived from Received Signal Strength (RSS), which attenuates over the distance and node connectivity, is, however, inaccurate and unpredictable in the real world due to problems caused by sensor motes and the environment of the sensor field. In this paper, through an empirical analysis, we present detailed radio signal properties of the 2.4GHz IEEE 802.15.4 radio module. We also provide the methodology of antenna design and mounting to alleviate the antenna orientation and RSS fluctuation problems, which are key factors that make RF-based ranging irregular in an obstacle-free environment. Our work is differentiated from previous work, which concludes with merely revealing the problems, ignoring them by assumptions, or even limiting the feasibility of RF utilization in localization.

1 Introduction

Although localization for Wireless Sensor Networks (WSN) has actively been studied in recent years, it is still a challenging issue. One of the simple methods for localization is to use a Global Positioning System (GPS) [1]. However, while GPS enables localization in an outdoor environment, it is costly and the energy consumption is significant. Using Received Signal Strength (RSS), or connectivity of radio communication, for localization in WSNs is attractive because of its low cost and low power consumption, and because it does not require any additional measuring devices other than the low-power radio module itself. Recently many RF-based localization algorithms have been proposed [2], [3], [4], [5], [6], [7], [8], [9]. These localization techniques, using the RSS or RF connectivity, theoretically work well in ideal conditions; however, in the real world the location error is too high to be useful in most cases. Therefore, the discrepancy of localization result between theoretical and practical conditions generates the belief that RF-based localization is useless. The main reason for the discrepancy is that most localization algorithms based on RSS or RF connectivity assume that the radio radiation pattern is perfectly circular or spherical in shape, and that the formula for RSS attenuation over distance is directly applicable. In the

K. Langendoen and T. Voigt (Eds.): EWSN 2007, LNCS 4373, pp. 309–324, 2007.

real world, the pattern of radio transmitted at the antenna is neither a circular nor a spherical shape, and the path loss model is not valid due to problems caused by the sensor mote and the environment of the sensor field. The study in [10] shows that the performance of RF-based localization degrades in the presence of an irregular radio range.

In this paper, we consider antenna orientation and the fluctuation of RSS as the major problems that make RF-based ranging inaccurate and unpredictable in an obstacle-free environment. Through extensive measurements, we analyze the cause of each problem and propose a methodology that eliminates the limits of RF-based localization in an obstacle-free environment. Instead of making the RF-based localization algorithm more complicated by combining with an error correction algorithm, which increases power consumption, we focus on antenna technology to solve these problems at the base level. To the best of our knowledge, our work is the first approach that shows that the irregularity of RF is not an inherent problem in WSN, and the RF irregularity can be eliminated with antenna design or mounting mechanisms. The experimental results with the various antennas clearly show the feasibility of a more accurate RF-based localization for WSN in practice.

The rest of the paper is organized as follows. Section 2 describes previous work that discusses RF irregularity. The empirical analyses of two main factors that make RF-based ranging inaccurate and the methodology for eliminating the RF irregularity with various antennas are presented in Sections 3 and 4. In Section 5, we analyze a critical consideration when deploying nodes with special antennas. In Section 6, we discuss an ideal antenna design for accurate RF-based ranging. Finally, we conclude the paper in Section 7.

2 Related Work

Early research, [11], [12], [13] mentioned link asymmetry and irregular radio range in WSNs. These phenomena were shown because of experiments to quantify the performance of packet delivery with the Berkeley Mica or Mica2 motes. They hypothesized that the irregularity of radio communication in WSNs was caused by differences in the quality of radio and hardware calibrations.

Zhou et al. [14] categorized the causes of radio irregularity into two main factors: the heterogeneous properties of devices and the non-isotropic properties of propagation media. Device properties include the antenna type (directional or ommidirectional), transmission power, antenna gains, receiver sensitivity, receiver threshold and the Signal-Noise Ratio (SNR). Media properties include the media type, background noise and various other environmental factors. They concluded that an asymmetric link is mainly caused by the variance in RF transmission power and the differences in path loss as a function of direction of propagation. However, the reason for an asymmetric link between two nodes that have the same transmitting power in an obstacle-free environment was not discussed in their work. They regarded the radio irregularity in WSNs as an inherent problem and consequently proposed the Radio Irregularity Model (RIM) to apply the radio irregularity to simulations.

Recently, Lymberopoulos et al. [15] provided a detailed analysis of radio properties of 2.4GHz RF using the IEEE 802.15.4 radio module and a monopole antenna. They used the CC2420 [16] radio module to characterize the properties of RSS and link asymmetry in obstacle-free and indoor environments. Through extensive measurements, they showed that antenna orientation greatly affects RSS and link asymmetry in indoor and outdoor scenarios, and confirmed the presence of antenna orientation and irregular RSS attenuation problems in practice. However, a method to solve these problems was not considered in their work.

3 Antenna Orientation

Many techniques, which determine the location of an unknown node using RF, have been proposed. Most of them, however, assume ideal conditions, where the pattern of horizontal radiation is circular and the radio range is the same for each node. However, because of the presence of antenna orientation problems inherent in a real world environment, these localization algorithms only work where the assumptions hold. Antenna orientation is a problem defined as the RSS of the receiver varies as the pair wise antenna orientations of the transmitter and the receiver are changed. In this section, we analyze the cause of antenna orientation problems in WSNs, and provide solutions based on antenna characteristics. We also provide data on how the link property improves between two nodes in conditions where an antenna orientation problem does not exist.

3.1 Cause of Antenna Orientation

Most off-the-shelf sensor motes use a $\frac{1}{4}$ wavelength monopole antenna, which is mounted in either an internal or external type configuration. A $\frac{1}{4}$ wavelength monopole antenna shows the same radiation pattern of a $\frac{1}{2}$ wavelength dipole antenna whose horizontal radiation pattern is omni-directional. However, this omni-directional radiation pattern is distorted when an antenna is mounted on sensor motes. An irregular radiation pattern means that the measured RSS may vary according to the orientation of the transmitting and receiving nodes, although both the transmitter and the receiver are located in a fixed position. To quantify the distorted radiation pattern, we measured average RSS values in 24 different degrees with a fixed receiver node and a rotating transmitter node at a 1.5m distance and output power of -10dBm using "Tmote Sky[1]" [17] in a relatively obstacle-free environment (No obstacles making reflections within three meters).

As shown in Figure 1(a), the radiation pattern of the internal antenna is so jagged that the difference in the measured RSS is up to 20dBm, which is impossible for use in obtaining propitious distance information for localization. In the case of

---

[1] All experiments using real sensor motes in this paper were conducted with "Tmote Sky" from the Moteiv cooperation.

¼ wavelength external monopole antenna, the radiation pattern is still biased and the maximum difference of RSS is 15dBm, as shown in Figure 1(b), although the pattern is more circular compared to the internal antenna case.

One of the main factors that cause the antenna orientation phenomenon is the small size of the ground plane inside the PCB (Printed Circuit Board). The widely-used ¼ wavelength monopole antenna is formed by replacing one half of a dipole antenna with a ground plane at right-angles to the remaining half. If the ground plane is large enough, the monopole behaves exactly like a dipole, as if its reflection in the ground plane formed the missing half of the dipole. The ground plane of a sensor mote, however, may not satisfy the ideal ground conditions. Another factor, which affects the radiation pattern, is the circuit design and devices on a sensor mote. In other words, the electric field of the antenna is distorted by the interference from other devices, which are close to it.

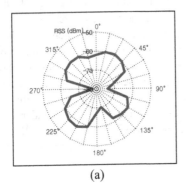
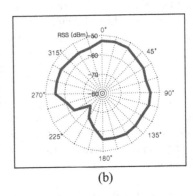

(a)   (b)

Fig. 1. Horizontal radiation patterns of (a) internal inverted-F ¼ wavelength antenna and (b) external ¼ wavelength monopole antenna mounted on a sensor mote

3.2 Length of Antenna

To validate whether the antenna orientation problem is indeed caused by interference from electric devices on a sensor mote, we kept the distance between the antenna and the sensor mote to a wavelength height (12.5cm at 2.4GHz) using a coaxial cable whose impedance is 50Ω. Since the vertical angle of radiation gets narrower as the length of the antenna gets longer from ¼ wavelength to ½ or ⅝wavelength [18], we also changed the length of the antenna to ½ and ⅝wavelengths. Three antennas of different lengths both with and without a coaxial cable are shown in Figure 2. Figure 3(a) shows the measured vertical radiation patterns for each antenna, which shows the longer antenna has narrower angle of vertical radiation. Measurements were conducted in the anechoic chamber, as shown in Figure 3(b), which does not generate a reflection of electromagnetic waves, and a device which takes a measurement of RSS from the antennas in every single degree used.

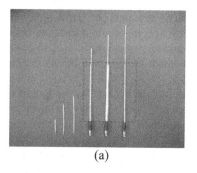 

(a)   (b)

Fig. 2. (a) ¼, ½, and ⅝wavelength monopole antennas with and without a coaxial cable. The area designated by the dotted-line indicates a wavelength coaxial cable. (b) A sensor mote with an external antenna.

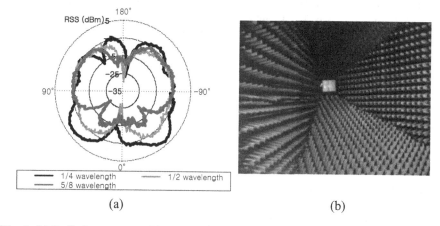

(a)   (b)

Fig. 3. (a) Radiation patterns of ¼, ½, and ⅝wavelength monopole antenna on side view. (b) Picture of the anechoic chamber where the measurements of radiation pattern were conducted.

Figure 4(a) shows that the null radiation zone, where a radically weaker radiation than in other areas occurs, is eliminated when the ¼ wavelength optimal antenna is mounted a wavelength height farther from a sensor mote. With a ½ wavelength monopole antenna, we obtained more circular radiation patterns, especially when the antenna was a wavelength away from the mote. In case of a ⅝wavelength antenna, it shows an almost perfect circular radiation pattern although it is mounted without a coaxial cable. Note that the radiation pattern gets more circular with a ½ or ⅝wavelength monopole antenna, however the RSS gets weaker when compared to a ¼ wavelength antenna.

As shown in Figure 4, the antenna orientation problem can be eliminated with a ½ wavelength monopole antenna, which keeps a wavelength distance away from a sensor mote or a ⅝wave length one. In other words, the antenna orientation problem can be solved by minimizing the electrical interference from devices of a sensor mote and matching the ground plane with the proper length of antenna. The horizontally omni-directional radiation pattern is obtained by simply keeping enough distance between an antenna and a sensor mote or changing the antenna to a longer one. In practice, however, the distance between an antenna and a sensor mote cannot be as far away as is theoretically needed.

Using a ½ or ⅝wavelength antenna is also inefficient because as the length of an antenna deviates from the optimal length, the antenna does not resonate at the given frequency. Figure 5 shows the resonant point, measured with a network analyzer, of three monopole antennas whose length is ¼, ½, and ⅝wavelength of 2.4GHz respectively. In Figure 5(a), the ¼ wavelength monopole antenna causes maximum resonance at the frequency of 2.4GHz, however, ½ and ⅝ones do not. The attenuation of RSS, which is caused by changing the antenna length from an optimal ¼ wavelength to others, is about 10dBm as shown in Figure 4. An antenna whose length does not match the given frequency receives weak signals, and consequently shortens the communication range. To solve this problem, an antenna that has an analogous radiation pattern to ½ or ⅝wavelength antenna without attenuation of RSS is required.

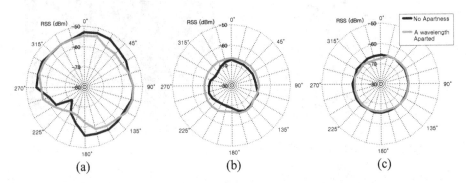

Fig. 4. The horizontal radiation patterns of (a) ¼ wavelength, (b) ½ wavelength, and (c) ⅝wavelength antenna mounted on a sensor mote. Measurements were conducted at a 1.5m distance between two motes and output power of -10dBm. Both the transmitter and receiver used exactly the same length of antenna.

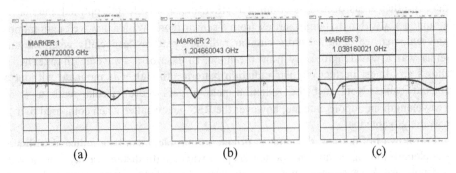

Fig. 5. Return loss of (a) ¼ wavelength, (b) ½ wavelength, and (c) ⅝ wavelength monopole antenna. The minimum peak indicates the return loss at maximum resonant frequency.

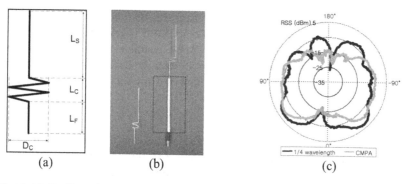

Fig. 6. (a) Configuration of collinear monopole antenna with loading coil, (b) Designed collinear monopole antenna. The area designated by the dotted-line indicates a wavelength coaxial cable, and (c) Vertical radiation pattern of the designed CMPA. Measurements of the vertical radiation pattern were conducted in an anechoic chamber.

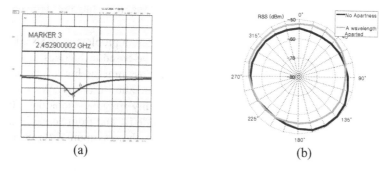

Fig. 7. (a) Return loss of designed CMPA. The minimum peak indicates the return loss at maximum resonant frequency. (b) Horizontal radiation pattern of the designed CMPA mounted on a sensor mote. Measurements were conducted at a 1.5m distance between two motes and an output power of -10dBm. Both the transmitter and receiver used exactly the same length of antenna.

3.3 Collinear Monopole Antenna

Since in spite of satisfying the regular radiation pattern, the longer than optimal length of antenna does not satisfy the normal communication range, we are required to find an antenna guaranteeing both a regular radiation pattern and no decrease in communication range.

The Collinear MonoPole Antenna (CMPA) is used to obtain a higher performance level [19]. It is composed of two linear wires connected with a loading coil and it has a narrower vertical radiation pattern than a ¼ wavelength default antenna. Figure 6(a) shows the configuration of a CMPA with a loading coil and Figure 6(b) shows the CMPA we have built where the length of the first antenna element L_F is 2.8cm, the length of the second antenna element L_S is 6cm, the uncoiled length of the coil arm L_C is 5.6cm, and the coil diameter D_C is 0.7cm. Figure 6(c) presents the measured vertical radiation pattern of our CMPA, which is narrower than a ¼ wavelength optimal monopole antenna. The resonant frequency of our CMPA is around 2.4GHz as shown in Figure 7(a). Figure 7(b) shows that the CMPA guarantees the omni-directional radiation pattern horizontally and the higher RSS than the case of measurement with not only ½ or ⅝wavelength monopole antenna but also a ¼ wavelength optimal one.

3.4 Asymmetric Link

Through the various experiments, we have discovered why the antenna orientation problem occurs and subsequently provided solutions through antenna design and mount methods. In this section, we show the improvement of link symmetry through antenna replacement. An asymmetric link is defined as one in which the connectivity of "node A" to "node B" is significantly different from that of "node B" to "node A" on condition that the transmission power of node A and B is the same. The link asymmetry is caused by factors such as the presence of obstacles, the asymmetric multi-path effect, and the antenna orientation. Since we consider the obstacle-free environment, we focus on the asymmetric link problem caused by antenna orientation.

The asymmetric link has been regarded as an inherent problem in WSNs. However, for accurate localization in both range-free and range-based techniques; it is essential that this issue be resolved. Figure 8 shows that the asymmetric link of the RSS problem can be eliminated by solving the antenna orientation problem. With a ¼ wavelength monopole antenna, which has the horizontally irregular radiation pattern, the maximum deference of RSS from "node A" to "node B" and from "node B" to "node A" is 15dBm as shown in Figure 8(a). Conversely, the maximum difference of RSS between two links is only 1.7dBm, as shown in Figure 8(b), for nodes with a ⅝wavelength monopole antenna, which transmits almost the same strength of radio signal to all horizontal directions. Consequently, the asymmetric link problem in WSNs is not an independent issue, but a problem that is dependent on the antenna orientation problem.

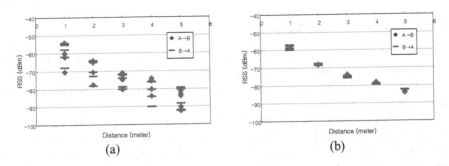

Fig. 8. Average RSS vs. distance plot for (a) ¼ wavelength monopole antenna and (b) ⅝wavelength monopole antenna. Nodes were placed with random orientation for each measurement. All measurements were conducted with a transmission power of -7dBm.

From the viewpoint of link connectivity, link symmetry, which is the most important factor in many range-free localization methods, can also be guaranteed with a horizontally omni-directional antenna. Srinivasan et al. [20] presented the relationship between RSS and Packet Reception Rate (PRR), which shows that PRR varies rather radically where RSS is less than -87dBm. Figure 9 shows the similar result, which is re-experimented. As shown in Figure 8(a), the difference in RSS is up to 15dBm where the antenna of sensor motes is $\frac{1}{4}$ wavelength monopole whose horizontal radiation pattern is irregular. Hence, a node may receive all packets or nothing according to the directions of the nodes in the case where the average RSS value is close to -87dBm, which is an entrance of a gray region. Conversely, an antenna that guarantees the horizontally omni-directional radiation pattern satisfies a certain level of PRR although the average RSS value is near -87dBm.

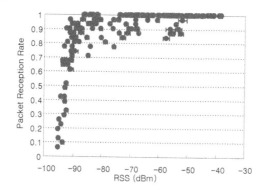

Fig. 9. RSS vs. Packet Reception Rate plot. 150 measurement cases were randomly picked where the distance between a transmitter and a receiver is 50 to 2000cm and the transmission power is -25 to 0dBm.

4 RSS Fluctuation

Theoretically, RSS attenuates over distance in free space. However, this is not valid in practice due to multi-path fading. In the real environment, RSS attenuates by a certain distance, and then starts fluctuating. This fluctuation leads to unreliable distance information because the same RSS can be measured at different distances. In this section, we validate that the distance guaranteeing RSS attenuation without fluctuation can be extended through antenna replacement. Based on an experiment using parabolic antennas, we also provide insight on how the accuracy of range-based ranging improves under the circumstance such that the cause of RSS fluctuation is eliminated through a special antenna.

4.1 Ground Reflection

Figure 10 shows the RSS values versus distance for five different output power levels. The measured RSS attenuates almost linearly by the distance d_R as shown. Here, d_R is a distance that guarantees the validity of the path loss model so that mapping RSS to distance information for localization can be possible within d_R. However, beyond this reliable distance, RSS begins fluctuating. Note that the RSS starts fluctuation at the same distance for all cases of different output power, and each peak for different output power after the distance of d_R is generated at the same distance. This implies that the output power of the transmitter is not a factor that affects d_R. Since the object, which generates multi-path fading, is only the ground in an obstacle-free environment, the ground reflection is the main factor which generates the RSS fluctuation problem.

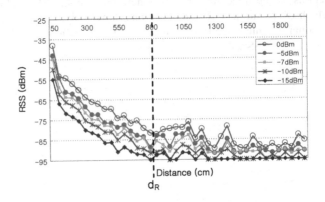

Fig. 10. RSS vs. distance for five different output powers on soil ground. Measurements were conducted with ¼ wavelength optimal monopole antennas. The top of the antenna was at 20cm height. -95dBm of RSS value indicates no communication between receiver and transmitter.

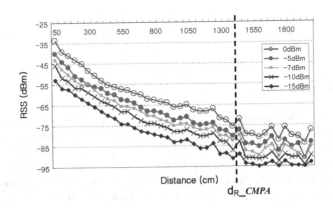

Fig. 11. RSS vs. distance for five different output powers on soil ground. Measurements were conducted with the designed CMPA. The top of the antennas was at 20cm height. -95dBm of RSS value indicates no communication between receiver and transmitter.

Since d_R depends on where the first reflection by ground occurs, extending the distance of the first reflection is required to extend d_R for obtaining useful distance information at a longer distance. We changed the antenna from an optimal ¼ wavelength monopole to CMPA in Figure 6(b) to extend d_R. The vertical radiation pattern of designed CMPA is narrower than an optimal $\frac{1}{4}$ wavelength monopole antenna as shown in Figure 6(c). Therefore, the angle of incidence of CMPA is narrower than a $\frac{1}{4}$ wavelength one. Since the narrower angle of incidence means that the reflection on the ground occurs at a greater distance and the reflected RF also interferes with directly-propagated RF at a further distance, d_R is extended.

Figure 11 shows the RSS values versus that of distance with CMPA. Compared with a $\frac{1}{4}$ wavelength monopole antenna, the distance that guarantees obtaining useful distance information directly from RSS is extended from 8m to 14m. Note that we adjusted the top of both antennas to the same height to minimize the side-effect caused by different antenna heights. The adjustment of antenna height was essential because the difference of $\frac{1}{4}$ wavelength monopole and the designed CMPA is about 7cm.

4.2 Experiment Using Parabolic Antennas

In the previous section, we validated that the distance, which guarantees the path loss model can be extended by changing into an antenna whose vertical radiation angle is narrower than the case of a $\frac{1}{4}$ wavelength optimal antenna. We now focus on how long d_R can be extended under the environmental conditions where the ground reflection does not exist. To measure RSS value over a distance satisfying the condition of no ground reflection, we used a parabolic antenna [21], which has a very sharp radiation pattern in both the horizontal and vertical planes.

We placed two sensor motes in an obstacle-free space, connecting them with parabolic antennas whose gain is 15dBi, and satisfying the line-of-sight as shown in Figure 12. The parabolic antenna transmits a radio signal to an extremely narrow direction so that the reflection of RF caused by ground almost never occurs. As shown in Figure 13, in the condition where there is no ground reflection, RSS attenuates linearly over distance without fluctuation. In an obstacle-free environment where the ground reflection is removed by using an antenna whose radio signal is not radiated to the ground, the reliable distance d_R can be extended to the communication range itself. In case of our experiment with the parabolic antenna of 15dBi gain, the reliable distance was over 50m.

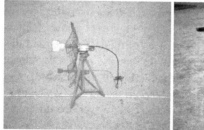

Fig. 12. An experimental setup for RSS measurement with parabolic antennas. The transmission power is 0dBm and the line of sight is satisfied at a height of 50cm.

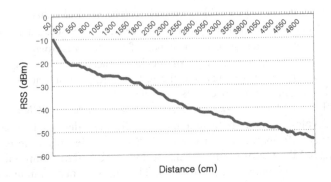

Fig. 13. RSS vs. Distance with parabolic antennas of 15dBi gain at a height of 50cm

Through this experiment, we noticed that remarkably accurate performance of localization can be achieved even with RSS-based localization techniques, which translate RSS to actual distance between nodes, provided that an antenna, which eliminates the RSS fluctuation problem is used.

5 Deployment Consideration

So far, we have validated that both antenna orientation and RSS fluctuation problems can be alleviated by changing the antenna into one whose vertical radiation pattern is less than a ¼ wavelength optimal antenna. Experimental results in a relatively flat and obstacle-free environment show better performance in terms of regular radiation pattern and obtaining a longer distance range which is applicable to the path loss model. The problem which is occurred when changing an antenna from a ¼ wavelength optimal one to an antenna with a narrower angle of vertical radiation, is that the RSS attenuation over distance is less reliable than the case of using a ¼ wavelength optimal monopole antenna in the environment where the heights of a transmitter and a receiver are different.

In order to analyze how the comparatively narrower vertical radiation than ¼ wavelength monopole antenna affects the localization performance in an environment where a height difference exists, we measured RSS over distance with different heights between a receiver and a transmitter. Figure 14 shows RSS values versus distance for four cases. The height differences of the transmitter and the receiver are 0cm, 40cm, 80cm, and 120cm respectively. In the case of a ¼ wavelength monopole antenna, the path loss model was valid for the height difference of 0cm, 40cm, and 80cm. For the height difference of 120cm, the measured RSS value at a 2m distance was weaker than the RSS value at a 4m distance. However, the difference of the RSS value was slight for 2dBm.

In the case of our CMPA, the path loss model was slightly broken at a height difference of 80cm, and the RSS difference between 2m distance and 4m distance was

10dBm at a height difference of 120cm as shown in Figure 14(b). To identify the height difference, which guarantees the path loss model, we measured RSS at the distance of 2m between a transmitter and a receiver by changing the height difference from 0 to 120cm. As shown in Figure 15, for a ¼ wavelength optimal antenna, the RSS value decreases dramatically at a height difference of 90cm. On the other hand, the RSS value starts dramatically decreasing at a height difference of 70cm for the CMPA. The vertical boundary which guarantees the path loss model can be represented about 24.5° for a ¼ wavelength monopole antenna and about 19.5° for the CMPA.

In an RSS-based localization technique, the ¼ wavelength optimal antenna consequently presents reliable localization performance where the angle with a transmitter and a receiver is only lower than 24.5°. Moreover, when using a special antenna such as the CMPA to alleviate antenna orientation and RSS fluctuation problems, more restrictions on node-deployable environment, in terms of height difference, are imposed because the vertical radiation angle gets narrower.

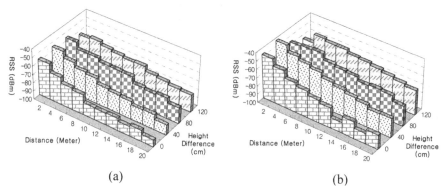

Fig. 14. RSS vs. Distance in four cases that the transmitter and receiver are placed at different heights for (a) a ¼wavelength monopole antenna and (b) our CMPA. Measurements were conducted with a transmitter of fixed height and a receiver on a tripod, which can adjust height.

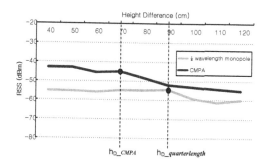

Fig. 15. RSS vs. height difference of the transmitter and receiver at 2m distance

6 Discussion

In Section 4.2, we showed that the RSS attenuates over distance without any fluctuation when using a parabolic antenna whose vertical radiation pattern is very sharp so that the reflection by ground does not occur. The problem of a conventional parabolic antenna is that it radiates RF only to the particular direction. Satisfying no RSS fluctuation caused by ground reflecting, some special antennas make it possible to obtain a horizontally omni-directional radiation pattern. Figure 16(a) shows the schematic diagram of omni-directional antenna with dual reflectors of a paraboloid and a cone [22]. Figure 16(b) shows another antenna design to satisfy both horizontally omni-directional and horizontal-only radiation, which consists of an ellipse and a paraboloid as a sub-reflector and a main-reflector respectively [23]. The problem in constructing an antenna including a paraboloid is the size of the paraboloid. Since the diameter of paraboloid requires it being larger than a wavelength of RF, it is not possible to apply a conventional dual reflector antenna directly to a WSN.

With a collinear antenna, it is also possible to reduce vertical radiation and increase antenna gain such as with dual reflector antennas by increasing the number of coils or loops. The problem with the collinear antenna, which satisfies the problem of a narrow angle of vertical radiation making no ground reflection, is the increased length of antenna. The length of collinear antenna used in this paper is about 10cm, and the length increases to 25cm if making an antenna that includes two loops to obtain 6dBi gain. The length of antenna may get longer over 100cm for much less vertical radiation. We expect that a ceramic antenna can solve this length problem because the size of an antenna made with ceramic can be over 60% smaller than a conventional monopole antenna [24], [25].

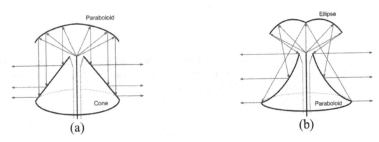

Fig. 16. Schematic diagram and radiation direction on side view of dual reflector omni-directional antenna consisting of (a) a paraboloid and a cone [22], and (b) an ellipse and a paraboloid [23]

7 Conclusions and Future Work

In this paper, we analyzed why the RF-based localization techniques do not work well in practice and the corresponding solutions. Based on extensive experiments with the widely-used CC2420 IEEE 802.15.4 compliant radio and various antennas, we conclude our work as follows:

- Factors involved with the antenna orientation problem include a small ground plane size and an electrical effect caused from other devices on a sensor mote. Therefore, the antenna orientation problem can be eliminated by mounting an antenna keeping a certain vertical distance away from a sensor mote or using an antenna which has less radiation toward the downside to minimize distortion of electrical fields.
- The asymmetric link in an obstacle-free environment is an incidental problem caused by antenna orientation. Hence, it can be easily solved by removing the cause of the antenna orientation.
- The RSS fluctuation is a problematic phenomenon in that the RSS attenuation over distance is not held out at a certain reliable distance, and is caused by multi-path fading, especially reflection by the ground in an obstacle-free environment. The reliable distance can be extended by replacing an antenna with one having a narrow vertical radiation pattern, which leads the first reflection of RF on the ground to occur at a greater distance.
- Dual reflector antenna or high-gain collinear antenna can be used for eliminating both antenna orientation and RSS fluctuation problems in cases where sensor motes are deployed in a relatively flat ground environment. We expect to reduce the size of those antennas by building them of ceramic.

In future work, we plan to make a ceramic collinear antenna, which has similar characteristics to that of a dual reflector antenna, satisfying the appropriate size specifications in WSNs. With a specially made antenna, we hope to analyze and evaluate the improvement of the accuracy in RF-based localization techniques for relatively flat and obstacle-free environments.

Acknowledgments

This work was supported by the National Research Laboratory (NRL) program of the Korea Science and Engineering Foundation (2005-01352), and the MIC(Ministry of Information and Communication), Korea, under the ITRC(Information Technology Research Center) support program supervised by the IITA(Institute of Information Technology Advancement)" (IITA-2006-C1090-0603-0015).

References

1. Hofmann-Wellenhof, B., Lichtenegger, H., and Collins, J.: *Global Positioning System: Theory and Practice*. 4th Ed., Springer Verlag (1997)
2. Patwari, N., and Hero III, A. O.: Using Proximity and Quantized RSS for Sensor Localization in Wireless Networks. ACM International Workshop on Wireless Sensor Networks and Applications (WSNA) (2003)
3. Savarese, C., Rabay, J., and Langendoen, K.: Robust Positioning Algorithms for Distributed Ad-Hoc Wireless Sensor Networks. USENIX Technical Annual Conference (2002)
4. Savvides, A., Park, H., and Srivastava, M.: The Bits and Flops of the N-Hop Multilateration Primitive for Node Localization Problems. ACM International Workshop on Wireless Sensor Networks and Applications (WSNA) (2002)

5. Shang, Y., and Ruml, W.: Improved MDS-Based Localization. INFOCOM (2004)
6. Ji, X., and Zha, H.: Sensor Positioning in Wireless Ad-hoc Sensor Networks with Multi-dimensional Scaling. INFOCOM (2004)
7. Bulusu, N., Heidemann, J., and Estrin, D.: GPS-less Low-Cost Outdoor Localization for Very Small Devices. IEEE Personal Communications Magazine (2000)
8. Niculescu, D, and Nath, B.: Ad hoc Positioning System (APS). IEEE GLOBECOM (2001)
9. Yedavalli, K., Krishnamachari, B., Ravula, S., and Srinivasan, B.: Ecolocation: A Sequence Based Technique for RF Localization in Wireless Sensor Networks. Information Processing in Sensor Networks (IPSN) (2005)
10. He, T., Huang, C., Blum, B. M., Stankovic, J. A., and Abdelzaher, T.: Range-Free Localization Schemes for Large Scale Sensor Networks. ACM International Conference on Mobile Computing and Networking (MobiCom) (2003)
11. Ganesan, D., Krishnamachari, B., Woo, A, Culler, D., Estrin, D., and Wicker, S.: Complex Behavior at Scale: An Experimental Study of Low-Power Wireless Sensor Networks. Technical Report, UCLA/CSD-TR 02-0013 (2002)
12. Cerpa, A., Busek, N., and Estrin, D.: SCALE: A Tool for Simple Connectivity Assessment in Lossy Environments. CENS Technical Report 0021 (2003)
13. Zhao, Y. J., and Govindan, R.: Understanding Packet Delivery Performance in Dense Wireless Sensor Networks. ACM Conference on Embedded Networked Sensor Systems (SenSys) (2003)
14. Zhou, G., He, T., Krishnamurthy, S., and Stankovic, J. A.: Impact of Radio Irregularity on Wireless Sensor Networks. International Conference on Mobile Systems, Applications, and Services (MobiSys) (2004)
15. Lymberopoulos, D., Lindsey, Q., and Savvides, A.: An Empirical Analysis of Radio Signal Strength Variability in IEEE 802.15.4 Networks using Monopole Antennas. European Workshop on Sensor Networks (EWSN) (2006)
16. CC2420 Data sheet. http://www.chipcon.com/files/CC2420_Data_Sheet_1_3.pdf.
17. MoteIV, Tmote-Sky-Datasheet, http://www.moteiv.com/products/docs/tmote-sky-datasheet.pdf.
18. Joseph, C. J.: *Practical Antenna Handbook*. 4th Ed., McGraw Hill (2001)
19. Taguchi, M., Yamashita, K., Tanaka, K., and Tanaka, T.: Analysis of coil-loaded thin-wire antenna. IEEE International Symposium on Antennas and Propagation (1989)
20. Srinivasan, K., and Levis, P.: RSSI is Under Appreciated. 3rd Workshop on Embedded Networked Sensors (EmNets) (2006)
21. Pacific Wireless, http://www.pacwireless.com/products/GD24_datasheet.pdf.
22. Orefice, M., and Pirinolli, P.: Dual Reflector Antenna with Narrow Broadside Beam for Omnidirectional Coverage. Electron Letters Vol. 29 (1993) 2158-2159.
23. Bergmann, J. R., and Moreira, F. J. S.: An Omnidirectional ADE Reflector Antenna. Microwave and Optical Technology Letters Vol. 40 (2004)
24. Choi, W., Kwon, S., and Lee, B.: Ceramic Chip Antenna using Meander Conductor Lines. Electronics Letters, Vol. 37, No. 15 (2001)
25. Moon, J., and Park, S.: Small Chip Antenna for 2.4/5.8-Ghz Dual ISM-Band Applications. IEEE Antennas and Wireless Propagation Letters, Vol. 2 (2003)

Radio Propagation-Aware Distance Estimation Based on Neighborhood Comparison

Carsten Buschmann[1], Horst Hellbrück[1], Stefan Fischer[1], Alexander Kröller[2], and Sàndor Fekete[2]

[1] Institute of Telemactics, University of Lübeck, Germany
{buschmann, hellbrueck, fischer}@itm.uni-luebeck.de
[2] Institute of Mathematical Optimization, Braunschweig University of Technology, Germany
{a.kroeller, s.fekete}@tu-bs.de

Abstract. Distance estimation is important for localization and a multitude of other tasks in wireless sensor networks. We propose a new scheme for distance estimation based on the comparison of neighborhood lists. It is inspired by the observation that distant nodes have fewer neighbors in common than close ones. Other than many distance estimation schemes, it relies neither on special hardware nor on unreliable measurements of physical wireless communication properties like RSSI. Additionally the approach benefits from message exchange by other protocols and requires a single additional message exchange for distance estimation. We will show that the approach is universally applicable and works with arbitrary radio hardware. We discuss related work and present the new approach in detail including its mathematical foundations. We demonstrate the performance of our approach by presenting various simulation results.

1 Introduction

In sensor networks self-localization is an important part of self-organization [1]. Location information is essential for the detection of events and the tagging of these events with their geographic origin. Considering a temperature sensing network where some nodes experience a sudden temperature rise, nodes can identify the bounding region of this incident with the help of their position. However, GPS receivers are costly and energy consuming, and thus conflict with major sensor node design goals: low price, tiny form factor and minimal energy consumption. Hence not all nodes can be equipped with GPS, and other techniques have gained popularity. These algorithms assume that a small number of devices, so called anchors, already know their location. The other nodes try to estimate their distances to the anchors and then infer their position through multilateration. Like this, distances became one of the key foundations for location estimation based on anchor nodes [13]. Furthermore, proximity is an intrinsically interesting property of environmental elements and other wireless sensor nodes.

Many different systems for distance estimation (often also called ranging) have been developed. Nearly all of them employ a sender-receiver-scheme: one node

K. Langendoen and T. Voigt (Eds.): EWSN 2007, LNCS 4373, pp. 325–340, 2007.
© Springer-Verlag Berlin Heidelberg 2007

emits some kind of signal, the other uses a special receiver to measure physical signal properties such as attenuation or time of flight. These techniques will be discussed in detail in the next section. If no direct range distance estimation is possible, multi hop accumulation of distance estimates along the route from anchor to the node is a common work-around (compare e.g. DV-Distance in [15]).

In this paper we present the neighborhood intersection distance estimation scheme (NIDES). This novel approach to distance estimation does not rely on special hardware or unreliable measurements of physical signal properties. Instead, it computes the distances from intersection of sets of adjacent nodes. It is based on the observation that close sensor nodes share more neighbors than distant ones. However, we show that the number of shared neighbors also depends on the radio propagation properties. Hence, we developed a scheme that is radio aware. We will show that the approach is generally applicable and will work with arbitrary radio models.

The remainder of this paper is structured as follows. In the next section we present related work that deals with distance estimation or employs neighborhood lists. We review different distance estimation techniques and discuss their advantages and disadvantages. In Section 3 we give an overview of different radio models and show how their properties can be expressed in so called radio model functions or probability functions. Section 4 then introduces the radio model aware neighborhood intersection distance estimation scheme. We elaborate on its mathematical foundations and discuss properties and factors of influence. In addition, we point out how NIDES can be implemented as a distributed network protocol. Section 5 reports the results of the simulative performance evaluation. The paper is concluded by a summary and directions for future work.

2   Related Work

A number of techniques to acquire distance estimates between nodes have been developed in the past.

One of the first approaches for distance estimation in ubiquitous computing systems was proximity detection. Examples are the Active Badge [21] and the Hybrid indoor navigation system [5]. They both use infrared light to periodically transmit beacons with unique identification. The recipients of these beacons - either the fixed infrastructure or the mobile devices - deduce proximity to the beacon since the range of infrared signals is limited to a few meters of distance. With increasing number of beacons a fine grained resolution is achievable. The downside of this distance estimation technique is the very high deployment effort and the need for a backbone infrastructure.

To enable infrastructure-less distance estimations, a broad range of techniques have been proposed, deployed and researched in the past, which can be classified into the following three categories: approaches based on (differential) time of flight, radio signal strength and connectivity.

The measurement of the *time of flight (ToF)* of a signal is a robust method to estimate distances which is used e.g. by GPS [12]. However, measurements

require a tight time synchronization of sender and receiver. Systems like Cala-
mari [22], Cricket [18], AHLoS [20] and others use a technique called "differential
time of arrival" (DTOA) to avoid complex time synchronization. They send out
two signals (usually ultra sonic sound and radio frequency signals) propagating
with different speeds and measure the difference in time of arrival. If both signal
propagation speeds are known, a distance can be derived from the delta of arrival. The raw difference measurements tend to yield average estimation errors
of about 74% [22]. Yet, quite good accuracies can be achieved by post-processing
of the measured data with techniques like noise canceling, digital filtering, peak
detection and calibration. While some authors report average range estimation
errors of 10% [22], others claim an error of about 1% at a maximum range of
9 m [19]. In [23] the authors report the increase of the maximum range to 12 m
with an error of 0.5%.

While these systems yield low estimation errors they have two limitations that
confine their applicability in real world deployments. The first is their limited
coverage: They are typically able to cover 3–15 m [20] which is only a fraction
of the communication range of radio frequency transmitters. The second and far
more severe is that they require a separate sender/receiver pair, which implies
negative effects on size, cost and energy consumption. All three collide with the
aim to design tiny, cheap and highly energy efficient nodes for wireless sensor
networks [1].

In order not to require additional hardware, different other schemes have
been developed using the radio interface itself to infer distances to other nodes.
These approaches use radio signal attenuation properties to model the distance
between nodes as a function of the *received signal strength indicator (RSSI)*.
Systems that rely on the RSSI as input parameter such as [4], [3], [2] tend to
be quite accurate for short ranges if extensive post-processing is employed, but
are imprecise beyond a few meters [14]. At short ranges, distance estimations
exhibiting errors of about 10% at the maximum range of about 20 m [23] are
feasible. The uncertainty of the radio propagation imposes problems like multi-
path propagation, fading and shadowing effects as well as obstacles in the line-
of-sight. These effects complicate the development of a consistent model [20]. As
a result systems relying exclusively on RSSI values remain inaccurage distance
estimators [8].

The idea presented in this paper is based on counting neighbors. Whether
communication with nearby node is possible depends also on a RSSI threshold
but NIDES inherently compensates RSSI inaccuracies by incorporating links to
many neighbors and merging the results instead of measuring the unreliable
RSSI values of a single link.

Another improvement of RSSI is presented in [14] where *radio interferometry*
techniques are used to achieve an average localization error of 3 cm and a range
of up to 160 m with a largest error of approximately 6 cm (which is about 0.04%).
However, radio interferometry seems to be susceptible to the effects of shadowing,
reflection and multi-path propagation. The downsides of the approach are the
high computational complexity of the algorithm and that it requires special

features of the radio chip. In addition the accuracy is achieved by long lasting measurements, which renders the approach impractical for mobile scenarios.

In [6], the authors present the idea to detect far away neighbors by comparing neighborhood lists. However, by determining the percentage of shared neighbors they do not estimate distances. Instead, that fraction influences the probability of forwarding a received flooding message. The fewer neighbors the sender and the receiver share, the higher the forwarding probability is. Thus, distant nodes have a higher probability to forward packets, increasing the coverage per packet sent. However, the authors limit usage of the neighborhood list to forwarding purposes.

3   Radio Model Properties

Not only due to the lack of hardware in real quantities but also for the sake of simplicity researchers in the area of wireless sensor networks are forced to use simulations for validation of algorithms and protocols. Therefore a number of radio models have been developed in the past that express the physical layer characteristics of the radio channel. The key characteristic to determine whether a node is able to receive a radio packet transmitted from a node are the location of sender and receiver, some models also include the status of the radio channel (busy, free with a noise level).

The unit disk graph model (UDG) is the most common model in wireless simulations and available in all network simulators due to its simplicity. It is backed by the observation that (for two dimensional scenarios) the signal strength of wireless communication transceivers fades with the square of the distance from the sender. Given a minimum signal strength required for reception, nodes within the radius of a disk can receive frames from sending nodes. It is rotationally symmetric, and hence yields bidirectional links. Figure 1(a) depicts the radio model function of the unit disk graph model. Here and in all following figures, the communication range has been normalized to 1.

However, experiments have shown that especially in wireless sensor networks with their simple transceivers fading is not circular [9], [25]. To cope with irregularities in the transmission range that is common to real world networks different new models have been proposed. The DOI-Model (DOI means for degree of irregularity) [10] introduces two limits: below the minimum range communication

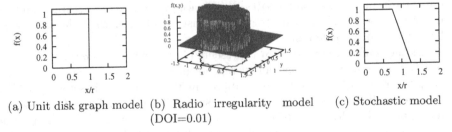

(a) Unit disk graph model   (b) Radio irregularity model   (c) Stochastic model
                              (DOI=0.01)

Fig. 1. Probability functions of different radio models

is always possible, above the maximum range communication always fails. In between the two the communication range varies depending on the angle. The DOI factor determines the maximum change in transmission range per degree and thus controls the irregularity of the radio shape (also see Figure 1(b)). In contrast to the circular shape of the unit disk graph model, the DOI model also yields unidirectional links. The radio irregularity model (RIM) [25] further extends the DOI-Model with individual variable sending power that influences the radius of the DOI-shape.

The radio irregularity model is still an oversimplification of the existing radio characteristics because wireless links tend to be error prone so that only a portion of packets is received successfully. Note that for the DOI model nodes within the transmission area receive 100% of the transmitted packets. Measurements in [9] show that packet reception probability decreases with distance but it has a fairly long tail (i.e. even nodes at distances far beyond r may occasionally receive packets). To address this fact Zuniga and Krishnamachari [26] developed a statistical radio model that describes a function for receiving probability fading with the distance. Like the radio irregularity model, it has two bounds. While reception is always possible below the first one, it never takes place above the second. Other than RIM it is rotiationally symmetric but still yield unidirectional links. Figure 1(c) shows a so called linear stochastic model where the change of the packet reception ratio is modelled by a straight line. The bounds are set to $0.75r$ and $1.25r$ here.

There are many other less commonly used radio models, including models a special areas e.g. for cellular network planning. However, these do not provide universal results and are not considered hence.

We will show that NIDES is a general approach for distance estimation that is able to work with arbitrary radio models including unit disk graph, RIM and stochastic radio models.

4   Radio Model Dependent Distance Estimation

The basic idea of the neighborhood intersection distance estimation scheme (NIDES) is to estimate the distance between neighboring nodes from the percentage of neighbors they share. It is based on the observation that two nodes have most of their neighbors in common if they are located close to each other while distant nodes will share fewer or no neighbors at all. For simplification of the model construction we assume a locally uniform node distribution and derive a relation between the percentage of common neighbors of two nodes and their distance. We will address this issue later on in Section 5.

We will show that the fraction of shared neighbors changes with the chosen radio model and will present a generic way to estimate distances with an arbitrary model.

For three different radio models illustrated in Figure 1, an example scenario with the shared neighbors (filled black circles) of two nodes (with an extra black ring) is depicted in Figure 2. Note that the two black nodes feature the same distance in all three cases, variations in the number of common neighbors date back to the radio model. In Figure 2(a) the unit disk graph radio model was employed. The two disks with radius r are indicated as thin circles. The two nodes share 26 neighbors. Figure 2(b) shows the use of the radio irregularity model, the two nodes have 27 common neighbors. The stochastic model was used in the scenario in Figure 2(c), the pair of circles around the two nodes indicates distances of $0.75r$ and $1.25r$. Here, 23 neighbors are shared.

It is evident that the fraction of common nodes varies with the chosen radio model. As a result, distance estimation based on neighborhood intersection without taking the radio model into account will be incorrect. The model should rather be considered as an integral factor of influence for neighborhood-based distance estimation. Hence we propose a scheme that is radio model-aware and incorporates its properties.

Neighborhood-based distance estimation requires a mapping between the fraction of shared neighbors s of two nodes and their expected distance d from each other that takes the radio model into account. In the following paragraphs we show how a distance estimation function $d(s)$ can be constructed from a given radio model, here described as a two-dimensional function.

The starting point of the construction is the radio model function $f : \mathbb{R} \times \mathbb{R} \to [0, 1]$. It describes the probability that a node that has a position offset of (x, y) to another node can receive its radio signals.

Some radio models provide only a one-dimensional function $f_1 : \mathbb{R} \to [0, 1]$ that models the communication probability as a function of the distance between two nodes (i.e. the radio model is rotationally symmetric). Examples are the unit disk graph or the stochastic radio model. In these cases, a two-dimensional function $f(x, y)$ can easily be constructed by rotating f_1 around the z-axis. The resulting function looks as follows:

$$f(x, y) = f_1(\sqrt{x^2 + y^2}) \tag{1}$$

The created function now also describes the probability that a node located at (x, y) can receive packets from the node at $(0, 0)$.

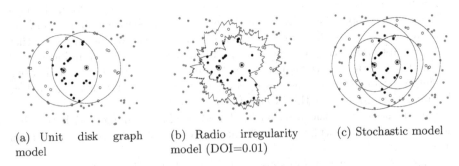

(a) Unit disk graph model

(b) Radio irregularity model (DOI=0.01)

(c) Stochastic model

Fig. 2. Number of common neighbors varying with the employed radio models

An example for f is shown in Figure 1(b). It depicts the communication probability function of the radio irregularity model with the degree of irregularity set to 0.01.

The estimation function $d(x)$ can now be calculated by convolving f. Because in the general case f is not rotationally symmetric, it must also be rotated during the convolution.

$$f_{rot}(x, y, \alpha) = f(x \; cos(\alpha) + y \; sin(\alpha), -x \; sin(\alpha) + y \; cos(\alpha)) \qquad (2)$$

describes f rotated around the z-axis by α. It is translated along the x-axis by d by subtracting d from x. (d will be the distance between the nodes).

The fraction of shared neighbors over distance is now given by $s : \mathbb{R}^+ \to [0, 1]$:

$$s(d) = \int_0^{2\pi} \frac{\int_{-\infty}^{\infty} \int_{-\infty}^{\infty} f_{rot}(x - d, y, \alpha) \; f_{rot}(x, y, \alpha) \, dx \, dy}{\int_{-\infty}^{\infty} \int_{-\infty}^{\infty} f_{rot}(x, y, \alpha) \, dx \, dy} \, d\alpha \qquad (3)$$

While we here integrate from $-\infty$ to ∞ for the sake of generality, the limits can be adopted to the area of the radio model that adds non-zero values to the integral.

If the radio model is rotationally symmetric like the unit disk graph or the stochastic radio model, the rotation within the convolution can be omitted. The function $s(d)$ is then given by

$$s(d) = \frac{\int_{-\infty}^{\infty} \int_{-\infty}^{\infty} f(x - d, y) f(x, y) \, dx \, dy}{\int_{-\infty}^{\infty} \int_{-\infty}^{\infty} f(x, y) \, dx \, dy}. \qquad (4)$$

In both cases $s(d)$ gives the expected fraction of shared neighbors for a certain distance d.

Figure 3 depicts the result for $s(d)$ of different radio models. For the radio irregularity model, it is depicted in Figure 3(a), the unit disk graph and stochastic model are shown in subfigure (b) and (c).

Because s describes the fraction of shared neighbors depending on the distance, its inverse function is required for distance estimation:

$$d(s) = s^{-1}(d) \qquad (5)$$

To obtain unique results, s_n needs to be monotonically decreasing. This is the case for all presented radio models.

So far we have shown how the distance estimation function $d(s)$ can be constructed from the radio model probability function $f(x, y)$. In order to employ NIDES in a real world wireless network, basically three steps must be taken:

1. The behavior of the employed communication hardware must be modeled, i.e. the radio model probability function must be determined. This can e.g. be done by conducting measurements. An alternative might be to consult data sheets of the manufacturer.

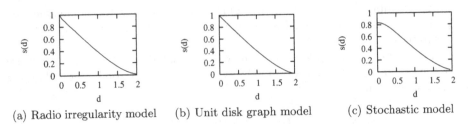

(a) Radio irregularity model   (b) Unit disk graph model   (c) Stochastic model

Fig. 3. $s(d)$ for different radio models

2. Once the probability function $f(x, y)$ is known, $s(d)$ can be calculated as described above. It can be used to obtain a lookup table for different distances d, the so called estimation table. It can be stored in the code segment of the target hardware, and hence does not consume any random access memory.
3. At runtime, only neighborhood information must be exchanged between the nodes. When distances need to be estimated, the estimates can be looked up in the estimation table.

Note that the first two steps are done prior to deployment. The generated table is part of the software of the nodes. In this way, every node can estimate the distances to its neighbors if it knows its own neighbors as well as the neighbors of its neighbors. To make sure all nodes have these pieces of information, each node must broadcast two data packets. Due to length limitation of this paper we will only consider distance estimation based on single-hop-neighborhoods here.

First, all nodes must send out a 'hello' packet that enables nodes in range to take notice of them. The sending nodes are inserted into the receivers' neighbor lists. Finally, all nodes have built up their own completed list from the hello packets received. This list must be kept in memory and will be augmented with information about the neighbor distances in the second step. For fast access, the neighbor list should be kept sorted by the node IDs. Unsigned 16 bit values should usually be sufficient to uniquely identify all neighbors. If memory is extremely scarce, neighbor addresses can be easily mapped to at least locally unique (maybe actually 8-bit) identifiers. Even in dense networks with 50 neighbors, this list requires only 100 bytes of memory.

In a second data packet, each node broadcasts its neighbor list. When an adjacent node receives it, it can calculate the number of shared neighbors n_{common}. Because both the received and the local list are sorted, it is enough to iterate once through both lists.

After n_{common} has been acquired, a second value n_{total} representing the overall number of neighbors needs to be determined in order to calculate the fraction s of common neighbors. We propose to employ the average neighbor count, i.e. the mean length of the received and the local neighbor list. Thus fluctuations in the node density and hence in the number of neighbors can be partially compensated for. Note that we do not consider the two nodes to be part of their own neighborhood, and hence omit them when calculating $s = \frac{n_{common}}{n_{total}}$.

Now the receiver can calculate the distance to the sender using $d(s)$ and store the value in a distance list at the index of the sender. Note that it is not required to store the received neighbor list permanently; it can be disposed after the distance has been computed. Only the local neighbor list and the corresponding distances must be kept in memory. To represent the distances, an unsigned 8 bit value should be sufficient.

In some cases, nodes will already have neighbor lists available although NIDES did not explicitly exchange hello messages. Examples for other software that collects neighbor information are routing protocols such as AODV [17], protocols for topology control like SPAN [7] or clustering schemes. When neighbor lists are available from other protocols, the step of broadcasting hello messages can be omitted. Nevertheless, the transmission of the list in the second packet is still required.

5 Simulative Evaluation

To evaluate the distance estimation accuracy of NIDES we ran an extensive set of simulations different scenarios using ns-2 [16]. We implemented the radio irregularity and stochastic communication model by extending the free space radio propagation model.

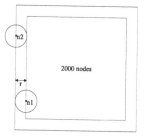

Fig. 4. Simulation scenario

We used the simulation scenario depicted in Figure 4. When analyzing the estimation accuracy, we only considered nodes that were located inside the dotted inner rectangle. The width of this inner area is $2r$ smaller than the simulation area, where r is the communication range. Thus the full communication range of the considered nodes resides within the simulation area (c.f. node n1). This avoids edge effects that would be caused by missing neighbors for node n2 on the left. In order to obtain simulation results for different network densities (i.e. different average neighborhood sizes) we calculated the size of the inner area depending on the desired network density so that a fixed number of nodes resided inside. The size of the full simulation area and the overall node number can then be calculated accordingly. Nodes were spread randomly over the full simulation area, i.e. their x and y coordinates where taken from a uniform random distribution. The average communication range was set to 100.

We iterated over all pairs of adjacent nodes inside the inner rectangle, estimated their distances using NIDES, and compared these estimates to their real Euclidean distances. To obtain statistically sound results, we averaged the results of 100 simulations with the same parameter set.

We focus on simulation results for the radio irregularity model, because it has been developed especially for wireless sensor networks and represents many properties that are typical for this network type. We later present results for the unit disk graph model and the stochastic model.

Depending on radio propagation properties, it is not uncommon that links between nodes are only uni-directional. This effect does not harm the protocol proposed above and also occurs in the simulative evaluation.

5.1 Radio Irregularity Model

Figure 5(a) shows an interquartile diagram of the estimation error over the average neighborhood size.

In an interquartile diagram, each bar describes a value distribution where only 25% of the values lie above the upper bound and below the lower bound of the bar. Figure 5(a) also includes the mean absolute error and the median. For the earlier the absolute error values were summed up for all considered distances and divided by their number, while for the latter a value is selected so that half of the errors are bigger and the other half is smaller. Hence the median indicates whether the estimates are biased.

The diagram was obtained through simulations with the radio irregularity model and the DOI set to 0.01, the estimation function depicted in Figure 3(a) was used. The error is expressed as a fraction of the communication range r.

The spread of the interquartiles decreases with increasing network densities, i.e. neighborhood sizes. As expected, the estimates get more exact with bigger neighborhoods. With many neighbors, the interquartile of the estimates lies within $0.07r$ around the correct distance (i.e. 50% of the estimates feature an

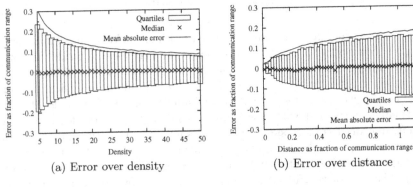

(a) Error over density   (b) Error over distance

Fig. 5. Error characteristic, uniform node distribution, radio irregularity model (DOI=0.01)

error of less than 7% of the communication range). For densities above 10 the
mean absolute error is below 20% of the communication range. Note that the median error is always very close to zero which means that NIDES has no tendency
at all to systematically over- or underestimate distances.

Research has shown that mobile ad-hoc networks tend to partition with high
probability if the density, i.e. the average neighborhood size, is below 10 [11].
Others proved that the density required for full connectivity depends on the
network size. The more nodes a network consists of, the higher the required
density is [24]. For a network comprising 300 nodes, a density of about 13 is
needed. Hence, we consider an average neighborhood size of 15 to be a reasonable
choice for wireless sensor networks.

With 15 neighbors, the mean error is about $0.15r$ with an interquartile spread
of about 0.2. This means that 50% of the estimates feature an error of $0.1r$ or
less. If not indicated differently, the simulation results presented in the remainder
of the paper feature a density of 15.

We then studied the dependency of the estimation accuracy on the actual
distance between the two involved nodes. Figure 5(b) depicts an interquartile
diagram of the error over the Euclidean node distance. Both distance and error
are expressed as a fraction of the communication range.

The mean absolute error and the interquartile spread increase with the real
distance between the two estimating nodes. The reason for that is the decreasing
absolute number of shared neighbors. Hence density fluctuation gains importance, and leads to an increased error spread. However, the interquartile spread
stays below $\pm 0.15r$ and the mean absolute error is always less than $0.18r$. If these
values are averaged over all distances, a mean error of $0.15r$ and an interquartile
spread of $\pm 0.1r$ result (as indicated in Figure 5(a) at x=15).

Finally we conducted simulations with non-uniform node distributions. An
example of a Gaussian node distribution over the simulation area is depicted in

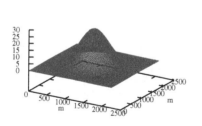
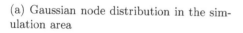
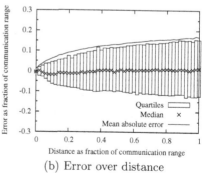

(a) Gaussian node distribution in the simulation area

(b) Error over distance

Fig. 6. Gaussian node distribution and resulting error characteristic for the radio irregularity model

Figure 6(a). It shows the node density at every point of the simulation area and results from averaging 100 simulations runs. As for the results discussed above, the average node density is set to 15. Different from the scenarios above, we considered all nodes including those at the edges of the network here.

The resulting error characteristic is presented in Figure 6(b). It closely resembles the results obtained with uniform distributions. The error decreases even a bit because of the increased density in the center of the simulation area. The median runs along the x-axis, so obviously the non-uniform distribution does not lead to biased results.

5.2   Linear Stochastic Radio Model

In this subsection we consider the influence of the stochastic model on distance estimation performance. We employed the linear variant with the bounds set to $0.75r$ and $1.25r$ (both as indicated in Figure 1(c)). The corresponding estimation function is depicted in Figure 3(c).

Figure 7 shows the according diagrams. Subfigure 7(a) indicates the distribution of the estimation error depending on the network density (again indicated as a fraction of the communication range r). The mean absolute error is below $0.20r$ for a density of 10 and goes down to 9% of the communication range for a density of 50 while the interquartile spread ranges between $\pm 0.17r$ and $\pm 0.07r$. For a density of 15, the mean absolute error is 16% of the communication range while half of the estimates exhibit an error within $0.12r$ and $0.14r$. The median is always very close to zero.

These values indicate a slightly lower accuracy as if the radio irregularity model was used. The reason for that can be found when looking at Figure 7(b). It indicates the influence of the real distance on the estimation error at a density of 15. While similar to the radio irregularity model for distances above $0.3r$, the stochastic model shows a different behavior below that. The reason is that even if nodes are very close to each other, their neighborhood can vary heavily because the radio model determines a significant fraction of neighbors randomly. This

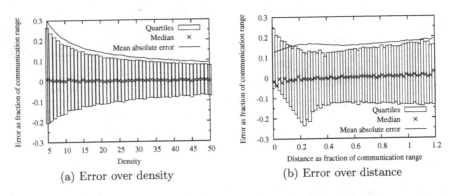

(a) Error over density   (b) Error over distance

Fig. 7. Error characteristic for the linear stochastic radio model

especially means that even if two nodes are located at the same spot, they will share only 83% of their neighbors on average (compare the distance estimation function depicted in Figure 3(c) at $x = 0$). If nodes have a distance in between each other but share 83% of their neighbors or more, NIDES will estimate their distance as 0, which leads to underestimations for small distances.

In addition, the run of the estimation function is quite flat for small values of x. Thus already minor changes in the fraction of shared neighbors lead to significant changes in the estimated distance. If nodes are close but share slightly less than 83% neighbors of their neighbors, NIDES will estimate a distance relatively far.

Together with the random selection of neighbors, this results in a relatively high error spread for small distances.

However, for small real distances, the negative estimation error is bound by the actual distance of the nodes. Hence also the lower interquartile can be no bigger than the real distance, as visible in Figure 7(b) for distances below $0.23r$.

The increased error for short distances has a negative impact on the overall error. However, this influence is bounded to about 1% of the communication range.

5.3   Unit Disk Graph Model

If the unit disk graph radio model is used, the performance of NIDES is very similar to the case when the radio irregularity model is used.

Figure 8 shows the according diagrams. We used the estimation function depicted in Figure 3(b).

Subfigure 8(a) indicates the influence of the average density on the estimation error (again indicated as a fraction of the communication range r). The mean absolute error is $0.27r$ for a density of 5 and goes down to 7% of the communication range for a density of 50 while the interquartile spread ranges between $\pm0.21r$ and $\pm0.06r$. For a density of 15, the mean absolute error is 15% of the communication range while 50% of the estimates exhibit an error of below $\pm0.12r$. These values indicate a slightly higher accuracy as if the radio irregularity model is used. The median is running along the x-axis.

Subfigure 8(b) indicates the influence of the real distance on the estimation error. Again, the behavior of the radio irregularity model is slightly mimicked except for a slightly higher accuracy.

However, the median is not centered for very short distances. It runs on a line that is defined by $g(x) = -x$ instead. This indicates that half of the estimates are 0 even though the nodes have a certain distance, i.e. their displacement is underestimated exactly by their Euclidean distance. The reason is that nodes that are very close to each other have a certain probability of sharing all neighbors. It is due to the fact the fractions of shared neighbors are discrete and only certain values occur (e.g. $\frac{15}{15}$ and $\frac{14}{15}$, but nothing in between) while the real node distance is continuous. This effect occurs again at about $0.55r$ and $0.8r$. Around there, different distances must be mapped on the same fraction.

The effect depends on the node density: the higher the density, the smaller the effect (because the denominator increases). It also appears with the stochastic

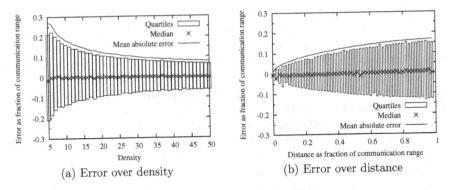

(a) Error over density   (b) Error over distance

Fig. 8. Error characteristic for the unit disk graph radio model

and the radio irregularity model but is not as clearly visible because it is averaged out by other stochastic effects. However, it never significantly influences the estimation accuracy.

6   Conclusion and Future Work

In this paper we presented the neighborhood intersection distance estimation scheme (NIDES). This novel approach computes distance estimates from intersection cardinalities of sets of adjacent nodes. In other words, its operation is based on the observation that nodes that are located close to each other share many of their neighbors whereas distant nodes share only few neighbors. While doing so, the presented scheme is radio model aware, i.e. the function that derives the actual distance estimate from the fraction of shared neighbors is constructed from the radio model and hence incorporates the radio properties.

Through simulations we assessed the accuracy of NIDES. While the scheme gets more accurate with increasing network density, it regardless of the radio model yields an average deviation of only about 15% of the communication range when nodes have about 15 neighbors.

Thus NIDES classifies in between existing approaches for distance estimation. It achieves a higher accuracy than estimates based on RSSI. Estimates based on differential time of flight feature a higher accuracy than NIDES but demand for specific hardware such as ultra sound emitters and receivers. These have negative effects on cost, size and power consumption, which seems disadvantageous especially for wireless sensor networks. In addition, these have only a very limited maximum range compared to NIDES. Radio interferometry features promisingly low errors but requires specific RF chip properties. Also, this approach needs long series of measurements and complex processing, two disadvantages that can be omitted when neighborhood intersection is used.

We are currently preparing large scale experiments with real sensor network hardware to further validate our simulation results. In the future, we plan to extend NIDES to consider two hop neighborhoods. This enables nodes to sort neighbors with regard to angle, which opens up new vistas for location estimation protocols. In addition, angles along multi hop paths can be estimated. Multi hop distance estimation will also be in the focus of future work.

References

1. I. F. Akyildiz, Y. S. W. Su, and E. Cayirci. Wireless sensor networks: A survey. *Computer Networks*, 38(4):393–422, Mar. 2002.
2. P. Bergamo and G. Mazzini. Localization in sensor networks with fading and mobility. In *Proceedings of the 13th IEEE International Symposium on Personal, Indoor and Mobile Radio Communications*, 2002.
3. J. Beutel. Geolocation in a picoradio environment, 1999.
4. N. Bulusu, J. Heideman, and D. Estrin. Gps-less low cost outdoor localization for very small devices. *IEEE Personal Communications*, 2000.
5. A. Butz, J. Baus, A. Krüger, and M. Lohse. A hybrid indoor navigation system. In *IUI '01: Proceedings of the 6th international conference on Intelligent user interfaces*, pages 25–32, New York, NY, USA, 2001. ACM Press.
6. J. Cartigny and D. Simplot. Border node retransmission based probabilistic broadcast protocols in ad-hoc networks. In *HICSS '03: Proceedings of the 36th Annual Hawaii International Conference on System Sciences (HICSS'03) - Track 9*, page 303, Washington, DC, USA, 2003. IEEE Computer Society.
7. B. Chen, K. Jamieson, H. Balakrishnan, and R. Morris. Span: an energy-efficient coordination algorithm for topology maintenance in ad hoc wireless networks. *Wirel. Netw.*, 8(5):481–494, 2002.
8. E. Elnahrawy, X. Li, and R. P. Martin. The limits of localization using signal strength: A comparative study. In *EEE SECON*, 2004.
9. D. Ganesan, B. Krishnamachari, A. Woo, D. Culler, D. Estrin, and S. Wicker. Complex behavior at scale: An experimental study of low-power wireless sensor networks, 2002.
10. T. He, C. Huang, B. M. Blum, J. A. Stankovic, and T. Abdelzaher. Range-free localization schemes for large scale sensor networks. In *MobiCom '03: Proceedings of the 9th annual international conference on Mobile computing and networking*, pages 81–95, New York, NY, USA, 2003. ACM Press.
11. H. Hellbrück and S. Fischer. Towards analysis and simulation of ad-hoc networks. In *Proceedings of the 2002 International Conference on Wireless Networks (ICWN02)*, pages 69–75, Las Vegas, Nevada, USA, June 2002. IEEE Computer Society Press.
12. B. Hofmann-Wellenhof, H. Lichtenegger, and J. Collins. *Global Positioning System: Theory and Practice*. Springer, 5 edition, 2001.
13. K. Langendoen and N. Reijers. Distributed localization in wireless sensor networks: a quantitative comparison. *Comput. Networks*, 2003.
14. M. Maroti, P. Völgyesi, S. Dora, B. Kusy, A. Nadas, A. Ledeczi, G. Balogh, and K. Molnar. Radio interferometric geolocation. In *SenSys "05: Proceedings of the 3rd international conference on Embedded networked sensor systems*, 2005.
15. D. Niculescu and B. Nath. Ad hoc positioning system (aps). In *Proceedings of GLOBECOM, San Antonio, November 2001.*, 2001.
16. The Network Simulator ns-2 (v2.29). http://www.isi.edu/nsnam/ns/, October 2001.

17. C. Perkins. Ad hoc On-Demand Distance Vector (AODV) Routing. Request for Comments 3561, Network Working Group, Internet Engineering Task Force, July 2003.
18. N. B. Priyantha, A. Chakraborty, and H. Balakrishnan. The cricket location-support system. In *MobiCom '00: Proceedings of the 6th annual international conference on Mobile computing and networking*, pages 32–43, New York, NY, USA, 2000. ACM Press.
19. J. Sallai, G. Balogh, M. Maroti, A. Ledeczi, and B. Kusy. Acoustic ranging in resource-constrained sensor networks. In *International Conference on Wireless Networks*, 2004.
20. A. Savvides, C.-C. Han, and M. B. Strivastava. Dynamic fine-grained localization in ad-hoc networks of sensors. In *MobiCom '01: Proceedings of the 7th annual international conference on Mobile computing and networking*, pages 166–179, New York, NY, USA, 2001. ACM Press.
21. R. Want, A. Hopper, V. Falcao, and J. Gibbons. The active badge location system. *ACM Transactions on Information Systems*, 10(1):91–102, 1992.
22. K. Whitehouse and D. Culler. Calibration as parameter estimation in sensor networks. In *WSNA '02: Proceedings of the 1st ACM international workshop on Wireless sensor networks and applications*, pages 59–67, New York, NY, USA, 2002. ACM Press.
23. K. Whitehouse, C. Karlof, A. Woo, F. Jiang, and D. Culler. The effects of ranging noise on multihop localization: an empirical study. In *The Fourth International Conference on Information Processing in Sensor Networks (IPSN "05)*, 2005.
24. F. Xue and P. R. Kumar. The number of neighbours needed for connectivity of wireless networks. *IEEE Wireless Networks*, 10(2):169–181, 2004.
25. G. Zhou, T. He, S. Krishnamurthy, and J. A. Stankovic. Impact of radio irregularity on wireless sensor networks. In *MobiSys '04: Proceedings of the 2nd international conference on Mobile systems, applications, and services*, pages 125–138, New York, NY, USA, 2004. ACM Press.
26. M. Zuniga and B. Krishnamachari. Analyzing the transitional region in low power wireless links. In *First IEEE International Conference on Sensor and Ad hoc Communications and Networks (SECON)*, October 2004.

Removing Systematic Error in Node Localisation Using Scalable Data Fusion

Albert Krohn[1], Mike Hazas[2], and Michael Beigl[3]

[1] Telecooperation Office, University of Karlsruhe, Germany
krohn@teco.edu
[2] Lancaster University, United Kingdom
[3] Distributed and Ubiquitous Computing Group, University of Braunschweig, Germany
beigl@ibr.cs.tu-bs.de

Abstract. Methods for node localisation in sensor networks usually rely upon the measurement of received strength, time-of-arrival, and/or angle-of-arrival of an incoming signal. In this paper, we propose a method for achieving higher accuracy by combining redundant measurements taken by different nodes. This method is aimed at compensating for the systematic errors which are dependent on the specific nodes used, as well as their spatial configuration. Utilising a technique for data fusion on the physical layer, the time complexity of the method *is constant and independent of the number of participating nodes*. Thus, adding more nodes generally increases accuracy but does not require additional time to report measurement results. Our data analysis and simulation models are based on extensive experiments with real ultrasound positioning hardware. The simulations show that the ninety-fifth percentile positioning error can be improved by a factor of three for a network of fifty nodes.

1 Introduction

In sensor networks, knowledge of physical node topology is important for packet routing, power control, location annotation of gathered sensor data, and to satisfy demands for specific application areas, such as mobile computing. A variety of solutions for node localisation have been proposed, concentrating on both sensing technologies and algorithms. These techniques have traditionally traded off performance attributes (such as accuracy and location update rate) with resource requirements (such as sensor node cost, power consumption, computational complexity, and communication overhead).

There has been a significant amount of effort invested in improving the accuracy of the location result while keeping the algorithm resource requirements to a reasonable level. More recently, some researchers have become concerned with characterising how the location result is affected by the error of the raw sensor measurement (such as radio signal strength, range, or angle-of-arrival) [1,2]. In this paper, we introduce a new method wherein the systematic measurement error typically found in localisation systems can be dramatically reduced without

K. Langendoen and T. Voigt (Eds.): EWSN 2007, LNCS 4373, pp. 341–356, 2007.

incurring additional computational complexity or communication overhead. In fact, as the number of nodes within sensing range increases, the communication overhead of the method stays constant, and the overall accuracy gain improves.

1.1 Related Work

A number of systems have been developed for tracking people and objects [3]. These have employed a variety of sensing media, including infrared, ultrasound, RF signal strength, ultra-wideband radio, computer vision, and physical contact. However, many of these systems have been designed for static deployment using dedicated infrastructure.

Other systems have been specifically designed for the processing, communication, power constraints, and dynamic deployments imposed upon sensor networks. Primarily, these have relied upon creating ranging estimates using the received signal strength indication (RSSI) provided by a sensor node's radio transceiver [4,5], or creating finer-grained (centimetre-scale) ranging estimates by measuring the time-of-flight of an acoustic signal [6,7,8]. Recently, it has been shown that competitive ranging accuracies are possible by measuring the phase offset between two slightly different radio carrier frequencies [9]. Some authors have also proposed measuring the angle-of-arrival of a signal, to be used to compute node orientation [7], or as a quantity to be used in triangulation to produce location results [10] (as opposed to *trilateration* which is applied using range measurements).

There has been a large focus on developing and comparing algorithms which take sensed ranges and compute location results with varying degrees of distributed operation [11]. Some of the algorithms do not require anchor nodes whose location is previously surveyed or known—these algorithms produce a set of *relative* coordinates which describe the spatial layout of the nodes with respect to one another, but not to any global reference point [12,13]. Relative location solutions are often sufficient for the purposes of network routing or analysing how sensor readings vary across the network (e.g. temperature and humidity in environmental monitoring). Researchers have also analysed the effects of ranging noise on the location results [1,14]. One paper in particular showed for multi-hop networks how ranging and angle-of-arrival measurement error creates accuracy bounds for the location result [2].

1.2 Motivation

Much in the spirit of the latter papers, our approach is informed by analysis of measurement error. However, rather than try to produce increasingly robust (and possibly resource-intensive) algorithms, we chose to address the measurement error, specifically the *systematic error* that is common in many sensor node localisation systems. This paper's contribution is twofold. First, it presents a method to reduce systematic errors usable for many sensor measurement settings. Second, a lightweight framework is proposed which requires minimal hardware, software and network resources and is able to support such error reduction even in scenarios where there are a large number of sensor devices.

Systematic errors appear as constant and repeatable error within measured quantities. This systematic error component can arise due to sensor decalibration (e.g. misalignment of an acoustic sensor) or environmental interference which is constant for that spatial distribution of nodes (e.g. a metal object is present near one of the nodes, affecting its radio RSSI measurements).

Because a large component of the systematic error is hardware-dependent or spatially-dependent and thus different for each node in the system, we propose fusing the measurements taken by different nodes together in order to "average out" this measurement offset. This can be done when the nodes are capable of independently computing estimates of the same spatial quantities. For example, if all nodes in a system are capable of independently estimating the range between two given nodes, then all of these range measurements could be combined to produce an inter-node range whose systematic error component is much reduced.

As more nodes join the system and are capable of measuring the same physical quantities, then the communication overhead required for each node to report its measurement can become prohibitively expensive, especially if measurement updates need to be provided at a high rate. To avoid this, our method accomplishes the averaging by using a physical layer data fusion technique called *synchronous distributed jam signalling* (SDJS). This allows all nodes to report their measurements for a given quantity simultaneously. Thus, the communication overhead for our method is constant and independent of the number of nodes in the system. The error models, proof-of-concept, and simulations are based on extensive data gathered using an ultrasonic relative positioning system [15].

1.3   Target Application Scenarios

Because our method relies upon averaging of measurements from different nodes to remove large systematic errors, it naturally grows more effective when there are greater numbers of nodes within measurement range of one another. High node densities are often envisioned for application scenarios such as environmental habitat monitoring and battlefield surveillance, and it is typical to consider high node densities in analyses of node localisation algorithms and error [2,11,13].

Another application area which envisions high node densities is that of mobile and ubiquitous computing. In such scenarios, it is assumed that everyday objects such as mobile phones, furniture, or even coffee cups are embedded with microcontrollers, sensors, and wireless communication. These *augmented objects* are thus able to sense, compute, communicate, and work together to aid people in their everyday tasks. Contextual data is often needed for this, and one of the most important types of context data is location information. Thus, accurate localisation is an important goal for the dense settings of sensors envisioned for mobile and ubiquitous computing.

2   System Operation

This section discusses the attributes and operation of the type of positioning sensor network that we consider in this paper. We begin with a notation for relative positioning systems and then discuss how nodes can locally estimate the same physical quantity. Throughout this paper, we focus on implementation and analyses of 2D localisation systems, such as the hardware platform in figure 1, but similar methods could be applied for 3D systems.

2.1 Relative Positions

Figure 2 depicts three sensor nodes which take measurements that can be used to estimate the nodes' relative positions. Each node in figure 2, denoted with a capital letter, defines its own local coordinate system, referenced to its sensor hardware. In figure 2 this is marked with the local (x,y) - coordinate systems that belong to each of the nodes. Relative positioning systems normally do not use anchor nodes or global coordinate systems, so we have to clarify a relative position (which is a vector) by always including the according reference coordinate system in the notation.

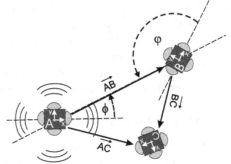

Fig. 1. A node used for ultrasonic relative positioning

Fig. 2. Relative positioning of nodes

For example, $\vec{AB}_A$ expresses the position of B (meaning the vector A to B) in the view of a local coordinate system of A. If we determine relative positions via multiple hops, we can just add the vectors together as long as we assure to use the same reference coordinate system for all vectors. Different views of positions (and therefore vectors) can be translated by simply transforming the according coordinate systems. The position of C in figure 2 in the view of A $(=\vec{AC}_A)$ can be combined through step by step summation of a vector chain from A to C:

$$\vec{AC}_A = \vec{AB}_A + \vec{BC}_A$$
$$\vec{BC}_A = \begin{pmatrix} \cos\rho & -\sin\rho \\ \sin\rho & +\cos\rho \end{pmatrix} \vec{BC}_B \tag{1}$$
$$\rho = \phi + (180° - \varphi)$$

2.2   Creating Local Estimates of the Same Physical Quantity

As described above, relative positions and orientations can be computed by applying trigonometry to measured ranges, angles-of-arrival, and angles-of-emission. The method proposed in this paper relies upon multiple nodes being able to independently create local estimates of a given physical quantity so that they can then be fused to improve accuracy. We now give two examples of how multiple distributed estimates of the same physical quantities would be created:

Ranging. For example, many observing nodes might independently estimate the range between two beaconing nodes A and B. To do this, an observing node (for example C) would need to minimally measure its range to A and B (d_{AC} and d_{BC}), as well as the angles-of-arrival of the ranging signals from both A and B (ϕ_{AC} and ϕ_{BC}). Applying the Law of Cosines, the observing node C could then estimate d_{AB} with only these locally-measured quantities. Using experimental data, Section 4.2 demonstrates that ranges locally estimated in this way by three observing nodes can be fused together to yield an improved range result.

Positioning. Alternatively, many nodes might each estimate the relative position of B with respect to A. As explained below in Section 5, an observing node is able to independently estimate this physical quantity by locally measuring the ranges to A and B, the angles-of-arrival of the ranging signals, as well as the angles-of-emission of the ranging signals. By way of simulations, Section 6 shows how an improved estimate of the relative locations of A and B can be created by fusing estimates from many observing nodes.

3   A Model for Measurement Errors

In general for measurement systems, the process of measuring can be understood as an operation based on the ground truth. For example, suppose we take a sensor observation $\tilde{r}$. It is based on the actual physical quantity being observed, the "ground truth" r. Incorporated in the observation is also an error due to the system status (e.g. spatial configuration of the nodes, or environmental conditions) which is described by a vector we want to call $\mathbf{t}$. Additionally, there is an independent part n influencing the measurement, which appears as random noise on the measurements. Thus, the overall sensor observation can be described as the sum

$$\tilde{r} = r + f(\mathbf{t}, r) + n. \qquad (2)$$

This model divides the influences on our measurement into the two types of *systematic* ($f(\mathbf{t}, r)$) and *statistical* (n) errors. *Statistical errors* come from random sources of noise, such as the thermal noise present in sensors and their supporting circuitry, or (particularly relevant to ultrasonic sensing) acoustic noise created by uncorrelated physical events in the environment. Statistical errors cannot be avoided but can be reduced by techniques such as cooling of electronic parts or aggressive filtering of the sensor signal. *Systematic errors* in a measurement system occur for a variety of reasons, including component ageing, wear-and-tear, or changing environmental conditions that affect the measurement process in a constant and repeatable way. To handle the systematic errors, the traditional approach is to either *model* the errors or *calibrate* the affected parts of the system. Modelling systematic error is e.g. done in ultrasonic ranging systems by taking temperature and humidity measurements to gain an accurate estimate of the speed of sound in air.[1] Methods for calibration on the other hand vary in difficulty and effectiveness, but a thorough calibration can be a tedious task requiring high precision. Moreover, re-calibration is often required during the life-time of a product, and this can also be very difficult and expensive to manage.

By analysing measurements from our ultrasonic localisation system, we discovered that a large component of the systematic error is dependent upon the *spatial configuration* of the nodes. Spatially-dependent systematic error has been shown to exist for other sensing modalities as well; examples include infrared light intensity [16] and radio RSSI [17]. We would expect that our methods can be applied to sensor network localisation systems based on infrared light, ultrasound, audible sound, or radio signals.

4 Removing Error in Measurements

In this paper, we focus on the low-labour technique of averaging; device-specific calibration and modelling can always be carried out and applied in addition to averaging. According to our error model (2), multiple measurements taken in the same system conditions will help to reduce the statistical error n (assuming the statistical error is non-biased). By contrast, the systematic part $f(\mathbf{t}, r)$ can not be averaged out in this way, since it represents the constant and repeatable error component.

4.1 Removing Systematic Error

One of the core ideas presented in this paper is a natural extension to averaging in location system. It is obvious that averaging of multiple measurements helps against statistical errors such as thermal noise in analogue components. In the same way, we want to use averaging on the systematic error. We can achieve this by *varying* the system state during multiple measurements. In our application of positioning systems, this would e.g. imply to vary the system states like temperature, orientation etc. In other words, if we are able to measure the same physical value under *varying* system states, we will not get a repeatable, but also varying systematic error, and thus the systematic error loses its *systematic* nature.

4.2 Analysis of Experimental Measurements

In figure 3, we see a plot of the errors of the angle-of-arrival of ultrasound pulses that were measured experimentally; our experimental analysis is based on data

---

[1] If the estimate of the speed of sound is too fast or too slow, then all measurements will suffer from a systematic over- or under-ranging.

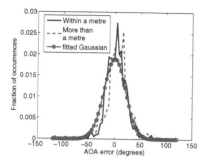

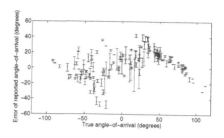

Fig. 3. Mean error for angles-of-arrival detected by five nodes in many different spatial configurations. The error characteristic in this plot is for measurements where the incoming ultrasound pulses were sensed on two or more of the node's transducers; this condition was true for over seventy percent of the successful measurements taken.

Fig. 4. Angle-of-arrival measurements taken by a single node in different spatial configurations. The error bars indicate the tenth and ninetieth percentile levels of the observed errors at a given angle. The angle-of-arrival error offsets for a given system state tend to be tightly constrained, and thus systematic.

gathered using five nodes placed in fifty spatial configurations, with favourable line-of-sight conditions [15]. The distribution is very similar to the Gaussian indicated in the same figure. But for a given node spatial arrangement, we are more interested in the specific error distribution rather than the total distribution for all nodes/configurations. Figure 4 shows the angle-of-arrival measurement errors reported by one node over many experimental settings. Each error bar shows the distribution of angle-of-arrival errors measured from a particular node in a particular location. While the error distribution for different nodes in different spatial configurations varies, the spread of errors for a given node in a given spatial configuration tends to be small. Thus, if measurements are taken by a node in the same system state ($\mathbf{t}$ is constant), the error tends not to vary much; it is repeatable, or systematic. This holds true for readings taken by all five nodes used in the experiments; ninety percent of the ninetieth percentile angle errors are within $16°$ of the median error.

For a particular node's repeated measurements, Figure 4 shows that the angle-of-arrival error tends to have a systematic offset. However, in order to motivate the use of averaging to compensate for systematic errors, it is necessary to show that the systematic errors of the nodes in a given spatial configuration are independent. Using the experimental data collected from five nodes in fifty spatial configurations, the range between two of the nodes was estimated by using data collected locally by the other three. The three estimates were then averaged together to create a fused estimate of the range between the two nodes. Figure 5 illustrates the result of fusing three locally-obtained range estimates. The ninetieth percentile accuracy improves by about 15 cm. The graph demonstrates that the device– and location-dependent systematic errors in the system are not

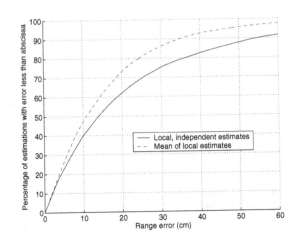

Fig. 5. Removal of systematic error using data collected from three nodes to estimate the range between two others

significantly correlated with one another; averaging the locally-estimated quantities, despite their individual systematic offsets, yields an improved result.

5 Multiple, Simultaneous Measurements

In our analysis of the measurements, we found that a large component of the systematic error depends on the particular signal angles-of-arrival at each node, which is in turn dictated by the relative locations of the nodes. Instead of carrying out a device-specific calibration, we propose choosing a physical quantity which is to be measured by many nodes to overcome the systematic nature. Because each node has its own systematic but specific error offset (dependent on the node's location, orientation, and particular hardware), the random spatial configuration of the nodes can be exploited to yield several estimates of the same physical quantity which have different systematic error offsets. These independent estimates can then be averaged together for an improved result.

Localisation nodes which are capable of measuring (1) the time-of-flight (i.e. a range), (2) the angle-of-emission, and (3) the angle of arrival of the signal can, using simple trigonometry, locally estimate the relative positions of any other two beaconing nodes (figure 2). Note additionally that in many sensor systems, any signals used for localisation (such as infrared, ultrasound, or ultra-wideband radio) are of a *broadcast* nature.

Thus, multiple measurements can be accomplished simultaneously by different nodes: whenever a node emits a localisation signal, a number N of other nodes can take a measurement. Provided these N nodes can all estimate the same quantity from their measurements (such as the range between two nodes A and B, or their relative location coordinates), then the scaling of taking measurements can be improved from $O(N)$ to $O(1)$.

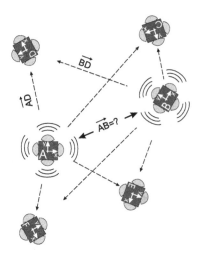

Fig. 6. Performing multiple measurements in a relative positioning system based on ultrasound

As shown in figure 6, if A and B both successively emit ranging signals, the other nodes present can individually and simultaneously compute results under different system states which can then be combined for improved positioning of A and B. For example, when A transmits, another node D can measure A's relative position using the angle-of-arrival and range to A. When B transmits, D similarly estimates its relative location. Since D has additionally logged the angle-of-emission of the signal from A, D can perform a rotation (1) of its locally-referenced coordinate system to express the location of B relative to A:

$$\overrightarrow{AB}_A = (\overrightarrow{AD}_D - \overrightarrow{BD}_D)_A. \tag{3}$$

Other nodes in the environment (C, E, and F) can do the same, simultaneously arriving at the relative position of B with respect to the local coordinate system of A ($\overrightarrow{AB}_A$). Thus after an ultrasonic emission from both A and B, there are $N = 4$ measurements of $\overrightarrow{AB}_A$. These estimates individually held by the nodes C, D, E, and F now need to be combined, ideally in a way which scales favourably as N increases.

5.1   Data Fusion with Multi-SDJS

We now hold N measurements $\tilde{r}_i$ of the same vector from A to B, which we want to collect for a data process such as averaging. With multi-SDJS, we are capable of collecting these vectors in a very efficient way. The important property is that the time required to perform SDJS is independent of the number of participants. Increasing the number of participants in multi-SDJS allows more observations to be incorporated into the fused data estimate, without impacting the amount of time required for the fusion process.

For the ease of understanding, we explain the protocol directly with our application of collecting the measured vectors from A to B; we called the measurement $\tilde{r}_i$. The SDJS process we utilise operates with *scalar* values in an a-priori *known interval*. Therefore, the $\overrightarrow{AB}_A$ measurements are expressed as polar coordinates $(\tilde{r}_i, \tilde{\varphi}_i)^T$, and multi-SDJS is performed for each component.[2] For the SDJS process, we assume that the nodes are within radio range of one another, since they have been able to perform the localisation measurements.

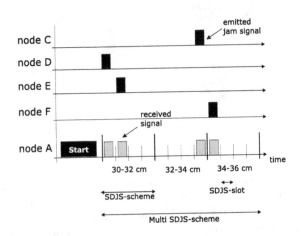

Fig. 7. The multi-SDJS process for collecting data using signalling on the physical layer of the nodes' radio

Figure 7 shows how the collecting of data works. Node A initiates the multi-SDJS scheme by broadcasting a start packet, which contains information about the upcoming SDJS communication. In this case, it specifies that three SDJS schemes will follow, each scheme containing four SDJS slots. The schemes correspond to the ranges 30–32 cm, 32–34 cm, and 34–36 cm. To lower the necessary slots and schemes, the ranges are based on the distance estimation that the initiating node A has.

After the start packet, each node selects the SDJS scheme which corresponds to their measurement. For example, if node D has a measurement of 31.2 cm, it would select the first SDJS scheme. Then, during the time of the first SDJS scheme, node D (and also node E) *randomly* select one SDJS-slot and emit a jam signal. Using these emissions, from D and E signal to A that they have a measurement that lies in the interval from 30 to 32 cm. Node A will receives the signals and can estimate the number of nodes based on counted signals and collisions. Node A does not simply *count* the number of jam signals but has to

---

[2] Note that averaging can only work using a polar coordinate representation $(r, \varphi)^T$, as the distribution of the measurement (as that shown in figure 10) is not bias-free in $(x, y)^T$. This is because the raw ultrasonic measurements themselves produce relative distances and angles, and not (x, y) coordinate results.

include possible collisions into its estimation. For a discussion on the estimation theory, the reader is referred elsewhere [18].

6   Simulation

Our simulation is based on an indoor scenario of a 5m by 5m room with up to 200 nodes.[3] The simulation error models for the range and angle-of-arrival accuracy were derived from our experiments, in which over half a million measurements were taken using five ultrasonic positioning nodes placed in fifty different spatial configurations [15]. The following models were used for the simulation:

Angles-of-arrival: a Gaussian systematic error with $\mu = 0°$ and $\sigma = 14°$; a Gaussian statistical error with $\mu = 0°$ and $\sigma = 1.4°$

Angles-of-emission: a uniform distribution in the interval $[-45° \ldots + 45°]$

Ranges: a right-sided half-Gaussian systematic error with $\mu = 0$ cm and $\sigma = 3.5$ cm; a Gaussian statistical error with $\mu = 0$ mm and $\sigma = 4.9$ mm

Simulation model for the SDJS process: The SDJS process influences the averaging process of the distributed measurements. It quantises the numbers (we used a resolution of 2 cm and 2°) and then the number estimation of the SDJS process can also introduce errors due to an inadequate range of possible values or due to using too few slots per scheme. For our simulation, we assumed that the SDJS process would be suitably parameterised such that the errors introduced with SDJS are negligible.

In the simulations, we compare "direct measurements" with the measuring process results of our framework. The direct measurements assume a measurement that is based on signals and data exchange only between the endpoint nodes. We always take the best possible solution here and let B transmit and A receive as the model for the angle-of-arrival (Gaussian, $\sigma = 14°$) is much more narrow than the transmit model (uniform $\pm 45°$).

6.1   Acquisition of the Relative Position Between Two Nodes

Figure 8 shows a simulated room with 50 nodes. We measured the relative location from node A $(150, 150)^T$ to B $(350, 350)^T$. We simulated 1000 runs of this scenario, varying the position of the 48 "helper" nodes. We looked at the error for the relative position of node B, meaning the error of $\overrightarrow{AB}_A$. In figure 9, we compare the results of direct measurements and our framework for the case of 50 nodes. The three plots show the relative occurrences of error values for the angle between A and B, the absolute position error of B and the error for the Cartesian coordinates (x,y) of the room. All three plots compare the distribution of the results of the direct measurements with those of our framework.

---

[3] The simulation was done using OMNet++. See http://www.omnetpp.org/.

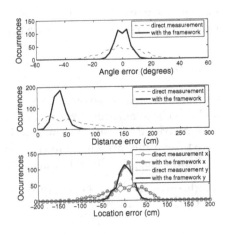

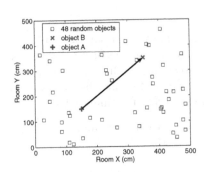

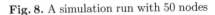

Fig. 8. A simulation run with 50 nodes

Fig. 9. The improvements using the framework for the measurements

For the direct measurements, the maximum error in positive x direction is given when node B is (wrongly) positioned on the same y-position like A in the room, then the x-position $\overrightarrow{AB}_A$ of B is 432 cm plus some noise, resulting in a x-position error of 82 cm plus noise. We can see this limit around 100 cm in the x-position errors of figure 9. The distribution of angles are symmetric to zero, which we expected. For all values, we see how the framework improves the overall results. The distribution are much more narrow. The error on the absolute location error gives the distribution of the distance of the results from the target position of B. We also see here, how the mean was shifted towards zero.

Figure 10 gives another illustration of one of our simulation runs. It shows how the distribution of the direct measurements are placed on a segment of a circle, as the error in the angle φ is much higher than on the radius r. After the averaging process of the 48 helper nodes, the distribution is much more concentrated around the target node B. We simulated 1000 runs, each run with a new topology, only the (x,y)-position of node A and B were held constant. Their orientation varied as well.

In table 1, we find the statistical characteristics of the distributions for the normal direct measurement process and the averaged values through our framework. The improvements are exceedingly visible in the decreasing of the standard deviation of the distributions. With the averaging, we achieve much more narrow distributions. The (x,y) coordinates describe the relative position error of node B in the view of node A. Φ denotes the angle under which B was estimated from the view of A. The row labelled "Euclidian" shows the absolute Euclidian position error in the location estimation of B from its real position at (350,350).

Table 2, demonstrates how adding large numbers of nodes improves the results of the system. Numbers are based on a simulation of the same situation, but with 198 "helper" nodes. One can see, how the standard deviations σ of

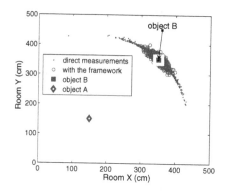

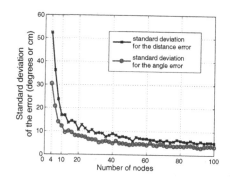

Fig. 10. 1000 simulations run with 50 nodes

Fig. 11. Gradual improvements of accuracy with increasing number of nodes N

Table 1. Statistical characteristics for N=0, 48

(μ/σ)	direct meas.	with framework (N=48)
Φ (degrees)	(-0.3/ 13.4)	(-0.1/ 4.9)
Euclidian (cm)	(53.6/ 38.8)	(38.5/ 10.8)
x (cm)	(-4.7/ 47.2)	(1.4/ 17.2)
y (cm)	(-2.6/ 46.0)	(1.6/ 17.7)

Table 2. statistical characteristics for N=0, 48, 198

$(\sigma/95\%)$	direct	N=48	N=198
x (cm)	(47.2/90.5)	(17.2/ 32.4)	(9.9/18.6)
y (cm)	(46.0/86.5)	(17.7/33.5)	(10.0/20.6)
Φ (degrees)	(13.4/35.6)	(4.9/9.8)	(2.8/5.5)
Euclidian (cm)	(38.8/125)	(10.8/56.3)	(5.2/44.1)

the resulting statistics decrease and the distribution becomes even more narrow. The tabulated ninety-fifth percentiles give the error values at which the corresponding cumulative distribution reached 0.95. In other words, 95% of all measurements will have an error equal or smaller than that value.

As a next step, we now want to look at the dependency of our achieved accuracy and the number of nodes. Table 2 already gives a hint on the clear convergence with increasing number of nodes N. We again simulated the same situation but now with a variable number of nodes from $N = [1..200]$. For each number of nodes, we simulated 100 random topologies in the 5 by 5 m room but kept nodes A and B at (x,y)-position (150,150) and (350,350) with random orientation. We numerically extracted mean and standard deviations from the results of the framework and plotted them against the number of nodes in Figure 11. We see how the standard deviation of the measurements decreases the more nodes that are involved. The gradient is especially high for the low number of nodes ($N < 10$). That means, that even with a comparably small number of nodes, we can already achieve great improvements in accuracy. But as the framework process time is independent of the number of participants, one would always include all available measurements from all nodes in the area.

7   Conclusion

This paper has described and evaluated a method for reducing device-dependent and spatially-dependent systematic error in localisation systems. Using this method, many nodes simultaneously gather measurements to create estimates of the same physical quantity, such as the relative location of one node with respect to another. In so doing, the systematic errors can be treated as statistical or random, since they depend on the nodes' independent locations and orientations. Averaging can then be applied to these independent estimates to improve the overall result.

Using the SDJS protocol, the time required for sensor measurements and data fusion is constant and *independent* of the number of nodes involved; the accuracy increases with a higher number of nodes involved, as long as this number stays in reasonable bounds. Some quantitative measures have been previously published [18]. As an example calculation, we want to parameterise a typical SDJS process for our application. With an initial estimate of the location of B relative to A, we may need for the next estimate a range of ±50 cm for the SDJS process with a resolution of 1 cm, resulting in one hundred SDJS schemes. Assuming a slot time with 18 μs (based on physical parameter from IEEE 802.11a) and fifty slots per value, we get a total time of $100 \cdot 50 \cdot 18\mu s = 90.0$ ms for the averaging process. Using fifty slots per value would allow the network to scale to upwards of 300 nodes, and the SDJS process would still return accurate fused estimates.

With these properties, our method is ideally suited for low-cost hardware that is densely distributed in the environment. With the method, we address both statistical and even severe systematic errors of the hardware through the fusion of measurements taken from different nodes in different locations and orientations.

Using a large number of measurements captured from five ultrasonic localisation nodes, we demonstrated that the systematic errors of locally-estimated ranges between any two nodes are independent and thus the overall error can be vastly reduced by fusing the local estimates; even with just three nodes performing the process, the ninetieth percentile range error can be improved by about 20 cm. With the error models derived from these real measurements, we also showed in simulations that the accuracy can be greatly improved using even more nodes. For this, we simulated a 5×5 m room with both 50 and 200 nodes and quantified the accuracy improvement. For example, the standard deviation of the determined relative angle was reduced from $\sigma_{\Phi,2} = 13.4$ for the direct measurement over $\sigma_{\Phi,50} = 4.9$ with a setting of 50 nodes to only $\sigma_{\Phi,200} = 2.8$ when using 200 nodes in the room.

Acknowledgements

The work presented in this paper was undertaken as part of a collaborative project, "Relate: Relative Positioning of Mobile Objects in Ad Hoc Networks." It is funded by the European Commission's FP6 IST Programme, project number 013790.

References

1. Kamin Whitehouse, Chris Karlof, Alec Woo, Fred Jiang, and David Culler. The effects of ranging noise on multihop localization: An empirical study. In *Proceedings of the Fourth International Symposium on Information Processing in Sensor Networks (IPSN)*, pages 73–80, Los Angeles, USA, April 2005.
2. Andreas Savvides, Wendy L. Garber, Randolph L. Moses, and Mani B. Srivastava. An analysis of error inducing parameters in multihop sensor node localization. *IEEE Transactions on Mobile Computing*, 4(6):567–577, November 2005.
3. Jeffrey Hightower and Gaetano Borriello. Location systems for ubiquitous computing. *IEEE Computer*, 34(8):57–66, August 2001.
4. Jeffrey Hightower, Roy Want, and Gaetano Borriello. SpotON: An indoor 3d location sensing technology based on RF signal strength. UW CSE 00-02-02, University of Washington, Department of Computer Science and Engineering, Seattle, WA, February 2000.
5. Kiran Yedavalli, Bhaskar Krishnamachari, Sharmila Ravula, and Bhaskar Srinivasan. Ecolocation: A sequence based technique for RF localization in wireless sensor networks. In *Proceedings of the Fourth International Symposium on Information Processing in Sensor Networks (IPSN)*, pages 285–292, Los Angeles, USA, April 2005.
6. Andreas Savvides, Chih-Chieh Han, and Mani B. Srivastava. Dynamic fine-grained localization in ad-hoc networks of sensors. In *Proceedings of the Seventh International Conference on Mobile Computing and Networking (MobiCom)*, pages 166–179, Rome, Italy, July 2001.
7. Nissanka B. Priyantha, Allen K. L. Miu, Hari Balakrishnan, and Seth Teller. The Cricket Compass for context-aware mobile applications. In *Proceedings of the Seventh International Conference on Mobile Computing and Networking (MobiCom)*, Rome, Italy, July 2001.
8. Masateru Minami, Yasuhiro Fukuju, Kazuki Hirasawa, Shigeaki Yokoyama, Moriyuki Mizumachi, Hiroyuki Morikawa, and Tomonori Aoyama. DOLPHIN: a practical approach for implementing a fully distributed indoor ultrasonic positioning system. In *Proceedings of the Sixth International Conference on Ubiquitous Computing (UbiComp)*, pages 347–365, Nottingham, UK, September 2004. Springer.
9. Miklós Maróti, Branislav Kusý, György Balogh, Péter Völgyesi, András Nádas, Károly Molnár, Sebestyén Dóra, and Ákos Lédeczi. Radio interferometric geolocation. In *Proceedings of the Third International Conference on Embedded Networked Sensor Systems (SenSys)*, pages 1–12, San Diego, USA, November 2005.
10. Dragoş Niculescu and Badri Nath. Ad hoc positioning system (APS) using AOA. In *Proceedings of the Annual Joint Conference of the IEEE Computer and Communications Societies (INFOCOM)*, pages 1734–1743, San Francisco, USA, March 2003.

11. Koen Langendoen and Niels Reijers. Distributed localization in wireless sensor networks: A quantitative comparison. *Computer Networks*, 43:499–518, August 2003.
12. Srdjan Čapkun, Maher Hamdi, and Jean-Pierre Hubaux. GPS-free positioning in mobile ad-hoc networks. *Cluster Computing Journal*, 5(2):157–167, April 2002.
13. Yi Shang and Wheeler Ruml. Improved MDS-based localization. In *Proceedings of the Twenty-Third Conference of the IEEE Communications Society (INFOCOM)*, Hong Kong, March 2004.
14. David Moore, John Leonard, Daniela Rus, and Seth Teller. Robust distributed network localization with noisy range measurements. In *Proceedings of the Second International Conference on Embedded Networked Sensor Systems (SenSys)*, pages 50–61, Baltimore, USA, November 2004.
15. Mike Hazas, Christian Kray, Hans Gellersen, Henoc Agbota, Gerd Kortuem, and Albert Krohn. A relative positioning system for co-located mobile devices. In *Proceedings of the Third International Conference on Mobile Systems, Applications, and Services (MobiSys)*, Seattle, USA, June 6-8 2005.
16. Albert Krohn, Michael Beigl, Mike Hazas, Hans Gellersen, and Albrecht Schmidt. Using fine-grained infrared positioning to support the surface-based activities of mobile users. In *Proceedings of the Fifth International Workshop on Smart Appliances and Wearable Computing (IWSAWC)*, Columbus, USA, 2005.
17. John Krumm and Eric Horvitz. LOCADIO: inferring motion and location from Wi-Fi signal strengths. In *Proceedings of the First Annual International Conference on Mobile and Ubiquitous Systems: Networking and Services (Mobiquitous)*, pages 4–13, Boston, USA, August 2004.
18. Albert Krohn, Tobias Zimmer, Michael Beigl, and Christian Decker. Collaborative sensing in a retail store using synchronous distributed jam signalling. In *Proceedings of the Third International Conference on Pervasive Computing*, Munich, Germany, 2005.

Author Index

Lecture Notes in Computer Science

For information about Vols. 1–4279

please contact your bookseller or Springer

Vol. 4327: M. Baldoni, U. Endriss (Eds.), Declarative Agent Languages and Technologies IV. VIII, 257 pages. 2006. (Sublibrary LNAI).

Vol. 4326: S. Göbel, R. Malkewitz, I. Iurgel (Eds.), Technologies for Interactive Digital Storytelling and Entertainment. X, 384 pages. 2006.

Vol. 4325: J. Cao, I. Stojmenovic, X. Jia, S.K. Das (Eds.), Mobile Ad-hoc and Sensor Networks. XIX, 887 pages. 2006.

Vol. 4323: G. Doherty, A. Blandford (Eds.), Interactive Systems. XI, 269 pages. 2006.

Vol. 4320: R. Gotzhein, R. Reed (Eds.), System Analysis and Modeling: Language Profiles. X, 229 pages. 2006.

Vol. 4319: L.-W. Chang, W.-N. Lie (Eds.), Advances in Image and Video Technology. XXVI, 1347 pages. 2006.

Vol. 4318: H. Lipmaa, M. Yung, D. Lin (Eds.), Information Security and Cryptology. XI, 305 pages. 2006.

Vol. 4317: S.K. Madria, K.T. Claypool, R. Kannan, P. Uppuluri, M.M. Gore (Eds.), Distributed Computing and Internet Technology. XIX, 466 pages. 2006.

Vol. 4316: M.M. Dalkilic, S. Kim, J. Yang (Eds.), Data Mining and Bioinformatics. VIII, 197 pages. 2006. (Sublibrary LNBI).

Vol. 4313: T. Margaria, B. Steffen (Eds.), Leveraging Applications of Formal Methods. IX, 197 pages. 2006.

Vol. 4312: S. Sugimoto, J. Hunter, A. Rauber, A. Morishima (Eds.), Digital Libraries: Achievements, Challenges and Opportunities. XVIII, 571 pages. 2006.

Vol. 4311: K. Cho, P. Jacquet (Eds.), Technologies for Advanced Heterogeneous Networks II. XI, 253 pages. 2006.

Vol. 4309: P. Inverardi, M. Jazayeri (Eds.), Software Engineering Education in the Modern Age. VIII, 207 pages. 2006.

Vol. 4308: S. Chaudhuri, S.R. Das, H.S. Paul, S. Tirthapura (Eds.), Distributed Computing and Networking. XIX, 608 pages. 2006.

Vol. 4307: P. Ning, S. Qing, N. Li (Eds.), Information and Communications Security. XIV, 558 pages. 2006.

Vol. 4306: Y. Avrithis, Y. Kompatsiaris, S. Staab, N.E. O'Connor (Eds.), Semantic Multimedia. XII, 241 pages. 2006.

Vol. 4305: A.A. Shvartsman (Ed.), Principles of Distributed Systems. XIII, 441 pages. 2006.

Vol. 4304: A. Sattar, B.-H. Kang (Eds.), AI 2006: Advances in Artificial Intelligence. XXVII, 1303 pages. 2006. (Sublibrary LNAI).

Vol. 4303: A. Hoffmann, B.-H. Kang, D. Richards, S. Tsumoto (Eds.), Advances in Knowledge Acquisition and Management. XI, 259 pages. 2006. (Sublibrary LNAI).

Vol. 4302: J. Domingo-Ferrer, L. Franconi (Eds.), Privacy in Statistical Databases. XI, 383 pages. 2006.

Vol. 4301: D. Pointcheval, Y. Mu, K. Chen (Eds.), Cryptology and Network Security. XIII, 381 pages. 2006.

Vol. 4300: Y.Q. Shi (Ed.), Transactions on Data Hiding and Multimedia Security I. IX, 139 pages. 2006.

Vol. 4299: S. Renals, S. Bengio, J.G. Fiscus (Eds.), Machine Learning for Multimodal Interaction. XII, 470 pages. 2006.

Vol. 4297: Y. Robert, M. Parashar, R. Badrinath, V.K. Prasanna (Eds.), High Performance Computing - HiPC 2006. XXIV, 642 pages. 2006.

Vol. 4296: M.S. Rhee, B. Lee (Eds.), Information Security and Cryptology – ICISC 2006. XIII, 358 pages. 2006.

Vol. 4295: J.D. Carswell, T. Tezuka (Eds.), Web and Wireless Geographical Information Systems. XI, 269 pages. 2006.

Vol. 4294: A. Dan, W. Lamersdorf (Eds.), Service-Oriented Computing – ICSOC 2006. XIX, 653 pages. 2006.

Vol. 4293: A. Gelbukh, C.A. Reyes-Garcia (Eds.), MICAI 2006: Advances in Artificial Intelligence. XXVIII, 1232 pages. 2006. (Sublibrary LNAI).

Vol. 4292: G. Bebis, R. Boyle, B. Parvin, D. Koracin, P. Remagnino, A. Nefian, G. Meenakshisundaram, V. Pascucci, J. Zara, J. Molineros, H. Theisel, T. Malzbender (Eds.), Advances in Visual Computing, Part II. XXXII, 906 pages. 2006.

Vol. 4291: G. Bebis, R. Boyle, B. Parvin, D. Koracin, P. Remagnino, A. Nefian, G. Meenakshisundaram, V. Pascucci, J. Zara, J. Molineros, H. Theisel, T. Malzbender (Eds.), Advances in Visual Computing, Part I. XXXI, 916 pages. 2006.

Vol. 4290: M. van Steen, M. Henning (Eds.), Middleware 2006. XIII, 425 pages. 2006.

Vol. 4289: M. Ackermann, B. Berendt, M. Grobelnik, A. Hotho, D. Mladenič, G. Semeraro, M. Spiliopoulou, G. Stumme, V. Svátek, M. van Someren (Eds.), Semantics, Web and Mining. X, 197 pages. 2006. (Sublibrary LNAI).

Vol. 4288: T. Asano (Ed.), Algorithms and Computation. XX, 766 pages. 2006.

Vol. 4287: C. Mao, T. Yokomori (Eds.), DNA Computing. XII, 440 pages. 2006.

Vol. 4286: P.G. Spirakis, M. Mavronicolas, S.C. Kontogiannis (Eds.), Internet and Network Economics. XI, 401 pages. 2006.

Vol. 4285: Y. Matsumoto, R.W. Sproat, K.-F. Wong, M. Zhang (Eds.), Computer Processing of Oriental Languages. XVII, 544 pages. 2006. (Sublibrary LNAI).

Vol. 4284: X. Lai, K. Chen (Eds.), Advances in Cryptology – ASIACRYPT 2006. XIV, 468 pages. 2006.

Vol. 4283: Y.Q. Shi, B. Jeon (Eds.), Digital Watermarking. XII, 474 pages. 2006.

Vol. 4282: Z. Pan, A. Cheok, M. Haller, R.W.H. Lau, H. Saito, R. Liang (Eds.), Advances in Artificial Reality and Tele-Existence. XXIII, 1347 pages. 2006.

Vol. 4281: K. Barkaoui, A. Cavalcanti, A. Cerone (Eds.), Theoretical Aspects of Computing - ICTAC 2006. XV, 371 pages. 2006.

Vol. 4280: A.K. Datta, M. Gradinariu (Eds.), Stabilization, Safety, and Security of Distributed Systems. XVII, 590 pages. 2006.